JACK THE RIPPER

-

NEWSPAPERS FROM HULL VOLUME 2

Copyright © 2015 Mike Covell

Layout Copyright © 2015 Creativia

Published 2015 by Creativia

Paperback design by Creativia (http://www.creativia.org)

ISBN: 978-1511618007

Cover art by http://www.thecovercollection.com

All rights reserved. No part of this book may be reproduced or transmitted in any form or by any means, electronic or mechanical, including photocopying, recording, or by any information storage and retrieval system, without the author's permission.

Contents

Introduction

Newspaper reports post 1888

Stop the Press - Editors Comments

Appendix I   The 1900 Hull Ripper Scare

Appendix II   The 1988 Hull Ripper Craze

Appendix III   Beverley Ripper Craze's

Appendix IV   Frederick Bailey Deeming in the Hull Press – 1890

Appendix V   Newspaper Reports featured

Bibliography and Further Reading

    Jack the Ripper General Reference

    Jack the Ripper – Press Associated

    Hull History

    Maps

    Acknowledgements

Mike Covell

Introduction

London's notorious East End was the scene of a number of brutal crimes commonly attributed to an unknown serial killer who has become known as "*Jack the Ripper*." Some theorize that the murderer had only five victims, these being Mary Ann Nichols, Annie Chapman, Elizabeth Stride, Catherine Eddowes, and finally Mary Jane Kelly. Some, however, argue that "*Jack the Ripper*" could have killed more before and after this date. These victims are categorized by most as "Whitechapel Murders" even though many did not die in Whitechapel. Another series of murders also ran alongside the crimes in Whitechapel and surrounding environs, these included the Torso Murders, where a number of body parts were found in the Thames, Whitehall, and elsewhere. All in all 1888 was a bloody year of murder, mutilation, and death. For many who look into the crimes of Jack the Ripper, 1888 is the be all and end all, but what happened next? How did the press cover the events after the murder of the victim named in the press as Mary Jane Kelly? This volume aims to answer those questions and more.

More Whitechapel Victims followed, and with these murders, the name "*Jack the Ripper*" continued to fill column inches in Hull, Britain, and even further afield. The Ripper was big business, and any headline covering the murderer would sell copies and create excitement.

In 2006 armed with a pen and a pad and a few dates I headed into Hull's local studies library, which at the time was situated in Hull City Council's Central Library, to try and find any articles in the Hull newspapers that covered the crimes of "*Jack the Ripper*." I expected to come away with a couple of articles, but nothing prepared me for the mass of material I gathered on that visit. My budget at the time wasn't very high so I got a few articles and made notes of the dates of the other reports for a later date. Eventually I returned and gathered a few more together, making notes of other reports for later visits. It is now almost 7 years later and I am still gathering reports from the Hull press on "*Jack the Ripper*." Some of the articles covered the murders, some covered the suspects, and some of them covered the scares and scandals that made it into the Hull press. My main aim was to collect articles on the case for the writing of *Jack the Ripper From Hell, From Hull?* But the more I collected the more I realized that I was onto something special. Many of the articles provided a new slant on an age old tale, with Hull having representatives in London at the time the reports were coming from Hull journalists.

In 2008 I was asked to write an article for *Ripperologist Magazine* on Hull Jack the Ripper Scares and Scandals between 1888 and 1988. The research for the article would include Hull based suspects, arrests in Hull on "*Jack the Ripper like conduct*," Jack the Ripper letters from Hull, Jack the Ripper letters to Hull, and Jack the Ripper letters from Hull.

With the material from the article I was able to create a lecture that was first presented at the Hull Heritage Centre at Carnegie Library to a packed crowd on December 9th 2009. Other venues followed, and on Tuesday May 9th 2010 I lectured at the newly opened multi million pound Hull History Centre. Once again the lecture was packed, with standing room only at the back and round the edges. It was also memorable because it attracted the 10,000th visitor to the Hull History Centre, which made it into *The Hull Daily Mail*. The visitor had mentioned that he came to my lecture!

With so much new material being discovered it felt like I needed to share it, but cramming the material from 1888 to 1988 in one volume would soon become problematic, purely because of the wealth of the material that I had uncovered. It was at that point, seeing a mammoth book in front of me that I decided to split the material into two volumes, not just because of the wealth of material, but I thought that perhaps there was another story to tell, a story beyond the usual events of 1888.

This volume will, therefore, look at the events after the year of 1888, featuring articles published in the Hull newspapers from the year 1889 until the year 1988. These articles will cover the murders of Alice McKenzie, the Pinchin-street torso, Frances Coles, as well as murderers linked to the case such as James Thomas Sadler, Frederick Bailey Deeming, and much more. We will also look at other local "*Ripper Scares*" including the full story behind the 1900 Hull Ripper Scare, the 1988 Hull Ripper Craze, and an in depth look at the Beverley Jack the Ripper Scares. I have also included the 1890 articles from the Hull press that cover Frederick Bailey Deeming's

Mike Covell

trial in Hull for fraud against Messrs. Reynoldson and Son, Jewelers of Whitefriargate, Hull.

Packed with thrilling stories published during these incredible scares, and supported by a wide range of primary sources and contemporary illustrations, it is time to take a trip back, and see what happened after "The Autumn of Terror."

Newspapers from Hull Volume 2

The story so far

As 1888 drew to a close the local and national press were featuring a number of retrospective articles looking at the events of the previous year. 1888 was unlike any other year in the history of the British press, and no event prior to the appearance of "Jack the Ripper" had seen so many newspaper articles appear looking at the numerous victims, suspects, and theories.

The serial killer, known as "Jack the Ripper" after a missive was sent to the Central News Agency, dated September 27th 1888, and signed *"Jack the Ripper,"* had begun his reign of terror on Friday August 31st 1888 when Mary Ann (Polly) Nichols was found brutally murdered on Buck's-row. Some theorists have argued that he could have been responsible for the earlier murder of Martha Tabram, who was found dead on Tuesday August 7th 1888, in George Yard Buildings, Whitechapel. Others have argued that Emma Elizabeth Smith, who was assaulted and died of her injuries days later on Tuesday April 3rd 1888, was also an earlier victim, but most believe the murderer started his reign with Nichols. A little over a week later the body of Annie Chapman was discovered, on Saturday September 8th 1888, in the rear yard of number 29 Hanbury-street. On Sunday September 30th 1888 the body of Elizabeth Stride was found murdered in Dutfield's Yard, a small entry next to the International Working Men's Club on Berner-street a little after 01:00. At 01:44, a short distance away, Constable Watkins discovered the body of Catherine Eddowes in Mitre-square, and at 02:55 Constable Long finds a blood stained apron and graffito at the Wentworth Model Dwellings. The graffito stated, *"The Juwes are The men That Will not be Blamed for nothing."* On Wednesday October 3rd 1888 the trunk of an unknown woman was found in the cellars of the Whitehall buildings that would house New Scotland Yard. Most theorists argue that the torso murders had no connection to *"Jack the Ripper,"* but the press seized on these grisly finds and connected them to the events in the East End. On the morning of Friday November 9th 1888 the body of a woman we have become to know as Mary Jane Kelly was discovered at 13 Miller's-court, off Dorset-street. Her body was badly mutilated, in fact it was the worst of the commonly accepted five victims, but her body was discovered inside in a small room that she had been renting. It was also on November 9th 1888 that the resignation of Sir Charles Warren was accepted.

This short introduction is just a short overview of the events that transpired in the autumn of 1888. Anyone wishing to dig a little deeper should consult *Jack the Ripper: Newspapers from Hull Vol. I.*

From August until November "*Jack the Ripper*" had filled column inches on a global scale, but more was to come, much more.

Hull was no different to any other town or city that had its own newspaper. It picked up on the crimes at a national level, but many of the articles reported on the case from a local perspective, adding the local slant to sell copies to gain, and keep, the public's attention. Local stories of people accused of "*Jack the Ripper like conduct*," and a local "*Jack the Ripper*" letter filled column inches, but the public were eager for more. It is a long established myth that the murders ended with the horrific murder of Mary Jane Kelly at number 13 Miller's Court, Dorset-street. Many people have assumed that the police, and thus the press, had ceased to cover "*Jack the Ripper*" anymore, and as soon as the monster had arrived, he had vanished.

These are, of course, myths, and whilst most people agree that "*Jack the Ripper*" had ended his crime spree, the name continued to creep into the local, national and international press, just as "*Saucy Jack*" had crept into the courts, alleys and entries of Victorian London.

Visiting the National Archives one can, with the correct permissions, view the "Whitechapel Murder File." This file, held at the Public Record Office, Kew, features two files, HO 144 220, and HO 144 221. The first file, HO 144 220, is split into three folios as follows:

A49301.A – Features the suspect file, which features letters and clippings.

A49301.B – Features paperwork on rewards.

A49301.C – Features paperwork concerning the police investigations into the murders.

The second file, HO 144 221, features 7 sub files, these are as follows:

Newspapers from Hull Volume 2

A49301.D – This file features material from the Foreign Office.

A49301.E – This file features material on the bloodhounds.

A49301.F – This file features a letter from Sir Charles Warren to Godfrey Lushington.

A49301.G – This file features records of payments to officers.

A49301.H – This file features material on the murder of Rose Mylett.

A49301.I – This file features material on the murder of Alice McKenzie.

A49301.J – This file does not exist.

A49301.K – This file features material on the Pinchin-street murder.

Other files exist at the Public Records Office that feature the Scotland Yard Files, these are split into three files, MEPO 3 140, MEPO 3 141 and MEPO 3 142.

MEPO 3 140 – Features reports, statements and other material on the victims, these include,

Martha Tabram

Mary Ann Nichols

Elizabeth Stride

Catherine Eddowes

Mary Jane Kelly

Rose Mylett

Pinchin-street Torso

Frances Coles

MEPO 3 141 – Features a series of letters, police reports, and interviews

MEPO 3 142 – Features a series of letters allegedly from the killer

Mike Covell

Whilst I am not here to cover the official files, this has been done previously in *The Ultimate Jack the Ripper Sourcebook*, [Stewart P. Evans and Keith Skinner, Robinson, 2001,] I do hope that this collection of files illustrates that there was more to the mystery than the events of 1888.

Newspapers from Hull Volume 2

Newspaper reports post 1888

The year of 1888 was out, but the local, national, and international press was still reporting on stories with any angle pertaining to either Whitechapel or Jack the Ripper. The first article to appear in the Hull press on the case appeared on January 1st 1889!

The Hull Daily Mail, January 1st 1889,

THE WHITECHAPEL MURDERER. SEARCH IN AMERICA. Inspector Andrews, of Scotland Yard, (The Daily Telegraph's correspondent says), has arrived in New York from Montreal. It is generally believed, so the correspondent says, that the inspector has received orders from England to commence his search in that city for the Whitechapel murderer. Mr. Andrews is reported to have said that there half a dozen English detectives, two clerks, and one inspector employed in America in the same chase. A few days ago Andrews took thither from England, Roland Gideon Israel Barnet, charged with helping to wreck the Central bank, Toronto, and since his arrival he has received orders which will keep him in America for some time. The supposed inaction of the Whitechapel murderer for a considerable period and the fact that a man suspected of knowing a good deal about this series of crimes left England for the other side of the Atlantic three weeks ago has produced the impression that Jack the Ripper is in America. Irish Nationalists pretend that the inspector hunting up certain evidence to be given before the Parnell Commission.

Note:

There are many Ripperologists that agree that the search for "Jack the Ripper" in America pertains to the suspect known as Francis Tumblety. Tumblety was due to appear at the Old Bailey on charges of gross indecency on November 20th 1888 but the case was postponed until December 10th. This postponement gave Tumblety enough time to flee and he left for France on the La Bretagne on November 24th 1888. He then fled France and arrived back in America on December 3rd 1888. Whilst some theorists argue that Tumblety was "Jack the Ripper," others disagree, arguing that the gross indecency charges were against

Mike Covell

> males and not females as one would expect. They also argue that Tumblety was a supporter of the Irish Nationalists and because of this was followed and watched closely by detectives. Whatever the case, Tumblety remains one of the most discussed and debated suspects in Ripperology.
>
> The New York Herald, dated December 23rd 1888, claimed that Inspector Andrews was searching for National League informers, but that his efforts had been unsuccessful.

The Hull Daily Mail, January 1st 1889,

> REMARKABLE DISCOVERY. A JACK THE RIPPER LETTER. Another correspondent telegraphs: - A remarkable story, which came to the knowledge of the Bradford police some time on Thursday, on the morning of which the boy John Gill was first missed, and regarding which they have kept the strictest silence, has come to light. On Wednesday night last a tailor living in the thoroughfare in the suburb where the body was found, but about half a mile further from the town, and in very isolated position, went to call his wife. Upon his return, about 10 o'clock on Thursday morning, an hour and a half after the boy was last seen, he found that his house had been entered. The furniture had been pulled about and turned upside down; a number of articles of various kinds had been thrown in a heap upon the table in the living room; and upon another table was a sight which struck him with horror. A couple of carving knives were placed crosswise on the table and upon them a card, on one side of which was written: "Half past nine. Look out. Jack the Ripper has been." On the other side were the words, "I have removed down to the Canal side. Please drop in. – Yours truly, "Suicide." There was a large tin can full of water on the same table, and the whole surface of the table was saturated with water. The clock in the dining room was stopped, and the fingers indicated the time stated on the card, half past nine. Nothing had been removed from the house except a bottle of rum, and another bottle of rum had been removed from the cupboard and some of its contents had been poured into two glasses, which were left upon the table almost empty.

> **John Gill:**
>
> John Gill's death has been linked with the "Jack the Ripper" murders since 1889, but in recent years a number theories have been put forth as to who the murderer was. One of the strangest came from Patricia Cornwell, who claimed in her book

> *Jack the Ripper: Case Closed, that John Gill was killed by the popular artist Walter Sickert!*
>
> *John Gill's Death is registered thus:*
> *Name: John Gill, Estimated Birth Year: abt 1882, Date of Registration: Jan- Feb- Mar 1889, Age at Death: 7, Registration District: Bradford, Inferred County: Yorkshire West Riding, Vol: 9b, Page: 84*
>
> *William Barrett's acquittal is registered thus: [HO27, P214, P205]*
> *Name: William Barrett, Date of Trial: Mar 8th 1889, Trial Year: 1889, Location of Trial: Yorkshire – West Riding, England, Sentence: Acquittal, Charge: Wilful Murder, Discharge Notes: Bill Ignored by Grand Jury. Not Guilty on the Coroner's Inquisition, Discharged.*
>
> *The National Archives holds a file on the case, it reads, [HO140/117]*
>
> *First name: William, Last name: Barrett, Age: 23, Year of birth: 1866, Occupation: Milkman, Date the court session started: 08 Mar 1889, Court: Town Hall Leeds, Area of court: Yorkshire, Victims: John Gill, Record source: A Calendar Of Prisoners Tried At The Assizes.*
>
> *A more detailed entry reads,*
>
> *No: 14, Name: William Barrett, Age: 23, Trade: Milkman, Degree of Instruction: Imp, Name and Address of committing magistrate: James G. Hutchinson, Esq. Coroner, Bedford, Date of warrant: Ditto, When received into custody: Ditto, Offence as charged in the indictment: Wilful Murder of John Gill at Bradford, on the 29th December, 1888, When tried: March 12, Before whom tried: Ditto, Verdict of the jury: Bill of indictment for wilful murder ignored by the Grand Jury. Not guilty on the Coroner's Inquisition, Particulars of previous conviction: [Blank], Sentence or order of the court: To be discharged, No: 14.*

The Eastern Morning News, 2nd January 1889,

> *THE WHITECHAPEL TRAGEDIES. SEARCH IN AMERICA. Inspector Andrews, of Scotland Yard (The Daily Telegraph's correspondent says) has arrived in New York from Montreal. It is generally believed that he has received orders from England to commence his search in this city for the Whitechapel Murderer. Mr Andrews is reported to have said that there are half a dozen English detectives, two clerks, and one inspector employed in America in the same chase. Ten days ago Andrews brought hither from England Roland Gideon Israel Barnet, charged*

> with helping to wreck the Central Bank, Toronto; and since his arrival has received orders which will keep him in America for some time. The supposed inaction of the Whitechapel murderer for a considerable period, and the fact that a man suspected of knowing a good deal about this series of crimes, left England for this side of the Atlantic three weeks ago, has produced the impression that "Jack the Ripper" is in America. Irish Nationalists pretend that the inspector is hunting up certain evidence to be given to the Parnell Commission.

The Hull Daily Mail, January 3rd 1889,

> OUTRAGE IN GLASGOW. IMITATION OF THE "RIPPER" METHOD. The Glasgow police report this morning that an attempted "Jack the Ripper" case has occurred, in Glasgow this morning in darkness. John Stevenson, enticed an unfortunate named Mary Mackenzie into Exchange Court. He threw his arms around her, and stabbed her on the neck and in seven places on the abdomen. She cried for help. The police caught Stevenson. McKenzie was removed to the Hospital, where she now lies in a precarious condition. Stevenson is aged 19. The Press Association's Glasgow correspondent, telegraphing later, says the man met the woman about one o'clock a.m., enticed her up a court in Queen-street, and stabbed her in the neck. A struggle ensued, in which the woman was stabbed in the abdomen seven or eight times. Her cries brought assistance, and after a short chase her alleged assailant was arrested. The woman was removed to the Royal Infirmary, and the man, who gave the name of John Stevenson, coachbuilder, Glasgow, was this morning remanded for 48 hours.

The Hull Daily Mail, January 10th 1889,

> THE "JACK THE RIPPER" CRAZE. MURDEROUS ATTACK ON A MOTHER AND BROTHER NEAR BARNSLEY. Yesterday, at Barnsley, the magistrates remanded a collier, named Thomas Roebuck, for unlawfully wounding his mother with a formidable carving knife at Wombwell. The prisoner resided with his mother, who is 71 years of age, and two brothers. He returned home at a late hour on Tuesday night, when the family had retired to rest, but he insisted on his mother coming down to get him some supper. On getting down she found prisoner with a carving knife in his hand, and was horrified to hear him declare he would "Jack the Ripper" all the lot of them. His mother quietly went to the cellar to get him something when he struck at her with the knife. The blow missed the old woman but passed through the panel of the cellar door. Mrs. Marsdin ran upstairs, followed by the prisoner, who inflicted a serious gash to her wrist. He next went to a bed where one of his brothers was sleeping, and struck at him with the knife. The blow missed the lad, but with such force was it dealt that it passed

through the bed clothes and through the bed into the mattress. An alarm was raised, and two policemen arrived and found the prisoner had undressed himself and quietly got into bed as if nothing had occurred. He was ordered to dress himself and was taken to the Wombwell Police Station. It is stated that although the prisoner had had something to drink he was not drunk, but seemed to be actuated by a fiendish desire to imitate "Jack the Ripper." A GIRL DRIVEN MAD. A Banbridge correspondent telegraphs that some time ago a young girl named Martha Memurrin, of Mullabrack, when in bed was much terrified at seeing standing at the bedside, a person dressed as a man, brandishing a weapon, and crying out, "I am Jack the Ripper." The girl never mentally recovered from the shock, and on Wednesday the police found it necessary to take the poor creature into custody. After being medically examined she was pronounced a dangerous lunatic, and removed to the Downpatrick Asylum. The perpetrator of the "joke" proved to be a female friend of the unfortunate girl.

Thomas Roebuck:

Thomas Roebuck's trial is registered thus: [Class HO27, P241, P192]

Name: Thomas Roebuck, Date of Trial: Feb 4th 1889, Trial Year: 1889, Location of Trial: Yorkshire – West Riding, England, Sentence: Imprisonment, Crime: Maliciously Wounding.

The National Archives holds a file on the case, [Ref: HO140/117] it reads,

First name: Thomas, Last name: Roebuck, Age: 27, Year of birth: 1862, Occupation: Collier, Date the court session started: 04 Feb 1889, Court: Court House Wakefield, Area of court: Yorkshire, Victims: Mary Marsden, Record source: A Calendar Of Prisoners Tried At The Adjourned General Quarter Sessions Of The Peace - Christmas

A more detailed entry in the same file reads,

Name: Thomas Roebuck, Age: 27, Trade: Collier, Degree of Instruction: Imp, Name and Address of committing magistrate: J. Dyson, Esq. Green Bank, Thurgoland, near Sheffield, H. Piggot, Esq. Barnsley, Date of warrant: Jan 14th When received into custody: Jan 14th, Offence as charged in the indictment: Unlawfully and maliciously wounding Mary Marsden, at Wombwell, on the 8th January, 1889, When tried: Ditto, Before whom tried: Ditto, Verdict of the jury:

Mike Covell

> Guilty of unlawfully wounding, Particulars of previous conviction: [Blank], Sentence or order of the court: The same for 12 calendar months, No: 4.

The Hull Daily Mail, January 11th 1889,

> AN EXTRAORDINARY "JACK THE RIPPER" CASE. A YOUNG WOMAN WOUNDING HERSELF. A Manchester correspondent telegraphs: - The Chief Constable f Manchester (Mr. C. M. Wood) yesterday reported to the Watch Committee an extraordinary case which had occupied the city police for some time with a remarkable result. On the 21st November last a young woman, about 19 years of age, reported to the police that she had received a threatening letter signed "Jack the Ripper," and couched in the usual language. Letters continued to arrive, some by post and others being put under the door. Nineteen letters in all were received threatening to take the girl's life and that of a companion. Some of the letters were stained with blood and others had a coffin crudely drawn upon them. Whilst the police were trying to discover the sender of the missives, some young women who work with the girl pointed out a man having followed them, and accused him of being the writer of the letters. The man was spoken to by the police, but turned out to be quiet innocent of the affair. Next day, however, the girl received a letter by post purporting to come from "Jack the Ripper," and saying that she thought she would get him "pinched," but that he had "squared the police," and again threatening to kill her. A companion of the complainant's also received two similar letters. The matter became more serious later on, for on the 21st December the girl reported that she had been stabbed. She stated that she went into the back yard at home with a jug to empty, and saw a man on the wall with a knife in his hand. He at once struck at her, and in order to save her face she put up her left arm, and received a cut near the wrist, up her left arm, and received a cut near the wrist. She then screamed, and her father ran out, but could not see no-one. She was taken to a surgery, when it was found that her arm was severely cut, and had to be stitched. The matter created great alarm and excitement in the neighbourhood, and at the Roman Catholic Chapel, where the complainant and the other girl who had received letters attended special prayers were offered for their safety, and that the man might soon be brought to justice, and the clergy paid frequent visits to both families. After the reports of the stabbing the police set a close watch on the two houses, and, from something recently discovered, the District Superintendent of Police sent for the complainant and questioned her, and ultimately she confessed that she had written the letters herself. As to the alleged attack in the backyard, she stated that she never went into the yard, and never saw any man. She herself cut her arm with a knife in the scullery and then set up a scream. The only explanation of her conduct she could give was that she was "unhappy at home." No action has been taken against her,

and the Watch Committee, in publishing the case as "probably a sample of other cases so far as the letters go," suppress the names of all parties concerned.

The Hull Times, January 12th 1889,

THE "JACK THE RIPPER" CRAZE. MURDEROUS ATTACK ON A MOTHER AND BROTHER NEAR BARNSLEY. On Wednesday, at Barnsley, the magistrate remanded a collier, named Thomas Roebuck, for unlawfully wounding his mother with a formidable carving knife at Wombwell. The prisoner resided with his mother, who is 71 years of age, and two brothers. He returned home at a late hour on Tuesday night, when the family had retired to rest, but he insisted on his mother coming down to get him supper. On getting down she found the prisoner with a carving knife in his hand, and was horrified to hear him declare he would "Jack the Ripper" all the lot of them. His mother quietly went to the cellar to get him something when he struck at her with the knife. The blow missed the old woman but passed through the panel of the cellar door. Mrs Maradin ran upstairs, followed by the prisoner, who inflicted a serious gash on her wrist. He next went to a bed where one of his brothers was sleeping, and struck at him with the knife. The blow missed the lad, but with such force was it dealt that it passed through the bed clothes and through the bed into the mattress. An alarm was raised, and two policemen arrived and found prisoner had undressed himself and quietly got into bed as if nothing had occurred. He was ordered to dress himself and was taken to the Wombwell police station. It is stated that although the prisoner had had something to drink, he was not dunk, but seemed to be actuated by a fiendish desire to imitate "Jack the Ripper." A GIRL DRIVEN MAD. A Banbridge correspondent telegraphs that some time ago a young girl named Martha Memurrin, of Mulabrack, when in bed was much terrified at seeing standing at the bedside, a person dressed as a man, brandishing a weapon, and crying out, "I am Jack the Ripper." The girl never mentally recovered from the shock, and on Wednesday the police found it necessary to take the poor creature into custody. After being medically examined she was pronounced a dangerous lunatic, and removed to Downpatrick Asylum. The perpetrator of the "joke" turned out to be a female friend of the unfortunate girl.

The Hull Times, January 12th 1889,

AN EXTRAORDINARY "JACK THE RIPPER" CASE. A YOUNG WOMAN WOUNDING HERSELF. A Manchester correspondent telegraphs:- The Chief Constable of Manchester (Mr. C. M. Wood) on Thursday reported to the watch committee an extraordinary case which had occupied the city police for some time with a remarkable result. On the 21st November last, a young woman, about 19 years of age, reported to the police that she had received a threatening letter signed "Jack the Ripper," and couched in an unusual language. Letters continued to arrive, some by post, and others being put under the door. Nineteen letters in all were received threatening to take the girls life and that of a companion. Some of the letters were stained with blood, and others had coffins crudely drawn on them. Whilst the police were trying to discover the sender of the missives, some young woman who worked with the girl pointed out a man having followed them, and accused him of being the writer of the letters. The man was spoken to by the police, but turned out to be quite innocent of the affair. Next day, however, the girl received a letter by post purporting to come from "Jack the Ripper," and saying that she thought she would get him "Pinched," but that he had "Squared the police," and again threatening to kill her. A companion of the complainant's also received two similar letters. The matter became more serious later on, for on the 21st December the girl reported that she had been stabbed. She stated that she went into the back yard at home with a jug to empty, and saw a man on the wall with a knife in his hand. He at once struck at her, and in order to save her face she put up her left arm, and received a cut near the wrist. She then screamed, and her father ran out, but could see no one. She was taken to a surgery, when it was found that her arm was severely cut, and had to be stitched. The matter created great alarm and excitement in the neighbourhood, and at the Roman Catholic Chapel, where complainant and the other girl, who had received letters attended, special prayers were offered for their safety, and that the man might soon be brought to justice, and the clergy paid frequent visits to both families. After the reports of the stabbing the police set a close watch upon the two houses, and, from something recently discovered, the District Superintendent of the Police sent for the complainant and questioned her, and ultimately she confessed that she had written the letters herself. As to the alleged attack in the backyard, she stated that she never went into the yard, and never saw any man. She herself cut her arm with a knife in the scullery and then set up a scream. The only explanation of her conduct she could give was that she was "unhappy at home." No action has been taken against herm and the Watch Committee, is publishing the case as "probably a sample of other cases so far as letters go," suppress the names of all the parties concerned.

The Hull and East Yorkshire and Lincolnshire Times, January 12th 1889,

TRAGEDIES. THE BRADFORD MURDER. MAGISTERIAL EXAMINATION. The magisterial investigation into the charge against Barrett on suspicion of the murder of the boy Gill was resumed at Bradford yesterday morning. The court was again crowded. – The Borough Analyst was first called, and spoke of the examination made by him of the clothes found in the prisoner's house and stable, *and the [illegible]. The witness was not cross examined. The Police surgeon, who was next called, deposed to seeing the disjointed remains after the discovery in Back Mellor-street. He could not then discovery any traces of blood. He made a post mortem examination on the day the remains were found, in company of Drs Major and Miall. In his opinion death was entered by a deep stab in the chest, which severed the aorta. He was of opinion that death was practically instantaneous. There was another stab in the chest. He was certainly not of the opinion that the boy was where the body was found. It was almost positively certain that the mutilation took place after death. It would require something heavier than a knife to sever some parts of the body. The body was blanched, all the blood having been drained away. The collar found on the body was blood stained but what struck him as remarkable was that the blood was more moist. Cross examined, the Police surgeon said, according to his knowledge, death might have been caused within 24 hours after he saw the body. All traces of blood were the boy was murdered could not have been removed without special provision. The ears and missing parts were removed as cleanly as witness could have done it. – Dr. Major was the next witness called, and he was also of opinion that death was caused by wounds in the chest. Witness was not cross examined. – Dr. Miall was of the same opinion. – This was the case for the prosecution, who submitted that on the evidence offered the Bench had no other alternative but to commit the prisoner for trial on the charge of the murderer of Gill. – The Bench retired at a quarter to one to consider their decision. The prisoner, meanwhile, left the dock. – The magistrates returned into court after an absence of nearly 40 minutes and the chairman said there would be an adjournment until three o'clock. THE ACCUSED DISCHARGED. When the Court re-assembled the Chairman said: - "The Bench felt to its fullest extent the importance of their duty on this occasion, and have carefully considered every point of the evidence, and they are unanimously of opinion that no prima facia case has been made against the prisoner. Prisoner will be discharged. SCENE AT THE TOWN HALL. Some 40 minutes after his discharge Barrett left the cells at the Town Hall. Crowds of people gathered at most of the entrances to the building, but Barrett got away without at first exciting such observation. When recognised, however, the people rushed up to him, and greeted him heartily. Accompanied by his brother and his friends, he jumped into a cab and drove in the direction of home, followed by crowds of cheering people. General satisfaction prevails as the result. The Bradford Coroner sat yesterday to decide when to resume the hearing of his inquiry into the Bradford murder. – The police were not prepared to proceed, and asked for an adjournment. – Barrett's solicitor said if necessary he was ready to defend fully before the magistrates, and the least time he would take would be four days. He had a considerable amount of evidence for the Coroner's jury, which the police had obtained but not used. – The inquest adjourned till Friday next. THE*

Mike Covell

> "JACK THE RIPPER" CRAZE. MURDEROUS ATTACK ON A MOTHER AND BROTHER NEAR BARNSLEY. Yesterday, at Barnsley, the magistrates remanded a collier, named Thomas Roebuck, for unlawfully wounding his mother with a formidable carving knife at Wombwell. The prisoner resided with his mother, who is 71 years of age, and two brothers. He returned home at a late hour on Tuesday night, when the family had retired to rest, but he insisted on his mother coming down to get him some supper. On getting down she found prisoner with a carving knife in his hand, and was horrified to hear him declare he would "Jack the Ripper" all the lot of them. His mother quietly went to the cellar to get him something when he struck at her with the knife. The blow missed the old woman but passed through the panel of the cellar door. Mrs. Marsdin ran upstairs, followed by the prisoner, who inflicted a serious gash to her wrist. He next went to a bed where one of his brothers was sleeping, and struck at him with the knife. The blow missed the lad, but with such force was it dealt that it passed through the bed clothes and through the bed into the mattress. An alarm was raised, and two policemen arrived and found the prisoner had undressed himself and quietly got into bed as if nothing had occurred. He was ordered to dress himself and was taken to the Wombwell Police Station. It is stated that although the prisoner had had something to drink he was not drunk, but seemed to be actuated by a fiendish desire to imitate "Jack the Ripper." A GIRL DRIVEN MAD. A Banbridge correspondent telegraphs that some time ago a young girl named Martha Memurrin, of Mullabrack, when in bed was much terrified at seeing, standing at the bedside, a person dressed as a man, brandishing a weapon, and crying out, "I am Jack the Ripper." The girl never mentally recovered from the shock, and on Wednesday the police found it necessary to take the poor creature into custody. After being medically examined she was pronounced a dangerous lunatic, and removed to Downpatrick Asylum. The perpetrator of the "joke" proved to be a female friend of the unfortunate girl.

The Hull Daily Mail, January 15th 1889 states that there has been a Jack the Ripper murder in Paris.

The Hull Daily Mail, January 17th 1889,

> THE ALLEGED ARREST OF THE WHITECHAPEL MURDERER. Tunis, Wednesday.- The man arrested here and reported by the Petit Journal to be "Jack the Ripper" is named Alfred Gray, and corresponds in several particulars with the description of the Whitechapel murderer. The British Consul informed the Foreign Office of the arrest.

> **_Alfred Gray_:**
>
> According to The Hornsey and Middlesex Advertiser, January 25th 1889, Alfred Gray had two tattoo's, with the letters "M" and "P". It was claimed that he stated they stood for Mary and Polly. According to The Manchester Times, February 2nd 1889 his real name was Boxhall and in early 1887 he was in the 3rd Battalion Rifle Brigade, but deserted.

The Hull Times, January 19th 1889,

> THE WHITECHAPEL HORROR. EXTRAORDINARY RUMOUR. On Tuesday, Le Petit Journal (Paris) published a telegram from Tunis, dated the previous day, stating that the police there had captured a band of robbers and assassins, and that it was suspected, the Whitechapel murderer was one of them. The British Consul saw a man in custody, and immediately afterwards telegraphed the authorities in London. The Press Association was informed on inquiry at Scotland Yard on Tuesday morning that nothing was known there of the reported capture at Tunis of a man resembling the supposed Whitechapel murderer. ANOTHER "RIPPER" CONFESSOR. A respectable looking man, named Walter Hill, was remanded at Dalton Police court, London, charged with disorderly conduct last night. He went up to a policeman and shouted that he was "Jack the Ripper" The constable promptly summoned assistance by means of an American alarm. An ambulance cart was brought from the station, and the man conveyed there within a few minutes.

> **Walter Hill:**
>
> The story of Walter Hill also featured in The Trewman's Exeter Flying Post or Plymouth and Cornish Advertiser, January 15th 1889, The Birmingham Daily Post, January 16th 1889, The Huddersfield Daily Chronicle, January 16th 1889, and The Daily News, January 17th 1889.

The Hull Daily Mail, January 22nd 1889 features another report on the Paris scare.

The Hull Daily Mail, February 6th 1889,

> CURIOUS CRUELTY CASE IN HULL. "JACK THE RIPPER" PERFORMING ON PIGS. This morning at the Hull Police Court, before Mr. E. C. Twiss, Joseph

Mike Covell

> J. Kelly was charged with maliciously killing and maiming certain animals, to wit, two pigs, and property of William Cawkill, between the 3rd and 4th inst. – Prosecutor, a pork butcher at 24, Holderness-road, stated, that he killed pigs at Pexton's slaughter house, Bright-street, on Sunday last. He had two pigs in an outhouse adjoining that slaughter house, and saw them safely locked up about 6 pm, that day. They were then well, and uninjured in any way, but on taking a friend to see them on the following day, he found one of the pigs lying dead, stabbed several times "right through the body." The other pig had also been stabbed in several places, and was just expiring, and to save it further pain prosecutor killed it at once. He then examined the place, and found the butcher's knife produced, lying on the ground alongside the pigs. On looking further he saw traces of blood on the ground up to the water tub, where the perpetrator of the offence had evidently washed his hands, as the water was tinged with blood, and there were every appearance of the man having cut his hand. There were traces of blood on the wall top and the spout, the man having come and gone away on the wall, as the door was found untouched. – Detective Marshall ascertained that the prisoner had gone to the Royal Infirmary to have his hand dressed for a severe cut. Prisoner, on being taken to the station and charged with the offence, said, "I never see'd the pigs, if I never stir from here." – The motive alleged for the act was that the prisoner had quarrelled with a butcher named Newton, and maimed the pigs in revenge, believing the pigs to be Mr. Newton's. – Prisoner was remanded for eight days.

The Cawkill Case:				
The 1881 Census, 4 Arundel-street, Southcoates, Drypool, Hull				
Sarah Cawkill	27	Head	Forewoman Milliner
Mary A. Cawkill	58	Mother	Provision Shop
John Cawkill	32	Son	Journeyman Butcher
William Cawkill	23	Son	Journeyman Butcher

Tom Cawkill	17	Son	Plumber Apprentice
Walter H. Eccles	25	Son	Commercial Clerk

[RG11, P4756, F27, P8, GSU1342149]

1891 Census, 24 Holderness-road, Southcoates, Drypool, Hull

William Cawkill	34	Head	Butcher
Kate Cawkill	42	Wife	
Annie Smith	21	Step Daughter	
Ada A Smith	19	Step Daughter	Drapers Assistant
Kate H Smith	17	Step Daughter	
Clarice M Smith	16	Step Daughter	
Dora G Cawkill	8	Daughter	
William A Cawkill	7	Son	
Vera Cawkill	4½	Daughter	

[RG12, P3923, F131, P37, GSU6099033]

Mike Covell

Atkinson's 1888 Trade Directory of Hull features an entry for Mrs. Mary A Cawkill, Pork Butcher, 24, Holderness-road

Searching further for the outcome on the case I came across several articles in the Yorkshire press.

The York Herald, February 7th 1889,

CURIOUS CRUELTY CASE IN HULL. This morning at the Hull Police Court, before Mr. E. C. Twiss, Joseph J. Kelly was charged with maliciously killing and maiming certain animals, to wit, two pigs, and property of William Cawkill, between the 3rd and 4th inst. – Prosecutor, a pork butcher at 24, Holderness-road, stated, that he killed pigs at Pexton's slaughter house, Bright-street, on Sunday last. He had two pigs in an outhouse adjoining that slaughter house, and saw them safely locked up about 6 pm, that day. They were then well, and uninjured in any way, but on taking a friend to see them on the following day, he found one of the pigs lying dead, stabbed several times "right through the body." The other pig had also been stabbed in several places, and was just expiring, and to save it further pain prosecutor killed it at once. He then examined the place, and found the butcher's knife produced, lying on the ground alongside the pigs. On looking further he saw traces of blood on the ground up to the water tub, where the perpetrator of the offence had evidently washed his hands, as the water was tinged with blood, and there were every appearance of the man having cut his hand. There were traces of blood on the wall top and the spout, the man having come and gone away on the wall, as the door was found untouched. – Detective Marshall ascertained that the prisoner had gone to the Royal Infirmary to have his hand dressed for a severe cut. Prisoner, on being taken to the station and charged with the offence, said, "I never see'd the pigs, if I never stir from here." – The motive alleged for the act was that the prisoner had quarrelled with a butcher named Newton, and maimed the pigs in revenge, believing the pigs to be Mr. Newton's. – Prisoner was remanded for eight days.

On March 2nd 1889 Joseph Jasper Kelly appeared at York charged with Maiming Cattle, he was found not guilty and acquitted. [HO27, P214, P204]

The York Herald, March 5th 1889,

NO BILL. The Grand Jury found "no bill" against Joseph Jasper Kelly, charged with maliciously maiming two pigs, belonging to William Corking, at Hull, on the 3rd February.

The Yorkshire Gazette, March 9th 1889,

CASES FROM HULL. The Grand Jury threw out a bill against Joseph Jasper Kelly, who was charged with maliciously maiming two pigs belonging to William Corking, at Hull, on the 3rd February.

The York Herald, March 9th 1889,

NO BILL. The Grand Jury found "no bill" against Joseph Jasper Kelly, charged with maliciously maiming two pigs, belonging to William Corking, at Hull, on the 3rd February.

The Hull Daily Mail, February 18th 1889 Jack the Ripper in Central America.

The Hull Daily Mail, February 19th 1889 Jack the Ripper in Central America.

The Hull Daily Mail, March 14th 1889 featured the following report about Jack the Ripper in Grimsby,

BRUTAL MURDER ON A GRIMSBY SMACK. REVOLTING AFFAIR. THE CAPTAIN STABBED TO DEATH. JACK THE RIPPER AT SEA. ARREST OF THE MURDERER. Grimsby, Tuesday, 11.35 am. Our Grimsby correspondent telegraphs: - Another of these shocking tragedies which are now and again reported in connection with the fishing trade, has just commenced. The trawl smack Doncaster, belonging to the Grimsby Ice Company, arrived at Grimsby this morning, and the second hand, Arthur Turnell reported having on board the dead body of the master, William Connelly, aged 46, residing at 116 Kent-street, who had been murdered when on the fishing grounds, 210 miles from Spurn. It appears that about six o'clock on the evening of Monday, the 6th, the second hand was standing near the companion in conversation with the master, when the cook, Walter Tennant Gempton, who was walking about the side of the vessel, suddenly rushed at the master with an open clasp knife, and stabbed him in the back of the neck. The master fell on the deck, saying, "Oh, he has stabbed me." The cook said, "You craft b--------- has that settled you? This is a bit of Jack the Ripper." The master was then taken into the cabin, and died in about ten minutes. The murderer was then secured and the vessel made for port, arriving this morning, when Gempton was handed over to the police. The body of the murdered man was removed to the Hospital Mortuary to await an inquest. Gempton is only 18 years of age, and it is thought that he cannot be sane, as there was no previous quarrel

Mike Covell

between him and the master. Connelly leaves a wife and two children. THE PRISONER BEFORE THE MAGISTRATES THIS DAY. FURTHER PARTICULARS. After the prisoner Gempton was locked up he was seized with a fit and became so ill that a doctor was sent for. He subsequently recovered, and was brought before the borough magistrates and charged with wilful murder. Supt. Waldram stated that the prisoner was cook on board the smack Doncaster, belonging to the Grimsby Ice Company. The deceased was the skipper of same smack, which sailed from Grimsby on Friday, the 22nd of last month. On Monday last they were about 240 miles from Spurn when the deceased and the second hand were on deck, and prisoner was walking on the port side of the deck. Without the slightest provocation prisoner rushed at the skipper and stabbed him in the back of the neck. The skipper fell upon the deck, and called out that he was stabbed. The prisoner fell on top of him. The second hand immediately took him off the skipper, who went into the cabin and laid down upon on his bunk. He called out to the second hand to put some flower on the back of his neck where he was stabbed in order to stop the bleeding, but it had no effect, and the skipper died about ten minutes afterwards. As soon as the boy had stabbed him he made use of this remark, "He wants to make off with the ship and all hands. He is Jack the Ripper." And after the skipper had got down into the cabin the lad shouted down the skylight, "There you crafty b---------- has that settled you. That is a bit of Jack the Ripper." Afterwards the second hand and the crew secured the prisoner in the cabin, and, of course, made for home, where they arrived at about 2.30 this morning. The body was removed to the Hospital, and the prisoner given into the hands of Dock Constable Lawton. The Coroner was acquainted with the facts. A remand was asked till Monday next. The Chairman (Mr. Palmer) to prisoner: Have you anything to say why you should not be remanded? Prisoner: No, sir. The Chairman: Then you will be remanded till next Monday. Prisoner: All right. The lad was then removed. The murdered man was the prisoner's uncle. FURTHER DETAILS. THE PRISONER'S MOTHER INTERVIEWED. HER STATEMENT. In the course of the interview with our representative Mrs. Gempton, the mother of the youth now in prison on a charge of murdering Connelly, said: My son has been subject to fits, and when he has them he is not responsible for what he does. He has actually tried to strangle me. That was only about six months ago. On that occasion he grasped me by the throat, and his hold was so firm that he did nearly strangle me. I consider my son is not responsible for his actions, and in fact all the neighbours know that he sometimes does things he ought not to do. Walter used to sail with his father, who was working out a vessel. When the vessel was taken from my husband Walter became anxious to go to sea in a vessel apart from any that his father might sail in, and he was allowed to go with his uncle, Mr. Connelly. THE KNIFE. The instrument with which the fatal wound was inflicted was an ordinary clasped pocket knife, such as anyone *might be expected to carry. The stab in the neck of the deceased has the appearance of having been done in a frenzy. It is on the right side of the neck, and though not in the form of a slash, it appears to have been dealt with considerable force. The knife has been handed to the police, and is covered with blood.* MRS CONNELLY INTERVIEWED. *Our reporter visited the wife of the deceased this afternoon. She lives at the house No. 106, Kent-road, and at the time of the call was made the blinds were drawn and every sign of mourning was apparent to those passing along the thoroughfare. The scene within was of a painful character. Mrs. Connelly appeared to have felt acutely the loss of her husband under the shocking circumstances through which he came by his death. She was sobbing as if her heart would break, and two ladies were present endeavouring to give her as much consolation as they could. Mrs. Connelly stated that her husband served a portion of his apprenticeship on board Hull vessels, but had been in Grimsby for the last twenty years. He was not interested financially in any smacks, and worked at his profession simply as a skipper. They had lived happily together, and for many years their home had been in the neighbourhood of Kent-street. The bereft woman added that she was the mother of two children, who are now alive.* THE STORY OF BURRELL. *Arthur Burrell, the second hand on board the smack Doncaster, says: - Connelly fell when he was struck by Gempton. When the skipper was lying on the deck the cook fell on top of him. I pulled the cook off the skipper, when then went below, pulled of his oil frock, and fell upon the locker. He said to me, "Put some flour on it and stop the blood. I did so, but the blood could not be stopped, and Connelly died ten minutes after he was assaulted by Gempton. After I pulled Gampton off the skipper on deck Gempton said to me, "He (referring to the skipper) wanted to make off with the ship, and that, too, because he is Jack the Ripper." He afterwards shouted through the skylight of the cabin, "There, you crafty b--------- has that settled you; that is a bit of Jack the Ripper." After that the rest of the crew helped me to secure Gempton in the cabin, and then we made sail for Grimsby.* THE POLICE REPORT. *The following is the official report of the tragedy which appears in the occurrence book at the Police station, Grimsby: - "P.C. Lawton reports that the trawl smack Doncaster, owned by the Grimsby Ice Company, arrived in dock this morning, the second hand Arthur Burrell, reported having on board the dead body of the master, William Connelly, aged 46, married, and who resided at 166, Kent-street, Grimsby. He said the skipper had been murdered when on the fishing grounds, about 240 miles from Spurn, about six o'clock on Monday evening, the 11th inst. It appears at the time and place the second hand was standing near the companion in conservation with the deceased, when the cook, Walter Tennant Gempton, who was walking aft to the port side of the vessel, suddenly rushed at the master with an open clasp knife and stabbed him in the back of the neck. The master fell on the dock, saying, "Oh! He has stabbed me." The cook said, "There, you crafty b---------, has that settled*

Mike Covell

> you; that is a bit of Jack the Ripper." The master was then taken into the cabin and died about 10 minutes after. The cook was afterwards secured and the vessel made for port, and arrives as already stated, when Gampton, the cook, was headed over to the police, the body of the deceased was afterwards landed and conveyed to the hospital to await the coroner's inquest and to allow time for the borough police to gain information. DESCRIPTION OF THE PRISONER. Gempton is of medium height, and has about him a rather vacant look; he was this morning dressed in his ordinary fishing clothes, which are somewhat dirty. At times he seems as if he is not responsible for his actions. This morning the superintendent of police for the borough thought that the accused did not seem conscious of what he had done. When he entered the dock at the Police Court he had his hat on. H was told to take it off, and in doing so he made one of those flourishes with his hand which are often indulged in by persons of unsound minds. Again when the Magistrates asked him whether he "had anything to say why he should not be remanded," he replied (with the utmost concern) "No, sir." He was then told that he would be remanded, and he replied "All right," and walked from the court with evident composure, and not realising the awfulness of the crime with which he was charged. We understand that he was very ill this morning when in the cell, and when Dr. Newby (Police Surgeon) examined him, he (the doctor) thought that the prisoner had been taking some poison or something to stupefy himself. Eventually Gempton was aroused from his lethargy, and excepting the pallor of his appearance he did not betray any symptoms of illness when in the dock at the Police Court. ADDITIONAL DETAILS. The murdered man was looked upon as one of the best and most trustworthy skippers sailing out of Grimsby. He was of a quiet and unassuming disposition, and what is often termed "a jolly good fellow." Little was known of the shocking occurrence in the port generally during to-day's forenoon, but the excitement created by the murder was great around the fishing docks. On the arrival of the early edition of the Daily Mail the news spread rapidly throughout the town, and the Mail was eagerly bought up, and soon there was not a paper to be had.

The Grimsby Case:

The Grimsby Case also featured in the following newspapers on the following days,
The Daily News, March 15th 1889
The Huddersfield Daily Chronicle, March 15th 1889
The Leeds Mercury, March 15th 1889

The Sheffield and Rotherham Independent, March 15th 1889 "Jack the Ripper" on a Grimsby Smack.
The Sheffield and Rotherham Independent, March 15th 1889
The Morning Post, March 15th 1889
The Standard, March 15th 1889
The York Herald, March 15th 1889
The Belfast News Letter, March 16th 1889
Birmingham Daily Post, March 16th 1889
The Huddersfield Daily Chronicle, March 16th 1889
The Leeds Mercury, March 16th 1889
Manchester Times, March 16th 1889
The Nottinghamshire Guardian, March 16th 1889
The Standard, March 16th 1889
The York Herald, March 16th 1889
The Leeds Mercury, March 19th 1889
The Lancaster Gazette and General Advertiser for Lancashire, Westmorland, and Yorkshire, March 20th 1889
Berrow's Worcester Journal, March 23rd 1889
The Newcastle Weekly Courant, March 23rd 1889
The Sheffield and Rotherham Independent, July 15th 1889

I decided to investigate further to ascertain if I could uncover more details on the Grimsby fishing smack involved. I searched the *Lloyds Shipping Registry*, covering the years 1889 – 1890. It stated:
Number: 269, Official Number: 75359, Name: Doncaster, Port of Registry: British, Hull, Tons/Gross: 165, Tons/Net: 216, Length: 160.5, Breadth: 18.7, Depth: 8.4, Built By: Martin Samuelson and Co, When: 1856, Owned By: Manchester, Sheffield, and Lincolnshire Rail.

The entry was far from conclusive.

The Grimsby Ice Company is, according to the *Hull and surrounding Environs Atkinson's Trade Directory of 1888*, situated in the Fish Dock.

The 1889 Kelly's trade directory of Lincolnshire lists
Great Grimsby Ice Company, Ltd., John Oliver Hawke, manager, Fish Dock Road

Birth:
Name: Walter Tennent Gempton, Date of Registration: Jan- Feb- Mar 1870, Registration District: Caistor, Inferred County: Lincolnshire, Vol: 7a, Page: 638

Mike Covell

1871 Census, 179 Kent-street, Grimsby			
Samuel Gempton	23	Head	Fisherman
Ellen Gempton	21	Wife	
Walter Gempton	1	Son	

[Class RG10, P3413, F59, P19, GSU839405]

1881 Census, 177 Kent-street, Grimsby

Ellen Gempton	29	Head	
Walter Gempton	12	Son	Scholar
Kate A Gempton	9	Dau	Scholar
Samuel Gempton	7	Son	Scholar
Susan E Gempton	7mo	Dau	

[Class RG11, P3269, F37, P20, GSU1341779]

1889 Criminal Register [HO 27, P213, P138]
Name: Walter Tennant Gempton, Date of Trial: July 12th 1889, Trial Year: 1889, Location of Trial: Lincolnshire, England, Sentence: Discharged the prisoner, sent to asylum, Crime: Murder.

1891 Census, Broadmoor Asylum, Easthampstead, Sandhurst,

Walter Tennant Gempton	20	Patient	Fisherman	B. Grimsby

Newspapers from Hull Volume 2

[Class RG12, P1008, F80, P19, GSU6096118]

The Death of Walter Gempton is registered thus:
Name: Walter T Gempton, Estimated birth year: abt 1871, Date of Registration: Jul- Aug- Sep- 1893, Age at death: 22, Registration District: East Hampstead, Inferred County: Berkshire, Vol: 2c, Page: 255

The Hull Daily Mail, March 18th 1889,

THE GRIMSBY MURDER CASE. LATEST PARTICULARS. THE PRISONER'S CONDUCT IN THE CELLS. FEELING IN THE TOWN. POLICE COURT PROCEEDINGS TO-DAY. (FROM OUR OWN CORRESPONDENT) THE PRISONER'S MOTHER IN COURT. At eleven o'clock this morning the following magistrates appeared in the Bench at the Grimsby Borough Police Court: _ The Mayor (Alderman Veal), Alderman Charlton, Mr. E. Bannister, Colonel Reed, and Mr. S. Oates. The minor cases having been disposed of, Walter Tennant Gempton, of Great Grimsby, fishing apprentice, was charged "On the information of Job Waldram, of Great Grimsby, head constable, that he on the 11th March instant, on the high seas, while on a fishing voyage from Great Grimsby to the North Sea and back, feloniously, wilfully, and of his malice afterthought did kill and murder one William Connolly against the peace of our Sovereign Lady the Queen, her Crown and Majesty. Prisoner, on being placed in the dock, looked about him with curiosity, and did not appear in any way depressed or alarmed as to his position. He wore an ordinary fisherman's dress. He was disfigured by abrasions of the skin over the right eye. During the giving of evidence, the prisoner fidgeted constantly with his cap. Arthur Turrel, 23, Duke-street, Clee, fisherman, said he sailed as second hand on the smack Doncaster. The prisoner, who was the skipper's nephew, sailed as cook. They left Grimsby on the 22nd of February last, and on the 11th March inst., about six o'clock in the evening, when they were on the fishing ground about 240 miles E.N.E. of Spurn, witness was on deck talking to the skipper. Prisoner and the deck hand were also on deck at the time. Prisoner was walking up and down on the port side of the deck with his hands in his pockets. Deceased was stood with his back to the prisoner. Without any warning the prisoner sprang at the skipper and struck him in the back of the neck. The deceased fell on the deck and prisoner on the top of him; and deceased cried out, "Oh, oh, he has murdered me; he has stabbed me." Witness pulled the prisoner off, and the skipper staggered down below, witness following. The prisoner said as witness was pulling him off. "He (the skipper) wanted to make away with the ship and all hands, he is Jack the Ripper." The deceased fell on a locker in the cabin and blood flowed from his neck. The skipper told him to put some flour on his neck to stop the bleeding, but it did not stop it. The last words the deceased said were,

Mike Covell

"Stop the blood, Jim, if you can, and I might live." He lost a large quantity of blood, and died about 10 minutes after. The prisoner was still on the deck, and shouted into the cabin, "You crafty -----, has that settled you? It is a bit of Jack the Ripper." To witness's knowledge there had been no quarrel between the two men, who appeared to be on friendly terms during the whole voyage. He was subject to fits, and had several during the voyage. He had one about four o'clock that afternoon but recovered. After the skipper died witness called to the prisoner and said, "Come down and look at the skipper now he is dead." He came down and looked, but made no remark. Witness then secured him without making any resistance, and sail was made for Grimsby. The Magistrates Clerk (Mr. William Grange): Has the prisoner anyone to represent him; a solicitor, or relative? Prisoner's mother was then brought into court, weeping, and on being asked whether she would rather stay inside or outside, intimated that she wished to stay in court. She was then accommodated with a seat near the prisoner. The Clerk, addressing the prisoner: Have you anything to say to this witness? Prisoner: I cannot remember handling the knife, sir. I cannot remember ever holding it. Henry Crow, deck hand, gave evidence similar to what he alleged at the coroner's inquiry. The prisoner being asked whether he wished to question the witness, replied: I cannot have had a void of sense when I did it. The Mayor (to witness): What sort of lad had he been on the voyage? Witness: Oh, all right, like the other boys. He did his duty as cook. Supt. Waldram then read extracts from a letter produced by Mr. James Davis, port missionary, written by the deceased to his wife whilst on the voyage, and delivered to Mrs. Connolly, at 130, Kent-street, the following being the passages. As written, relating to the prisoner:- "Walter has had no less than four fits since we came out, 3 in one day worst you never know when they are coming on...I have save that bottle with [illegible] in for when Walter goes off and I clap it under his nose he gets about two or three good sniffs it soon brings him to his feet but he is long kind of silly after." Dr. Stevenson having given evidence similar to that at the arrest. Dock Constable Lawton said that at 3.30 on Thursday, the 14th instant, he was on duty at the Fish Dock, and went on board the trawl smack Doncaster. He saw the witness Turrell in charge of the vessel, who reported that he had been on board the dead body of the master. A knife was also shown to him, which witness now produced in court, and the prisoner was given into his custody. He took him into the King Edward-street [illegible] police office, and after cautioning him, charged him with wilful murder. He said "It's all right." The body of the deceased was then conveyed to the mortuary. Witness went on board the vessel and found there the neckerchief (produced), which was saturated with blood, and had a mark through it as though it had been pierced with a knife. The Clerk, having administered the usual caution, said: Do you wish to say anything in answer to the charge? Prisoner: I do not know I have anything to say, gentlemen. The Mayor: It is a painful duty to

us, but we have only one course to take, and that is to commit you to the next Assizes to take your trial on the charge of wilful murder, and if there is any question as to your sanity, you know, the judge will take care you have every advantage and protection. Most probably you will be examined by a medical man, bit we have no alternatives; we are bound to commit you. The prisoner was then removed in custody, and the Court rose. OPINION OF THE MANAGER. Mr. J. Hawke, manager of the Great Grimsby Ice Company, who are the owners of the smack Doncaster, states to our representative that the crew of the Doncaster were as a whole very well behaved, and that the deceased skipper had of late years been for the most part exemplary in his conduct. The prisoner Gempton had never given any trouble to speak of before. The police state that the deceased and his wife had not been altogether unhappy in their union, several children having died. Several records were against him on the police books, but at such a time matters of this sort are no doubt best passed over. THE SCENE AT THE COURT. As early as ten o'clock small knots of seafaring men gathered in the neighbourhood of the Town Hall waiting for the opening of the Police Court. On the public being admitted the area of the court was immediately filled with men and woman of the fishing population. Before the prisoner was placed in the dock a fisherman named William Chafer was brought up on a charge of being drunk and disorderly. Superintendent Waldram stated that the defendant had rendered great assistance to the police in watching over the boy Gempton whilst in prison. The Mayor said that as the defendant had rendered such assistance he would be discharged. The man thanked the magistrates, and withdrew. THE CONDUCT OF THE ACCUSED IN PRISON. The prisoner has behaved in an orderly and satisfactory manner whilst under remand at Grimsby, and by this time shows clear indications of understanding thoroughly the serious nature of the charge brought against him. He has had two or three fits since being confined in the cells, but yesterday he passed the day quietly, without exhibiting any signs of epileptic attack. On Saturday, however, he had two fits, which the police describe as being, so far as they can judge, of an epileptic nature, the prisoner falling down flat without a moment's notice, and on recovering consciousness he presents a half dazed appearance, resembling that of an imbecile or half-witted person. It is suggested that the recurrence of the fits have an influence on his nervous system, and that he is liable as fits of frenzy at moments when he feels the seizure upon him, being during these violent intervals only partly conscious of and possibly wholly irresponsible for what he does. THE FEELING IN THE TOWN. The prevalent feeling in Grimsby as to the merits of the case is one of deep sympathy with the afflicted family in their distress at the painful occurrence. In as much as no sinister motive has been adduced which can have prompted the lad Gempton to the act, there is an almost entire absence of vindictiveness or anger against the prisoner, and the suggestion already indicated in our pages, that the accused

Mike Covell

> *murderer may prove to be not wholly responsible for his actions, grows stronger as the matter is more fully considered. No new feature has been brought to light since the inquest in the direction of additional evidence to be brought forward at the prisoner's trial; indeed, it is considered that there was hardly room for any beyond the depositions of Lawton, one of the railway police, as to the apprehension of the prisoner. It is stated that the widow of the deceased has absolutely no means of maintenance either for herself or her two children, and the misfortune is on that account the more deplorable.*

The Hull Daily Mail, March 20th 1889,

> "JACK THE RIPPER" AT PORTSMOUTH. MURDEROUS OUTRAGE ON A WOMAN. *A painful sensation was occasioned at Portsmouth on Tuesday, when it became known that a murderous attack on a woman had been made on the previous night in circumstances recalling the recent terrible crimes in the East End of London. The victim is a woman named Rawson, wife of an artificer in the Royal Navy, and who had been living for some time past with a pensioner in Little Charlotte-street. It appears that about 10 o'clock on Monday night, the woman was standing outside a public house when she accosted by a sailor, who asked her to take him home. She did so, and on arriving at the house he gave her a schilling. They had not been there many minutes before the woman was horrified to find that the man was assaulting her with some sharp instrument which he had concealed in his hand. After a severe struggle she reached the front door, staggered a few yards into the street, followed by her assailant, and fell to the ground senseless. The man then made off, and shortly afterwards the outraged woman, weltering in blood, staggered into an adjoining public house and said she had been stabbed. An alarm was raised, and the police were soon on the spot. Dr. Lysander Maybury, police surgeon, was summoned, and staunched the wounds, from which blood was still flowing copiously when he arrived. By direction of Dr. Maybury she was afterwards conveyed to the hospital, where she was received by Dr. O'Connor, the house surgeon, who found that the unfortunate woman had sustained a would below the abdomen two and half inches in length and from a quarter to half an inch deep, and which had been inflicted by a knife or other sharp instrument which had been used with great force. There was also a severe bruise on the body, the result of a violent blow or kick. The wound was sewn up by Dr. O'Connor, and the haemorrhage was stopped. In the opinion of the medical staff, no constitutional disturbance has occurred; but owing to the great loss of blood to the system, the woman lies in a very critical condition. She does not know the name of her assailant, and indeed, states that she is not aware that she has ever seen him before. A diligent search has been made for the weapon with which the crime was committed, but, so far, without success.*

> **Dr. Lysander Maybury:**
>
> *The 1887 UK Medical Register*, features the following [P. 720] Name: Lysander Maybury, Address: 15, Commercial-road, Southsea, Hants. Date and Place of Registration: 1879, Feb 5, E, Qualifications: Mem. R. Coll. Surg. Eng., 1877. Lic. Soc. Apoth. Lond. 1878, M.D., Mast. Surg., Lic. Midwif. 1878, Q. Univ. Irel

The Hull Daily Mail, April 8th 1889, featured another article on the Grimsby Jack the Ripper scare,

> GRIMSBY INTELLIGENCE. BOROUGH POLICE. MONDAY: *Before Messrs. E. Bannister, (presiding) J. P. Atkinson and S. Oates. – William Daynes, fisherman, was summoned by Frances Boyle, a young woman, for assaulting her. – Boyle said she was a rag picker. The defendant lodged at their house for a fortnight six months ago. On the 4th ult., the defendant came to her mother's house, and after using disgusting language, struck her in the face, - Two witnesses corroborated, and said the defendant hit the young woman in her own house whilst her mother was gone for a policeman. He came back at midnight and smashed the windows, saying he would "Play Jack the Ripper," – Defendant said he was standing in the yard talking to some friends, when Frances Boyle ran out and struck him between the eyes again with a poker. – Daynes fined 21s, including costs, and the case against Boyle was dismissed.*

The Hull Daily Mail, April 30th 1889,

> SUICIDE OF A GIRL IN THE REGENT'S CANAL. EXTRAORDINARY RESULT OF FORTUNE TELLING. AFRAID OF "JACK THE RIPPER." *At an inquest at St. Pancras, London, on Monday evening, on the body of a young woman named Annie Masters, aged 21, who was found drowned in the Regent's Canal, it was stated that the deceased had been told by a fortune teller that "Jack the Ripper" would probably get hold of her. She was greatly agitated, and told her mother she would never become a victim of "Jack the Ripper." She disappeared three weeks ago, and last Saturday was found in the canal.*

> **Annie Masters:**

Mike Covell

> Annie Masters Death is registered thus,
> Name: Annie Masters, Estimated Birth Year: abt 1868, Date of Registration: Apr- May- Jun- 1889, Age at Death: 21, Registration District: Pancras, Inferred County: London, Vol: 1b, Page: 4
>
> The case was covered in several British Newspapers of the period, but only one, the *Lloyd's Weekly Newspaper* (London, England), dated May 5th 1889, reported that she resided at 5, Clarence-gardens, Regent's-park, and was 22 years old at the time of her death. The jury at her inquest returned a verdict of "Suicide while temporarily insane."

The Hull Daily Mail, June 4th 1889,

> HORRIBLE OUTRAGE IN LONDON. REVOLTING MUTILATION. HALF A WOMAN'S BODY FOUND. JACK THE RIPPER AGAIN AT WORK. *Two men named Regan and Kelly have found a parcel by the Thames, near St. George's Stairs, Horsleydown, which was found to contain the lower half of a woman's body which had been cut in half. The remains, which bore no signs of decomposition, were wrapped in wrapped in an apron. Information was at once given to the Thames police, who took charge of the remains, and will no doubt make enquiries with a view to finding the other parts. It will be seen that this sensational affair bears a strong resemblance to the Jack the Ripper outrages.* MORE HORRIBLE DISCOVERIES. *Further details show that other parts of the body were found near the same place, and that part of a thigh has been picked up in the river at Battersea. The woman was evidently of fair complexion. The police surgeons of the district are making an examination of the remains at Wapping. The police affect to regard the discovery as an ordinary "Thames mystery," and say that the mutilated fragments were placed in the water by a medical student.*

The Hull Daily Mail, June 7th 1889,

> MORE LETTERS FROM "JACK THE RIPPER." *A correspondent writes to the St. James's Gazette:- A circumstance, which was not at first regarded in any serious light, but which derives a certain amount of importance taken in connection with subsequent events, has occurred at Leman-street Police Station. Three days previous to the discovery of the mutilated remains in the Thames a letter was received at the above mentioned police station, headed, "He is not dead, but liveth." It was signed "Jack the Ripper," and conveyed an intimation that the writer was about to "recommence operations" in that neighbourhood. As stated, no particular attention was paid to this missive at the time; but the subsequent discovery of the remains of a woman supposed to have been murdered*

again drew attention to the matter, and yesterday morning another letter, of which the following is a copy, was received:- "I see you have been finding the pieces, How is it you have not caught me yet? Look out for more pieces." The letter is signed "Jack the Ripper."

The Hull Daily Mail, June 11th 1889,

A GRAND CHANCE FOR THE POLICE. We have received the following extraordinary letter:- TO THE EDITOR OF THE "HULL DAILY MAIL." SIR,- Allow me, through your valuable paper, to recommend every person (male and female) to do all they can to discover "Jack the Ripper," and then, I think, this wholesale murderer will soon be caught. AN OLD SUBSCRIBER. We should recommend the police to communicate with the writer of the above. There is no saying what may be in store for them.

The Hull Daily Mail, June 17th 1889,

BOROUGH POLICE. MONDAY. – Before the Mayor, (Alderman Veal) Colonel Reed, and Messrs J. P. Atkinson and Oates. William Jackson, labourer, was charged on remand with cutting and wounding Mary Ann Fairlee, who deposed that the defendant dragged her down his passage in King Edward-street, and stabbed her with a knife in the arm three times, saying he would "Jack the Ripper" her." She had to go to the hospital. – Mr. Brown defended, and in reply to him prosecutrix said Jackson was not cutting tobacco with his knife. He ill-used her on the Saturday night before. – Albert S. Kitching, Customs Officer, said he was going home along King Edward-street on the night of the 11th inst. when he saw the prisoner striking the woman on the arm with the knife. – Ellen Burman, of No. 5 Shipman's-buildings, was called for the defence, and said she lived with the prisoner. Prosecutrix formerly lived in the same house with her. On Tuesday night, about ten o'clock, she was talking to Jackson, when prosecutrix came up and struck him in the face with something blunt, like a key, and witness then went for a policeman. – John Saunderson, of the New Inn beerhouse, King Edward-street, said that on the night of the 11th he saw Fairlee at his house several times. She had a big key in her hand, and said she was "going to give Yorkey (the prisoner) one, two, two." She was a very violent tempered woman. – Committed to sessions. Bail allowed – two sureties in £50 and self in £50.

Mary Ann Fairlee:

Mike Covell

Mary Ann Fairlee was quiet a character, going by the contemporary press reports and other primary sources. Her earliest appearance occurred then *The Hull Packet and East Riding Times*, dated February 3rd 1882, reported that Mary Ann Fairlee was up before the Borough Police in Grimsby on a charge of felony. She was described as a prostitute, and had stolen 3s and a purse. The charge was dismissed due to lack of evidence. In 1883 the following entry appeared in the trial manuscripts, it states, [HO27, P196, P277]

Name: Mary Ann Fairlee, Date of Trial: Oct 18th 1883, Trial Year: 1883, Location of Trial: Yorkshire – East Riding, England, Sentence: 8 Months Imprisonment, Crime: Occasioning Actual Bodily Harm.

The Hull Packet and East Riding Times, dated August 24th 1883, reported that Mary A Fairlee had assaulted a female prison officer at Hull Gaol, she appears at the Hull Police Court, but is later told she must appear at the next quarter sessions. *The York Herald*, dated October 20th 1883, reported that Mary Ann Fairlee was brought before the Hull Borough Sessions for assaulting a prison officer, named Marion Grace Bedding in Hull Prison. Fairlee was committed for offences in Grimsby.

The Hull Packet and East Riding Times, dated September 11th 1885, reported that Mr. Saunderson, of the New Inn, King Edward-street, Hull, kicked Mary Ann Fairlee out for using foul language. She was fined 21s or face 28 days in Hull Gaol. It was the same Mr. Saunderson that appeared in the report above!

In 1886 Mary Ann Fairlee appeared in another trial, the entry states, [HO27, P205, P262]
Name: Mary Ann Fairlee, Date of Trial: Jul 1st 1886, Trial Year: 1886, Location of Trial: Yorkshire – East Riding, England, Sentence: Acquittal, Crime: Larceny, one previous conviction.

The National Archives has a file on this incident, it reads, [HO140/113]

First name: Mary Ann, Last name: Fairlee, Age: 29, Year of birth: 1860, Date the court session started: 22 Oct 1889, Court: Grimsby, Area of court: Lincolnshire, Victims: John Sanderson, Record source: A Calendar Of Prisoners Tried At The General Quarter Sessions Of The Peace - Michaelmas

A more detailed entry reads,

Newspapers from Hull Volume 2

No: 13, Name: Mary Ann Fairlee, 7 Days, 19 December, 1881, stealing a weight, Grimsby Petty Sessions, 8 c. mos, h. l., 19 October, 1883, assault on a female warder, Hull session, and 16 times for drunk c., 10 times for assault, &c, 3 times for obscene language and once for wilful damage, from 1880 to 1889, Age: 29, Trade: None, Degree of Instruction: None, Name and Address of committing magistrate: Ditto, Date of warrant: 25th July, When received into custody: 25th July, Offence as charged in the indictment: Wilfully damaging certain windows and other articles, the property of John Sanderson, at Grimsby, on the 20th day of July, 1889, When tried: 22nd Oct, Before whom tried: The Earl of Yarborough, Verdict of the jury: Pleaded Guilty to wilful damage, Particulars of previous conviction: [Blank], Sentence or order of the court: 1 Calendar Month, H.L., Hull Prison, No: 13.

The Hull Daily Mail, June 26th 1889,

THE THAMES MYSTERY. IDENTIFICATION OF THE BODY. A SUPPOSED VICTIM OF "JACK THE RIPPER." After more than a fortnight of patient and unremitting inquiries and investigation, the Metropolitan Police have at length been able to place practically beyond doubt the identity of the woman, the portions of whose mutilated remains have been found in the Thames from time to time since the 4th inst. All the important portions of the body, with the exception of the head, are still preserved in spirit at the Battersea Mortuary. It was feared that in the absence of the head it would be impossible to establish the identity of the unfortunate victim of what was evidently a foul crime; but by means of certain scars, and by the portions of clothing in cautiously or recklessly left by the murderer, a number of persons have been enabled to declare in the most positive manner that the murdered woman was Elizabeth Jackson, a homeless woman, well known in some of the common lodging houses in the Chelsea district. Elizabeth Jackson was last seen alive on the 31st of May. Since then she has not been in any of her accustomed haunts, and a number of convergent facts in the possession of the police leave little doubt that upon the evening of that day the wretched woman met her murderer. The various articles of clothing found with portions of the body have been identified by a number of women who knew Elizabeth Jackson intimately, and were in fact her companions. All identified them without hesitation as having belonged to Jackson, who it appears, was also pretty well known to the police in the Chelsea district. The police on their past traced the woman's movements up to the hour almost of her disappearance. She certainly has not since been in any of the common lodging houses, nor an inmate of any of the casual wards, workhouses, or hospitals in London. Living from hand to mouth she must have been without means to leave London except on foot, and her physical condition made it practically impossible for her to go on tramp. She disappeared

Mike Covell

> on the evening of the 31st of May, and upon the morning of the 4th of June the first of the dreadful discoveries was made at Battersea and at Horselydown. It is noteworthy that the houses in which Elizabeth Jackson lodged from time to time and the thoroughfares which she used mostly to frequent are all within a short distance of Battersea Bridge, where the lighter parts of her body were evidently thrown into the river, and Battersea Park, where the upper portion of the trunk was found. There is even reason to believe that the murder was committed in a lonely part of the park after the gates had been closed for the night. The murderer, locked in with the girl, would have had little difficulty in completing the ghastly work of dismemberment before daylight, supposing he had previously provided himself with the necessary implements. There is, in truth serious ground for connecting the murder of Elizabeth Jackson with the Whitechapel atrocities, which startled London on and off all last year. Indeed, there was certain mutilations of the corpse which, though it was thought desirable at the time to suppress them, immediately suggested the handiwork of that most monstrous of murderers. The theory that the victims died from the effects of an unlawful operation performed upon her has been altogether abandoned.

The Hull Daily Mail, July 17th 1889,

> FIENDISH TRAGEDY IN WHITECHAPEL. MURDER OF A WOMAN IN THE STREET.GHASTLY DISCOVERY. REAPPEARANCE OF "JACK THE RIPPER." GREAT EXCITEMENT. THREE ARRESTS THIS MORNING. Another horrible murder and mutilation, similar in all its revolting details to the service which startled the whole world towards the end of last year, took place in Castle-alley, off Wentworth-street, Commercial-street, Whitechapel, at an early hour this morning. The victim in this case, as in all the others, was an unfortunate, and well known about the streets and alleys of Whitechapel. As the policeman on the beat was passing up Castle-alley, which leads into High-street, Whitechapel, and is only a stone's throw from Dorset-street, where the last murder took place, he came upon the murdered and mutilated corpse of a woman about 40 years of age under a gas lamp in front of Messrs. David King and Son's, [illegible] street warehouse, at ten minutes to one o'clock this morning. Her throat was cut from ear to ear, and her clothes being disarranged. It was also found that she had been severely gashed by a sharp instrument in the lower part of the abdomen. Evidently, however, the murderer had not had time to finish his ghastly work, as she was not so badly mutilated in the lower parts as some of the previous victims. A force of police and detectives soon on the spot, and the body was conveyed to the Montagu-street Mortuary, where it now lies. The police authorities do not for a moment seek to dispute the obvious inference that this is another victim of "Jack the Ripper." No arrest has yet been made. The neighbourhood in which the

murder took place is in a state of great excitement. The Press Association learns that three men are in custody in connection with the murder of a woman in Castle-alley, Whitechapel, but the police decline to give any information, and profess to attach little importance to the clue obtained. Recently the police have received several letters, signed "Jack the Ripper," stating that he should commence operations in July. It is believed the murderer was disturbed in his horrible work. LATEST PARTICULARS. The Press Association, in a later despatch, says: - From inquiries made this morning in the neighbourhood of last night's murder it does not appear that the identity of the victim has yet been determined. On this point, however, the police profess not to have reliable information, and what they do know they are not willing to communicate. The constable, who first discovered the body, was on his beat, and about one o'clock was passing through Castle-alley when he saw the woman lying on the pavement near a lamp post. At first he regarded her as simply one of the homeless class, either drank or asleep on the ground, but on approaching her noticed blood in considerable quantity, and then saw, on closer inspection, the woman's throat was cut. He immediately summoned other constables to his assistance, and the divisional surgeon was at once sent for. It was then found that the woman was dead, and the body was removed to the mortuary. Further examination disclosed a severe wound on the abdomen, inflicted evidently with a sharp instrument. Blood has flown copiously from this wound. So far as can be ascertained, however, there was no attempt at further mutilation, and in this respect the crime differs from the previous shocking murders in the East End. It is surmised that the murderer may have been disturbed in his horrible work. Castle-alley, where the body was found, is approached from High-street, Whitechapel, near to Commercial-street, by a narrow passage, and the alley itself is about 18 feet wide, leaving another and wider approach from the direction of Spitalfields. The crime, therefore, was perpetrated within the quarter of a mile radius common to the previous murders, and within a stone's throw of and between the scenes of the death place of Catherine Eddowes in Mitre-square, and that of the Miller's Court murder. The buildings in the locality are mostly workshops, and the body was almost directly in front of some public warehouses. The victim was about 45 years of age and five feet four inches in height, brown hair and eyes, and fair complexion, but has not yet been identified. She had on a brown linsey petticoat, black stockings, button boots, and Paisley shawl, but no hat or bonnet. Part of the nail of the thumb of the left hand is deficient. It has been reported that two or three persons have been arrested, but it has been ascertained but no one at present is retained in custody. Soon after discovery of the body the Chief Commissioner of Police and Superintendent Arnold of the local division, were on the spot, and later Chief Inspector Swanson and Inspector Moore, of Scotland Yard, have been making investigations, but no clue to the perpetrator of the crime has been so far obtained. It would appear that the murderer had enticed

Mike Covell

his victim to a spot which was under the shadow of a lamp and partly hidden also by a large waggon standing close by. So far as present information foes no one seems to have heard any cries or to have seen either the murderer of the victim enter the court. Hundreds of persons have visited the locality and great excitement has been caused by the outrage. The constable who found the body was Police constable Andrews (272H), and it is considered probable that the murder was committed in a doorway in front of the premises of Messrs. David King and Sons, builders and contractors. The scene is overlooked by a row of houses, so that any cries for aid would have aroused the inmates. Moreover, the vicinity has been placed under special patrol by reserve men, owing to it being a neighbourhood affording opportunities for the perpetration of crimes such as those for which Whitechapel has obtained notoriety. On one side of the road the lower windows of the houses are screened by a boarding, but on the side on which the discovery was made there is a continuous row of large warehouses and buildings. According to a statement of a man, resident in Castle-alley, who was called to the spot by Constable Andrews, the woman was poorly clad, and her clothes were all crushed upon her chest, the lower limbs being exposed. The wound in the throat was like a stab or thrust, and the only other wound on the body was below the right breast. There was a blood mark on the face, and on the left thigh as if by a blood covered hand. The Press Association in a later despatch says since the finding of the body this morning two arrests have been made, the first being at two o'clock. The man was loitering in the locality of the crime when apprehended, and was taken to Commercial-street Station, but after two hours detention, his statements being satisfactory, he was discharged. The second arrest was about 10 o'clock, but the man in this case was detained less than an hour. Up to noon the body remained unidentified, although it had been seen by a large number of poorer people from the neighbourhood of Spitalfields. The mortuary shed is entered by two large gates in Eagle-court, and a crowd of poor ill clad men and women crowded the narrow approach waiting to gain admission to see the body. The injuries inflicted are less revolting in character than in former murders in this part of London. On the left side of the throat is a wound extending from about three inches at the side of the neck, and not in front. The stab is wide and deep, this indicating that the weapon was probably a large knife with a wide and sharp point. The cut in the stomach extends from the waist nearly to the pit of the abdomen, but the intestines are in no way disturbed, as was the case in previous mutilations. Life was quiet extinct at the time of the discovery of the body. An ex member of the Metropolitan Police, who was standing talking with a friend at the corner of Castle-alley, not more than 40 yards distant, about the time of the occurrence, saw and heard nothing of the affair. The special patrol on this beat did not see anything to cause suspicion. Only forty minutes previously an officer left the Castle-alley at the Aldgate (High-street) end, where he had been on special duty. It is stated that

> *some fifty extra constables from other districts were withdrawn from this neighbourhood within the past few weeks, while there is a general belief among the police that the murderer has been accosted in the district. There is another equally strong opinion that the author of these horrible crimes is a foreign butcher. The inquest on the woman has been fixed for five o'clock this afternoon. At present the body is unidentified. She was a woman of the poorest class, and the official description accords with that given in previous telegrams. It is stated that she had been employed occasionally in the public wash houses in that alley, and that she gave the name of Kelly on such occasions. But the police do not believe this was her actual name, as inquiries have failed to elicit that any person of that name resided in that alley. London, Wednesday, 3.30 p.m. Some of those who have seen the body declare the woman was known in the neighbourhood as Alice, and was a charwoman. A sergeant of the X Division arrived at noon at Commercial-street Station with a woman from Nottingdale, who stated that she knew a woman called "Liverpool Liz," who formerly lived at Nottingdale, and migrated about Easter to Whitechapel. She, however, failed to identify the body. Mr. Superintendent Arnold, of the H. Division, accompanied by the surgeon to the City Police and other officers, have visited the mortuary in pursuit of their investigations. Several detectives from Scotland-yard have been out since early this morning inquiries into the affair in different places, but up to one o'clock there was no result beyond the information that has already been made public. There is no person now in custody.*

The Hull Daily Mail, July 18th 1889,

> *The nation has once more been shocked and startled by another of those revolting outrages upon defenceless women, for which the neighbourhood of Whitechapel, London, some time ago became notorious. The particulars of this latest example of a brutal and inhuman murder resemble very much of the details of the horrible crimes of a like nature that have from time to time been committed in the same locality. In the early hours of yesterday morning the body of a woman was found lying in one of the numerous courts which abound in Whitechapel. The victim was quiet dead, and the body was fearfully mutilated, though hardly to the extent of some of the previous murders, which would seem to suggest that the author of this atrocious crime was disturbed in his ghastly work. In this, as in so many other cases, the victim is a poor woman, a member of the unfortunate class who are so numerous in the particular portion of London indicated, and who from their wretched calling become comparatively easy victims of the monster who performs this diabolical work. The most singular part of these extraordinary outrages is that the perpetrator carries out his fiendish purpose with such caution and complete success that no trace is left behind likely to afford a clue to his detection.*

Mike Covell

> *Not unnaturally this last dreadful crime is generally attributed to the notorious individual who has become known under the nom de plume of "Jack the Ripper," the mystery surrounding whom renders the atrocious crimes attributed to him still more terrible and appalling. It is to say the least somewhat of a reflection upon the elaborate and costly police system of the Metropolis that such a long list of heinous crimes should be committed with impunity, but we should be committed with impunity, but we would venture to express a hope that are long this monster in human shape will be brought to justice.*

The Hull Daily Mail, July 19th 1889,

> *THE LONDON MURDERS. THE ADJOURNED INQUEST. The inquest was resumed on Thursday before Dr. Wynne Baxter, - The Coroner announced that he should [illegible] the recognisance of four jurors for not attending. Detective Inspector Reid stated he was called to Castle-alley at five minutes past one. On arriving he saw the body of the deceased on the pavement. There was a cut on the side of the throat, and blood was flowing from the head. After examination by the doctor the body was conveyed on an ambulance to the mortuary. He produced a short clay pipe found underneath the body. He also found a bronze farthing stained with blood. The inspector then described the position and surroundings of Castle-alley, which he said was alighted by five lamps. [Three missing jurors here entered, and the coroner remitted their fines.] Two constables constantly patrolled the alley, which was rather a broad turning out of Wentworth-street for foot passengers only. There was no doubt as to the name of the deceased. He had made inquiries at Gunn-street, and had ascertained from Deputy Ryder that "Mogg Cheeks," mentioned on the previous day, stayed with her sister that night. He found deceased's clothing in a very dirty condition, and thought she belonged to the very lowest class. He had no doubt deceased was murdered exactly where she was found. The position of the body was such that it could be seen only by a person going along the pathway. Witness considered the locality was sufficiently lighted. The cut on the throat could not be seen except by the constables' lamps. Mrs. Smith, wife, of the superintendent of the wash houses, Castle-alley, said the baths were usually closed at 10 o'clock. Dr George Baxter Phillips, divisional surgeon to the H Division, stated that on being called to Castle alley, about ten minutes past one, he saw the body lying about two feet six inches from the wall on the footway, the head being turned eastward towards Whitechapel, and the feet in the opposite direction towards the gas lamp. Her clothing was raised over the abdomen and crushed down over the chest. The right arm and hand were covered by the shawl, but the left arm was uncovered. Between the body and the wall was a quantity of coagulated blood, some of which was carried into the gutter by the rain. The blood came from a wound on the left side of the woman's throat, and*

had not been disturbed except by the rain. Having inspected the body he had it removed to the mortuary shed in Pavillion-yard. He had since made a post-mortem examination at the shed, which was very ill adapted for such a purpose. The rigor mortis was well marked, especially in the limbs. The body was still warm in the region of the abdomen. The face and forearms were freckled. Below the left collar was a bruise about the size of a shilling, and a larger bruise below the junction of the collar bone with the breast bone. There was a superficial wound seven inches long below the right nipple, and trailing off from this were scored wounds extending from the large wound, but only skin deep. The top of the right thumb was missing. The wound in the neck was four inches long, and almost divided part of the muscles. It extended to the front part of the neck below the chin. There was a second incision joining the first over the carotid artery, which was severed down to the membrane covering the vertebra. He had not the slightest doubt that the cause of death was syncope, arising from loss of blood through the carotid vessels, and that death was almost instantaneous. The Coroner said the doctor would reserve other points for the present, as it was unavoidable that there must be an adjournment. Margaret Cheek, of 50, Gun-street, wife of Charles Cheek, bricklayer, said deceased lived with her 18 months. She saw her on the morning of Tuesday, but not at night. Margaret Franklin, costermonger's widow, of Flower and Dean-street, said deceased lived 15 years in the locality, and was a married woman. She saw deceased between 11.30 and 12 o'clock on Tuesday night. The witness sat on the steps of a barber's shop with other girls at the top of Flower and Dean-street, when deceased came along and exchanged words with her. Deceased seemed to be sober, and went towards Whitechapel. Mrs Catherine Hughes, married woman corroborated the previous witness, and the proceedings were adjourned till August 14th.

Margaret "Mogg" Cheeks:

According to press reports Margaret "Mogg" Cheeks was the estranged wife of Charlie Cheeks but so far efforts to trace either in official documentation have been in vain.

The Hull Daily Mail, July 19th 1889,

THE WHITECHAPEL MURDER. ANOTHER ALLEGED ATTACK ON A WOMAN. Early yesterday morning, a woman reported at a police station in Walworth, South London, that she was accosted the previous night in Bishopsgate by a man who said he lived in Walworth, and persuaded her to accompany him

Mike Covell

> there. As they passed along an unfrequented thoroughfare, he attempted to force her down on the ground, and, when she screamed, drew a long bladed knife and threatened to rip her up. She, however, continued to call for help, and, as footsteps were heard approaching, her assailant decamped. He was pursued by a passer-by, but succeeded in escaping. The woman described the man as of dark complexion about five feet nine inches in height, and wearing black clothes. The description has been circulated throughout the Metropolitan districts. The police authorities decline to state whether they consider the incident may afford any help in elucidating the Whitechapel mystery.

The Hull Daily Mail, July 22nd 1889,

> The difficulty of the police in Whitechapel are greatly augmented by the false alarms of the capture of "Jack the Ripper," and by the disposition of the women who frequent the streets to imagine, or profess to imagine, that every man who speaks to them is the mysterious murderer. It is admitted that their apprehensions are natural, and just nor it may truly be affirmed that those who pursue their fearful calling carry their lives in their hand. But only a few who read about the crimes in Whitechapel know the character of the women among whom "Jack the Ripper" seeks his victims. They are human beings indeed, but this is all that can be said of some of them. Dissolute and dirty, they steal when they can, and many use their fists or their nails freely if they quarrel with their associates. The sailors, who are generally their most welcome "pals," may not be well behaved but compared with the women who parade the East end thoroughfares, they are not only respectable but refined.

The Hull Daily Mail, July 23rd 1889,

> THE LATEST WHITECHAPEL VICTIM. The funeral of Alice McKenzie, the last Whitechapel victim, has been postponed until Wednesday, at Plaistow.

The Hull Daily Mail, July 23rd 1889,

> THE WHITECHAPEL MURDERS. DR. FORBES WINSLOW'S PLAN. We recently stated that last year Dr. Forbes Winslow communicated with Sir Charles Warren a plan for tracing the Whitechapel murderer. Sir Charles stated that the plan was not one which the police could take up officially, but it was open to Dr. Forbes Winslow to do so in his private capacity. That gentleman has recently received so many communications from all parts of the country urging him to take action in the matter that he has resolved to put his scheme into operation as soon as possible. The work, however, will involve too much correspondence and money

outlay for one individual to undertake, and it is proposed to form a small committee and to obtain the service of a secretary. All persons desirous of cooperating in this movement are requested to communicate by letter only with Dr. Forbes Winslow, 70, Wimpole-street, London, W.

The Hull Daily Mail, July 24th 1889,

THE WHITECHAPEL MURDERS. FUNERAL OF THE LATEST VICTIM. *The funeral of Alice McKenzie, the latest victim of the Whitechapel murderer, took place this afternoon at Plaistow Cemetery. Many of the inhabitants of the neighbourhood in which the murder was committed assembled outside the public house to which the remains were brought from the mortuary at 1.30 o'clock. There was no excitement. The coffin was placed in an open hearse, and followed by two mourning coaches, containing three of four friends of the deceased. The funeral expenses were defrayed by local subscription.*

Alice McKenzie:

Alice McKenzie's death was registered thus;
Death: Name: Alice McKenzie, Estimated Birth Year: abt 1849, Date of Registration: Jul- Aug- Sept- 1889, Age at Death: 40, Registration District: Whitechapel, Inferred County: London, Vol: 1c, Page: 204

The Hull Daily Mail, July 29th 1889,

A THOUGHT – READER'S DREAM OF "JACK THE RIPPER." Mr. Stuart Cumberland, the thought – reader, has dreamt dreams and seen visions of the Whitechapel murderer. He publishes a portrait of the gentleman in the current number of the Mirror. Mr. Cumberland thus describes the murderer's face: - "It was thinnish and oval in shape. The eyes were dark and prominent, showing plenty of white. The brow was narrow, and the chin somewhat pointed. The complexion was sallow – somewhere between that of a Maltese and a Parsee. The nose was somewhat Semetic in shape, and formed a prominent feature of the face. The formation of the mouth I could not very well see: it was shaded by a black moustache. Beyond the hair on the upper lip the face was bare. It was not a particularly disagreeable face, but there was a wild intensity about the dark full eyes that fascinated me as I gazed into them. They were the eyes of the mesmerist! The man of my dream wore a short crowned chimney pot hat; he stooped in the shoulders, and although there was a wiry look about such portion of his figure

Mike Covell

> *that was visible to me, he did not have the appearance of a man of muscular build."* Mr. Stuart Cumberland thinks the assassin will commit yet another murder (the ninth) and will then be caught.

Stuart Cumberland:				
1881 Census, shows Cumberland as a visitor in Oxford. Class RG11, P1499, F80, P8, GSU1341362			
Robert Garner		Head	50	Farmer
Sarah E. Garner	Wife		49	
Walter E. Garner	Son		23	Farmer, Father's Assistant
Elizabeth M. Garner	Dau		25	
Henry Thame	Visitor		40	Farmer, Retired
Stuart C. F. Cumberland	Visitor		24	Literature and Lecturer	b. abt 1857 London

Marriage:
Name Stuart Charles F. Cumberland, Date of Registration: Jul- Aug- Sep 1882, Registration district: Hendon, Inferred County: Middlesex, Vol: 3a, Page: 195

Marriage Banns: [DRO/11, Item 012]
Name: Stuart Charles Francis Cumberland, Estimated Birth Year: abt 1856, Age: 27, Spouse: Laura Nina Webb, Spouse age: 28, Record Type: Marriage, Event Date: September 5th 1883, Parish: Edgware, Borough: Barnet, Father Name:

> *Robert Cumberland, Spouse Father Name: George Webb, Register Typoe: Parish Register.*
>
> 1891 Census, shows Cumberland and his family residing in Kensington. Class RG12, P31, F136, P40, GSU6095141

Stuart C. F. Cumberland	Head	34	Author and Editor b. abt 1857
Laura N. Cumberland	Wife	34	
Richard B. L. Cumberland	Son	6	
Anna Fischer	Governess	17	School Governess

> 1901 Census, shows the family in Lambeth, at 8 Herne Hill Mansions, Class RG13, P432, F89, P25

Stuart Cumberland	Head	41	Living on Own Means b. abt 1860
Laura Cumberland	Wife	40	
Richard Cumberland	Son	16	

> 1911 Census, shows the family in Lambeth, at 8 Herne Hill Mansions, Class RG14, P2087

Stuart Cumberland	Head		51 Author
Laura Cumberland	Wife		50

Mike Covell

| Richard Cumberland | Son | 25 |

Probate:
Charles Stuart Cumberland of 1 Sydney-place, Chelsea, Middlesex, died February 28th 1922 at St. George's Hospital, Mayfair, Middlesex. Administration London June 24th to Richard Lorne Cumberland, Engineer. Effects £38. 5s.

On March 3rd 1922 *The Times* ran a lengthy article on the life, and death, of Stuart Cumberland. It stated that Cumberland was an expert thought and muscle reader, and had worked with the Society for Psychical research with many of his papers being signed by Edmund Gurney. Cumberland published *That Other World: Personal Experiences of Mystics and Their Mysticism*. Cumberland claimed no supernatural powers, but that he simply took notice of small indications and put together deductions based upon them. His defining act was reading names written on paper that were crumpled into small balls, he did this by watching the movements on the pencil as the writer wrote their names! Cumberland's other notable works include, *From Ocean to Ocean*, (1887) *The Vasty Deep*, (1889) and *What I think of South Africa*, (1896)

The Hull Daily Mail, August 27th 1889,

LETTER FROM "JACK THE RIPPER." It is reported that the London police have during the past few days received a "Jack the Ripper" letter, to which they are deposed to attach considerable importance. The purport of the communication is kept secret, but it is said to have caused a flutter among the Scotland Yard men, and inquiries in a new direction are being made in the Whitechapel and other districts of the Metropolis.

The Hull Daily Mail, September 10th 1889,

ANOTHER WHITECHAPEL TRAGEDY. HORRIBLE OUTRAGE. A WOMAN MURDERED AND MUTILATED. THE BODY FOUND IN A SACK. The Press Association says: - At an early hour this morning the inhabitants of Whitechapel were thrown into a state of wild excitement by a rumour to the effect that the notorious criminal known as "Jack the Ripper" had again been at his work in their midst. It was about six o'clock this morning when the news first became noised abroad, and within half an hour of that time a great and excited crowd had collected in the neighbourhood of Pinchin-street, St. George's, the locality in which the tragedy was said to have been committed, and which was in close proximity to the scene of the outrages which have given Whitechapel its evil reputation. From inquiries made by the Press Association reporters, it appears that, while a murder has undoubtedly been committed, there is, so far as at present can be ascertained, no resemblance in it to those which have previously been perpetrated. The constable on his beat in Pinchin-street, which lies between Commercial-road and Leman-street, noticed something in a sack lying beneath one of the arches of the London, Tilbury and Southend Railway. The sack appeared to have been deposited just at the mouth of the archway, which is partially protected by some broken fencing, not such as to offer any obstruction to a person desiring to enter. On opening the sack the officer found that it contained the body of a woman minus the head, legs, and arms. There was no blood about the place, and the trunk appeared to have been brought from elsewhere. The constable despatched a messenger for an ambulance, and the body was conveyed to St. George's Mortuary, Cable-street, where it lies awaiting the post mortem examination. The Coroner (Mr. Wynne Baxter,) was also notified of the discovery. The police state that the woman appears to have been dead four or five days, and that much of the flesh is decomposed. They are unable to say whether the trunk is mutilated farther than being dismembered. It is impossible to give the age of the woman, and up to the present there is no clue to her identity. Three arrests were made this morning, but no importance is attached to them. They were two sailors and a shoeblack found sleeping under the arches, not far from where the body was found. It was reported about a quarter to nine that some clothes stained with blood had been found in Hooper-street nearby, and an excited crowd collected round a warehouse yard there. Some material bearing blood stains was certainly found, but whether it is connected with the mystery is only matter of conjecture. The crowd set to work to see if they could find any trace of missing limbs, but without an apparent result. The scene of the tragedy is a railway arch which forms part of the new Great Eastern Railway goods depot in Bishopsgate-street. A later account says: - Shortly after five o'clock Police constable Jannett (239 H) was patrolling his best when by the light of breaking day he noticed a bundle under the archway. He found it contained the body of a woman with the arms attached, but with the head and legs missing. It was slightly decomposed. The stomach had been cut in a brutal manner. Jannett called assistance, and in a short time Superintendent Arnold and a large body of plain clothes and uniformed officers were on the spot with an ambulance and medical assistance. It was certified that the mutilated trunk was that of a woman who had been dead at least four days, but only deposited beneath the archway during the night. Opinion is divided in the district as to whether the crime is another of the series which has made the name of "Jack the Ripper" a terror in the East End. The spot where the body was found is only a few yards from Berner-street, where, exactly a year ago almost to a day, the mutilated remains of a woman were found. A representative of the Press

Mike Covell

> *Association this morning had an interview with Constable Jannett. He stated that he was on duty near the railway arches in Pinchin-street after five o'clock this morning. When turning his lantern into one of the arches, he was horrified to discover a woman's body minus the head and legs. The trunk was naked with the exception of a small piece of calico or linen resembling a chemise, and appeared to have been carried in some coarse cloth or sacking. The remains were somewhat decomposed, and the woman must have been dead some time, and the policeman states that he passed the place where the body was found a short time before, and it positive that there was nothing there then, so that it would appear that it had been carried to the spot. A visit to the mortuary shows that the abdomen is split completely up. The severed flesh is dark coloured, decomposition having set in consequent on exposure to the air. An examination of the abdomen by Dr. Phillips assistant showed that nothing had been removed from the intestines or any other part of the stomach. The motive for the crime is less apparent in this case than in several which have preceded it. There was nothing by which the remains could be identified, nor anything to show the woman was married or single. The Scotland Yard authorities are assisting the local police, and the detective force has been increased. The Press Association, telegraphing at one o'clock, says: - It is now generally believed by the police that the crime does not owe its origin to Jack the Ripper. In many respects it bears a striking resemblance to that known as the Thames mystery, during the early part of the summer, when the dismembered remains of a woman, enveloped in scanty underclothing, were found on successive days in and around the Thames at Battersea. In view of these facts it was this morning deemed advisable that Detective Inspector Tonbridge, who conducted the investigations into the Thames mystery, should be called in. Accordingly, in company with the Chief Constable, Colonel Monsell, he this morning visited the scene of the discovery, and viewed the remains at the St. George's mortuary. Dr. Clarke, Dr. Neville's assistant, found that the legs had been cut off very cleanly. The stomach was cut upwards, but the contents had not been disturbed. The deceased was apparently about 40 years of age, was well nourished, and from 9st to 10st weight. Her hands did not bear evidence of having done hard work, being clean and smooth.*

The Hull Daily Mail, September 11th 1889,

> *THE WHITECHAPEL TRAGEDY. THE INQUEST. This morning Mr. Wynne E. Baxter, coroner, for the South Eastern division of the County of London, opened an inquest at the Vestry Hall, Cable-street, St. George's, concerning the death of a woman, unknown, whose mutilated trunk was discovered on Tuesday, under a railway arch in Pinchin-street, Back Church-lane, Whitechapel. The first witness called the Constable Pennett, who said that he went on duty at ten o'clock*

Monday night. His beat took him half an hour to cover. He always entered Pinchin-street at the same end, and usually returned along the thoroughfare again. At about 5.25 on Tuesday morning, coming along Pinchin-street towards Back Church-lane, he crossed over the road to the railway arches for the purpose of inspecting them. Before crossing, however, he noticed a bundle, such as Jews in the neighbourhood might have, but on inspecting it he saw that it was not such a parcel. It was about four yards from the footway and close to the right hand wall. There were only two or three pieces of rag covering the body; otherwise it was naked. He noticed that the head and legs were missing. The trunk was lying on the stomach under the arch. There was a quantity of dust so that footmarks would not be visible. Witness saw no drops of blood. After waiting a minute or two, witness saw a scavenger whom he sent for another constable telling him "he had got a job." Two constables came up promptly, and an inspector from the station was sent for. A search of the arches was then [illegible] had two men, apparently sailors, were found sleeping in the next arch but one. In the middle arch was a shoeblack, also sleeping. The three men were taken to the station. – Questioned as to when he last passed the arch before finding the body, witness said "Just before five o'clock," and there was then nothing under the arch. At no time during the morning had he seen anybody carrying a bundle or a strange vehicle of any kind. Within half-an-hour of the first alarm the Assistant Divisional Police Surgeon visited Pinchin-street, and saw the body. – In reply to the jury, witness said the body appeared to have been carried in a sack, then taken out, and placed where it was found. If witness or any other constable had seen a person carrying such a bundle at night, or early morning, he would have stopped him. – Inspector Pinhorn having some formal evidence bearing upon some points in the previous witness's examination, stated that a general search of the whole neighbourhood afforded no fresh information to the authorities. The men who had been sleeping in the arches had said that they heard nothing during the night, and they did not notice the trunk on going in. – At this point the Coroner said that Dr. Phillips and other medical gentleman were regarded in making their post mortem examination. The body had not been identified, but it was not a hopeless, although very difficult task. He would, therefore, adjourn the inquiry until the 21st inst. THE SCENE OF THE DISCOVERY. Pinchin-street, where the discovery took place, is a very lonely thoroughfare just off Back Church-lane. There is not a house in the lane, on one side being the railway arches, and on the other a long hoarding with two or three open spaces leading to narrow streets and courts. All these railway arches are boarded up, but boards are not intact, and in the arch where the trunk was placed a board sufficient to enable a person to crawl through had been taken away. PREVIOUS WHITECHAPEL ATROCITIES. Nine women have now been mysteriously murdered in the East End of London by the still undiscovered demon known as Jack the Ripper. This number is exclusive of crimes supposed to have

Mike Covell

> been committed by this individual, or individuals, as, for instance, the recent discovery of portions of a female body in the Thames. Five of the victims were done to death within a period of eight weeks. The following are the dates of the crimes and the names of the victims so far as known:-
> 1. – Christmas Week, 1887 – An unknown woman found murdered near Osborne and Wentworth-streets, Whitechapel.
> 2. – August 7, 1888 – Martha Turner found stabbed in 31 places on a landing in model dwellings known as George Yard buildings, Commercial-street, Spitalfields.
> 3. – August 31 – Mrs. Nicholls, murdered and mutilated in Buck's-row, Whitechapel.
> 4. – September 7 – Mrs. Chapman, murdered and mutilated in Hanbury-street, Whitechapel.
> 5. – September 29 – Elizabeth Stride, found with her throat cut in Berner-street, Whitechapel.
> 6. – September 29 – Catherine Eddowes, murdered and mutilated in Mitre-square, Aldgate.
> 7. – November 9 (after midnight) – Mary Jane Kelly, nicknamed "Fair Emma," murdered and mutilated in a house in Miller's-court, Dorset-street, Commercial-street, Whitechapel.
> 8. – July 17 – Alice Mackenzie, murdered and mutilated in Castle-alley, High-street, Whitechapel.

The Sunday Times, September 15th 1889, features a Hull Ripper scare that is not what it seems, it states,

> AN EXCITING INCIDENT. – An exciting incident occurred near Burton-on-Trent yesterday. An electrician named Thomas Heywood, in the employ of Lord Burton, at Rangemore, Hull, whose home is at Wednesfield, is stated to have become suddenly mad, rushing off into an adjoining wood, declaring that he was "Jack the Ripper." A party was ordered to search the wood, but in the meantime Heywood denuded himself entirely of his clothing, and travelled some miles before being captured, when he was found apparently attempting to swim in the middle of a road. He was temporarily lodged in Burton workhouse.

> **Rangmore Hall and Thomas Heywood:**
>
> Due to none of the locations being familiar to me I searched for the locations but discovered that none of them existed in Hull. There was also no evidence of a

Thomas Heywood in Hull. I searched deeper and discovered that "Rangemore, Hull," actually refers to Rangemore Hall. Rangemore Hall situated in a village in the Borough of East Staffordshire, and situated approximately 4 miles/6km west of Burton upon Trent. The hall was built in the late 1850's and was occupied in 1860.

The Hull Daily Mail, September 16th 1889,

THE RECENT WHITECHAPEL OUTRAGE. The Press Association learned on inquiry at Whitechapel on Saturday that there was nothing new to report in connection with the Pinchin-street mystery. The detectives have nothing whatever to work upon. ANOTHER ALLEGED TRAGEDY. UNFOUNDED RUMOUR. It was rumoured in London early on Saturday that another murder had been committed in the East End. On inquiry, however, the Press Association learns that the report is entirely unfounded.

The Hull Daily Mail, September 19th 1889,

THE WHITECHAPEL TRAGEDIES. A STARTLING RUMOUR. The Chairman of the Whitechapel Vigilance Committee, Mr. Albert Backert, informed the Press Association to-day that the police at Leman-street Station having received a letter stating that it has been ascertained that a tall strong woman had for some time been working at different slaughter houses attired as a man, searching inquiries have this morning been made at the slaughter houses in Aldgate and Whitechapel by the police. It is presumed that this has something to do with the recent Whitechapel murders, and it has given rise to a theory that the victims may have been murdered by the hands of a woman. It is remarked that in each case there is no evidence of a man being seen in the vicinity at the time of the murder.

The Hull Daily Mail, September 20th 1889,

THE WHITECHAPEL OUTRAGE. DR. LAWSON TAIT ON THE NEW THEORY. "JACK THE RIPPER" SUPPOSED TO BE A LONDON LUNATIC BUTCHER. Dr. Lawson Tait, the eminent women's surgeon, having read the suggestion circulated by the Press Association yesterday that the Whitechapel murderer might be a woman, this morning stated in conversation with a Pall Mall Gazette reporter that the murders, not only in Whitechapel, but in Battersea and Chelsea, are the work of the same individual, who is a lunatic, and butcher, and a London butcher. The cuts were made in a fashion peculiar to the London butcher. They would have been made quite different if the operator had hailed from Dublin or Edinburgh. He or she undoubtedly suffered from fits of epileptic fury, which in women are more regular than men.

Mike Covell

Dr. Lawson Tait:

Lawson Tait, was born Robert Lawson Tait on May 1st 1845.
The 1883 Medical Register, P. 839
Name: Robert Lawson Tait, Address: 7 Great Charles-street, Birmingham, Registered: May 16 1866 Scotland, Qualifications: Lic. R. Coll. Surg. Phys. Edin., 1866. Lic. 1866. Fell. 1870. R. Coll. Surg. Edin. Mem. R. Coll. Surg. Eng., 1870. Fell. R. Coll. Surg. Eng., 1871

The 1887 Medical Register, P. 1001
Name: Robert Lawson Tait, Address: 7 The Crescent, Birmingham, Registered: May 16 1866 Scotland, Qualifications: Lic. R. Coll. Surg. Phys. Edin., 1866. Lic. 1866. Fell. 1870. R. Coll. Surg. Edin. Mem. R. Coll. Surg. Eng., 1870. Fell. R. Coll. Surg. Eng., 1871

The 1891 Medical Register, P. 1099
Name: Robert Lawson Tait, Address: 7 Great Charles-street, Birmingham, Registered: May 16 1866 Scotland, Qualifications: Lic. R. Coll. Surg. Phys. Edin., 1866. Lic. 1866. Fell. 1870. R. Coll. Surg. Edin. Mem. R. Coll. Surg. Eng., 1870. Fell. R. Coll. Surg. Eng., 1871

The 1895 Medical Register, P. 1263
Name: Robert Lawson Tait, Address: 7 Great Charles-street, Birmingham, Registered: May 16 1866 Scotland, Qualifications: Lic. R. Coll. Surg. Phys. Edin., 1866. Lic. 1866. Fell. 1870. R. Coll. Surg. Edin. Mem. R. Coll. Surg. Eng., 1870. Fell. R. Coll. Surg. Eng., 1871

Dr. Robert Lawson Tait died on June 13th 1899 at Llandudno, Wales. His official death entry reads,
Name: Robert Lawson Tait, Estimated Birth Year: abt 1845, Date of Registration: Apr- May- Jun- 1899, Age at death: 54, Registration District: Conway, Inferred County: Caernarvonshire, Vol: 11b, Page: 370

An obituary was featured in *The Daily News*, dated June 14th 1899, and *The Standard*, dated June 14th 1899.

The views of Tait hit the headlines on September 20th 1889, when he was interviewed by *The Pall Mall Gazette*. He claimed that he had studied the murders in Whitechapel, Battersea, and Chelsea, and came to the conclusion that they were created by the same hand. He also claimed that the perpetrator must have been a lunatic. He goes on to claim that the murderer must have had past experience with the knife and cutting meat, but that the work was not done by a surgeon, but a London butcher. He rules out the possibility that it was a butcher from anywhere else and goes on to suggest that the police look for male and females with access to slaughter houses. Tait mentions that he has visited Whitechapel, and seen butchers walking around the district with packages of meat.

The interview caused quite a sensation, and was featured in several other national and international newspapers including:
The Trewman's Exeter Flying Post or Plymouth and Cornish Advertiser, September 20th 1889, *The Birmingham Daily Post*, September 21st 1889, *The North Eastern Daily Gazette*, September 21st 1889, *The Dundee Courier and Argus*, September 21st 1889, *The Leeds Mercury*, September 21st 1889, *The Manchester Times*, September 21st 1889, *The Sheffield and Rotherham Independent*, September 21st 1889, *The Hampshire Advertiser*, September 21st 1889, *The Aberdeen Weekly Journal*, September 23rd 1889, *The Aberdeen Weekly Journal*, September 25th 1889, *The Evening Post*, (NZ) October 14th 1889, *The Star*, (NZ), October 14th 1889, *The Poverty Bay Herald*, (NZ), October 14th 1889, *The Press*, (NZ), October 14th 1889, *The Otago Daily Times*, (NZ), October 14th 1889, *The Fielding Star*, (NZ), October 15th 1889, *The Wanganui Chronicle*, (NZ), October 15th 1889, *The Otago Witness*, (NZ), October 17th 1889, *The Launceston Examiner*, (Aus) November 6th 1889, *The South Bourke and Mornington Journal*, (Aus) November 6th 1889, *The Nelson Evening Mail*, November 13th 1889, *The Wanganui Chronicle*, (NZ), November 22nd 1889, and *The North Otago Times*, (NZ) December 18th 1889

Lawson Tait was also asked to comment on the James and Florence Maybrick case, and he appeared in the national and international press discussing the matter on several occasions.

The Hull Daily Mail, September 30th 1889,

THE WHITECHAPEL MURDERS. ALLEGED LETTER "JACK THE RIPPER,"
On Saturday evening the Press Association received a letter, bearing the East London post mark, purporting to be from "Jack the Ripper." The envelope was apparently addressed by a different person to the writer of the letter, which was written on a torn single sheet of notepaper, and was as follows:-
"E. 28 September,
"Dear Editor. – I hope to resume operations about Tuesday or Wednesday night. Don't let the "coppers" know. Jack the Ripper."

Mike Covell

> The envelope was smeared with red ink, and the signature was underlined with red ink.

The Hull Daily Mail, October 14th 1889,

> WHITECHAPEL AGAIN. ANOTHER "JACK THE RIPPER" LETTER. On Saturday night a post card was received by the Islington police bearing the following words: - "Jack the Ripper, Mischief again. On a hall vestryman in Wray-crescent, Hanley-road, Tollington Park, on Monday, Amen." Not much importance is attached to the matter, but certain precautions have been taken. Mr. Albert Backet, chairman of the Whitechapel Vigilance Committee, on Saturday received the following letter: - "Whitechapel, 9th October, 1889, - Dear Boss – I write you these few lines to let you know, as you are the boss of the Vigilant Society, that the last job wasn't me, for I shouldn't have made such a "Botch" of it. Never mind young man, you can keep your lamps open for the 18th October; I am on the job again. There's no blood knocking about, or I let you see some. Never mind, look out old man. You're a brave sort. You thought you had me once. Don't forget the 18th. – Yours in haste. "Jack the R."
> The envelope bears the East London post mark, and was posted on Saturday. The writing corresponds with that in the letters previously received by Mr. Backet.

The Hull Daily Mail, October 14th 1889,

> IN WOMAN'S ATTIRE. A "JACK THE RIPPER" SCARE. – TIMELY APPEARANCE OF THE POLICE. At the Thames Police Court to-day Edward Hambler, 61, a ship's joiner, was charged with disorderly conduct and with being dressed in female attire. – Inspector Ferrett said he saw a crowd on Sunday evening in Bromlwy-street, Ratcliff, and found the prisoner dressed in women's clothes. The people round were calling him "Jack the Ripper," and he would have been badly hurt bad not witness arrived. – Hambler, who said it was a freak, was bound over.

The Hull Daily Mail, October 18th 1889,

> ANOTHER JACK THE RIPPER SCARE. An extra watch was kept in Whitechapel last evening in consequence of the receipt of a threatening letter published by the Press Association last Saturday, but no untoward incident occurred. The low women of the locality, undeterred by the warnings of the police, swarmed the streets last night.

The Hull Daily Mail, October 28th 1889,

Newspapers from Hull Volume 2

> *MURDEROUS ENCOUNTER WITH A BURGLAR. POLICEMAN STABBED WITH A DOUBLE – EDGED DAGGER – DESPERATE STRUGGLE. Yesterday morning at three o'clock, while Police constable Dennis Pryor was on his beat in Harvest-lane, Sheffield, he noticed two suspicious looking men carrying a bag. The fellows immediately made off, taking different directions. Pryor followed one up a lane which ended in a blind wall. The ruffian turned at bay, and, exclaiming "I will Jack the Ripper you," drew a double edged ten inch dagger and stabbed the policeman in the face, neck, and body seven times, one blow just missing the jugular vein and another passing near the heart, but glancing off by the clothing. Pryor struck out with his truncheon and then closed with the ruffian, seizing the dagger, both falling to the ground, where a desperate struggle ensued. His assailant pulled the dagger through Pryor's hands, cutting his fingers severely, and, getting on his feet, resumed his fight. The officer followed until, weakened by loss of blood from his wounds, he dropped. In answer to his whistle, another constable saw a person running and captured him, though the man with the dagger got off for a time. The bag, which was picked up by a railway guard, was found to contain an excellent set of housebreaker's tools. Three men named Walter Redfearn, Thomas Johnson, and William Smith are now in custody on suspicion of being concerned in the outrage. The officer is most severely wounded and confined to bed. He is going on fairly well. The officer says he found his baton useless against the dagger, which caused him to close with the fellow. The struggle took place in a crowded locality and lasted some time, but no assistance was rendered him, disturbances after Saturday night being too frequent to excite attention.*

The Hull Daily Mail, January 8th 1890,

> *EXPECTING JACK THE RIPPER. WATCHING THE CATTLE BOATS. During the past few days there has been an increase of vigilance on the part of the East London Police owing to "information received." A number of the police have been watching some cattle boats which have arrived at the docks from the United States, and a very strict look out is being kept at night in the neighbourhood where the recent tragedies were committed by "Jack the Ripper."*

The Hull Daily Mail, January 13th 1890 features a report on the Vienna Ripper scare.

The Hull Daily Mail, January 13th 1890,

> *"JACK THE RIPPER" ALLEGED LIBEL BY THE NEW YORK HERALD. At the Thames (London) Police Court, this morning, a young man, who stated he was the*

Mike Covell

> chairman of the Whitechapel Vigilance Committee, applied for a warrant on summons against the editor of the New York Herald for alleged libel. Applicant stated that in Saturday's and Sunday's issues of the paper in question, under the heading "Jack the Ripper," it was imputed that the writer of a number of letters was suspected by the police, and he believed the remarks referred to him. – Applicant was referred to the chief clerk of the Court.

The Hull Daily Mail, March 19th 1890,

> HE KNOWS "JACK THE RIPPER." Charles Cooper (59) a well-dressed man, described as a railway sub-contractor, was charged at the Westminster Police Court this morning with being a lunatic at large. He accosted a constable near Buckingham Palace yesterday afternoon, and said he wanted an introduction to the Queen as he could tell her where "Jack the Ripper" was to be found. He reiterated his desire to the magistrate, who, however, remanded him.

The Hull Daily Mail, April 8th 1890,

> IMITATING "JACK THE RIPPER." Thomas Watterson was charged at Oldham yesterday with stabbing a woman named Jane Rourke, whom he met in a public house and asked to accompany him. On her refusing he drew a knife and ripped up her abdomen. She remains in a dangerous state in the infirmary. Prisoner was remanded for a week.

> **Thomas Watterson:**
>
> Thomas Watterson's trial was registered thus, [Class HO27, P216, P53]
> Name: Thomas Watterson, Date of Trial: May 3rd 1890, Trial Year: 1890, Location of Trial: Lancashire, England, Sentence: 5 years Imprisonment, Crime: Wounding with intent to do grievous bodily harm.

The Hull Daily Mail, April 9th 1890,

> IMITATING "JACK THE RIPPER." Thomas Watterson was charged at Oldham yesterday with stabbing a woman named Jane Rourke, whom he met in a public house and asked to accompany him. On her refusing he drew a knife and ripped up her abdomen. She remains in a dangerous state in the infirmary. Prisoner was remanded for a week.

The Hull Daily Mail, July 11th 1890,

THIS DAY'S POLICE. *Before Mr. E. C. Twiss, Stipendiary Magistrate. ALLEGED BRUTAL CONDUCT OF A HUSBAND. Isaac Walmsley, a labourer, residing in Woodhouse-street, was charged with assaulting his wife, Mary Ann Walmsley, on Thursday night. – The complainant, who was in a shocking condition, her face being hardly recognisable, said that her husband came home from work on the previous evening, and without any provocation ill-used her in a brutal manner. He threw her on the floor and kicked her in the face. He was wearing heavy nailed boots at the time and threatened to do for her when it was dark. She was afraid that he might do something serious to her. – P.C. Rodmell, who arrested the prisoner, heard him threaten to "Jack the Ripper" his wife. – The prisoner denied this, and said he received great provocation, his wife constantly aggravating him. He wished to be remanded in order to call evidence to this effect. – Mr. Twiss remarked that whatever provocation he had received nothing justified brutality. – Remanded for seven days.*

Isaac Walmsley:

Isaac Walmsley, a labourer, residing in Woodhouse-street,
wife, Mary Ann Walmsley,
P.C. Rodmell,

AAIsaac1 Daily Gazette for Middlesborough, July 19th 1890
AAIsaac2 Leeds Mercury, July 19th 1890

1891 Census, No. 10 Trippett-street, Hull

Isaac Walmsley	56	Head	Dock Labourer
Mary A Walmsley	36	Wife	
Annie Walmsley	5	Dau	
Elizabeth Walmsley	14	Dau	

Mike Covell

| Florence Walmsley | 12 | Dau | |

[Class RG12, P3935, F71, P19, GSU6099045]

The Hull Daily Mail, July 25th 1890,

REPORTED ARREST OF "JACK THE RIPPER." The Press Association is authorised to state that there is absolutely no foundation for the report that "Jack the Ripper" has been arrested in London. The whole story decried by the officials at Scotland Yard as a ridiculous concoction.

The Hull Daily Mail, September 17th 1890,

A FOOLISH "JACK THE RIPPER" JOKE. The residents of Moss-lane, Walton, a suburb of Liverpool, have been scared for some time by the operations of an individual who, until yesterday, managed to escape. Bottles, bricks, empty jars, and other missiles were hurled at the houses, and the windows broken. Letters, signed "Jack the Ripper" were sent to some of the residents, and something like a reign of terror ensued. The police, however, have succeeded in apprehending the offender, who proves to be a domestic servant, and whose only explanation is that it was a joke.

The Hull Daily Mail, October 2nd 1890,

A WARNING FROM "JACK THE RIPPER." The Exchange Telegraph Company learns that the Metropolitan Police have had another intimation from "Jack the Ripper" in the shape of a letter delivered at Whitechapel, in which the usual warnings are given.

The Hull Daily Mail, October 3rd 1890 Jack the Ripper scare in France.

The Hull Daily Mail, October 14th 1890,

"JACK THE RIPPER" AND HIS NEW KNIFE. "BUSINESS TO COMMENCE DIRECTLY." A discovery has just been made which, although in all probability a hoax, was yet considered by the police authorities of sufficient importance to be telegraphed to every station in the metropolitan district. It appears that a labourer found on a piece of waste land in Love-lane, Wandsworth, on old butcher's knife, upon which were stains of blood. To the handle was attached a piece of paper

> *bearing the words, "I have finished with this old knife, but have got another, and mean to commence business directly – Jack the Ripper."*

1891 The year of Francis Coles and James Sadler

The Hull Daily News, February 7th 1891,

> *THURSDAY "JACK THE RIPPER" CONDUCT John Rouse, labourer, was charged with being drunk and disorderly on the day previous.- From the evidence it appeared that the prisoner was seen following children about and seizing hold of them. He had two knives in his possession and was threatening people with them. He was also using disgusting language to females, and a gentleman Mr. R. Elder took several children from him, and eventually gave him into the custody of P.C. Wardell (171).- Mr Twiss imposed a fine of 20s and costs, in default 30 days. His Worship commended Mr. Elder for his prompt action in the matter.*

> **John Rouse:**
>
> The court case of John Rouse can be found in the Hull History Centre in the Minute Book that covers January through to April in the year 1891. It bears the reference CDPM/2/6 and on page 70 it states,
> Police Officer Number: 171
> Case Number: 314
> Name of Defendant: John Rouse
> Informant: Police
> *When: February 3rd*
> Offence: Drunk and Disorderly in Linnaeus-street
> Statement of PC Wardell:
> At 4 pm I saw prisoner with a child – a little boy – he was threatening the child, I liberated the child, he threatened me, I knocked him down, he squared up to me. I took him into custody, he was drunk and disorderly.
> Statement of W. Taylor (12): I saw the prisoner yesterday at Anlaby-road, he put his hand in his pocket and pulled a knife out, he got me by my collar, he frightened me.
> Paid: 1
> Cost: 5.6
> 30 days in gaol

The Hull Daily Mail, February 13th 1891, P. 2

Mike Covell

> THIS MORNING'S MURDER. The Whitechapel fiend has returned. It was only yesterday that we published the ingenious theory of an inventive correspondent that "Jack the Ripper" had committed suicide, but this morning he is credited with another atrocious crime. His lust for blood is unslaked. The circumstances of the murder described in another column leave no room for doubt as to who is the perpetrator of the murder. The ghastly story, in all its main details, bears a marvellous resemblance to the eight or nine other crimes that have made the East End of London notorious. First of all, the victims is an "unfortunate;" the hour was about two o'clock in the morning; a lonely railway archway is the scene of the crime; a policeman comes up within a minute or two after the victim was struck down, and "Jack the Ripper" vanishes into thin air! These crimes are getting almost stereotyped in their character and their incidents, and not only in these respects, but even in their surroundings. The resemblance of one crime to another smacks of the supernatural. If we were a superstitious people we should say the foul fiend himself had a hand in them. For look at the manner in which the Whitechapel murderer controls time, circumstance, and place, and bends them to his will. No other criminal has committed a series of crimes in which the victims, the scenery, the incidents, and the accessories have been so nearly akin to each case. And then the marvellous power of escape! In this latest crime it seems more marvellous than ever. The constable discovered the victim before her pulse had ceased beating, but of clue to her mysterious assailant there was no trace! The officer had a few moments before passed the same spot, and apparently he had not seen the woman, to say nothing of her murderer, nor does his attention seem to have been attracted by any unusual circumstances. In the space of two minutes the crime must have been committed. The energy displayed by the fell stroke of the assassin is shown by the nature of the wound. A very sharp knife was drawn rapidly with great force from ear to ear. The same hand displayed the old cunning – the same swiftness and sureness of stroke. "Jack the Ripper" never gives his victims a chance. He always strikes home; he invariably selects an "unfortunate," and he generally chooses a dark passage or an archway for his foul and ghastly work. But he seems to have had a narrow escape this time. He had barely time to get clear of his victim before the constable made the horrible discovery. No cry broke the stillness of the winter morning as the "Ripper's" knife did its grim work. These are silent crimes; they are crimes of ruthless savagery and darkest violence, but yet silent. That adds to their mystery and their eeriness. Fir fifteen months the East End Fiend has rested from his butcheries, but at a time when the world was trying to forget all about him he has reminded us that he is in our midst, and with his blood lust as strong upon him as ever.

The Hull Daily Mail, February 13th 1891, P. 4

LATEST NEWS. ANOTHER WHITECHAPEL OUTRAGE. "JACK THE RIPPER," STILL ALIVE. MURDER AND MUTILATION OF A WOMAN. HORRIBLE DISCOVERY THIS MORNING. THE VICTIM FOUND LYING IN A POOL OF BLOOD. ARREST OF A MAN. IDENTIFICATION OF THE VICTIM. *(Press Association Telegram.)* London, Friday, 6 a.m. Shortly after two o'clock this morning a woman was found in Leman-street, Whitechapel, with her throat horribly cut and having other injuries. She was quiet dead. The body was first found by a policeman on the beat. He immediately raised an alarm. Assistance arrived, and the body was removed to the mortuary. There is little doubt that the victim belonged to the unfortunate class. Detectives are inquiring at the hotels and lodging houses in search of a clue to the murderer. The locality and the precautions taken to escape detection are in all respects similar to those on previous occasions. 6.30 a.m.

The murder is evidently another of the series of crimes associated with East London, although in this case the revolting features which have characterised the former atrocious murders are happily absent. Nevertheless, the circumstances of the crime, the character of the victim, and the mysterious features by which the deed is environed, undoubtedly place it in the same category.

It appears that shortly after two o'clock this morning, at 13 minutes past the hour as nearly as can be ascertained, Constable 240H., while passing through an archway of the Great Eastern Railway, two thoroughfares running parallel with the Whitechapel-road, but lying more towards the river, observed a woman extended on her back in the centre of the thoroughfare. He had passed the spot fifteen minutes previously, and there was no one there. On turning his lamp on the prostrate figure he was horrified to find the woman lay in a pool of blood, which was flowing from a terrible wound in the throat, extending literally from ear to ear. He immediately sounded his whistle for assistance, and within a few minutes he was joined by Constable 327 H, whose beat is adjoining. The woman gave no sign of life, but the body was quiet warm, and the constable felt that the pulse was beating faintly. A messenger was despatched to the residence of Dr. Philips, surgeon to the division, who resides near at hand. In the meantime the police allowed the body to remain undisturbed, in accordance with instructions issued during the panic at East End nearly two years ago, and took careful note of the surroundings, with the view to tracing any possible clue. The deceased woman was about 27, and lay in the roadway, her feet being towards the footpath, and crossed one over with the other. One arm was bent over her breast and the other lay extended by her side. A black crape hat lay beside her, and several pieces of crape or black lace, were found in her dress pocket. On the arrival of Dr. Philips he pronounced, after a brief examination, that the woman, although not quiet

Mike Covell

dead, was fast expiring. In fact, before preparations could be made to remover her on a stretcher which was brought from Leman-street Police Station, she died. By direction of the medical men the body was conveyed to the Whitechapel Mortuary to await on inquest. Intelligence of the murder was telegraphed to the adjacent police stations as soon as possible, and Superintendent Arnold, Inspector Reid, and several detectives and police were soon on the scene, investigating the crime. Swallow-gardens and Ormon-street are narrow, badly lighted thoroughfares, and not much frequented after midnight. The arch under which the body was actually discovered is about 50 yards in length, and lighted by lamps at each end, but in the centre, where the deed was committed, it is dark. One side of the archway, which is boarded off, is used as a builder's store. Women of the unfortunate class frequent the spot, and last night two women were apprehended for loitering there. The deceased was known to the police in the locality, and had been seen during the evening about Leman-street. A Great Northern Railway shunter passed through the archway a few minutes past two o'clock, and a City detective passed some minutes later. The theory of the police is that deceased was lured into the archway and there murdered, and that the murderer was scared by someone approaching before he could commit further outrage on the body. No money was found on the deceased but on searching the ground two shillings were found behind a pipe for carrying off rainwater from the railway. Shortly before five o'clock this morning Chief Inspector Swanson, of Scotland Yard, arrived, and, with Inspector Arnold, made a searching examination of the spot, and the walls and boarding surrounding it. No marks of any kind were, however, found. A portion of the blood in the roadway was, by direction of Mr. Swanson, collected and preserved for analysis. The archway was then opened for traffic. Chief Inspector Swanson is charged with the further investigation of the crime. Early information of the murder was sent to Mr. Macnates, Chief Superintendent of the Eastern Police District, who arrived at Leman-street soon after five o'clock. After consultation with Supt. Arnold, he gave instruction as to the course to be followed in the inquiry. An official description of the woman is as follows: - Age, about 25; length, 5 feet; eyes and hair brown; complexion pale; dress black diagonal jacket, skirt black, satin bodice, white chemise and drawers, button boots, black ribbon around neck; black vulcanite earrings, and black crape hat. In pocket three pieces of black crape, one striped stocking, and a comb. The clothing was considerably worn and dirty, and the lobe of the left ear bore a mark of an ear-ring having been torn from it. The body was fairly well nourished. LATEST PARTICULARS. VISIT TO THE SCENE OF THE MURDER. A Press representative who has visited the scene of the murder writes: - In the minds of the police officials who have been summoned this morning in Whitechapel, there is now practically no doubt that it is the handiwork of the terrible miscreant who has earned the name of "Jack the Ripper." All the important details correspond, and the absence of fiendish *mutilation is only to be accounted for by the supposition that the murderer was interrupted before the completion of his full intentions. The selection of the scene of the tragedy, the appearance of the victim, and the way in which her death was brought about all correspond with the series of mysterious and, as yet, totally unexplained crimes which was thought to have closed with the discovery in September, 1889, of the trunk of a woman in Pinchin-street. It should be stated, however, that there was some doubt as to whether this discovery had any connection with the previous murders, and making allowance for this uncertainty the record of the crimes included eight outrages. The one brought to light this morning is therefore the ninth. HOW THE BODY WAS DISCOVERED. So far as can be ascertained, the facts upon which the police are at present able to base their inquiries are of a meagre character. It seems that a police constable belonging to the H Division, engaged perambulating the district under his surveillance, was passing through the thoroughfare known as Swallow Gardens, when he was horrified to discover the dead body of a woman still warm. Casting his lantern upon the body he at once saw that the unfortunate woman's throat had been cut almost completely round the front from ear to ear. The blood had flowed profusely, and formed a ghastly pool under and about the body. He at once communicated with Leman-street Police-station, and in a short space of time several officers were on the spot. ARRIVAL OF THE POLICE SURGEON. Dr. Phillips, the divisional surgeon, who has had to do with most, if not all, of the similar occurrences in and around the district was quickly summoned. When he arrived he was able to confirm what was only too apparent that life was extinct, and that DEATH HAD BEEN ALMOST INSTANTANEOUS. Careful note having been made of the state of the body and its condition when found, it was removed on an ambulance. DESCRIPTION OF THE WOMAN. The woman apparently was only 23 years of age, her height being about five feet, her hair and eyes were of light brown. On the knuckle of the third finger of the left hand was an enlargement. She wore black clothes, and to all appearances was in mourning. A SUPPOSED NEW CLUE. EXTRAORDINARY DISCOVERY. One of the most extraordinary discoveries, which suggests a totally new clue, was the finding of a woman's hat on the body, besides the crape hat which she had evidently been wearing. It must be said that this fact has caused no little surprise to the police, for it goes to support the suggestion that THE CRIME MIGHT HAVE BEEN PERPETRATED BY A WOMAN or at any rate a man in female attire. The local police officers quickly recognised the gravity of the occurrence, and saw that it was one of no ordinary character. Communications to this effect were telegraphed to the headquarters of Scotland-yard. THE POLICE ON ALERT. At an early hour Mr. Macnaghten (acting chief constable), with a large number of the most experienced detectives in the force, was soon in the locality. Mr. Macnaghten, accompanied by other officials, paid a visit to the spot where the body had been* found, and made himself familiar with the surroundings. It must be admitted, however, that little came under the keen scrutiny of the detectives to make them sanguine of an elucidation of the mystery surrounding the coming and going of the murderer. SWALLOW GARDENS. Swallow Gardens has nothing in its condition to bear out its name. it is little more than a passage through a railway arch, so narrow that when a vehicle goes past the pedestrian has to keep close to the wall to prevent contact with the wheels. The railway arch has been divided by a hoarding run up through it forming on one side some sheds used as old storehouses for bricks and railway debris, on the other side being the narrow passage referred to. It is very dark even at the best times, the only light showing in from the ends of the arch in Royal Mint-street and Chamber-street. At the Royal Mint-street end are some other goods offices of the Midland Railway, but nothing in the way of houses for some distances. Chamber-street is a narrow thoroughfare, one side of which is taken up by railway arches, of which the entrance to Swallow Gardens is one, and the other side has some small houses and a church school. At the end of the street are some more railway arches. It is almost impossible to give in words an adequate idea of the conglomeration of arches, courts, passages, and winding narrow streets; but even a cursory examination demonstrates the case with which even a person unacquainted with the district could quickly disappear into some larger thoroughfares without leaving a trace behind. But how much more easy it must be to a person who had carefully selected the spot for the perpetration of murder needs no proofs. A quarter past two is the time fixed as the time of the discovery, and it is said that not long before two A WOMAN WAS SEEN LOITERING ABOUT THE ARCHWAY. Whether this was the poor unfortunate creature who met such a tragic fate soon after cannot, of course, be stated at present. WHO IS THE VICTIM? The victim's identity is at the time of writing shrouded in complete mystery, and towards the unravelling of this first knot the detectives are now devoting every care. On the hoarding in the archway against which the body was found lying the police have SCRATCHED A CROSS, and this is practically all that there is to gratify the morbid curiosity of the crowd gathered around the spot discussing the case and its predecessors. ANOTHER STATEMENT AS TO THE DISCOVERY. A later telegram states that it is now said that the body was first found by two carters in the employ of the Great Northern Railway Company named Tim Sullivan and C. Clarke. It is also stated that the woman was seen at about half past one o'clock in the morning talking to a man outside a house in Chamber-street. POLICE CONFERENCE. Since 10 o'clock a conference has been in progress at the Leman-street Police Station between the local police officers and those officers who have been sent from Scotland-yard to direct the operations of the plain clothes staff, which is being increased. The officers sent from Scotland-yard include Detective Inspectors Swanson and Moore, both of *whom have had experience in the series of horrible murders which have occurred in the neighbourhood or Whitechapel. The object of the conference is to arrive, if possible, at some tangible clue to the perpetrators of the crime. WHERE IS THE MURDERER? It is suggested after one of the former "Ripper" murders that the perpetrator had probably escaped in one of the cattle boats lying in the Thames, but in this case the Thames Police have ascertained that since finding the body no person has left the shore to board the Spanish and Oporto cattle ships, and that the crews on board the vessels were all accounted for satisfactorily. It is therefore concluded that the criminal is now hiding in the vicinity. ARREST OF A MAN. About nine this morning a man of dejected appearance was arrested and taken to Leman-street Police Station, where he was charged on suspicion and detained pending inquiries. IDENTIFICATION OF THE VICTIM. London 1.15 p.m., The deceased woman has been recognised as an unfortunate well known in the neighbourhood of Tower Hill as "Carrotty Nell." LIST OF THE WHITECHAPEL MURDERS.*

1. – Christmas Week, 1887 – An unknown woman found murdered near Osborne and Wentworth-streets, Whitechapel.
2. – August 7, 1888 – Martha Turner found stabbed in 31 places on a landing in model dwellings known as George Yard buildings, Commercial-street, Spitalfields.
3. – August 31 – Mrs. Nicholls, murdered and mutilated in Buck's-row, Whitechapel.
4. – September 7 – Mrs. Chapman, murdered and mutilated in Hanbury-street, Whitechapel.
5. – September 29 – Elizabeth Stride, found with her throat cut in Berner-street, Whitechapel.
6. – September 29 – Catherine Eddowes, murdered and mutilated in Mitre-square, Aldgate.
7. – November 9 (after midnight) – Mary Jane Kelly, nicknamed "Fair Emma," murdered and mutilated in a house in Miller's-court, Dorset-street, Commercial-street, Whitechapel.
8. – July 17 – Alice Mackenzie, murdered and mutilated in Castle-alley, High-street, Whitechapel.
9. – September 10 1889, woman unknown; body found under Railway Arch in Pinchin-street, Whitechapel.
10. –February 13 1891, a woman found with throat cut, under railway arch in Leman-street, Whitechapel.

The Hull and East Yorkshire and Lincolnshire Times, February 14th 1891, P. 5,

Mike Covell

> *"JACK THE RIPPER" AGAIN. ATROCIOUS TRAGEDY IN WHITECHAPEL. MURDER OF A WOMAN. THE BODY FOUND LYING ON A POOL OF BLOOD. AN ARREST ON SUSPICION. SUPPOSED IDENTIFICATION OF THE VICTIM. COMPLETE DETAILS OF THE CRIME. London, Friday, 6 a.m. Shortly after two o'clock this morning a woman was found in Leman-street, Whitechapel, with her throat horribly cut and having other injuries. She was quiet dead. The body was first found by a policeman on the beat. He immediately raised an alarm. Assistance arrived, and the body was removed to the mortuary. There is little doubt that the victim belonged to the unfortunate class. Detectives are inquiring at the hotels and lodging houses in search of a clue to the murderer. The locality and the precautions taken to escape detection are in all respects similar to those on previous occasions. 6.30 a.m.*
>
> *The murder is evidently another of the series of crimes associated with East London, although in this case the revolting features which have characterised the former atrocious murders are happily absent. Nevertheless, the circumstances of the crime, the character of the victim, and the mysterious features by which the deed is environed, undoubtedly place it in the same category.*
>
> *It appears that shortly after two o'clock this morning, at 13 minutes past the hour as nearly as can be ascertained, Constable 240H., while passing through an archway of the Great Eastern Railway, two thoroughfares running parallel with the Whitechapel-road, but lying more towards the river, observed a woman extended on her back in the centre of the thoroughfare. He had passed the spot fifteen minutes previously, and there was no one there. On turning his lamp on the prostrate figure he was horrified to find the woman lay in a pool of blood, which was flowing from a terrible wound in the throat, extending literally from ear to ear. He immediately sounded his whistle for assistance, and within a few minutes he was joined by Constable 327 H, whose beat is adjoining. The woman gave no sign of life, but the body was quiet warm, and the constable felt that the pulse was beating faintly. A messenger was despatched to the residence of Dr. Philips, surgeon to the division, who resides near at hand. In the meantime the police allowed the body to remain undisturbed, in accordance with instructions issued during the panic at East End nearly two years ago, and took careful note of the surroundings, with the view to tracing any possible clue. The deceased woman was about 27, and lay in the roadway, her feet being towards the footpath, and crossed one over with the other. One arm was bent over her breast and the other lay extended by her side. A black crape hat lay beside her, and several pieces of crape or black lace, were found in her dress pocket. On the arrival of Dr. Philips he pronounced, after a brief examination, that the woman, although not quiet dead, was fast expiring. In fact, before preparations could be made to remover her*

on a stretcher which was brought from Leman-street Police Station, she died. By direction of the medical men the body was conveyed to the Whitechapel Mortuary to await on inquest. Intelligence of the murder was telegraphed to the adjacent police stations as soon as possible, and Superintendent Arnold, Inspector Reid, and several detectives and police were soon on the scene, investigating the crime. Swallow-gardens and Ormon-street are narrow, badly lighted thoroughfares, and not much frequented after midnight. The arch under which the body was actually discovered is about 50 yards in length, and lighted by lamps at each end, but in the centre, where the deed was committed, it is dark. One side of the archway, which is boarded off, is used as a builder's store. Women of the unfortunate class frequent the spot, and last night two women were apprehended for loitering there. The deceased was known to the police in the locality, and had been seen during the evening about Leman-street. A Great Northern Railway shunter passed through the archway a few minutes past two o'clock, and a City detective passed some minutes later. The theory of the police is that deceased was lured into the archway and there murdered, and that the murderer was scared by someone approaching before he could commit further outrage on the body. No money was found on the deceased but on searching the ground two shillings were found behind a pipe for carrying off rainwater from the railway. Shortly before five o'clock this morning Chief Inspector Swanson, of Scotland Yard, arrived, and, with Inspector Arnold, made a searching examination of the spot, and the walls and boarding surrounding it. No marks of any kind were, however, found. A portion of the blood in the roadway was, by direction of Mr. Swanson, collected and preserved for analysis. The archway was then opened for traffic. Chief Inspector Swanson is charged with the further investigation of the crime. Early information of the murder was sent to Mr. Macnates, Chief Superintendent of the Eastern Police District, who arrived at Leman-street soon after five o'clock. After consultation with Supt. Arnold, he gave instruction as to the course to be followed in the inquiry. An official description of the woman is as follows: - Age, about 25; length, 5 feet; eyes and hair brown; complexion pale; dress black diagonal jacket, skirt black, satin bodice, white chemise and drawers, button boots, black ribbon around neck; black vulcanite earrings, and black crape hat. In pocket three pieces of black crape, one striped stocking, and a comb. The clothing was considerably worn and dirty, and the lobe of the left ear bore a mark of an ear-ring having been torn from it. The body was fairly well nourished. VISIT TO THE SCENE OF THE MURDER. A Press representative who has visited the scene of the murder writes: - In the minds of the police officials who have been summoned this morning in Whitechapel, there is now practically no doubt that it is the handiwork of the terrible miscreant who has earned the name of "Jack the Ripper." All the important details correspond, and the absence of fiendish mutilation is only to be accounted for by the supposition that the murderer was interrupted before the

Mike Covell

completion of his full intentions. The selection of the scene of the tragedy, the appearance of the victim, and the way in which her death was brought about all correspond with the series of mysterious and, as yet, totally unexplained crimes which was thought to have closed with the discovery in September, 1889, of the trunk of a woman in Pinchin-street. It should be stated, however, that there was some doubt as to whether this discovery had any connection with the previous murders, and making allowance for this uncertainty the record of the crimes included eight outrages. The one brought to light this morning is therefore the ninth. HOW THE BODY WAS DISCOVERED. So far as can be ascertained, the facts upon which the police are at present able to base their inquiries are of a meagre character. It seems that a police constable belonging to the H Division, engaged perambulating the district under his surveillance, was passing through the thoroughfare known as Swallow Gardens, when he was horrified to discover the dead body of a woman still warm. Casting his lantern upon the body he at once saw that the unfortunate woman's throat had been cut almost completely round the front from ear to ear. The blood had flowed profusely, and formed a ghastly pool under and about the body. He at once communicated with Leman-street Police-station, and in a short space of time several officers were on the spot. ARRIVAL OF THE POLICE SURGEON. Dr. Phillips, the divisional surgeon, who has had to do with most, if not all, of the similar occurrences in and around the district was quickly summoned. When he arrived he was able to confirm what was only too apparent that life was extinct, and that DEATH HAD BEEN ALMOST INSTANTANEOUS. Careful note having been made of the state of the body and its condition when found, it was removed on an ambulance. DESCRIPTION OF THE WOMAN. The woman apparently was only 23 years of age, her height being about five feet, her hair and eyes were of light brown. On the knuckle of the third finger of the left hand was an enlargement. She wore black clothes, and to all appearances was in mourning. A SUPPOSED NEW CLUE. EXTRAORDINARY DISCOVERY. One of the most extraordinary discoveries, which suggests a totally new clue, was the finding of a woman's hat on the body, besides the crape hat which she had evidently been wearing. It must be said that this fact has caused no little surprise to the police, for it goes to support the suggestion that THE CRIME MIGHT HAVE BEEN PERPETRATED BY A WOMAN or at any rate a man in female attire. The local police officers quickly recognised the gravity of the occurrence, and saw that it was one of no ordinary character. Communications to this effect were telegraphed to the headquarters of Scotland-yard. THE POLICE ON ALERT. At an early hour Mr. Macnaghten (acting chief constable), with a large number of the most experienced detectives in the force, was soon in the locality. Mr. Macnaghten, accompanied by other officials, paid a visit to the spot where the body had been found, and made himself familiar with the surroundings. It must be admitted, however, that little came under the keen scrutiny of the detectives to make them sanguine of an elucidation of the mystery surrounding the coming and going of the murderer. SWALLOW GARDENS. Swallow Gardens has nothing in its condition to bear out its name. it is little more than a passage through a railway arch, so narrow that when a vehicle goes past the pedestrian has to keep close to the wall to prevent contact with the wheels. The railway arch has been divided by a hoarding run up through it forming on one side some sheds used as old storehouses for bricks and railway debris, on the other side being the narrow passage referred to. It is very dark even at the best times, the only light showing in from the ends of the arch in Royal Mint-street and Chamber-street. At the Royal Mint-street end are some other goods offices of the Midland Railway, but nothing in the way of houses for some distances. Chamber-street is a narrow thoroughfare, one side of which is taken up by railway arches, of which the entrance to Swallow Gardens is one, and the other side has some small houses and a church school. At the end of the street are some more railway arches. It is almost impossible to give in words an adequate idea of the conglomeration of arches, courts, passages, and winding narrow streets; but even a cursory examination demonstrates the case with which even a person unacquainted with the district could quickly disappear into some larger thoroughfares without leaving a trace behind. But how much more easy it must be to a person who had carefully selected the spot for the perpetration of murder needs no proofs. A quarter past two is the time fixed as the time of the discovery, and it is said that not long before two A WOMAN WAS SEEN LOITERING ABOUT THE ARCHWAY. Whether this was the poor unfortunate creature who met such a tragic fate soon after cannot, of course, be stated at present. WHO IS THE VICTIM? The victim's identity is at the time of writing shrouded in complete mystery, and towards the unravelling of this first knot the detectives are now devoting every care. On the hoarding in the archway against which the body was found lying the police have SCRATCHED A CROSS, and this is practically all that there is to gratify the morbid curiosity of the crowd gathered around the spot discussing the case and its predecessors. ANOTHER STATEMENT AS TO THE DISCOVERY. A later telegram states that it is now said that the body was first found by two carters in the employ of the Great Northern Railway Company named Tim Sullivan and C. Clarke. It is also stated that the woman was seen at about half past one o'clock in the morning talking to a man outside a house in Chamber-street. POLICE CONFERENCE. Since 10 o'clock a conference has been in progress at the Leman-street Police Station between the local police officers and those officers who have been sent from Scotland-yard to direct the operations of the plain clothes staff, which is being increased. The officers sent from Scotland-yard include Detective Inspectors Swanson and Moore, both of whom have had experience in the series of horrible murders which have occurred in the neighbourhood or Whitechapel. The object of the conference is to arrive, if *possible, at some tangible clue to the perpetrators of the crime. WHERE IS THE MURDERER? It is suggested after one of the former "Ripper" murders that the perpetrator had probably escaped in one of the cattle boats lying in the Thames, but in this case the Thames Police have ascertained that since finding the body no person has left the shore to board the Spanish and Oporto cattle ships, and that the crews on board the vessels were all accounted for satisfactorily. It is therefore concluded that the criminal is now hiding in the vicinity. ARREST OF A MAN ON SUSPICION. About nine this morning a man of dejected appearance was arrested and taken to Leman-street Police Station, where he was charged on suspicion and detained pending inquiries. IDENTIFICATION OF THE VICTIM. London 1.15 p.m., The deceased woman has been recognised as an unfortunate well known in the neighbourhood of Tower Hill as "Carrotty Nell." Telegraphing at 2 p.m., a Press Association representative says the police have not been able to ascertain definitely the identity of the woman. Like so many of her class, she was not known to many of her acquaintances by any regular name, and they are also ignorant as to where she was in the habit of living. Two or three women have, however, been able to identify the body as that of a young woman whom the Salvation Army had endeavoured to reclaim, and who frequently slept at the Army shelter in the Whitechapel-road. These women saw her alive for the last time on Monday. The mortuary is now being frequently visited by females, and some pathetic scenes have been witnessed. The women have come out after seeing horrible injuries the victim has sustained. Shortly before three o'clock a woman presented herself to the mortuary, and stated that she wished to view the body, as she believed she could recognise it. She was, however, informed that she would have to get an order from the police before she could be permitted to view the remains. Accordingly, she went to Leman-street Police Station, and, having satisfied the authorities that her request was a bona-fide one, was taken by Sergeant Doden to the mortuary. On seeing the body, she asserted that it was that of a woman who was in the habit of walking the streets, and who some time ago lived in Thrall-street, Spitalfields. Her name was either Francis or Frances, and whether it was a surname or a Christian name the woman could not say. She had not, she added, seen the deceased for some time. SIR EDWARD BRADFORD'S OPINION. Sir Edward Bradford, Chief Commissioner of the Police, stated this afternoon that he felt convinced, from the evidence of the previous murders in Whitechapel, that the murdered woman found this morning was the victim of the same assassin who had previously struck terror in the East End. Whilst in India Sir Edward was particularly famous in devising means for putting down "thuggism" (a form of silent murder by strangulation with a whipcord noose), and he will utilise his experience in that respect in a searching for the miscreant in the present case. Sir Edward has now at his disposal all the smartest detectives of the Criminal Investigation Department, and he will make use of them in the service of elucidating the latest mystery. LATEST PARTICULARS. IMPORTANT EVIDENCE. Considerable energy was shown in endeavouring to discover the identity of deceased, but for some time little could be learned beyond the fact that some police officers believed they recognised her as an unfortunate in the habit of frequenting the neighbourhood of Tower Hill and Whitechapel. As news of the crime spread, many people came forward with stories as to having seen a woman talking to a man near where the body was found, either late at night or in the early morning, and many of these were obviously of little value, but the officials were careful not to hastily discard any suggestions likely to be of the slightest assistance. The more credible statements were made by a man commonly known in that district as "Jambo," and by William, Frida, John, and Joe Knapta, in the employ of the Great Northern Railway Company, who asserted that they saw the murdered woman speaking to a man at 1.23 a.m. at the corner of Rosemary-lane, near the scene of the murder. The man they describe as wearing a brown coat and a brown hat, his height being about four feet four inches, and he was of stout build. The three last named men went to some stables close by, where they remained for about 35 minutes, and on returning found a constable in charge of the body. According to one man who resides in the locality, the murdered woman was seen in company with another woman drinking in a public-house, near Swallow-gardens, at about half-past 12 on Thursday night. The deceased is stated to have said, "Make haste, because I have to meet someone at the Arch at the half-hour." "What Arch?" asked the other woman; to which the deceased responded, "The shed-way arch, School-end." This man states that he knew the murdered woman as "Carrotty Hannah," a declaration which is borne out by some other persons. The statement given goes to show that the woman kept her appointment, which in all probability was with her murderer. As the day wore on the police received many applications from persons anxious to view the body In and around the mortuary not a few strange and pathetic scenes were witnessed, and for the greater portion of the day the entrance to the mortuary was surrounded by a motley throng of men and woman of the poorest class. Now and then two or three women would be conducted by a detective into the mortuary for the purpose, if possible, of identifying the body. THE FLIGHT OF THE MURDERER. This seems to have been the most remarkable in the completeness of the mystery surrounding it. The night watchman at the pierhead of St. Catherine's Docks named Wm. Paris stated to as representative of the Press Association yesterday that he had to call up his foreman and other men two hours before high tide. He reached the Royal Mint-square, which almost overlooked the scene of the tragedy, about ten minutes past two a.m. he saw no one about, and heard no noise. He tapped at the window of his foreman's apartments, and, receiving his answer, left. As he was returning to the docks a constable turned his light on him, and, recognising the watchman, said he was looking for "Jack the Ripper," as*

Mike Covell

there had been another murder. When he reached the scene there were three or four policemen arrived, and Dr Phillips was already in attendance. It was perfectly dark, and the only light shown was that from the constables lamps. He was not permitted to go near the body, but could see that the woman was lying on her back in the centre of the road. All was quiet in the neighbourhood, and he saw no one about but policemen. At the Royal Mint Square, which is close to Swallow Gardens, an officer in plain clothes was doing duty. He saw nothing of the murderer, although the latter, judging from the condition of the body when found, must have hurriedly escaped by one end of the thoroughfare as the officer entered at the other. By whichever end of the street the murderer escaped, he must have run the risk of meeting railway workmen, the dock watchman, and the plain clothes policeman, as well as the constable in uniform. At three o'clock yesterday afternoon, the police authorities circulated an announcement that the crime was supposed to be the work of "Jack the Ripper," and ordered all docks, wharves, and stairs to be searched. This was promptly carried out by Detective Inspector John Regan, of the River Police, whose efforts, combined with those of his men, soon disposed of the theory that the murderer might be connected with the cattle boats or some steamer lying in the port of London. There were none of the former in the dock, and the men of the other vessels were satisfactorily accounted for. Having concluded that, so far as the river boats were concerned, the murderer had not left land, a conference of detective officers was summoned. THE INQUEST. The inquest will be opened before Mr Gwynae E. Baxter this (Saturday) afternoon, and after formal evidence has been taken will probably be adjourned till Monday. LIST OF THE WHITECHAPEL MURDERS.

1. – Christmas Week, 1887 – An unknown woman found murdered near Osborne and Wentworth-streets, Whitechapel.
2. – August 7, 1888 – Martha Turner found stabbed in 31 places on a landing in model dwellings known as George Yard buildings, Commercial-street, Spitalfields.
3. – August 31 – Mrs. Nicholls, murdered and mutilated in Buck's-row, Whitechapel.
4. – September 7 – Mrs. Chapman, murdered and mutilated in Hanbury-street, Whitechapel.
5. – September 29 – Elizabeth Stride, found with her throat cut in Berner-street, Whitechapel.
6. – September 29 – Catherine Eddowes, murdered and mutilated in Mitre-square, Aldgate.
7. – November 9 (after midnight) – Mary Jane Kelly, nicknamed "Fair Emma," murdered and mutilated in a house in Miller's-court, Dorset-street, Commercial-street, Whitechapel.

8. – July 17 – Alice Mackenzie, murdered and mutilated in Castle-alley, High-street, Whitechapel.
9. – September 10 1889, woman unknown; body found under Railway Arch in Pinchin-street, Whitechapel.
10. –February 13 1891, a woman found with throat cut, under railway arch in Leman-street, Whitechapel.

Mike Covell

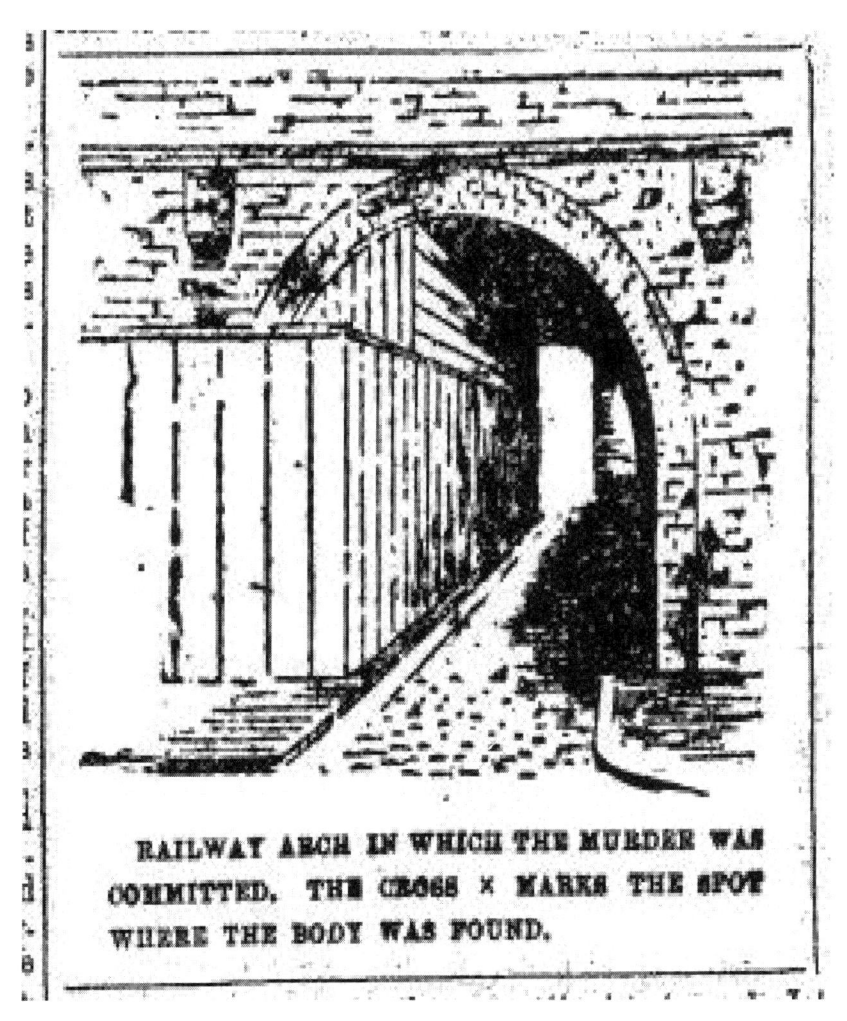

RAILWAY ARCH IN WHICH THE MURDER WAS COMMITTED. THE CROSS × MARKS THE SPOT WHERE THE BODY WAS FOUND.

Contemporary sketch from *Lloyd's Weekly Newspaper*, dated February 15th 1891, showing the scene of the crime.

VIEW OF THE ARCH AT NOON ON FRIDAY.

Contemporary sketch from *Lloyd's Weekly Newspaper*, dated February 15th 1891, showing the scene of the crime.

The Hull Daily Mail, February 16th 1891, P. 2

> *America is nothing if not enterprising. Not to be outdone by Whitechapel, Brooklyn has its "Jack the Clipper" – a mysterious personage, who sneaks up behind young women and appropriates their curls.*

The Hull Daily Mail, February 16th 1891, P. 3

> THE WHITECHAPEL TRAGEDY. THE ARREST OF SADLER. ALLEGED STRONG CASE AGAINST HIM. THE ACCUSED VISITS THE MORTUARY. THE

> *IDENTIFICATION OF THE MURDERED WOMAN. In connection with the Whitechapel murder, James Thomas Sadler, who was taken into custody on Saturday morning and detained on suspicion, is said to have been seen in the company of the deceased woman on Thursday. This is admitted by Sadler, who adds that they had a drunken orgy together. In the course of their rambles Sadler was assaulted by a number of men and woman, and also robbed of his watch. He was severely kicked and bruised, blood flowing and staining a cap he was wearing. He was treated for his injuries at the London Hospital at six o'clock on Friday morning. At first great importance was attached to the detention of this man, but his statements have been corroborated. STRONG CASE AGAINST SADLER. The case against Sadler is regarded by the police as being so strong that early this morning they formally charged him with the murder, and he will be brought before the magistrates during the day. The fact that he must consider himself in custody on the charge was communicated to him by the officer on duty, and he is understood to have declared his innocence. On being questioned as to whether anything had been discovered to connect the man with other crimes attributed to "Jack the Ripper," a high police official said "Well, we will see all about that as soon as we have stated what we know about him in connection with the present crime." ANTECEDENTS AND MOVEMENTS OF THE ACCUSED. The most absorbing interest naturally attaches to the investigation into the movements and antecedents of the man James Thomas Sadler, who remains detained at Leman-street Police Station on suspicion that he is not the murderer, and it is probable the man will not be detained for a much longer period. On Saturday afternoon, accompanied by detectives, Sadler visited the mortuary, and at once, without hesitation, identified the body as that of the woman in whose company he had been some hours previous to the murder. Sadler is about 50 years of age, but he looks older. He is about five feet six inches in height, stoops a little, and is fair, and even ruddy when washed. He wears a moustache and a goatee on the chin. He is dressed in a pilot cloth pea jacket and serge trousers, and has a black cloth cap with a leather peak but not of the shape called a cheese-cutter. The only blood found on his belongings was a little on the lining of his cap, the clothes showing no blood stains at all. The stains on the cap are such as may well be accounted for by the rough treatment he had received on Thursday night and early on Friday morning, and are more evidence of the truth of the story he tells of a wild drunken spree than of his connection with the woman Francis Coleman. A fairly full account of Sadler's recent movements is now in the possession of the police, whose activity and skill in this matter cannot be too highly praised. On the day preceding the murder Sadler had just arrived in London from Turkey on board the steamer Fez, and renewed a former acquaintance with the now deceased woman. On Wednesday night he slept with her in Dorset-street, and they left that house about noon on Thursday. Subsequently going on a heavy drinking*

bout, they visited in company a number of taverns in the district, drinking at most houses gin and cloves, varied occasionally with rum and milk. Among other well-known public houses which they visited were the Royal Standard, in Winter-row, and the Marlborough in Brick-lane. Late in the afternoon Sadler went with the woman to a haberdasher's in White's-row, where the deceased bought a hat for 1s 4 ½d. Sadler remarked, in the hearing of the shopkeeper, "You had better by half have some underclothing, for what you have is old and dirty." After another series of "drinks," the couple went on to Thrawl-street. The deceased refused to go into a house there, proposing that they should return to Dorset-street, Sadler refused, and, it is averred, said, "We will go to Thrawl-street; I'm afraid of nothing." They then went down Thrawl-street, and there some low women attacked Sadler and knocked him about the head until he fell to the ground insensible. While prostrate some male friends of the women beat and kicked him about the head, blacked his eyes, and robbed him of his watch and money. This assault would fully account for the scratches found by the police upon him, and it is probable this is the full explanation of how he got damaged. He soon recovered from the blows, and seeing the deceased close by had a row with her for allowing the other men and women to maltreat him. Sadler states that he finally left the deceased about nine o'clock on Thursday night, and proceeded to the London Dock's with the intention of going on board the Fez. But, being drunk, the police sergeant at the gate refused him admittance. He then abused the officers at the gate, and also had an altercation with some dockers who were hanging about. IS THE MURDERER LEFT HANDED? It is stated that the throat has been cut by a left handed person. It will be remembered that the appearance of the wounds on the previous victims went to prove that the murderer was left handed. SALVATIONISTS AS DETECTIVES. It is understood that the reasonable heads of the Salvation Army social and rescue work in the East End have under consideration the advisability of doing something through their organisation towards tracing terrible "Jack the Ripper." The notion is, that it might be possible through the Salvationist organisation, which gets so thoroughly into the nooks and by-ways and recesses of East-end life, to obtain some clue which might lead to the discovery of the miscreant. The slum sisters who go out among the very poorest dwellers in the East-end, the rescue girls who endeavour to seek out and reclaim fallen women, the prison gate brigade, those three agencies of the Salvation Army, it is felt, might go a fair way towards getting on the track of "The Ripper." A scrap of rumour might be picked up here by a slum sister, a point of information somewhere else by a rescue sister, or there might be carried to the knowledge of the Salvationist workers information which a wretched man or woman, in terror of self-apprehension, would not dare to convey to the police. In this way it is conceivable that something might be achieved for the ends of justice, only the Salvationists are slow to take any step which could give provocation for the

Mike Covell

> *charge that they were going outside their province. THE INQUEST. DREADFUL SPECTACLE. Mr. Wynne Baxter, coroner for East London, opened an inquest on Saturday on the body of the woman. A large crowd gathered around the Working lads Institute, and the excitement of the district was general, on account of the arrests made during the last two hours. The body presented a dreadful spectacle when viewed by the jury at the mortuary. The main arteries of the throat are all severed, and the woman must have died within a short time. After hearing the evidence of the police the inquiry was adjourned, Mr. Baxter stating that the body had not yet been properly identified.*

The Hull Daily Mail, February 16th 1891, P. 4

> *THE TRAGEDY IN WHITECHAPEL. SENSATIONAL DISCOVERY. SADLER'S KNIFE TRACED: A BLOOD-STAINED WEAPON. THE ACCUSED AT THE THAMES POLICE COURT. INTENSE EXCITEMENT IN THE EAST END. THE CHARGE AGAINST SADLER. The following is the entry on the charge sheet at Thames-street: - "John Thomas Sadler, marine fireman, residing at Victoria lodging houses, Upper East Smithfield, charged by Detective Inspector Moore, of the Criminal Investigation Department, with wilfully causing the death of Frances Coles by cutting her throat with a knife or some sharp instrument, at Swallow Gardens, on the 13th." THE TRACING OF SADLER'S KNIFE. A knife which Sadler owned has, by the exertions of Sergeants Record and Ward, been traced. It is stated that about 11 o'clock on Friday morning Sadler went to Well-street Sailors' Home, Whitechapel, and showed to another sailor named Duncan Campbell, a peculiarly shaped knife, which he offered to sell for 1s. Campbell bought the knife, and afterwards noticed it was blood stained. He sold it to another man, from whom the police have obtained it. INTENSE EXCITEMENT. Telegraphing at half past 11, the Press Association says it now appears unlikely that Sadler will be brought up before two o'clock, when only formal evidence will be taken. The news of the charge made against the prisoner and his expected removal to Thames-street caused the greatest excitement in the East-end. The police Court is surrounded by a vast crowd, and a strong body of police has been told off to keep the approaches to it clear. THE DECEASED'S FATHER. Detective Sergeants Record and Kuhrd discovered the father of the deceased – James William Cole (not Coles) – in the Bermondsey Workhouse, where he has been living for eight years, and Mary Ann Cole, her sister, who lives in Kingsland. The old man, who is very feeble, was brought to the mortuary in a cab, and had no difficulty in identifying the body. Another sister, named Selina, is also known to be living at Kingsland. The deceased was at one time engaged as a labeller at a wholesale chemist's factory in the Minories. She left her lodging in Thrawl-street about five weeks ago, but on Thursday last, between nine and ten o'clock,*

> *returned and asked her landlady, Mrs. Hague, to let her come back, and promised to pay what she owed. She then went away, but Mrs. Hague subsequently saw her in a public house at the corner of Montague-street. She was with a man who was treating her to drink. He was of fair complexion and had alight moustache. Mrs. Hague has also identified the body. THE ACCUSED BEFORE THE MAGISTRATE. At the Thames Police Court, this afternoon, before Mr. Mead, John Thomas Sadler, 55, marine fireman, Victoria lodging houses, Upper East Smithfield, was charged with wilfully causing the death of Frances Coles by cutting her throat with a knife or some sharp instrument, at Swallow Gardens, on the 13th of this month.*

The Hull Daily Mail, February 17th 1891, P. 4 Sad 6.0 – 6.6

> *LATEST NEWS. THE WHITECHAPEL MURDER. RESUMED INQUEST. This morning at the Working Lads' Institute, Whitechapel, Mr. Wynne Baxter, Coroner, for East London, resumed the inquest upon the body of Frances Coles (25), the woman who was found with her throat cut in Chamber's-street on Friday morning, and for whose murder a man named James Thomas Sadler is in custody. Amongst the officials of the police present were Superintendent Arnold, Chief Inspector Swanson, and Inspector Moore. The Coroner in the course of discussing the question of the future arrangement with the jury, was afraid that they had a protracted time before them, and that they were likely to have a lot of minute evidence. He also thought they would have the assistance of the Treasury in the matter, which was very unusual, but very desirable. At this stage Mr. Charles Matthews, barrister, entered, and, on behalf of the Public Prosecutor, placed himself at the disposal of the coroner, to render assistance. It was decided that Mr. Matthews should examine the witness. James William Coles said: - I am an inmate of the Bermondsey Workhouse. I went to the mortuary at Whitechapel between 10 and 11 on Saturday night. I then saw the dead body of a woman. I identified the body as that of my youngest daughter Frances. As near as I can say her age was about 26. I last saw her alive on Friday, the 6th February. She was at the workhouse on that day. She was in the habit of visiting me on Fridays. She deceived me as to where she was living. She told me it was 42, Richard-street, Commercial-road, but I found that was wrong. I did not know but what she was working for her living in the Minories at a wholesale chemist's. She had a sister, Mary Anne, living at 32, Wear-street, Kingsland-road. My daughter had a mark in the left ear; it looked to me as if it was torn by an ear-ring. I noticed that mark for three or four years. The knuckles of her hands were peculiar. There were great lumps of hard flesh on them, which she told me she had come from doing hard work. When I saw her on Friday, the 6th, she told me she would come on Sunday. She came on most Sunday's to go to church with me. The Coroner said that an*

Mike Covell

offer had been received from the Common Lodging-house Mission to bury the deceased. Witness said he would like to accept the offer. Mary Ann Coles said: I am single, and live at 32 Wear-street, Kingsland-road. I have been to Whitechapel Mortuary. I went on Sunday, and I there saw the body of the woman which I identified as that of my sister, Frances. I last saw her on the Friday after Christmas that would be the 26th December. She was then in good health, but very poor indeed, and she looked very dirty. I gave her some tea and bread and butter. She told me she lived on Richard-street, Commercial-road, and had buried a child three years ago. She also said that she worked in the Minories. I had noticed during her life that the lobe of her left ear was torn, and she said it was done by the little girl. I noticed last Sunday for the first time the lumps on her knuckles, which she said was done by her work, and she said that they were very painful. I recognised the clothing at the Mortuary. I had given her some of it, and had noticed her wearing a black satin bodice, a hat trimmed with crape, and a long black jacket. The name of the chemist she worked for was Hoare. She said she had left because there was not much work there in the winter. She said she had earned from 6s to 7s a week. I occasionally noticed that she smelt of drink. I did not know any of my sister's friends, and I never visited her. Peter Lorenzo Hawkes said: I am an assistant to my mother, a milliner, at 25, Nottingham-street, Bethnel Green. Between seven and eight o'clock on the evening of Thursday last, a woman came into my mother's shop. Last Friday I went to the Mortuary and saw the dead body of that woman. When she came to the shop, at her request I showed her several hats, and she bought one for 1s 11½d. After I told her the price of it she went outside of the shop and went away a short distance with a man who had been looking into the window. I noticed the man, and that is all. I could only see his face through the bonnets in the window. After walking away with the man she returned into the shop alone and tendered two shillings. I gave her the hat and halfpenny change. At that time she was wearing a black cape hat. The list which I hold here I put into a bag with my mother's name on it. When at the mortuary on Friday I saw and identified the hat which I sold her, and also saw there a hat similar to the one which she wore when she visited the shop. On Sunday, the 13th, I went to Leman-street Police Station, Whitechapel. I was there shown 20 men or more. I identified amongst them and picked out the man who had looked through my mother's shop windows on Thursday evening. By the newspapers I learn that he has given the name of James Thomas Sadler. By the Coroner: I was able to identify the hat, for it was one of our own manufacture. A Juryman: Was she sober when she came to the shop? She was what I should call "three sheets in the wind." (laughter). By the Coroner: I identified the man at once. Charles Gyver, said, I am a night watchman, and live at a common lodging house, 8, White's Row, Spitalfields. I have lived there for the last four years. For the past three years I have known a woman who has gone by the name of Frances. She came to *the house as a casual lodger, staying there a night at a time. She would sometimes come twice a week, and then not come for a time. She was a prostitute. She used to bring different men to sleep with her at the house. Samuel Harris said: I am a fish curer, employed by Mr. William Abrahams, 30, Virginia-road, Bethnal Green. Last Thursday evening I was lodging at 8, White's-row, Spitalfields. About half past nine the on that night I arrived home, and on going into the kitchen saw a woman I know by the name of Frances, sitting by the fire, with her head on the table as if asleep. About half past eleven while we were both there, a man dressed as a sailor came into the kitchen and looked round. He then sat down by the side of Frances on a form. He asked her if she had any money for her lodging, to which she – who had become awake – replied, "No." He then said, "I have been robbed. If I knew who had done it I would do for 'em." He asked me if I would let him go up to bed till to-morrow morning, thinking I was the Governor of the house. He showed me a certificate showing that he was entitled to £4 odd. I told him I had nothing to do with the letting of beds. He then asked me to mind the certificate till to-morrow morning, and I told him I could not do it. About half past twelve this morning this man left the house, and three or four minutes afterwards I saw Francis go out, after putting a black crape hat under her dress. She also wore a hat. I went to bed about a quarter to two, and saw nothing more that night of the man or the woman. The next I saw of her was at the mortuary, when I identified her dead body on the afternoon of Friday, the 13th. When did you next see that man? When I caught him (commotion). That was about half past eleven on Saturday morning, in the Phoenix public house, Upper East Smithfield. He was drinking in the house alone, and I was accompanied to the Phoenix by two police constables, to whom I had given information previously. I went inside the house alone, and identified the man at once. I then went outside and spoke to the constables. One of them went into the house and remained outside with the other some distance off. The man came out with the constable, and the man and the two constables proceeded to Leman-street Station, I walking behind. I went into the station. The officer questioned the man in my hearing, and he answered him. When I left at half past three the man remained behind. I am positive that this was the man who I saw in the kitchen of the lodging house as described. When he came into the kitchen and said he had been robbed I noticed a scar over the left eye. It was bleeding, and appeared to be a fresh one. When I saw him in the Phoenix on Saturday he had, in addition to this mark, two black eyes and a cut on his head, which cut I think was on the right hand side. I did not notice stains of blood on the man's clothes before he left the lodging house, neither did I notice any blood on his clothes on the Saturday morning. He did not on that occasion show any signs of recognising me. I had never seen the man before the occasion in the kitchen. He was then intoxicated and when I saw him in the Phoenix on Saturday he looked "half and half." By the Jury: I had known Frances as an occasional lodger at the*

Mike Covell

house for 18 months. The witness Syner (re-called) said: I have now seen a body and clothes, which I identify as those of a woman I knew as Frances for three years. I remember Frances coming to the house about 10 to 10.30 on the night of Wednesday, the 11th. She was with the man whose name I now know to be Sadler. She stood by the office window (where they pay), and he stood by the staircase door. I cannot say which paid for the bed. After this I took them upstairs to a bed, and they slept there that night. He asked me to call him at seven o'clock on Thursday morning, the 12th. I did so, but could not get him up. I went again about nine o'clock, and they were still in bed. I then went to bed myself, and did not see them again till Thursday evening. Frances came into the kitchen about ten o'clock that night alone, when she was very drunk. She went and sat on the form and fell asleep with her head on the table. While she was there in that position, Sadler came into the kitchen, and he too was the worse for drink. I asked him if he was looking for the young woman he was stopping with last night. He replied "Yes, I was Frances." I said, "There she is, asleep." Sadler tried to arouse her, but she was too drowsy. Sadler told me he had been robbed in Thrawl-street of 3s 6d. His face was bleeding, and I told him to go in the yard and wash the blood off his face. He looked as if he had been thrown down, for he had got gravel on the cheek bone. There was not particularly much blood, just a little running down his face; his clothes were smothered with dust as if he had been in a fight. I did not notice any blood on his clothes. After washing himself in the back yard he returned to the kitchen and kicked up a disturbance, wrangling with other lodgers. I advised him to go to bed. He said he had given Frances 1s to pay for the bed. The deputy said she had not paid him, I went upstairs, and when I came down again he was still wrangling. I then led him out. He was not violent at all. This was a little before 12 o'clock. Frances remained till about half past one or a quarter to two. I am positive she remained till after one o'clock, at any rate there was a clock in the office which I went by; besides I know the time by the amount of work I had got through. I am sure there was an interval of quiet an hour between the time of Sadler going out and the deceased leaving. Just before she went out she was sitting on the floor nursing a kitten. As I wanted to clean this kitchen she went away to another one. She was getting more sober then. When she first came into the house at ten o'clock she had two hats. I saw her throw one of them, a crape hat, into the fire, and it was just beginning to burn when a woman took it off and trampled on it. It was then hung up on one of the hat rails. I did not see this hat in her possession again. The one she wore was a different one. She never returned to the house after leaving it on this occasion. It was just after three o'clock on Friday morning, when I was going to go and call a man up, when Sadler came back to the house. The door was open, and he came into the garage. He asked me to let him come into the kitchen. I said it was more than I dare do, and he had better ask the deputy, Mrs. Fleming. Blood was running down his face, and he *said he felt faint. I said, "What have you been at?" and he replied, "I have been knocked down and robbed in the Highway," meaning "Ratcliffe Highway." I said, "I thought you told me as you had been robbed of 3s 6d in Thrawl-street, and that was all you had." He replied, "They thought I had got some money about me, but I did not have more." The deputy asked him what he wanted, and he asked to be allowed to go in the kitchen, as he felt so faint, but she declined. The man continued to lean against the wall, and again asked me to let him go into the kitchen, but I said I could not let him do so. I advised to go to the London Hospital, as blood was running down his forehead and face. His clothes looked as if he had been on the ground. Again I walked into the kitchen to finish my work, and left him leaning against the partition. In a minute or two Mrs. Fleming called me to turn him out. As I approached him to do so he walked out himself. It was then close on half past three, and I never saw him again till Sunday morning, the 15th between 11 and 12, at the Leman-street Police-station. He was then among a number of other seamen, and I at once identified him. I next saw him at the Thames Police Court. I have no doubt that he is the man who I saw at the lodging house under the circumstances described. Y the Jury: When he returned to the lodging house, at 3 a.m., he said nothing about Frances. The slightly burnt hat, which was thrown on the fire, is now in the mortuary. I saw it this morning there. When he came back at three, his clothes were not only dirty but disarranged. Mr. Matthews thought that this would be a convenient stage to adjourn, as they wished to sift and arrange the other evidence. The inquiry was then adjourned until 10 o'clock next Friday.*

The Hull Daily Mail, February 18th 1891, P.4

ANOTHER LONDON TRAGEDY. ATTEMPTED MURDER OF A WOMAN. ARREST OF THE ASSAILANT. At Southwark Police Court this morning Thomas Powell, labourer, was remanded charged with attempting to murder Elizabeth Collins, his paramour, by cutting her throat yesterday morning. Prisoner declared that the woman committed the injury herself, and that he dressed her and took her to the hospital, but the medical evidence showed that the injuries were not self-inflicted

Mike Covell

THE ACCUSED (JAMES SADLER).
<u>Contemporary sketch of James Thomas Sadler, taken from *The Western Mail*, dated February 18th 1891.</u>

The Hull Daily Mail, February 18th 1891, P.4

> THE WHITECHAPEL MURDER. FURTHER ARRESTS PROBABLE. *The Press Association's representative was informed by Inspector Moore, at Whitechapel, this morning, that there had been no new development in connection with the Frances Coles murder. Inquiries are being made into Sadler's antecendents, and also in other directions. It is probable there may be other arrests. The inquest will probably proceed beyond Friday next.*

The Hull Daily Mail, February 19th 1891, P. 3

THE WHITECHAPEL MURDER. SADLER'S ANTECEDENTS. PORTRAIT OF THE ACCUSED. The Press Association says the antecedents of the accused man Sadler have now been ascertained as far back as March 1887, and from this information it is indisputably shown that with half the series of crimes attributed to the East End miscreant he could have had absolutely nothing to do. It appears that on the 24th of March, 1887, he joined the Georgian at Newport, and remained with her until the 5th of May following, when he left her in London. From this latter date until August he was in England, and presumably in the Metropolis. It was during this period that the murders commenced, as an unknown woman was found during Christmas week near Osborne and Wentworth streets, and Martha Turner being stabbed in 39 places on August 7, 1888, in some model dwellings in Commercial-street, Spitalfields. It must be said that certainly the occurrence of these two crimes during the man's stay on land lends colour to the original suspicion. But the times of happening of succeeding crimes on the other hand supply a good answer to the suggestion. Sadler went away to sea again on the 17th of August, 1888, in the Winestead, and did not reach London until the evening of the 1st October following. During his absence no less than four murders were committed, two of them, strange to say, being on the morning of the day immediately preceding his arrival in the Thames. These murderers were discovered

SADLER, THE ACCUSED.

on the 31st of August in Buck's-row, and on the 7th of September in Mitre-square and Berner-street. In order to see if it was possible for Sadler to have left his ship so as to be in London on September 30 the logbook was inspected, and this clearly showed that such a thing would have been impossible as the vessel did not arrive until eight o'clock in the evening of the 1st of October. During his stay after his voyage the peculiarly atrocious murder of Mary Jane Kelly, on November 9, occurred, the victim being done to death in her own room and mutilated in a way

> *far exceeding in complete ferocity the foregoing crimes. On the 8th of May, 1889, having been in England for over seven months, Sadler went on another voyage, his ship this time being the Bilboa. His absence lasted until the 7th day of July. Ten days after his return the murder of Alice Mackenzie in Castle-alley took place, this being the last of the Whitechapel horrors preceding the one now absorbing attention. Summing up these facts, therefore, and carefully comparing dates, it is seen that Sadler was in this country when four murders took place, and that he was absent when a similar number were perpetrated. If the widespread supposition that the crimes be of common origin is accepted, then it is self-evident that Sadler cannot be regarded as responsible for them in the slightest degree. SADLER ON A HULL STEAMER. Further inquiry into Sadler's antecedents, made by the Daily Telegraph, reveals that he has a wife at Chatham, and he is believed to have been in the Hong Kong police, and also, in the intervals of his voyages, to have acted as a tram driver and conductor in the East of London. Amongst the vessels in which he sailed was the Winestead (Messrs. Bailey and Leetham's). He signed on at Gravesend on August 17th 1888, went to the Mediterranean, and was discharged at London on October 1st, in the same year. THE ACCUSED KNOWN AT GOOLE. It is stated that Sadler is also known at Goole, to which place he traded in 1889 between May 8th and July 7th in that year. He was a fireman on board the steamer Balboa, which ran between Goole and London between those dates for the Jescott Company. He left the Bilboa on her arrival from Goole on the 7th July. Mr. Speak, the Goole representative of the Jescott Company, remembers a man of the name being on board the Balboa, and that he was a fireman, but, so far has he knows, there was nothing especially noticeable in his conduct.*

The Hull Daily Mail, February 20th 1891, P. 2

> *NOTES AND REFLECTIONS. TOPICS OF YESTERDAY AND TO-DAY. SADLER'S WIFE. It is impossible not to feel sympathy with the man Sadler, now in custody on the charge of murdering the woman Coles, in Whitechapel, a few days ago for statements were published yesterday which cannot but seriously prejudice the mind of the public against the suspected murderer. One or two of our contemporaries, including the usually sober and decorous Standard, have undoubtedly been guilty of a grave impropriety in publishing the interview which a reporter has had with Sadler's wife. This interview is full of damaging suggestion; in fact, if all be true it contains, it points to one conclusion, and to one conclusion only – that Sadler is the real fiend of the East End. Sadler, according to his wife's outspoken statement, possesses most of the diabolical attributes assigned to the infamous "Jack." By many subtle and crafty touches Mrs. Sadler conveys (undesignedly, no doubt) the impression that her husband and no other*

> man, is the veritable "Ripper." We do not say that Mrs. Sadler made the statement with a view of further implicating her husband in the last Whitechapel crime, and it is stated this morning that she is "annoyed" at the sensational tone of the reported interview. She must be acquitted of any desire or intention to paint her husband blacker than he really is, or to prejudice him in the opinion of the public. But the effect of the statement will be just the same. The attention of the Home Secretary was called to the subject yesterday, and Mr. Matthews strongly condemned the publication of statements of this kind. Sadler wrote the letter which we published last evening before the interview with his wife had been made known, and he has now more cause than ever to bemoan his friendless condition, for he will imagine (wrongfully, probably), that even his wife is ranged on the side of his enemies. The appeal from Sadler that appeared in the Daily Mail yesterday, however, has not been in vain. A firm of solicitors has been instructed in his case, and the best that legal skill can accomplish will be done for him. But the impropriety of publishing incriminatory statements like that alleged to have been made by Mrs. Sadler is manifest without a moment's reflection. The statement is peculiarly and palpably suggestive, and as it is not made on oath, it should have no moral weight or effect. Yet it is calculated to bias – and to bias violently and unfairly – made public opinion against the accused, and as the case is now subjudice it is a question whether the Standard and other of our contemporaries were not guilty of contempt of Court in admitting such a statement to their columns. Mrs. Sadler's description of the peculiarities of her husband's disposition and character; her references to his strange, sudden and startling movements; the possession of a long sharp knife, his intimate knowledge of Whitechapel, and the whole colouring and tone of the interview, are more recklessly suggestive than anything we have read for a long time concerning an untried man in custody on a charge of committing a capital crime.

SCENE OF THE MURDER.

Contemporary sketch showing the scene of the murder, taken from *The Manchester Times*, dated February 20th 1891

The Hull Daily Mail, February 20th 1891, P. 4, first column,

> LATEST NEWS. THE WHITECHAPEL MURDER. SADLER'S ACQUAINTANCESHIP WITH THE DECEASED. RESUMED INQUEST TO-DAY. *The inquest into the circumstances attending the death of Frances Coles, who was found murdered in Whitechapel a week ago, was resumed this morning, at the Working Lads' Institute, Whitechapel, before Mr. Wynne Baxter, coroner for East London. Mr. Charles Matthews appeared for the Treasury, and Mr. Lawless now represented the man Sadler, who is at present detained in Holloway Gaol, charged with the murder. The first witness was Mrs. Anne Shuttleworth, an eating house keeper, living at 4, Welper-street. Replaying to Mr. Matthews, she said she had not seen the body, but a woman whom she knew as Frances went to*

Mike Covell

her shop on the day before the murder and said she would wait for a man. The man soon followed, and the woman spoke to him. The two left about a quarter to six, and she saw no more of them. They were quiet sober. She did not notice any injury to the man's face. The Coroner said he should not like to connect the deceased with the woman Frances, and witness was sent to the Mortuary to see the body. Mr. Steer, barman at the Bell public house, Middlesex-street, Whitechapel, was in the meantime examined. He said he remembered the deceased drinking with a man in his house on the afternoon of the 12th. He added that the man told him he was a sailor, and was intimate with the neighbourhood. The witness's evidence was very indefinite, and he, too, was sent to see the body. On the return of Mrs. Shuttleworth she said the body was that of Frances Coles, and added that the man wore a peak cap, a pilot coat, and looked like a sailor. Sarah Treadway, wife of the proprietor of the Marlborough Head Public house, said that prior to Thursday, the 12th, she had known a man named Thomas Sadler, who was a customer. On that night Thomas Sadler was in the house with a woman, whom witness had identified as the deceased. Mr. Matthews at this point said: I may say that the prisoner has made a statement. He says he went to the Bell public house in the course of that afternoon, from the Bell to Mrs. Shuttleworth's from Mrs. Shuttleworth's to Mrs. Treadway's; that he had been to these three houses in which he was with this unhappy woman on this afternoon. With the desire, where it is possible, to corroborate that statement, I am calling these witnesses, so that you may be able to judge what amount of credence you can give to his statement. The Coroner: I should tell you, Mr. Matthews, we have no prisoner here. Mr. Matthews: Well, I will say the accused man; the man who is at the present moment accused of the crime. Mrs. Fleming, deputy of the lodging house, 8, White's-row, Spitalfields, said the deceased and accused slept there together on the Wednesday night. She did not see Sadler go out on the Thursday night, but Frances left shortly after twelve o'clock, and Sadler came in at three in the morning. He had blood on his face and hands, and complained of having been robbed. Mr. Matthews: Did he say anything about the deceased? – Yes; the first thing he said to me when he came to the house was, "Has that young woman Frances been in?" The Coroner: It is very important. What did you say? – I said I have not seen her since she went out a little after 12. The Coroner: Did he say anything more about her? – No; he never mentioned her again. He was drunk, and could not stand or speak. Constable Bogan said that at 1.15 on the morning of February 13th he saw a sailor like man at the entrance to the London Docks. The man was lying in the gateway. Witness roused him, and he said, "I want to get my ship." Witness told him he was too drunk to go into the docks. Some dock labourers came out and inquired what was the matter and offered to pay the man's lodgings. The man said "I don't want your money, you dock rats." At two o'clock the same morning witness saw the man in Mint-street, and he then said he

> had been assaulted at the docks. He had his hand on his right ribs, and said he had been kicked. Witness, continuing, said it would take a man four or five minutes to walk from where he last saw Sadler, at 10 or 12 minutes past two, to Swallow-gardens, (it will be remembered that the woman was found dying here at a quarter past two.) Replying to Mr. Lawless, witness said when he saw Sadler there were several dock labourers about.

The Hull Daily Mail, February 20th 1891, P. 4, third column,

> SADLER IN PRISON. LETTER TO A FRIEND. DECLARATION OF INNOCENCE. John Thomas Sadler, the man in custody on the charge of murdering Florence Coles at Swallow-gardens, Whitechapel, last Friday, has addressed the following letter to a man named Wildgoose, of the Seamen's Union, from the Prison Hospital at Holloway, under Wednesday's date: -
>
> "Mr. Wildgoose, from T. Sadler, a stoke and member of your Union, Burnt Island Branch, No. 311. (My last payment was made at Tower-hill, last Friday, 13th.) Wishing prosperity to the Union, I must apply to you to act as my friend, as I have no claim on anyone else in particular. My wife has always a doubtful friend. My mother is too old, and I have no brother or sister or public house pals. WORTH A DAMN. I should like a reporter connected with Seafaring or the Star to watch over me. The police will hurry my case to suit their own ends. Anything turning up in my favour will be squashed. All the money and sense of Scotland-yard will be used to hurry me to a finish. What a God-send my case will be to them if they can only conduct me, INNOCENT AS I AM, to the bitter end. The whole detective system of Scotland-yard will be whitewashed in the sight of the whole world. Money presents will roll in to them. But on the other hand, if I have any true friend in a reporter to see that I am not tacked down or sat upon entirely by the police and the Court, I hope to walk out as I desire to. THE KNIFE BUSINESS IS FALSE. I have neither bought or sold any knife. I had one knife and fork only, a pair given me by my old mother a few months ago. J. T. Sadler.

Mike Covell

Contemporary sketch of James Thomas Sadler, taken from *The Hampshire Telegraph and Sussex Chronicle etc*, February 21st 1891

The Hull and East Yorkshire and Lincolnshire Times, February 21st 1891, P. 7,

THE WHITECHAPEL TRAGEDY. ACCUSED BEFORE THE MAGISTRATES. REPORTED FINDING OF HIS KNIFE. THE CORONER'S INQUIRY. SADLER'S ANTECEDENTS. At the Thames Police Court, on Monday, before Mr. Mead, John Thomas Sadler, 55, marine fireman, Victoria lodging houses, Upper East Smithfield, was charged with wilfully causing the death of Frances Coles by cutting her throat with a knife or some sharp instrument, at Swallow Gardens, on the 13th of this month. [The short column that follows is illegible with the print very poor.] This morning at the Working Lads' Institute, Whitechapel, Mr. Wynne Baxter, Coroner, for East London, resumed the inquest upon the body of Frances Coles (25), the woman who was found with her throat cut in Chamber's-street on Friday morning, and for whose murder a man named James Thomas Sadler is in custody. Amongst the officials of the police present were Superintendent Arnold, Chief Inspector Swanson, and Inspector Moore. The Coroner in the course of discussing the question of the future arrangement with the jury, was afraid that they had a protracted time before them, and that they were likely to have a lot of minute evidence. He also thought they would have the assistance of the Treasury in the matter, which was very unusual, but very desirable. At this stage Mr. Charles Matthews, barrister, entered, and, on behalf of the Public Prosecutor, placed himself at the disposal of the coroner, to render assistance. It was decided that Mr. Matthews should examine the witness. James William Coles said: - I am an inmate of the Bermondsey Workhouse. I went to the mortuary at Whitechapel between 10 and 11 on Saturday night. I then saw the dead body of a woman. I identified the body as that of my youngest daughter Frances. As near as I can say her age was about 26. I last saw her alive on Friday, the 6th February. She was at the workhouse on that day. She was in the habit of visiting me on Fridays. She deceived me as to where she was living. She told me it was 42, Richard-street, Commercial-road, but I found that was wrong. I did not know but what she was working for her living in the Minories at a wholesale chemist's. She had a sister, Mary Anne, living at 32, Wear-street, Kingsland-road. My daughter had a mark in the left ear; it looked to me as if it was torn by an ear-ring. I noticed that mark for three or four years. The knuckles of her hands were peculiar. There were great lumps of hard flesh on them, which she told me she had come from doing hard work. When I saw her on Friday, the 6th, she told me she would come on Sunday. She came on most Sunday's to go to church with me. The Coroner said that an offer had been received from the Common Lodging-house Mission to bury the deceased. Witness said he would like to accept the offer. Mary Ann Coles said: I am single, and live at 32 Wear-street, Kingsland-road. I have been to Whitechapel Mortuary. I went on Sunday, and I there saw the body of the woman which I identified as that of my sister, Frances. I last saw her on the Friday after Christmas that would be the 26th December. She was then in good health, but very poor indeed, and she looked very dirty. I gave her some tea and bread and butter.

Mike Covell

She told me she lived on Richard-street, Commercial-road, and had buried a child three years ago. She also said that she worked in the Minories. I had noticed during her life that the lobe of her left ear was torn, and she said it was done by the little girl. I noticed last Sunday for the first time the lumps on her knuckles, which she said was done by her work, and she said that they were very painful. I recognised the clothing at the Mortuary. I had given her some of it, and had noticed her wearing a black satin bodice, a hat trimmed with crape, and a long black jacket. The name of the chemist she worked for was Hoare. She said she had left because there was not much work there in the winter. She said she had earned from 6s to 7s a week. I occasionally noticed that she smelt of drink. I did not know any of my sister's friends, and I never visited her. Peter Lorenzo Hawkes said: I am an assistant to my mother, a milliner, at 25, Nottingham-street, Bethnel Green. Between seven and eight o'clock on the evening of Thursday last, a woman came into my mother's shop. Last Friday I went to the Mortuary and saw the dead body of that woman. When she came to the shop, at her request I showed her several hats, and she bought one for 1s 11½d. After I told her the price of it she went outside of the shop and went away a short distance with a man who had been looking into the window. I noticed the man, and that is all. I could only see his face through the bonnets in the window. After walking away with the man she returned into the shop alone and tendered two shillings. I gave her the hat and halfpenny change. At that time she was wearing a black cape hat. The list which I hold here I put into a bag with my mother's name on it. When at the mortuary on Friday I saw and identified the hat which I sold her, and also saw there a hat similar to the one which she wore when she visited the shop. On Sunday, the 13th, I went to Leman-street Police Station, Whitechapel. I was there shown 20 men or more. I identified amongst them and picked out the man who had looked through my mother's shop windows on Thursday evening. By the newspapers I learn that he has given the name of James Thomas Sadler. By the Coroner: I was able to identify the hat, for it was one of our own manufacture. A Juryman: Was she sober when she came to the shop? She was what I should call "three sheets in the wind." (laughter). By the Coroner: I identified the man at once. Charles Gyver, said, I am a night watchman, and live at a common lodging house, 8, White's Row, Spitalfields. I have lived there for the last four years. For the past three years I have known a woman who has gone by the name of Frances. She came to the house as a casual lodger, staying there a night at a time. She would sometimes come twice a week, and then not come for a time. She was a prostitute. She used to bring different men to sleep with her at the house. Samuel Harris said: I am a fish curer, employed by Mr. William Abrahams, 30, Virginia-road, Bethnal Green. Last Thursday evening I was lodging at 8, White's-row, Spitalfields. About half past nine the on that night I arrived home, and on going into the kitchen saw a woman I know by the name of Frances, sitting by the fire, with her head on the *table as if asleep. About half past eleven while we were both there, a man dressed as a sailor came into the kitchen and looked round. He then sat down by the side of Frances on a form. He asked her if she had any money for her lodging, to which she – who had become awake – replied, "No." He then said, "I have been robbed. If I knew who had done it I would do for 'em." He asked me if I would let him go up to bed till to-morrow morning, thinking I was the Governor of the house. He showed me a certificate showing that he was entitled to £4 odd. I told him I had nothing to do with the letting of beds. He then asked me to mind the certificate till to-morrow morning, and I told him I could not do it. About half past twelve this morning this man left the house, and three or four minutes afterwards I saw Francis go out, after putting a black crape hat under her dress. She also wore a hat. I went to bed about a quarter to two, and saw nothing more that night of the man or the woman. The next I saw of her was at the mortuary, when I identified her dead body on the afternoon of Friday, the 13th. When did you next see that man? When I caught him (commotion). That was about half past eleven on Saturday morning, in the Phoenix public house, Upper East Smithfield. He was drinking in the house alone, and I was accompanied to the Phoenix by two police constables, to whom I had given information previously. I went inside the house alone, and identified the man at once. I then went outside and spoke to the constables. One of them went into the house and remained outside with the other some distance off. The man came out with the constable, and the man and the two constables proceeded to Leman-street Station, I walking behind. I went into the station. The officer questioned the man in my hearing, and he answered him. When I left at half past three the man remained behind. I am positive that this was the man who I saw in the kitchen of the lodging house as described. When he came into the kitchen and said he had been robbed I noticed a scar over the left eye. It was bleeding, and appeared to be a fresh one. When I saw him in the Phoenix on Saturday he had, in addition to this mark, two black eyes and a cut on his head, which cut I think was on the right hand side. I did not notice stains of blood on the man's clothes before he left the lodging house, neither did I notice any blood on his clothes on the Saturday morning. He did not on that occasion show any signs of recognising me. I had never seen the man before the occasion in the kitchen. He was then intoxicated and when I saw him in the Phoenix on Saturday he looked "half and half." By the Jury: I had known Frances as an occasional lodger at the house for 18 months. The witness Syner (re-called) said: I have now seen a body and clothes, which I identify as those of a woman I knew as Frances for three years. I remember Frances coming to the house about 10 to 10.30 on the night of Wednesday, the 11th. She was with the man whose name I now know to be Sadler. She stood by the office window (where they pay), and he stood by the staircase door. I cannot say which paid for the bed. After this I took them upstairs to a bed, and they slept there that night. He asked me to call him at seven o'clock on*

Mike Covell

> *Thursday morning, the 12th. I did so, but could not get him up. I went again about nine o'clock, and they were still in bed. I then went to bed myself, and did not see them again till Thursday evening. Frances came into the kitchen about ten o'clock that night alone, when she was very drunk. She went and sat on the form and fell asleep with her head on the table. While she was there in that position, Sadler came into the kitchen, and he too was the worse for drink. I asked him if he was looking for the young woman he was stopping with last night. He replied "Yes, I was Frances." I said, "There she is, asleep." Sadler tried to arouse her, but she was too drowsy. Sadler told me he had been robbed in Thrawl-street of 3s 6d. His face was bleeding, and I told him to go in the yard and wash the blood off his face. He looked as if he had been thrown down, for he had got gravel on the cheek bone. There was not particularly much blood, just a little running down his face; his clothes were smothered with dust as if he had been in a fight. I did not notice any blood on his clothes. After washing himself in the back yard he returned to the kitchen and kicked up a disturbance, wrangling with other lodgers. I advised him to go to bed. He said he had given Frances 1s to pay for the bed. The deputy said she had not paid him, I went upstairs, and when I came down again he was still wrangling. I then led him out. He was not violent at all. This was a little before 12 o'clock. Frances remained till about half past one or a quarter to two. I am positive she remained till after one o'clock, at any rate there was a clock in the office which I went by; besides I know the time by the amount of work I had got through. I am sure there was an interval of quiet an hour between the time of Sadler going out and the deceased leaving. Just before she went out she was sitting on the floor nursing a kitten. As I wanted to clean this kitchen she went away to another one. She was getting more sober then. When she first came into the house at ten o'clock she had two hats. I saw her throw one of them, a crape hat, into the fire, and it was just beginning to burn when a woman took it off and trampled on it. It was then hung up on one of the hat rails. I did not see this hat in her possession again. The one she wore was a different one. She never returned to the house after leaving it on this occasion. It was just after three o'clock on Friday morning, when I was going to go and call a man up, when Sadler came back to the house. The door was open, and he came into the garage. He asked me to let him come into the kitchen. I said it was more than I dare do, and he had better ask the deputy, Mrs. Fleming. Blood was running down his face, and he said he felt faint. I said, "What have you been at?" and he replied, "I have been knocked down and robbed in the Highway," meaning "Ratcliffe Highway." I said, "I thought you told me as you had been robbed of 3s 6d in Thrawl-street, and that was all you had." He replied, "They thought I had got some money about me, but I did not have more." The deputy asked him what he wanted, and he asked to be allowed to go in the kitchen, as he felt so faint, but she declined. The man continued to lean against the wall, and again asked me to let him go into the*

kitchen, but I said I could not let him do so. I advised to go to the London Hospital, as blood was running down his forehead and face. His clothes looked as if he had been on the ground. Again I walked into the kitchen to finish my work, and left him leaning against the partition. In a minute or two Mrs. Fleming called me to turn him out. As I approached him to do so he walked out himself. It was then close on half past three, and I never saw him again till Sunday morning, the 15th between 11 and 12, at the Leman-street Police-station. He was then among a number of other seamen, and I at once identified him. I next saw him at the Thames Police Court. I have no doubt that he is the man who I saw at the lodging house under the circumstances described. Y the Jury: When he returned to the lodging house, at 3 a.m., he said nothing about Frances. The slightly burnt hat, which was thrown on the fire, is now in the mortuary. I saw it this morning there. When he came back at three, his clothes were not only dirty but disarranged. Mr. Matthews thought that this would be a convenient stage to adjourn, as they wished to sift and arrange the other evidence. The inquiry was then adjourned until 10 o'clock next Friday. AN OFFICIAL FROM THE TREASURY VISITS MRS. SADLER. DAMAGING ADMISSION. A Chatham correspondent says that Mrs Sadler was visited on Thursday afternoon by an official from the Treasury. Mrs Sadler, it is stated, admits that it is perfectly true that on more than one occasion Sadler had stood over her for more than a quarter of an hour with a long knife in his hand. SADLER IN PRISON. LETTER TO A FRIEND. DECLARATION OF INNOCENCE. John Thomas Sadler, the man in custody on the charge of murdering Florence Coles at Swallow-gardens, Whitechapel, last Friday, has addressed the following letter to a man named Wildgoose, of the Seamen's Union, from the Prison Hospital at Holloway, under Wednesday's date: - "Mr. Wildgoose, from T. Sadler, a stoke and member of your Union, Burnt Island Branch, No. 311. (My last payment was made at Tower-hill, last Friday, 13th.) Wishing prosperity to the Union, I must apply to you to act as my friend, as I have no claim on anyone else in particular. My wife has always a doubtful friend. My mother is too old, and I have no brother or sister or public house pals. WORTH A DAMN. I should like a reporter connected with Seafaring or the Star to watch over me. The police will hurry my case to suit their own ends. Anything turning up in my favour will be squashed. All the money and sense of Scotland-yard will be used to hurry me to a finish. What a God-send my case will be to them if they can only conduct me, INNOCENT AS I AM, to the bitter end. The whole detective system of Scotland-yard will be whitewashed in the sight of the whole world. Money presents will roll in to them. But on the other hand, if I have any true friend in a reporter to see that I am not tacked down or sat upon entirely by the police and the Court, I hope to walk out as I desire to. THE KNIFE BUSINESS IS FALSE. I have neither bought or sold any knife. I had one knife and fork only, a pair given me by my old mother a few months ago. J. T. Sadler. SADLER'S

Mike Covell

ANTECEDENTS. *The Press Association says the antecedents of the accused man Sadler have now been ascertained as far back as March 1887, and from this information it is indisputably shown that with half the series of crimes attributed to the East End miscreant he could have had absolutely nothing to do. It appears that on the 24th of March, 1887, he joined the Georgian at Newport, and remained with her until the 5th of May following, when he left her in London. From this latter date until August he was in England, and presumably in the Metropolis. It was during this period that the murders commenced, as an unknown woman was found during Christmas week near Osborne and Wentworth streets, and Martha Turner being stabbed in 39 places on August 7, 1888, in some model dwellings in Commercial-street, Spitalfields. It must be said that certainly the occurrence of these two crimes during the man's stay on land lends colour to the original suspicion. But the times of happening of succeeding crimes on the other hand supply a good answer to the suggestion. Sadler went away to sea again on the 17th of August, 1888, in the Winestead, and did not reach London until the evening of the 1st October following. During his absence no less than four murders were committed, two of them, strange to say, being on the morning of the day immediately preceding his arrival in the Thames. These murderers were discovered*

SADLER, THE ACCUSED.

on the 31st of August in Buck's-row, and on the 7th of September in Mitre-square and Berner-street. In order to see if it was possible for Sadler to have left his ship so as to be in London on September 30 the logbook was inspected, and this clearly showed that such a thing would have been impossible as the vessel did not arrive until eight o'clock in the evening of the 1st of October. During his stay after his voyage the peculiarly atrocious murder of Mary Jane Kelly, on November 9, occurred, the victim being done to death in her own room and mutilated in a way far exceeding in complete ferocity the foregoing crimes. On the 8*th* of May, 1889, having been in England for over seven months, Sadler went on another voyage, his ship this time being the Bilboa. His absence lasted until the 7*th* day of July. Ten days after his return the murder of Alice Mackenzie in Castle-alley took place, this being the last of the Whitechapel horrors preceding the one now absorbing attention. Summing up these facts, therefore, and carefully comparing dates, it is seen that Sadler was in this country when four murders took place, and that he was absent when a similar number were perpetrated. If the widespread supposition that the crimes be of common origin is accepted, then it is self-evident that Sadler cannot be regarded as responsible for them in the slightest degree. THE TRACING OF SADLER'S KNIFE. A knife which Sadler owned has, by the exertions of Sergeants Record and Ward, been traced. It is stated that about 11 o'clock on Friday morning Sadler went to Well-street Sailors' Home, Whitechapel, and showed to another sailor named Duncan Campbell, a peculiarly shaped knife, which he offered to sell for 1s. Campbell bought the knife, and afterwards noticed it was blood stained. He sold it to another man, from whom the police have obtained it. INTENSE EXCITEMENT. Telegraphing at half past 11, the Press Association says it now appears unlikely that Sadler will be brought up before two o'clock, when only formal evidence will be taken. The news of the charge made against the prisoner and his expected removal to Thames-street caused the greatest excitement in the East-end. The police Court is surrounded by a vast crowd, and a strong body of police has been told off to keep the approaches to it clear. THE DECEASED'S FATHER. Detective Sergeants Record and Kuhrd discovered the father of the deceased – James William Cole (not Coles) – in the Bermondsey Workhouse, where he has been living for eight years, and Mary Ann Cole, her sister, who lives in Kingsland. The old man, who is very feeble, was brought to the mortuary in a cab, and had no difficulty in identifying the body. Another sister, named Selina, is also known to be living at Kingsland. The deceased was at one time engaged as a labeller at a wholesale chemist's factory in the Minories. She left her lodging in Thrawl-street about five weeks ago, but on Thursday last, between nine and ten o'clock, returned and asked her landlady, Mrs. Hague, to let her come back, and promised to pay what she owed. She then went away, but Mrs. Hague subsequently saw her in a public house at the corner of Montague-street. She was with a man who was treating her to drink. He was of fair complexion and had a light moustache. Mrs. Hague has also identified the body. SALVATIONISTS AS DETECTIVES. It is understood that the reasonable heads of the Salvation Army social and rescue work in the East End have under consideration the advisability of doing something through their organisation towards tracing terrible "Jack the Ripper." The notion is, that it might be possible through the Salvationist organisation, which gets so thoroughly into the nooks and by-ways and recesses of East-end life, to obtain some clue which might lead to the

> *discovery of the miscreant. The slum sisters who go out among the very poorest dwellers in the East-end, the rescue girls who endeavour to seek out and reclaim fallen women, the prison gate brigade, those three agencies of the Salvation Army, it is felt, might go a fair way towards getting on the track of "The Ripper." A scrap of rumour might be picked up here by a slum sister, a point of information somewhere else by a rescue sister, or there might be carried to the knowledge of the Salvationist workers information which a wretched man or woman, in terror of self-apprehension, would not dare to convey to the police. In this way it is conceivable that something might be achieved for the ends of justice, only the Salvationists are slow to take any step which could give provocation for the charge that they were going outside their province.*

The Hull Times, February 21st 1891,

> ANOTHER LONDON TRAGEDY. At Southwark Police Court on Wednesday Thomas Powell, labourer, was remanded charged with attempting to murder Elizabeth Collins, his paramour by cutting her throat on Tuesday morning. Prisoner declared that the woman committed the injury herself, and that he dressed her and took her to the hospital, but the medical evidence showed that the injuries were not self-inflicted.

Mike Covell

JAMES THOMAS SADLER, THE ACCUSED.   FRANCES COLES, THE VICTIM.

Two contemporary sketches, showing James Thomas Sadler and Frances Coles, taken from the *Reynolds's Newspaper*, dated February 22nd 1891

The Hull Daily Mail, February 23rd 1891, P. 4

LATEST NEWS. THE WHITECHAPEL MURDER. RESUMED INQUEST. FURTHER IDENTIFICATION OF THE ACCUSED. SADLER'S KNIFE PRODUCED IN COURT. SENSATIONAL EVIDENCE. The inquest into the circumstances attending the death of Frances Coles, who was found with her throat cut in Whitechapel on the morning of the 13th inst., was resumed this morning at the Working lads' Institute, Whitechapel, before Mr. Wynne Baxter, coroner. Mr. Charles Mathews represented the Treasury, and Mr. Lawless appeared for the man Sadler, who is charged with the crime. Charles Littlewood and Stephen Longhurst said that at half past six on the morning of Friday, the 13th, a man came into their coffee shop, 173, Whitechapel-road, and had some coffee. There was blood on his wrists. They identified Sadler as the man. Frederick Smith, employed at Lockhart's coffee-house on Tower Hill, said that about five minutes to two – he could not be quiet certain about the time – on Friday morning, he saw a man coming from the Mint pavement. He heard the man complain that he had been knocked about, and saw him walk away in the direction of the Minories. Joseph Haswell, fish porter, said he knew the deceased as a customer of Mr.

> Shuttleworth. He last saw her alive at half past one on the morning of the 13th, when she went into the shop alone and asked for three ha'porth of mutton and some bread. She stayed a quarter of an hour. Witness said to her, "Do you mind getting out of the shop, as we want to shut the doors?" He had to say this two or three times. "She said to him, "Mind your own ---- business." He had to put her out. There were several customers in the shop." By Mr. Lawless: They were all women. She had something to drink. SADLER'S KNIFE PRODUCTION OF THE WEAPON. Duncan Campbell, sailor, said that on Friday, the 13th, he was staying at the Sailors' House in Wells-street. He was in the hall of the house at a quarter past 10 o'clock, and he saw Sadler. Sadler said he had been robbed and was dying for a drink. He pulled out a pocket knife (produced) and said to witness, "Will you buy it?" Witness gave him a shilling for it and a bit of tobacco. Witness added, "I said to him, "This is not an English knife." He said, "No, I bought it in America." He did not stay, but went straight into Leman-street. At 11 o'clock I heard that a murder had been committed. I went into the lavatory of the Sailors' Home and examined the knife. I washed it in clean water, which was afterwards of a salmon colour. When Sadler sold me the knife he said it has cut many a model. On Sunday I gave a description of the man, and I took the police officers to the shop where I sold the knife. I picked out Sadler from a number of others at the police station.

The Hull Daily Mail, February 25th 1891, P. 4

> THE WHITECHAPEL TRAGEDY. SADLER BEFORE THE MAGISTRATES. A FURTHER REMAND. John Thomas Sadler was charged on remand at the Thames Police Court on Tuesday with the murder of Frances Coles at Whitechapel, and was formally remanded until Tuesday next. – on Sadler being placed in the dock Mr. Mathews asked Mr. Mead, the magistrate, if it would be convenient and right to remand the prisoner until the evidence before the coroner's jury, whose inquiry it was imagined would terminate on Friday, was completed. He asked for a remand until this day (Tuesday) week. He was happy to say his friend, Mr. Lawless, joined in the application. – Mr. Mead said that under the circumstances he should certainly grant the remand. The prisoner was remanded accordingly.

The Hull Daily Mail, February 25th 1891, P. 4

> A DARK SPOT. A MEMENTO OF THE LAST WHITECHAPEL MURDER.

Mike Covell

The archway in which Sadler is alleged to have murdered Frances Coles, the "unfortunate".

The Hull Daily Mail, February 26th 1891, P. 3

DISTRICT INTELLIGENCE. THE WHITECHAPEL MURDER. – *Sadler's Movements: Diary and Illustrated Sketch of his Wanderings on the Night of the Tragedy.* – Hull Times, Next Saturday.

The Hull Daily Mail, February 26th 1891, P. 4

STRANGE DEATH OF A WITNESS IN THE WHITECHAPEL CASE. POST MORTEM ORDERED. Dr. Macdonald, M. P., coroner for North East London, received information this morning of the sudden death of Charles Guyver, 8, White-row, Spitalfields, one of the principle witnesses at the inquest on the body of

> *the murdered woman Frances Coles. He was 34 years of age. Dr. Dukes, who was fetched, being unable to certify the cause of death, the coroner has ordered a post mortem examination of the body.*

The Hull Daily Mail, February 27th 1891, P. 3,

> *STRANGE DEATH OF A WITNESS IN THE WHITECHAPEL CASE. POST MORTEM ORDERED. Dr. Macdonald, M. P., coroner for North East London, received information this morning of the sudden death of Charles Guyver, 8, White-row, Spitalfields, one of the principle witnesses at the inquest on the body of the murdered woman Frances Coles. He was 34 years of age. Dr. Dukes, who was fetched, being unable to certify the cause of death, the coroner has ordered a post mortem examination of the body.*

The Hull Daily Mail, February 27th 1891, P. 3

> *DISTRICT INTELLIGENCE. THE WHITECHAPEL MURDER. – Sadler's Movements: Diary and Illustrated Sketch of his Wanderings on the Night of the Tragedy. – Hull Times, Next Saturday.*

The Hull Daily Mail, February 27th 1891, P. 4

> *THE WHITECHAPEL MURDER. RESUMPTION OF THE INQUEST. UNIMPORTANT TESTIMONY. This morning Mr. Baxter resumed the inquest concerning the murder of Frances Coles, the last Whitechapel victim. The proceedings took place at the Working Lads' Institute, Whitechapel. Mr. Matthews appeared on behalf of the Treasury whilst Mr. Lawless represented the accused man Sadler. Detective Sergeant George Butcher, of the Criminal Investigation Department, produced plans of the locality affecting the case. He said there were eight modes of getting away from the archway where the body of the murdered woman was found. John Johnson, deputy at the Victoria Lodging House, Upper East Smithfield, said that about a quarter past one in the morning of Friday, the 13th inst., Sadler came to the house and wanted a bed. Witness refused, as he was drunk. After abusing him Sadler went away. There was a scratch on his face. He returned in the evening, and his head had then been bandaged. Thomas Johnson, seamen, said that he had been taken to Leman-street Police Station, and there identified Sadler as the man he had seen leaving the Sailors' Home, after having sold a knife to a man named Duncan Campbell on the Friday morning. In reply to Mr. Lawless, witness said that he saw other men pick out Sadler before he identified him. On another day witness had taken to the Thames Police Court, and there saw Sadler. When he saw Sadler at the Sailors' Home he was going out.*

Mike Covell

> *Detective Inspector Moore deposed that when formally charged on Sunday, the 15th inst., Sadler said, "The old man has made a mistake about that knife; I never saw him before." When being removed to the cells he added, "Make it as light as you can, gentlemen." Ellen Calloran said that at about half past one on Friday morning she had the deceased, Frances Cole, met a man in Commercial-street. He spoke to witness. He was a short man with a moustache. It was not Sadler whom witness had seen earlier that day. Witness refused to go with the man, and he then spoke to deceased, who consented to go with him and walked away with him towards the Minories. Witness advised her not to go with the man, but Coles said she should. Answering Mr. Matthews, witness denied she had said this happened at three o'clock. William Friday, carman, said that at about 10 minutes to two on the Friday morning he saw a man and woman together in Royal Mint-street, about 30 yards from Swallow-gardens. He was going to speak to the woman, as he thought she was Kate McCarthy, but he found it was someone else. The woman was dressed in black and had a crape hat.*

The Hull Daily Mail, February 27th 1891, P. 4

> THE LAST OF FRANCES COLES. SCENE AT THE GRAVE SIDE. DISGRACEFUL CONDUCT OF THE CROWD. *The funeral of Frances Coles, the victim of the last Whitechapel murder, was made the occasion of the gathering of vast crowds in the East End and in the East London Cemetery, where the internment took place on Wednesday. A brisk trade was done in "In Memoriam" cards, and the kerbstone vocalists invited patronage by their rendering of the latest patriotic songs of the day. The funeral arrangements had been entrusted by the father of the deceased to the London Common Lodging-house Mission, and it was from the offices of this society in Ludgate-circus that three carriages started. The first contained Mr. Coles, the father, and Miss Mary Ann Coles, the sister of the murdered woman; Mr. A. H. Shepherd, one of the vice-presidents of the mission; Mr. John Harvey, the hon. Secretary; and the Rev. D. Thomas, of Grove-road, Victoria Park. In the second were Mrs. Harvey, Mrs Bordman, and Mrs. Day, representing the lady workers of the mission; and in the third Mr. F. C. Paynter, honorary solicitor; Mr. Maysmith, and Mr. Johnson. About 500 people marched on each side of the hearse, which fully exposed the polished elm and white metal mounted coffin to view. The plate was simply inscribed with the name of the deceased, the date of her death, and her age (26). A few wreaths were placed about it, one of them having been sent from Maidstone. In the cemetery fully 20,000 people had assembled, and the majority of these, when it was noticed that the hearse was taking a lower road through the grounds, made a wild stampede across the grass, tumbling down in their haste, shrieking and laughing in the most unseemly manner. The site assigned to the last resting place of*

> *Frances Coles is within a few yeards of the graves of Mary Ann Nicholls, Annie Chapman, Elizabeth Stride, and Mary Jane Kelly, four of the women murdered in Whitechapel and Spitalfields during the year 1888; and close by lie buried the mutilated remains of the unknown woman whose dismembered body was discovered in Pinchin-street in the autumn of 1889. The burial service was short and simple, being conducted by the Rev. D. Thomas, who in prayer supplicated the Almighty "to bring to the bar of justice the cruel hand that smote the death blow," so that right might be done, and "that which cried from the very ground for vengeance might be heard and answered." In a short address, the reverend gentleman appealed to the people present to take warning by the event. The rev. gentleman's discourse was interrupted by fervent "Amen's." – Mr. Harvey, the next speaker, was also listened to attentively. – Mr. Paynter, the hon. Solicitor, added a few words, saying that Mr. Coles had assured him that his daughter had never given him any trouble or pain during her life. The father, who appeared in a feeble state and shed tears abundantly, took a last look at the coffin, and was then led away to the carriage in waiting. Happily, he did not see the crowd surge over the ropes and nearly throw the two attendant policemen into the open graves.*

The Hull and East Yorkshire and Lincolnshire Times, February 28th 1891,

> *THE WHITECHAPEL MURDER. SADLER'S MOVEMENTS. DIARY AND PLAN OF HIS WANDERINGS ON THE NIGHT OF THE MURDER. The accompanying plan will give the reader some idea of Sadler's movements as detailed in the evidence on the day before and morning of the murder of Frances Coles ion the archway of Swallow-gardens. The evidence supplies (with some light variations as to time,) the following diary:*

Mike Covell

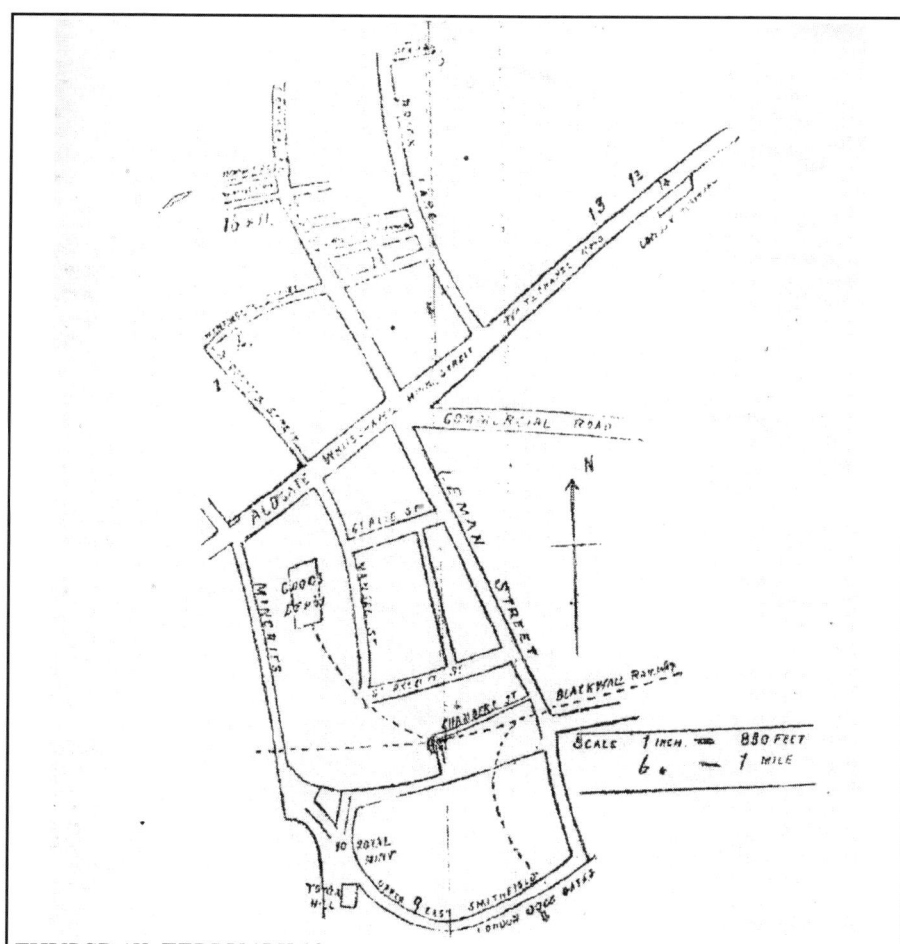

THURSDAY, FEBRUARY 12.
1. 1.30 p.m. – Sadler and Frances drinking at the Bell, Middlesex-street.
2. 5.15 p.m. – Sadler and Frances Coles were at Mrs Shuttleworth's cook shop, 4, Wentworth-street.
3. 6 to 7 p.m. – Both drinking at the Marlborough Head, Pelham-street, Brick-lane.
4. BETWEEN 7 AND 8 p.m. – Frances and Sadler at the milliner's shop, Nottingham-street, Bethnal-green, buying a hat.
5. ABOUT 8 p.m. – Back again together drinking at the Marlborough Head, Pelham-street.

6. *10.30 p.m. – Frances alone in the kitchen of the lodging house, 8, White's-row, Spitalfields.*
7. *11 p.m. – Sadler arrived in the kitchen of the lodging house. According to Gyver's evidence he left about 12.30 a.m. Frances did not leave till 1.30 or 1.45 a.m.*
FRIDAY, FEBRUARY 13.
8. *ABOUT 1.15 a.m. – Sadler drunk at the main entrance to the London Docks. At 1.30 he fought with Dooley, and at 1.45 he was seen by Police constable Sessions going in the direction of Tower Hill.*
9. *1.30 a.m. – Sadler entered kitchen of lodging house, 18, Upper East Smithfield, where he was again seen by Dooley, and the lodging house keeper ejected him.*
10. *SHORTLY BEFORE 2 a.m. – Police-constable Edwards saw Sadler on the Mint pavement going in the direction of the Minories. Other witnesses corroborate, but one says it was 12 minutes past two. This is denied by other constables, who say it was not later than three minutes past two.*
[2.15 a.m. – Murder discovered at spot marked X. The body was not there at 2.12 when Shunter Guthrie passed.]
11. *3 a.m. – Sadler re-appears in kitchen of lodging house in White's-row.*
12. *3.30 a.m. – Sadler seen opposite London Hospital, Whitechapel-road.*
13. *4.5 to 4.15 a.m. – Sadler ejected from a coffee house in Whitechapel-road.*
14. *4.45. – Sadler had his wounds dressed at the London Hospital.*
The numbers on the plan coincide with the numbered paragraphs.

RESUMED INQUEST. SADLER'S KNIFE PRODUCED IN COURT. *The inquest into the circumstances attending the death of Frances Coles, who was found with her throat cut in Whitechapel on the morning of the 13th inst., was resumed this morning at the Working lads' Institute, Whitechapel, before Mr. Wynne Baxter, coroner. Mr. Charles Mathews represented the Treasury, and Mr. Lawless appeared for the man Sadler, who is charged with the crime. Charles Littlewood and Stephen Longhurst said that at half past six on the morning of Friday, the 13th, a man came into their coffee shop, 173, Whitechapel-road, and had some coffee. There was blood on his wrists. They identified Sadler as the man. Frederick Smith, employed at Lockhart's coffee-house on Tower Hill, said that about five minutes to two – he could not be quiet certain about the time – on Friday morning, he saw a man coming from the Mint pavement. He heard the man complain that he had been knocked about, and saw him walk away in the direction of the Minories. Joseph Haswell, fish porter, said he knew the deceased as a customer of Mr. Shuttleworth. He last saw her alive at half past one on the morning of the 13th, when she went into the shop alone and asked for three ha'porth of mutton and some bread. She stayed a quarter of an hour. Witness said to her, "Do you mind getting out of the shop, as we want to shut the doors?" He had to say this two or three times. "She said to him, "Mind your own ---- business." He had to put her out. There were several customers in the shop." By Mr. Lawless: They were all women. She had something to drink. Duncan Campbell, sailor, said that on Friday, the 13th, he was staying at the Sailors' House in Wells-street. He was in the hall of the house at a quarter past 10 o'clock, and he saw Sadler. Sadler said he had been robbed and was dying for a drink. He pulled out a pocket knife (produced) and said to witness, "Will you buy it?" Witness gave him a shilling for it and a bit of tobacco. Witness added, "I said to him, "This is not an English knife." He said, "No, I bought it in America." He did not stay, but went straight into Leman-street. At 11 o'clock I heard that a murder had been committed. I went into the lavatory of the Sailors' Home and examined the knife. I washed it in clean water, which was afterwards of a salmon colour. When Sadler sold me the knife he said it has cut many a model. On Sunday I gave a description of the man, and I took the police officers to the shop where I sold the knife. I picked out Sadler from a number of others at the police station. By Mr Lawless: Sadler, when witness identified him, was wearing a cap with a cloth peak (several witnesses have already sworn that Sadler wore a cap with a glazed peak.) He was not certain that Sadler was the man who sold him the knife until he saw the scar on his forehead. He did not think at the time that the water was stained with blood, and his suspicions were not aroused by it. Thomas Robinson, marme store dealer, said he bought the knife from Campbell for 6d. Witness said to Campbell that the knife looked like "Jack the Ripper's" knife. Campbell said it had cut out many a model. Witness sharpened the knife, and eat his supper that night and dinner on the Sunday with it. By Mr Lawless: The knife was very blunt when he bought it, and he had to sharpen it before he could cut his meat and bread. Erard Delafosse, a deputy superintendent at the Shipping Offices, Tower Hill, deposed to Sadler presenting a wags account for £4 15s 1d. The paper had blood upon it, and Sadler accounted for that by saying that he had been knocked about and robbed of a watch. Chief Inspector Swanson, of the Criminal Investigation Department, said that when Sadler was taken to the station he asked, "Am I arrested for it?" Witness said, "Certainly not, but it is necessary to take a statement from you to help us to throw some light upon the matter." Sadler then made a statement, which was taken down in writing. – The Court then adjourned for luncheon. On the Court resuming at half past two o'clock, Mr Matthews proceeded to read the statement in which Sadler said he was discharged from his ship the Fez, on the 11th inst. On the same day he met a woman whom he had known for 18 months in the Princess Alice public house, Whitechapel. Her name was Frances. He slept with her that night. On the following day he went with the deceased to buy her a new bonnet. During the day he was knocked down by a woman, and was at once surrounded by some men who kicked him severely. He had a row woman Francis, because he thought she might have helped him. He was discharged because he* *had no money to pay for a bed, all he had having been stolen. Sadler then went on to say how he tried to get to his ship, and the remainder of the statement was practically borne out of the evidence already given. He denied ever having carried a knife, and said after he failed to get into the docks he wandered about all night in a drunken condition. Detective Sergeant Dodd who arrested Sadler in the Phoenix public house, read a statement made by the accused at the time, in which Sadler said he had been in a row with Frances, as he believed it was through her he had been assaulted. Medical evidence was then called which has already appeared in our columns. The inquiry was adjourned until Friday. YESTERDAY'S PROCEEDINGS. THE VERDICT: NO CASE AGAINST THE ACCUSED. Yesterday the inquest was again resumed. Mr Matthews appeared on behalf of the Treasury, whilst Mr Lawless represented the accused man Sadler. Detective Sergeant George Butcher, of the Criminal Investigation Department, produced plans of the locality affecting the case. He said there were eight modes of getting away from the archway where the body of the murdered woman was found. John Johnson, deputy at the Victoria Lodging House, Upper East Smithfield, said that about a quarter past one on the morning of Friday the 13th inst., Sadler came to the house and wanted a bed. Witness refused, as he was drunk. After abusing him Sadler went away. There was a scratch on his face. He returned in the evening, and his head had then been bandaged. Thomas Johnson, seamen, said that he had been taken to Leman-street Police Station, and there identified Sadler as the man he had seen leaving the Sailors' Home, after having sold a knife to a man named Duncan Campbell on the Friday morning. In reply to Mr Lawless, witness said that he saw other men pick out Sadler before he identified him. On another day witness was taken to the Thames Police Court, and there saw Sadler. When he saw Sadler at the Sailors' Home he was going out. Detective Inspector Moore deposed that when formally charged on Sunday, the 15th inst., Sadler said, "The old man has made a mistake about that knife; I never saw him before." When being removed to the cells he added, "Make it as light as you can gentleman." Ellen Calloran said that at about half past one on Friday morning she and the deceased, Frances Cole, met a man in Commercial-street. He spoke to witness. He was a short man with a moustache. It was not Sadler whom witness had seen earlier that day. Witness refused to go with the man, and he then spoke to deceased, who consented to go with him and walked away with him to the Minories. Witness advised her not to go with the man, but Coles said she should. Answering Mr Matthews, witness denied she had said this happened at three o'clock. William Friday, carman, said that at about 10 minutes to two on Friday morning he saw a man and woman together in Royal Mint-street, about 50 yards from Swallow-gardens. He was going to speak to the woman, as he thought it was Kate McCarthy, but he found it was someone else. The woman was dressed in black and had a crape hat. Other evidence being called, the Coroner, at* *considerable length, summed up the evidence for and against Sadler. He pointed out that if Dr Oxley's opinion was sound Sadler at the time of the murder was physically incapable of committing the crime, even if he had desired to do so. The jury returned a verdict of "Murder against some person or persons unknown." The jury added that the police had done their duty in detaining Sadler. SADLER BEFORE THE MAGISTRATES. John Thomas Sadler was charged on remand at the Thames Police Court on Tuesday with the murder of Frances Coles at Whitechapel, and was formally remanded until Tuesday next. – on Sadler being placed in the dock Mr. Mathews asked Mr. Mead, the magistrate, if it would be convenient and right to remand the prisoner until the evidence before the coroner's jury, whose inquiry it was imagined would terminate on Friday, was completed. He asked for a remand until this day (Tuesday) week. He was happy to say his friend, Mr. Lawless, joined in the application. – Mr. Mead said that under the circumstances he should certainly grant the remand. The prisoner was remanded accordingly. A DARK SPOT. A MEMENTO OF THE LAST WHITECHAPEL MURDER.*

THE ARCHWAY IN WHICH SADLER IS ALLEGED TO HAVE MURDERED FRANCES COLES, THE "UNFORTUNATE." STRANGE DEATH OF A WITNESS. Dr. Macdonald, M. P., coroner for North East London, received information this morning of the sudden death of Charles Guyver, 8, White-row, Spitalfields, one of the principle witnesses at the inquest on the body of the murdered woman Frances Coles. He was 34 years of age. Dr. Dukes, who was fetched, being unable to certify the cause of death, the coroner has ordered a post mortem examination of the body. BURIAL OF THE VICTIM. SCENE AT THE GRAVESIDE. The funeral of Frances Coles, the victim of the last Whitechapel murder, was made the occasion of the gathering of vast crowds in the East End and in the East London Cemetery, where the internment took place on Wednesday. A brisk trade was done in "In Memoriam" cards, and the kerbstone vocalists invited patronage by their rendering of the latest patriotic songs of the day. The funeral arrangements had been entrusted by the father of the deceased to the

Mike Covell

> London Common Lodging-house Mission, and it was from the offices of this society in Ludgate-circus that three carriages started. The first contained Mr. Coles, the father, and Miss Mary Ann Coles, the sister of the murdered woman; Mr. A. H. Shepherd, one of the vice-presidents of the mission; Mr. John Harvey, the hon. Secretary; and the Rev. D. Thomas, of Grove-road, Victoria Park. In the second were Mrs. Harvey, Mrs Bordman, and Mrs. Day, representing the lady workers of the mission; and in the third Mr. F. C. Paynter, honorary solicitor; Mr. Maysmith, and Mr. Johnson. About 500 people marched on each side of the hearse, which fully exposed the polished elm and white metal mounted coffin to view. The plate was simply inscribed with the name of the deceased, the date of her death, and her age (26). A few wreaths were placed about it, one of them having been sent from Maidstone. In the cemetery fully 20,000 people had assembled, and the majority of these, when it was noticed that the hearse was taking a lower road through the grounds, made a wild stampede across the grass, tumbling down in their haste, shrieking and laughing in the most unseemly manner. The site assigned to the last resting place of Frances Coles is within a few yeards of the graves of Mary Ann Nicholls, Annie Chapman, Elizabeth Stride, and Mary Jane Kelly, four of the women murdered in Whitechapel and Spitalfields during the year 1888; and close by lie buried the mutilated remains of the unknown woman whose dismembered body was discovered in Pinchin-street in the autumn of 1889. The burial service was short and simple, being conducted by the Rev. D. Thomas, who in prayer supplicated the Almighty "to bring to the bar of justice the cruel hand that smote the death blow," so that right might be done, and "that which cried from the very ground for vengeance might be heard and answered." In a short address, the reverend gentleman appealed to the people present to take warning by the event. The rev. gentleman's discourse was interrupted by fervent "Amen's." – Mr. Harvey, the next speaker, was also listened to attentively. – Mr. Paynter, the hon. Solicitor, added a few words, saying that Mr. Coles had assured him that his daughter had never given him any trouble or pain during her life. The father, who appeared in a feeble state and shed tears abundantly, took a last look at the coffin, and was then led away to the carriage in waiting. Happily, he did not see the crowd surge over the ropes and nearly throw the two attendant policemen into the open graves.

The Hull Times, February 28th 1891,

> THE MAYBRICK MURDER. The Baroness Von Roques, mother of Mrs Maybrick, arrived in England on Monday last from France, and had a long interview on Wednesday with her solicitor (Mr. Pooley, of Sloane Street, London). The Baroness claims to be in possession of documents which fully corroborate Mrs Maybrick's statement at her trial that she had used for a long period for toilet purposes a

> *prescription containing arsenic. It is understood that another effort will be made to re-open the case.*

James Maybrick:

James Maybrick was a Liverpool cotton merchant, born in 1838, who became sick and died in May 1889. At the time it was claimed that his young wife, Florence Maybrick, was responsible for his death. A trial took place, under Sir James Fitzjames Stephen, who was the father of "Jack the Ripper" suspect J. K. Stephen, and Florence Maybrick was found guilty. Uproar followed, as Stephen claimed to grasp many aspects of the case, and after spending 15 years in prison was released and died in America in 1941.

James Maybrick was associated with the Ripper case in the early 1990's when an alleged diary was revealed to the world. Opinion was divided on the journal, which comprised of sixty three handwritten pages, and experts failed to provide proof it was either genuine or a forgery. Efforts have been made to ascertain whether the ink used is genuine, whether the journal is from the period, whether the handwriting is that of James Maybrick, and whether the events in Maybrick's life match those in the diary. Ripperologists have also looked at the "Jack the Ripper" side of the diary to see whether the claims match the known details. Linguistic experts have also looked at the language used to ascertain whether it is contemporary. Opinion is also divided on the conclusions reached by the experts who carried out these tests and checks.

Months after the press reported on the Maybrick/Ripper Diary a watch surfaced which was owned by a Mr. Albert Johnson. Inside the Henry Verity Watch, made in 1846, were the scratched words, "*J. Maybrick,*" and "*I am Jack,*" along with the initials of Mary Nichols, Annie Chapman, Elizabeth Stride, Catherine Eddowes, and Mary Kelly. The watch, like the diary, is still the subject of fierce debate over its authenticity.

Since then a great number of books and even a documentary, presented by the late Michael Winner, have been released that look at all sides of the argument and present the facts of the case.

The Hull Daily Mail, March 2nd 1891, P. 4,

Mike Covell

> *INQUEST ON THE WHITECHAPEL WITNESS. DEATH FROM EXCITEMENT. At the inquest in London to-day on the body of Charles Guiver, aged 34 years, lately acting as night watchman at a common lodging house in White's-row, Spitalfields, who died suddenly on Wednesday, it was shown that death was due to apoplexy, accelerated by excitement. Deceased was one of the principal witnesses in the inquiry into the circumstances attending the murder of Frances Coles in Swallow Gardens, and had suffered from pains in his head since he identified the body.*

The Hull Daily Mail, March 4th 1891, P. 4,

> *DISCHARGE OF SADLER FROM CUSTODY. At the Thames Police Court on Tuesday, John Thomas Sadler, who was charged with the murder of Frances Coles, at Swallow Gardens on the 13th ult,, was, on the application of the Treasury, discharged from custody.*

The Hull Times, March 7th 1891,

> *SADLER FREE. At the Thames Police Court on Tuesday, John Thomas Sadler, who was charged with the murder of Frances Coles, at Swallow Gardens on the 13th ult,, was, on the application of the Treasury, discharged from custody.*

The Hull Times, and The Hull Daily News, both dated, March 7th 1891,

> *ANOTHER LONDON MYSTERY. Today's Star says:- The left leg and right hand and arm of a woman were found at Regent's Canal at Bethnal Green on Monday, under the arch where Cambridge Heath Road crosses it. The limbs were wrapped in a thick, coarse material and looked as though they had been in the water for several days. They were immediately taken charge of by the police and conveyed to Hackney Mortuary. It is intended to drag the canal. Another correspondent says:- A barge man on the Regents Canal on Monday came across the mutilated and decomposed remains of a human being in the water near Cambridge Heath Bridge, Bethnal Green. Dr White, divisional surgeon, made an examination, and found that the body was apparently that of an adult female. All the bones of the skull, with the exception of three or four pieces, were missing, as were the spinal column, ribs, breastbone, haunch bones, right thigh and leg. All the intestines were gone, and the body was in an advanced stage of decomposition. The doctor is of the opinion that the bones had been rudely dragged from the body. The body had probably been in the water for six to eight months, and it is not likely any clue to its identity will be found.*

The Hull Daily Mail, April 7th 1891, P. 4

At the Maidenhead Police Court this morning William Sadler, the man who was charged in London with being the perpetrator of the last Whitechapel murder, was sentenced to seven days' hard labour for having been drunk in the town last night. Sadler behaved in a strange manner when in the dock.

The Hull Daily Mail, April 30th 1891, P. 3

THE WHITECHAPEL CRIMES. A SENSATIONAL STORY FROM WIMBLEDON. HAS THE MURDERER COMMITTED SUICIDE. A singular rumour has been circulated in the neighbourhood of Wimbledon, to the effect that the East End murderer has committed suicide. It appears that about three weeks ago a person of gentlemanly appearance committed suicide on Wimbledon Common by shooting himself with a revolver. The deceased was not identified at the inquest, which was held on the 9th inst., and his remains were subsequently buried at the expense of the parish. Since his death everything has been done by the authorities to trace the identity of the deceased, but without success, and the affair has until lately remained a complete mystery. There is now, however, a report that the deceased is no other than the notorious murderer. It is declared that the appearance of the deceased corresponds strangely with the description given of the perpetrator of the Whitechapel crimes. Several blank sheets of note paper of a similar kind, it is said, to that used for the written warnings which were posted in various parts of London for a short time previous to many of the Whitechapel murders were found on the body. The suicide appears to have been committed in a most determined manner, and everything that could have led to the man's identification seems to have been intentionally destroyed.

The Hull Daily Mail, May 1891,

ANOTHER LONDON MYSTERY. Tuesday's Star says:- The left leg and right hand and arm of a woman were found in Regent's Canal at Bethnal Green on Monday, under the arch where Cambridge Heath road crosses it. The limbs were wrapped in a thick, coarse material, and looked as if they had been in the water for several days. They were immediately taken charge of by the police and conveyed to Hackney mortuary. It is intended to drag the canal. Another correspondent says:- A bargeman on the Regent's Canal on Monday came across the mutilated and decomposed remains of a human being in the water near Cambridge Heath Bridge, Bethnal Green. Dr White, divisional surgeon, made an examination, and found that the body was apparently that of an adult female. All the bones of the skull with the exception of three or four pieces, were missing, as were the spinal

Mike Covell

> *column, ribs, breastbone, haunch bones, right thigh and leg. All the intestines were gone, and the body was in an advanced stage of decomposition. The doctor is of the opinion that the bones had been rudely dragged from the body. The body had probably been in the water for six or eight months, and it is not likely any clue to its identity will be found.*

The Hull Daily Mail, May 20th 1891,

> *THE AMERICAN "RIPPER" TRAGEDY. FRENCHY ON HIS TRIAL. A Desperado of a Degraded Class. "Frenchy" was on Monday indicted by the grand jury of New York for murder of the first degree. He is implicated in what is known as the "Jack the Ripper" murder. The prisoner is variously named as Ben Ali, Frank Sherlick, Frenchy and in the indictment as George Frank. He is an Algerian of the most degraded class, whose habits and practices are unutterably filthy, and it could only be an advantage to the community to get rid of him. At the same time there is not a one fair minded person who believes him guilty of the butchery of Carrie Brown. As he stated in a previous despatch the reporters who were actually on the scene before the detectives, failed to discover the alleged track of blood from the prisoners room. If it were there it might have just as readily have been caused by the man who accompanied the woman and who in departing had to pass the prisoners door. The only other important evidence is the fact that there were bloodstains on the wall of the prisoners room on his hands, and under his fingernails. This says little, as these scoundrels are cut throat desperadoes, and are seldom free from stains of blood. In the meantime the question is asked- Where is the man who was last seen with the victim? Should he not turn up, and it begins to seem as though he would not, George Frank will in all probability be found guilty.*

The Hull Daily Mail, May 21st 1891,

> *IS "FRENCHY" THE REAL "JACK THE RIPPER?" SUPPOSED DISCOVERY OF THE WHITECHAPEL FIEND A Story with an Air of Probability about it. According to advices received at Plymouth yesterday the police authorities of Jersey City, State of New York, believe they have in custody the real "Jack the Ripper" It will be remembered that a woman named Carrie Brown was murdered at the River Hotel, and that the police of New York arrested for the crime a man known as "Frenchy No 1" The individual now charged with committing the act is supposed to be an Algerian sailor, and a cousin of "Frenchy No. 1," passing generally under the alias of "Frenchy No. 2" Strangely enough, he in many ways corresponds with the published descriptions of "Jack the Ripper", and follows the occupation in which the notorious criminal is believed to be engaged- a boss*

> *cattle driver on the tramp cattle ships. What also tends to strengthen the belief that the man in gaol and "The Ripper" are one and the same person is that fact that he was arrested in London (England) and imprisoned several weeks for one of the Whitechapel murders, but the authorities had to release him because of their inability to identify him with the perpetrator of those horrible crimes.*

> ***Frenchy - Ameer Ben Ali:***
>
> It was claimed that Ameer Ben Ali, known in the press as Frenchy, and Frenchy 1, was the murderer of Carrie Brown. Carrie Brown was killed in New York on April 24th 1891. She was a prostitute, and known as Old Shakespeare in the press due to her love of Shakespearean quotes. Her body was mutilated and dumped in a dumpster at the East River Hotel. The case was reported in the press as a Jack the Ripper murder and the hunt was on for a suspect. Ameer Ben Ali, an Algerian, was staying in a room in the hotel, and it was claimed that a bloodstain led from her room to his, a "fact" that several sources on the scene denied, and Ali was charged with Brown's murder. He subsequently appeared at court and was sentenced to life imprisonment after the jury found him guilty of second degree murder.
>
> ***Further Reading:***
> *A Tale of Two Frenchy's*, Michael Conlon
> *An Investigation into the Carrie Brown Murder*, Larry Barbee
> *The Carrie Brown Murder Case: New Revelations*, Michael Conlon

The Hull Daily Mail, May 22nd 1891,

> *A GERMAN "JACK THE RIPPER" A Death bed Confession. A prisoner in the penitentiary of the city of Erfurt, suffering from blood poisoning, and thinking his last hour had come has just made a confession to the effect that he is the long sought for German "Jack the Ripper", who on Good Friday of 1890, butchered a woman of bad character in the barrack grounds of Erfurt. He says three other men and one woman assisted him in the "job", which was executed according to the descriptions of the London "Ripper" murders. One of the men implicated, a farmer named Polaresk, living in Evershagen, has been arrested. The others, who heard of the warrants out for their arrest, have escaped, but are being pursued by the police. The farmer was formerly a butcher. He has a large family, and up to the present time has borne a good reputation.*

Mike Covell

The Hull Daily Mail, June 30th 1891, P. 5,

> A "VIGILANT" CHAIRMAN. FIVE SHILLINGS OR FIVE DAYS. *Alfred Bachert, the chairman of the so-called Whitechapel Vigilance Committee, who described himself as an engraver and report, was charged at Thames-street Police Court to-day with disorderly conduct in High-street, Whitechapel. A constable deposed that the defendant was fighting, and another witness said Bachert often got drunk, mostly on Mondays and Tuesdays. Defendant was fined 5s or five days' imprisonment.*

The Hull Daily Mail, July 3rd 1891, P. 4,

> *At the Thames Police Court this morning, Mr. Bachert (chairman of the Whitechapel Murder Vigilance Committee), who was fined on Tuesday for alleged disorderly conduct, applied for the process for perjury against a witness in the case. The Stipendiary told the applicant he must prepare a written information before the matter could be considered.*

> **Albert Bacchert**
> 1887 Electoral Register
> 3717 Bachert, Albert, One room first floor unfurnished, 13 Newham Street, Mr. John Bachert Same Address
>
> 1888 Electoral Register
> 3950 Bachert, Albert, One room first floor unfurnished, 13 Newham Street, Mr. John Bachert Same Address
>
> 1889 Criminal Case, HO27, P212, P181
> Name: Albert Backert, Date of Trial: Nov 30 1889, Trial Year: 1889, Location of Trial: Essex, England, Sentence: Acquittal, Crime: [illegible] Counterfeit coin twice on same day.
>
> 1893 Electoral Register
> 3677 Bachert, Albert Edward, One room second floor unfurnished, 13 Newham Street, Mr. John Bachert Same Address

The Hull Daily Mail, August 7th 1891,

Newspapers from Hull Volume 2

> *LATEST NEWS. IS IT "JACK THE RIPPER" AGAIN? ANOTHER WHITECHAPEL OUTRAGE. ATTEMPT TO MURDER A WOMAN. DESPERATE STRUGGLE FOR LIFE. On old woman named Woolf, about 70 years of age, was brought to the London Hospital this morning suffering from a severe gash in the throat, and her injuries are so serious that her depositions have been taken. It appears that early this morning she was in Cannon-street, St. George's, when a man attacked her with a knife. He managed to inflict a desperate wound in her throat, but she struggled with her assailant to such a successful purpose that he at last ran away, not however, before he had inflicted some severe cuts about her arms. The police have arrested a man on suspicion of being the woman's would be murderer, but it is not yet known whether the authorities have any evidence in their possession which will conclusively identify the prisoner with the crime.*

The Hull Daily News, August 8th 1891,

> *LATEST NEWS. A WHITECHAPEL TRAGEDY. On old woman named Woolf, about 70 years of age, was brought to the London Hospital this morning suffering from a severe gash in the throat, and her injuries are so serious that her depositions have been taken. It appears that early this morning she was in Cannon-street, St. George's, when a man attacked her with a knife. He managed to inflict a desperate wound in her throat, but she struggled with her assailant to such a successful purpose that he at last ran away, not however, before he had inflicted some severe cuts about her arms. The police have arrested a man on suspicion of being the woman's would be murderer, but it is not yet known whether the authorities have any evidence in their possession which will conclusively identify the prisoner with the crime. FURTHER PARTICULARS. THE WOMAN'S STATEMENT. – DESCRIPTION OF HER ASSAILANT. The Press Association, in a later telegram, says the attention of the police was first called to Woolf, who is of German nationality, by two men, who found her lying on a doorstep in Cable-street. She was taken to the hospital immediately, and attended by Mr Williams, house surgeon, who saw that her recovery was almost hopeless. Superintendent Arnold accordingly sent for Mr Mead, the magistrate for the division, who took the woman's depositions. She spoke with considerable difficulty, and her statement was interpreted by one of the nurses. She said that as she did not feel well she went for a walk before going to bed. A man whom she did not know came up, seized hold of her, and cut her in the arm and throat. She said he was a man of medium height, and about 30 years of age, and had a full face and black moustache and beard. When he caught hold of her he did not say anything, and she was too frightened to call out, and, although saw a knife in his hand, it was too dark for her to distinguish the kind of knife it was. After the man, who wore a short jacket and black felt hat had cut her throat he ran away in the*

> *direction of the Vestry Hall, Cable-street, and she fell on a doorstep, where she remained for some time. Several persons passed her, and she called to them, but not being able to speak English, they took no notice and passed on. At last, however, two men noticed that she was wounded and apprised the police. A thorough search was made of the district with the result that at the bottom of Dellow-street a razor was discovered lying in some blood, and a man who was taken into custody, at five o'clock, was at noon still detained at Harbour-square Police-station. The police do not appear to attach much importance to the arrest. The man has evidently been drinking heavily, and he threatens to commit suicide. It has been ascertained that the woman's real name is Catherine Gertrude Wohler. SUPPOSED ATTEMPTED SUICIDE. A representative of the Press Association learns, as the result of further inquiries, that the police are now inclined to believe that it is a case of attempted suicide. Wohler is a respectable woman, but she is very eccentric and, despite her rambling statements, it is thought that her injuries are self-inflicted. The police subsequently released the man taken into custody for the attack on Mrs Wohler, his explanation being regarded as satisfactory. The woman was, last night, in a critical condition at the London Hospital.*

The Hull Daily News, August 10th 1891,

> THE OUTRAGE IN WHITECHAPEL. THE ATTEMPTED SUICIDE THEORY DISCREDITED BY THE DOCTORS. *Latest accounts respecting the alleged attempted murder in Whitechapel, says: - Throughout on Friday the police officials of the Shadwell district, assisted by officers from the central detective office, were busy investigating the circumstances attending the outrage. They, as previously stated, have come to the conclusion that the injured woman attempted to commit suicide. The medical attendants of the woman, however, state that the wounds are such as could not have been self-inflicted. The police have found no clue to lead to the discovery of the man. Dr Williams states that his patient remains very weak; and though the wounds of themselves might not be sufficiently severe to cause the death of a younger person, the shock to the system of the old woman has been so great that he fears there is no chance of her recovery; he thinks she will probably live from two to three days.*

The Hull Daily Mail, August 10th 1891, P. 4,

> THE WHITECHAPEL MYSTERY. THE THEORY OF SUICIDE STILL BELIEVED. *The woman Wohler, who was found with her throat cut in Whitechapel on Friday, continues to improve, and there seems little doubt now but*

> *that she will recover. The police still adhere to the belief that is a case of attempted suicide.*

Katherine Gertrude Wohler:

The curious case of Katherine Gertrude Wohler, alias Catherine Wohler, alias, Catherine Woolf, alias Catherine Woolfe, alias Catherine Wolf, made headline news when the, still unsolved incident, occurred in August 1891. The story made national news in the following publications in Great Britain:

The North Eastern Daily Gazette, August 7th 1891, *Daily Gazette for Middlesborough*, August 7th 1891, *Nottingham Evening Post*, August 7th 1891, *Gloucester Citizen*, August 7th 1891, *Yorkshire Evening Post*, August 7th 1891, *Portsmouth Evening News*, August 7th 1891, *Sunderland Daily Echo and Shipping Gazette*, August 7th 1891, *Derby Daily Telegraph*, August 7th 1891, *The Belfast News Letter*, August 8th 1891, *The Blackburn Standard and Weekly Express*, August 8th 1891, *The Cheshire Observer*, August 8th 1891, *North Eastern Daily Gazette*, August 8th 1891, *Freeman's Journal and Daily Commercial Advertiser*, August 8th 1891, *The Hampshire Advertiser*, August 8th 1891, *Exeter and Plymouth Gazette*, August 8th 1891, *The Yorkshire Gazette*, August 8th 1891, *The Yorkshire Herald and York Herald*, August 8th 1891, *The Leeds Mercury*, August 8th 1891, *The Times*, August 8th 1891, *The Liverpool Mercury*, August 8th 1891, *The Sheffield and Rotherham Independent*, August 8th 1891, *Western Times*, August 8th 1891, *Portsmouth Evening News*, August 8th 1891, *Gloucester Citizen*, August 8th 1891, *Manchester Courier and Lancashire General*, August 8th 1891, *The Daily Gazette for Middlesbrough*, August 8th 1891, *Bucks Herald*, August 8th 1891, *Shields Daily Gazette*, August 8th 1891, *Lloyd's Weekly Newspaper*, August 9th 1891, *Manchester Courier and Lancashire General Advertiser*, August 9th 1891, *The Pall Mall Gazette*, August 10th 1891, *The Times*, August 10th 1891, *Gloucester Citizen*, August 10th 1891, *Aberdeen Evening Express*, August 10th 1891, *Portsmouth Evening News*, August 10th 1891, *Shields Daily Gazette*, August 10th 1891, *Yorkshire Evening Post*, August 10th 1891, *Derby Daily Telegraph*, August 10th 1891, *Aberdeen Weekly Journal*, August 11th 1891, *Birmingham Daily Post*, August 11th 1891, *Freeman's Journal and Daily Commercial Advertiser*, August 11th 1891, *The Huddersfield Daily Chronicle*, August 11th 1891, *Western Times*, August 11th 1891, *Portsmouth Evening News*, August 11th 1891, *Manchester Courier and Lancashire General Advertiser*, August 11th 1891, *Shields Daily Gazette*, August 11th 1891, *Sheffield Daily Telegraph*, August 11th 1891, *Sunderland Daily Echo and Shipping Gazette*, August 11th 1891, *The*

Mike Covell

> *Hampshire Advertiser*, August 12th 1891, *North Devon Journal*, August 13th 1891, *The Morning Post*, August 13th 1891, *Western Gazette*, August 14th 1891, *Stamford Mercury*, August 14th 1891, and the *Worcestershire Chronicle*, August 15th 1891.
>
> Internationally, the case drew attention, and appeared in newspaper reports across the world in the following newspapers:
> *Daily Northwestern*, August 7th 1891, *St. Paul's Daily News*, August 7th 1891, *The Atchison Daily Globe*, August 7th 1891, *The Daily Evening Bulletin*, August 7th 1891, *Bangor Daily Whig and Courier*, August 8th 1891, *Evening Star*, August 8th 1891, *The Galveston Daily News*, August 8th 1891, *The North American*, August 8th 1891, *The Emporia Daily Gazette*, August 8th 1891, *Rocky Mountain News*, August 8th 1891, *Middletown Daily Times*, August 8th 1891, *New York Times*, August 8th 1891, *Philadelphia Record*, August 8th 1891, *Chicago Tribune*, August 8th 1891, *The Morning Herald*, August 8th 1891, *The Brooklyn Eagle*, August 8th 1891, *Luxemburg Wort*, August 8th 1891, *Bismarck Daily Tribune*, August 10th 1891, *Paterson Daily Press*, August 13th 1891, *Stevens Point Daily Journal*, August 15th 1891
>
> Her death is registered thus,
> Name: Catherine Gertrude Wolf, Quarter: Oct – Nov – Dec, Year: 1891, County: St George in the East, Vol: 1C, Page: 276
>
> *Ripper Notes*, 24, October 2005, PP. 105-107

The Hull Daily Mail, November 16th 1891, P. 4,

> AN ANTI – "RIPPER" IN TROUBLE. "GOT UP AND MANUFACTURED BY THE POLICE." *At the Thames Police Court this morning, Albert E. Backert, chairman of the so – called Whitechapel Murder Vigilance Committee, was charges with being drunk and disorderly in the East India Dock-road. Defendant, in answer to the charge, said that it was a conspiracy got up by the police and manufactured by them. He called many witnesses, who stated they saw a policeman push Backert. – The Magistrate said he would give defendant the benefit of the doubt and discharged him.*

The Hull Daily Mail, December 17th 1891, P. 3,

> ANOTHER WHITECHAPEL TRAGEDY. A WOMAN MURDERED. AN ARREST. *The man arrested last night on a charge of murdering a woman at Great Nicholl-street, is named Miaa. He is a shoemaker of middle age, and had been living with*

> *the deceased as her husband. The case will be investigated by the police court to-day. The wound inflicted by the prisoner was in the breast, and jealousy is stated to have been the motive of the crime.*

1892 – The year of Frederick Bailey Deeming

With 1891 over, it looked as though the newspaper reports were settling down, but in March of 1892 all that would change, with a new Ripper suspect name, and a new collection of victims. 1892 got off with a bang with numerous reports in the Hull press covering Frederick Bailey Deeming. This wasn't the first time that Deeming was in the Hull press he had earlier appeared in a criminal trial in 1890 when he defrauded Thomas Reynoldson at his jewellery store on Hull's Whitefriargate. (See: Appendix IV) For anyone wishing to read more about that event I would recommend reading *Mike Covell's Jack the Ripper – From Hell, From Hull, Vol: II*

The Hull Daily Mail, March 16th 1892, P. 3,

> *THE MELBOURNE MURDER. SUPPOSED SIMILAR CASE AT LIVERPOOL. A PROBABLE DISCLOSURE. A Liverpool correspondent telegraphs that, in connection with the supposed murder near Melbourne, of a woman named Williams or Mather, whose body was found buried under the floor of a suburban villa at Windsor, near Melbourne, inquiries at Rainhill, Lancashire, on the part of detectives from Scotland Yard, point to the probability of SIMILAR CRIMES and similar disposal of the bodies of a woman and two children, who mysteriously disappeared previous to William's departure to Australia in the company of the woman Mather, whose murdered remains were found, as already stated. Mather's mother is a newsagent and tobacconist at Rainhill, and had the letting of a house which Williams occupied at Rainhill, called Durham Villa. Here, it is said, he spent a good deal of his time lifting the bottom floors of the villa, which were afterwards filled up with cement. This house has been untenanted since Williams left it last July; and yesterday, Superintendent Keeley had under consideration the advisability of lifting the floor. It is said that a charwoman once remarked to Williams that there was a strong smell of chloride of lime, to which the latter replied he was merely trying to remedy bad drainage. On several occasions Williams was visited by woman, whom he introduced as his sisters; and these are supposed to have been DONE TO DEATH in "Jack the Ripper" fashion by Williams, who spent a part of his time drinking freely at the Commercial Hotel, Rainhill, and in doing mysterious work at his villa, which was partly furnished by a Liverpool furnishing establishment. It is this villa which will, in the course of a*

Mike Covell

> few days, be thoroughly explored by the police, and which in its results, may form a feature in the antecedents of the man Williams, charged with the Melbourne murder. It may be added that Williams left behind him a Gladstone bag, distinctly saturated with blood, which is now in the hands of the police, and that, after an interval, he re-appeared at Rainhill, dressed in strange habiliments, ill fitting, and such as might be obtained at any second hand clothes shop, the worse for wear, and moth eaten. These facts are being freely discussed, and commented upon in the village, in connection with the murder just brought to light at Melbourne.

The Hull Daily Mail, March 16th 1892 P. 4,

> THE MELBOURNE TRAGEDY. FURTHER INVESTIGATIONS AT LIVERPOOL. SENSATIONAL DISCOVERY TO-DAY. THREE BODIES FOUND. The Press Association's Liverpool correspondent telegraphs that the police at Rainhill this morning commenced an examination of Durham Villa House, occupied some months ago by the man Williams, who is now under arrest at Melbourne for the murder of his wife. When he occupied the house he was visited by a lady and two children, who suddenly and mysteriously disappeared, Williams saying at the time that she had gone to join her husband at Port Said. He afterwards purchased a quantity of cement, and cemented the hearthstone, calling in a plasterer to complete the job which he had commenced. It is alleged that there was then an odour of chloride of lime in the house which has not been tenanted since Williams went away, and a portmanteau left by Williams at the Rainhill Hotel bears marks which are apparently BLOOD STAINS. There now appears to be no doubt that the woman murdered in Australia was Miss Mather, to whom Williams was married just before he sailed. The news from Melbourne came as a great shock to many friends of Miss Mather, and the greatest sympathy is expressed for her widowed mother, who gave her last unmarried daughter to one whom she regarded as an honourable suitor. Mrs. Mather, it appears, was the agent for Dinham Villa, and it was while negotiating with Mrs. Mather for the house that he became acquainted with the young lady whom he married, and about whose fate there is such painful anxiety. While stopping at the Commercial Hotel, Rainhill, Williams CHARMED EVERYONE by his gentlemanly bearing and courteous demeanour, and it is stated that after sleeping at Dinham Villa some nights he returned to the hotel, saying he could not rest alone at the house. He was then told that he could not have his bedroom, and went to London. Williams, while at Rainhill, dazzled the inhabitants with profusion of his wealth, sporting diamond rings and nuggets of gold, and on one occasion he flourished bank notes to the value of £1,100; and letters have been received from various ports at which Mr. and Mrs. Williams called giving the most glowing descriptions of their journey and their happiness together. Telegraphing at 12.30 the same correspondent says: The operations at

Rainhill are being conducted with the greatest secrecy. The doors of the house are barred and the windows have been frosted in order to prevent anything being seen from the outside. The work is being done by the police officers from Widnes, acting under the direction of the authorities at Scotland Yard. ON THE POINT OF DISCOVERY. The work of breaking up the cement under the hearth stone had proceeded for about half an hour when a sickening smell began to emanate from the hole, and it was evident the police were on the verge of an important discovery. As the work proceeded the stench became so intolerable and sickening that the man had to suspend operations for a time just as they had come upon a table cloth and a woman's apron. FINDING THE BODIES. The Press Association's Liverpool correspondent telegraphs this afternoon that the police have found the bodies of a woman and two children in the house at Rainhill, where the man Williams was visited by a lady and two children, whom he reported to be his sister and her children.

The Hull Daily Mail, March 17th 1892, P. 2,

THE RAINHILL ROMANCE. The revelations at Rainhill and in Melbourne, Australia, seem to point to a horrible crime, and outdoing Dumas in its lurid romance. Last summer a mysterious stranger arrived at Rainhill, near Liverpool. He had all the customary appurtenances of such a weird visitant. He had wealth – for he wore diamond rings and flourished thousand pound bank notes – he had "style" – for his manners were gentlemanly – he had position – for he wore a suit of regimentals. More than all this, he won the daughter of a Mrs. Mather. But while he lived at Rainhill, some strange business went on. The opulent and mysterious "military man" took a large house and had the floors of one or two rooms concreted. He complained of the sewage and of unpleasant smells. There was nothing remarkable in this – bad sanitation is common enough – but there was, in fact that Mr. Williams would persist in doing the concreting himself. Upon one occasion and woman and two children came to the house and then disappeared in an unaccountable way.. Now Williams has been arrested in Australia on a charge of crime. Five bodies have already been found in the floor catacomb. The question now exercising the minds of the people of Rainhill is: - What other secrets does that concreted floor contain? More dead bodies?

The Hull Daily Mail, March 17th 1892, P. 3,

THE RAINHILL HORRORS. GHASTLY DISCOVERIES. MURDERS WHOLESALE. A KITCHEN TURNED INTO A GRAVEYARD. VICTIMS BURIED IN CEMENT. REVELATION FOLLOWS REVELATION. A GRUESOME STORY. A quiet little village of Rainhill, about nine miles distant from Liverpool, which is *upon the London and North Western route, and is known only as being the locale of the county lunatic asylum, was thrown into a state of intense excitement by the discovery that murders on a wholesale scale had been perpetrated in its midst. The first suspicion arose from a telegram, dated Melbourne, March 11, which was as follows: - Great excitement has been caused here by the recent discovery in an empty house in a suburb of this city of a woman's body, under circumstances which leave no doubt that she was the victim of a cruel murder. The body was found buried in a quantity of cement under a fireplace in one of the rooms. It was completely doubled up and firmly secured in that position with a stout cord, and a nearer examination showed that the woman's throat had been cut and her skull fractured. The investigations of the police led to the identifications of the remains as those of a woman who had passed as the wife or a man named Williams, who formerly occupied the house, and it is believed that the murder must have been committed at about Christmas time. Williams has now been arrested on suspicion in Western Australia, and he will be formally charged with murder. It is reported that the unfortunate woman formerly had a bookseller's or stationer's shop in Liverpool, and resided with her mother at New Brighton. She arrived in Melbourne on December 15th last on board the Norddeutscher Lloyd's Kaiser Willhelm II. INQUIRIES AT RAINHILL. Inquiries at New Brighton disclosed that nothing was known there of the woman or Williams, but a later telegram stated that the woman came from Rainhill, where she had been married to Williams, who has now been charged with the murder by the Melbourne police, who have him in custody. Further inquiries led to the discovery that the woman was Miss Mather, daughter of an old and respected resident of Rainhill, who had lived there with her widowed mother. In July last Mr. A. O. Williams arrived in Rainhill, and p up at a local hostelry, describing himself as an Inspector of Regiments. Mrs. Mather, who kept a stationer's shop, was entrusted with the letting of a house, Dinham Villa, and this house Williams agreed to take. During the negotiations he became acquainted with Miss Mather. A day or two after Mr Williams's arrival a lady, accompanied by two children, came on the scene, and visited Williams on one or two occasions, and had tea and lunch with him. Then the woman disappeared, and Williams explained that she was his sister, and had gone to meet her husband at Port Said. ANTECEDENTS OF WILLIAMS. Williams, who appeared to have plenty of money, went to the villa for a few days, and then leaving for London. He was away a fortnight, and then came back dressed in regimentals and flush of money. He entertained some of the residents to dinner, and announced that he was about to marry Miss Mather, a statement which caused some surprise. The wedding took place at eight o'clock one morning in September last in Rainhill Parish Church, and the bride and bridegroom left immediately afterwards for London, en route to India and Australia. Letters were received by Mrs Mather from various places, describing the journey and stating that they were very happy.*

These, however, ceased for a whole, and then came the telegram of the discovery of the body in Melbourne. The police at Scotland Yard communicated with the police of Widnes, in which division Rainhill is situated, and inquiries led to the above facts being ascertained, and also to the disclosure that during his stay at Rainhill Williams had CEMENTED THE FLOOR of the kitchen of the villa, which had remained empty ever since he left. Williams had commenced cementing himself, but got a local plasterer to complete it. Suspicion was at once aroused that some horrible mystery was hidden beneath this cemented floor, and the police decided to take up the flags and cement. The task was performed yesterday under the direction of Inspector Keighley, of Widnes, who was formerly in the Liverpool Police Force. The inspector arrived at Dinham Villa a few minutes before one o'clock, and the hearthstone flag in the back kitchen was at once raised, and a couple of constables set to work with pickaxes. Before they had been at work a quarter of an hour a sickening smell emanated from the floor, and those present were at once convinced that they were about to come upon some buried remains. It was evident that a deep hole had been dug in the kitchen floor, and that several barrels of cement had been used. This had been poured into a mass solid and hard as concrete, and the work of excavating it was painfully slow. As the man proceeded the SICKENING GRAVEYARD SMELL became horribly intensified, and after half an hour's digging, when the earth and cement had been excavated to the depth of about a foot, a confirmatory discovery was made. The corner of a white damask table-cloth, and what appeared to be a woman's apron or shawl, were disclosed to view. The stench had now become so overpowering that the constables were compelled to cease work for a time and go to the door for fresh air. When the work was recommenced, not many minutes elapsed before the police were able to take out the bodies of two children. Both were lying face downwards, with their little bodies simply covered with a night shirt, and with their legs perfectly bare. The first body taken out was that of a boy about five years of age. He wore a striped print shirt, and his head was wrapped in what appeared to be a piece of old linen. When the body was taken up, the stench, which previously been intolerable, became infinitely worse. Those present dared not breathe unless they went to a window to do so, and every window in the house had to be thrown open. The body of the first child discovered was immediately taken upstairs into one of the bedrooms. When the head-wrap was removed it was discovered that not only was there a fearful wound on the head, but that the throat had been cut, and the HEAD NEARLY SEVERED FROM THE BODY. The remains were dreadfully decomposed at the extremities of the arms and legs. The body of a fair-haired little girl of about seven years was next brought out, her throat also being terribly cut. After removing the bodies of the two children the police began to excavate further for the body of the woman, who, it now became apparent, was deeply embedded in cement. Slowly the work proceeded, but ultimately one foot peeped above the

Mike Covell

earth. It was covered with a soft house-shoe. Then the figure became apparent, but it was only in outline. Great difficulty was found in extracting the body, as it was to firmly embedded in the cement. It was seen that the woman had a rope around her neck, the ends of which were cut sharply off, as if she had been hanged and cut down. A policeman tugged at the rope, but it gave way, and the digging operations commenced again, the body being ultimately removed. Whole the men were at work digging around the body of the woman they made an unexpected discovery of the body of a baby girl lying at the foot of the woman. Soon afterwards A FOURTH CHILD, a girl of about 10 years, was found lying beside the woman. The body of the woman was wrapped in an eider-down quilt, and tied lightly round with rope. She was fully dressed with the exception of a boot and stocking on one foot, all her clothes being of very fine quality. She had on a print morning dress. The throat was cut. She was of very dark complexion, and had short black hair, suggestive of her being half-caste. On her left hand was a wedding ring and keeper. All the bodies were in an advanced stage of decomposition, and the work of getting them out was completed only after great difficulty. The burial of bodies had been carried out in a very systematic and complete manner. A deep hole had been dug and the bodies of the woman and two children placed in it, the cement being poured on them. Flags were then laid upon the top of the hole, and over all was a layer of six inches of cement, which ENXTENDED OVER THE ENTIRE KITCHEN. On the removal of the last of the bodies they were all laid out in an upper room, and work was discontinued for the day. The police, however, entertained the belief that no more bodies were interred in the kitchen. The greatest excitement prevailed in Rainhill and neighbourhood, and the wildest rumours were afloat as to other missing females, who, it is stated, had visited Williams and had not been seen since. These stories are being inquired into by the police, and the work of exploring the house will be resumed to-day. IS WILLIAMS "JACK THE RIPPER?" Many people who knew Williams when he was in Rainhill believe that he will be found to be no other than "Jack the Ripper." One important fact in this connection is that the notorious Whitechapel murders commenced about the time that Williams was supposed to have first arrived in England, and that since July last, when Williams put in an appearance at Rainhill, there had been no more East End outrages of that description. WILLIAMS AND HIS PICTURES: A REMARKABLE CIRCUMSTANCE. A very remarkable circumstance connected with the affair is related by some London and North Western railway officials at St. Helens, who state that on the 6th of October last an oil painting, described as "Two Dogs," by the artist Bolland, arrived at St. Helens, addressed to "Williams, to be called for." It had been consigned by Williams from King's Cross, London. Two or three days after a man with high cheek bones, heavy moustache, sallow complexion, and soft hat of the Yankee style, and wearing massive rings studded with diamonds, well dressed, but *nevertheless slovenly, giving the name of Williams and residence as Rainhill, called and said he was the consignee of the picture, which he stated was a valuable one, and had been in the Paris Exhibition. It had therefore been insured for £100 against damage in transit. Before accepting it Williams insisted upon examination, and when opened, the corners of the frames were found to be disjointed and slightly chipped and the beading displaced. He refused to accept the picture, and sent in a claim through a solicitor for £50. Mr James, the chief clerk, in reporting the matter to Mr Shaw, the district superintendent, said there was something VERY STRANGE ABOUT THE TRANSACTION. The sender and receiver were the same person, and, that being so, why not have the pictures sent from Euston to Rainhill direct, instead of sending it over the Great Northern and having it transferred to the London and North Western Railway? Williams stated that he wanted an immediate settlement, as he had taken a passage for himself and five others to Australia, and would sail on the 17th of October. Mr James, however, recommended a strict and searching investigation. The picture was badly packed, was evidently of little value, and had apparently been damaged before consignment. It was therefore sent back to the Leeds Hotel, Finsbury-square, London, to the address Williams gave, but so far as is known at St. Helens he sailed without the £50. It is stated that Williams did his best to get into society at Rainhill and Hayton, but although he displayed gold and diamonds in profusion they were not sufficient recommendation. ANOTHER WOMAN AND TWO CHILDREN MISSING. According to a further report from Australia, it is stated that in addition to the body of Miss Mather, which had been discovered, a woman and two children had been missing for some time. If these cases be connected with Williams they bring up the total number of murders to nine.*

The Hull Daily Mail, March 17th 1892, P. 4,

THE RAINHILL MYSTERY. THE MURDERER'S CONNECTION WITH HULL. SUPPOSED IDENTITY. ACTIVITY OF DETECTIVE SUPERINTENDENT CLAPHAM. Our representative waited on Detective-Supt. Clapham at the Central Police Station, Hull, this afternoon, and found the officer engaged on a letter which he was writing to the superintendent of police at Rainhill. Mr. Clapham stated that on reading in the newspapers the description of the Rainhill murderer, he recognised a strong resemblance to the man Lawson, who was convicted in 1890 for obtaining jewellery, amounting to £286, from Messrs Reynoldson and Son, Hull. The prisoner was a man with an intellectual forehead, high cheek bones, long moustache, and had a sallow complexion. Mr. Clapham further stated that he knew Lawson had a wife and two or three children living at Birkenhead at the time he married Miss Matheson, of Beverley. He intends sending a photograph of Lawson with the letter, and by that means hopes to prove or disprove the

Mike Covell

allegation that Lawson and Williams are one and the same. CORROBORATION FROM LIVERPOOL. A Liverpool correspondent says the murdered woman at Rainhill has been identified as Marie Deeming, who was employed at a Liverpool fishmonger's shop. Williams courted her, and married her in the name of Deeming, describing himself as a mining engineer. They left Liverpool and went to Hull, where Williams was convicted of forgery, and sent to gaol. After he came out of gaol he married a young woman at Hull, and wished her to go abroad, but she declined, and he deserted her and returned to his first wife. They afterwards went to Cape Town, but returning to England they went to Birkenhead, where they resided for some time. The deceased woman has three brothers and two sisters living at Birkenhead. HAS WILLIAMS BEEN AT BEVERLEY? There is grave reason for supposing that the man Williams now in custody at Melbourne, and at whose former residence the police are making such terrible discoveries, is the man who in 1890 married a young lady at Beverley, and deserted her, when warrants were obtained for his apprehension. Early in that year a man, who gave the name of Harry Lawson, and described himself as a wealthy cattle dealer from Australia, made the acquaintance of a young lady named Matheson, whose mother, respectably connected, then lived in the New Walk. He took apartments in Mrs. Matheson's house and gave the impression that he had plenty of money. In February he married Miss Matheson, and they left Beverley for the honeymoon, but they then found that he had purchased a quantity of jewellery from Messrs Reynoldson, of Hull, which were paid for by cheque on the Saturday afternoon. When presented on the following Monday at the bank it was discovered he had withdrawn all his money and had absconded. Warrants were obtained for his apprehension, and the aid of the Foreign Office having been obtained he was arrested at Monte Video in April, and brought back to Hull, where at the Borough Sessions in October he was sentenced to nine months' hard labour. During the time he was in prison it was found that he had a wife living at or near Birkenhead named Dean or Deeming, and as the case was a very heartless one it was decided to prosecute him for bigamy. It turned out, however, that by the law of extradition with the state of Uruguay a person can only be tried for the offence with which he was charged with when taken into custody, and the prosecution had to be abandoned. He left the Hull Prison on the 15th July, 1981, and remained a few days in Hull, when he left for Liverpool. His communications from that locality soon ceased, and nothing was heard from him again until he arrived in Australia, the last letter which reached Beverley from him only arriving a few days ago. It is known in Beverley that he purchased a picture in Antwerp of two dogs. INVESTIGATIONS AT LIVERPOOL This morning the police resumed digging operations at Dinham Villa, Rainhill, taking up the floor of the scullery which, like the kitchen, had been covered with a thick layer of cement. Arrangements have been made to hold the inquest on the bodies at the Inn, near the station, where

Williams used to stay. The Coroner has been communicated with this morning, and the date of the inquest will be fixed in the course of the day. WHO ARE THE MURDERED CHILDREN? AN IMPORTANT LINK. *The Press Association's Liverpool correspondent telegraphing at one o'clock, says the police have discovered in the house at Rainhill, to-day, a child's copybook, which bears the name of "Bertha Deeming." The greatest excitement prevails in the village, and a large crowd has assembled round the house awaiting the result of the search. "Deeming" was one of the aliases by which Williams was known in Australia. It was stated in answer to inquiries at the Leeds Hotel, 39 Finsbury-square, London, where Williams stopped for a few days during his honeymoon that his manner created suspicion whatever, and that he and his wife appeared happy together. When they left for Melbourne the luggage was taken to the railway station in a van ordered by Williams himself.* WILLIAMS'S BOX. *The large heavy box sent from Rainhill by Williams has been discovered at Plymouth. It was consigned to Mrs. A. Holds, Plymouth – to be called for; from A. W. Wilson, Ashton-road, Prescot. As it was not called for the railway authorities wrote to Wilson, Prescot, but the letter was returned through the dead letter office. The railway officials at Plymouth are now in communication with the Lancashire police on the subject.* THE CHILDREN IDENTIFIED. *Our Liverpool correspondent says: - A gardener living next door to Dinham Villa says he saw the woman whom he recognised as the deceased in the yard of the Villa on Sunday after the August Bank Holiday. On the Monday he heard the screams of children proceeding from the Villa. He never saw either woman or children after. A man named Deeming from Liverpool has identified the children.*

The Hull Daily Mail, March 18th 1892, P. 3

THE RAINHILL MURDERS. WILLIAMS AT BEVERLEY. MRS. MATHESON INTERVIEWED. *The representative of a contemporary visited Beverley yesterday, and called in at Mrs Matheson's shop, when he found that lady somewhat and not unnaturally perturbed by the latest development of this highly emotional case. Mrs. Matheson complains of the activity of the local gossips, not, be it understood, in reference to this unexpected turn of events, for of that they were as yet ignorant, but it seems that the mere fact of her daughter having been so suddenly deserted, coupled with the subsequent conviction of Lawson, has again given occasion for no small comment, and she was therefore anxious to have the truth of the matter set plainly forth. She stated at the outset that the first intimation of the man arrested at Melbourne being the supposed husband of her daughter was conveyed to her by a customer at her shop yesterday, and she was exceedingly startled by the information. She had, however, by the time the representative waited upon her, recovered a certain degree of composure and answered the question readily and*

Mike Covell

fully. "When was the first time you saw Lawson (for that is the name by which he was known to Mrs. Matheson)? – "The first time," she said, "was towards the end of 1889 – about October. We had an announcement in the window "Apartments to let," and seeing this he walked in." "What did he say?" – "Well, he said he had been looking round Beverley for apartments, and he thought he should like to stay at our house. It seemed a nice sort of place, he said, and he rather liked it." Mrs. Matheson then mentioned that his appearance was that of a man who had spent some time abroad in a warm climate, his face was tanned, though not sallow, as described in recent reports. His complexion was naturally fair, his hair was of a chestnut tinge, his eyes blue, and he walked with a peculiar posture of the shoulders, which are drawn up almost close to his ears. His manner was suave and engaging, and altogether he seemed the last person one would have suspected to be capable of committing any crime. Notwithstanding also his profuse display of jewellery and the easy manner in which he seemed to regard money he drove as hard a bargain for his apartments as even the neediest seeker of what are called "diggings" might be expected to do. At length, however, an agreement was arrived at, and "Lawson" at once took up his abode with the family. "What did he say he was?" – "He told us that he was an Australian sheep farmer, and that he was over here looking after wool sales." "What were his general habits?" "Well, he seemed to conduct himself in a way that no one would have noticed anything strange about. He spent a good deal of his time in writing letters – he wrote a lot of letters – and at night he would go out a bit, or sometimes, when he got my permission, would take to the girls to a place of amusement, or in the afternoon take them out for a drive." "Did he receive any letters?" – "No, he didn't," says Mrs. Matheson, "that was what I noticed, and I asked him about it. He said he got telegrams – one from a Mr. Brock, of Rockhampton, who, he said, was a partner of his." Mrs. Matheson, after "Lawson's" return and his conviction at Hull, became aware of his having a wife and family at Birkenhead, and would have preferred the charge of bigamy – or rather seen that her daughter did so – but for the flaw in the Extradition Treaty, about which she still feels indignant. "What's the good of it?" she asks. "It might as well have been a murder." The one point on which she is peculiarly emphatic is the question of the dates when "Lawson" was released from Hull and when the cement was purchased in Liverpool. She believes that while "Lawson" may be the man arrested, he may not be the man guilty of the Rainhill murders. "That's the point," she things, and she believes he was not likely to commit any such deed. "He would out with my daughters," she says "on the road, and lived with us in a house situate in a very quiet part, he being the only man in the house. He could have murdered the lot of us if he had liked, and he never gave any sign of violence." "There's been a lot of talk." Mrs. Matheson adds, "but, as a lady in Beverley remarked, What girl in the town would not have been glad of the chance of him?" What is there to lead anybody to suppose there was anything wrong about him?" She says he left the house sometimes for a day or so, and now believes that it was for the purpose of seeing his wife and family at Birkenhead. "It has been stated that he was illiterate: was that so?" – "Not so far as I saw – at all events: he talked very well, and appeared to have read a lot. He went down to the station every day for the London and some local papers." "Lawson" from the first showed his apparent liking for Miss Nellie Matheson, who was then something over 21 years of age, an accomplished young lady who had been brought up with her grandfather in Scotland, and as his intentions seemed honourable enough, it is not too much to say that the attachment was mutual, and, as already stated, resulted in the marriage of the parties at St. Mary's Church, in Beverley, in February, 1890. Before that time "Lawson" paid a visit to several continental towns, and stayed among other places at the Hotel de l'Europe. While there he happened an accident which confined him to his room, and so pathetic was the account of the misfortune which he sent to Beverley that Miss Matheson and her mother went over and nursed him, that, as the latter lady on Thursday remarked, being only what they might be expected to do considering the relationship existing between them, and the fact that "Lawson" had no one to look after him. It is believed that it was during his sojourn at Antwerp that he purchased the picture "The Two Dogs" which has been mentioned in the Press. Mrs. Matheson gave an interesting account of the honeymoon trip. After the wedding "Lawson," who behaved with the greatest kindness, started off with his wife for the South of England, staying at Bournemouth and Plymouth for two or three weeks. One morning he suddenly suggested a return to Hull as his account at one bank was overdrawn, and he wished to transfer some of his money. They accordingly returned to the Station Hotel, Hull, on a Friday, and on the next day he and his wife drove over to Beverley. "He was an excellent whip," Mrs. Matheson says: and in fact this, like everything else that he did, seemed to fit in with his story so aptly that she never doubted his bona-fides. Arrived at the house they discussed whether they should spend Sunday at Hull or Beverley, and Miss Matheson preferring the former place "Lawson" acquiesced. They went back to Hull, and that night for the first time he showed her the diamond bracelet which he had obtained from Messrs Reynoldson and Son. He seemed in perfectly good spirits, and in response to a request that he should give it to his wife then jocularly remarked, "No, I'll give it to you tomorrow." He ordered the waiter to send in tea to the coffee-room for his wife, stating that he was going into the town, but would be back shortly. He never came: all that night she waited at the hotel, and inquiries were instituted by the police to see if anything had befallen the mysterious individual. Nothing could be learnt, and the truth came out when the warrant was issued for his arrest at the instance of Messrs Reynoldson and Son. He left the hotel in quiet an off-hand way:

Mike Covell

> *his luggage was at Southampton, and he did not think it necessary to take even his great coat, which he left in the hanging room.*

The Hull Daily Mail, March 18th 1892, P. 4, Latest News

> THE RAINHILL MURDERS. FURTHER DEVELOPMENTS OF THE MYSTERY. MORE ABOUT WILLIAMS. *The circumstances surrounding the Rainhill murders are becoming more and more sensational, and especially as regards Hull. Yesterday the name of Harry Lawson, was convicted at the Hull Quarter Sessions in October, 1890, for obtaining jewellery from Messrs Reynoldson, was associated with the crimes, and the police have been more remarkably active in their endeavours to establish the identity of Williams with Lawson. So far as the inquiries have proceeded, the facts point strongly to Lawson, whose modus operandi as known to the Hull police is precisely similar to the tactics which have been adopted by the man Williams. Furthermore, it was well known to the Hull police that Lawson had several aliases, one of which was Deeming, that he always gave the impression he was extremely wealthy, and that he had an important connections with the colonies. Dinham Villa, the house in which the victims were buried, was leased to Williams or Deeming, on the 23rd of July, just one week after "Lawson" was liberated from the Hull Gaol. Mrs. Deeming, sister to the woman murdered at Rainhill, informs a Liverpool Daily Post reporter that Williams married her sister eleven years ago at Birkenhead. He was always mysterious in his movements, and a few years ago went to Australia. Upon his return he gave it out that he had amassed a fortune through gold mines and always seemed flash of coin. Continuing Mrs. Deeming stated, "We were unfortunately aware that he was sentenced to nine months' imprisonment at Hull, where he had contracted a bigamous marriage; but when he returned to his home at Birkenhead my poor sister did not like to prosecute him as she had a family of young children dependent upon him. He left Birkenhead in July last, and his wife told me that they were going to live at Rainhill; only, however, for a short time, as it was their intention to reside in foreign parts. There were away on Saturday, and my sister came back to Birkenhead on the Sunday, and told me that her husband, Frederick Deeming, had taken a very nice villa at Rainhill, where they were to remain for a short time. I never saw my sister again. We heard from a friend that she and her husband and family had gone to Calcutta, and, therefore, I did not consider it necessary to make inquiries about her. I have no doubt at all that Williams is Frederick Deeming. When my sister first met she lived in Liverpool, and he was staying at Birkenhead. I think Old Nick was in him. I never cared for him much, but I never thought things would come to this terrible end. He was a man slightly under the middle size, with lightish hair, a reddish moustache, and big, round shoulders." Other remarkable facts are given by the brothers Deeming. In the*

> course of a statement with reference to the history of Frederick Deeming, alias Williams, alias Lawson, they state that after his marriage in February, 1887, he took his wife to Cape Town. About two years ago Mr and Mrs Deeming returned to England, and took a house to Birkenhead, which was furnished in fairly good style. Here they lived for some time, and here their youngest child, Marie, one of the murdered little ones, was born. Deeming afterwards disappeared, and it was during this interval that he was apprehended on a charge of stealing jewellery at Hull, and sentenced to nine months' imprisonment. At the time "Lawson's" term of imprisonment expired at Hull – viz., on the 15th July, 1891 – Messrs Smith and Sons, auctioneers, of Argyle-street, Birkenhead, received instructions from a Mrs Deeming to sell a house of furniture at Bridge-street, Birkenhead, the reason for the sale being that her husband was coming home from abroad – believed to be from Australia – and she did not want him to get hold of the furniture. After the sale she went with her four children to live at Rainhill, where she was joined by Williams, and where she met a tragic fate. When Mrs Deeming left to go to Dinham Villa to join her husband she stated to her sister and brother in law that she intended to settle in Rainhill. Nothing further was heard of her or her family until the present discovery. Not hearing from him subsequently, the brothers concluded that he and his wife had again gone abroad.

The Hull Daily Mail, March 18th 1892, P. 4,

> HIS MOVEMENTS IN HULL AND AT BEVERLEY. It has been ascertained beyond doubt that the man who married Miss Matheson at Beverley in February, 1890, is the same who married at Tranmere, under the name of "Frederick Deeming, bachelor, mariner, aged 27," nine years before. Mrs Deeming visited him while he was in prison at Hull, and after his release it is believed he remained in the neighbourhood for a few days, and then left for Birkenhead and Liverpool. His wrote frequently from those places to Miss Matheson up to the month of September, and informed her that any communication for him must be inserted in the Standard to the end of September, and he should see it. He next wrote from Australia and the last letter from him arrived to Beverley only about a week ago, bearing the Sydney postmark. It should be stated that after the portrait which has been published was taken he grew a beard, and it was with this addition that he was known in Beverley. His habits while there were extravagant, in illustration of which it may be stated that he purchased £3 worth of books within a short period, although he was not much given to literature. One curious fact in connection with his marriage to Miss Matheson is worth recording. The ceremony took place during the Holy Thursday Horse Fair, which is held near St. Mary's Church, and the personal appearance of the bridegroom aroused many unflattering comments among the bystanders, one remarking he was probably the man who broke a

Mike Covell

window in London two days before and stole a quantity of jewellery; another that if he was judged by his features he deserved 10 years penal servitude. It is also correct that the Beverley police, although they had no information respecting him, kept him under notice until he left the railway station with his bride, and that he manifested some uneasiness when he found he was being watched. "Lawson" was also a troublesome customer while in the Hull prison. He spoke insultingly to the Governor and to the Visiting Justices, and his conduct induced the authorities to take the precaution of confining him to his cell during the whole period of his detention. Considerable satisfaction is expressed in Beverley that his earlier marriage became known to Miss Matheson before he was released. It is assumed, with very grave reason, that had he induced her to leave Hull with him she would have shared the same fate as the poor creatures whose deaths are now the subject of investigation. DIGGING GRAVES FOR THE VICTIMS. Our Liverpool correspondent says there is again great excitement at Rainhill to-day, the little village being crowded by a morbid throng. Doctors M'Clellan and Hutchinson commenced a post mortem of the bodies in Dinham Villa, the approaches to which were jealously guarded by a force of police Grave-diggers are busy digging graves for the victims in the Parish Churchyard, where the funerals will take place this afternoon. STATEMENT BY A RELATIVE. A relative of the murdered woman states that when the latter made Deeming's acquaintance she was an assistant in the employ of a local fishmonger. Shortly after their marriage they went to Cape Town, Deeming holding out that he was engaged there in connection with some mining enterprise. While living at Cape Town, Mrs. Deeming wrote to her friends in Liverpool and Birkenhead stated that they were getting on most prosperously, and that her husband was making money rapidly. About two years ago, Mr and Mrs Deeming returned to England and took a house in Birkenhead, which was furnished in fairly good style. Here they lived for some time, and here their youngest child, Marie, one of the murdered little ones, was born. About eighteen months ago Deeming represented while living at Liverpool both to his wife and his acquaintances, that he was about to return to the Cape, to resume his mining operations. It has, however, been since ascertained that he went to Hull, where he made the acquaintance of a young woman belonging to Beverley, whom he married. Whilst living in Hull he obtained jewellery by false pretences, and was sentenced to nine months' imprisonment, under circumstances narrated elsewhere. Upon his liberation the young lady, who was of respectable family, declined to leave Hull with him. Deeming then went back to his wife, who in the meanwhile had been staying at Birkenhead. He, it is stated, told his wife of the Hull marriage, and asked her, in case any inquiries were made, to deny that she was his wife, but the poor woman, although anxious to screen him, refused to deny that he was her husband. It is stated that the murdered woman was aware that her husband had taken Dinham Villa, he at the same time retaining his residence at

> *Birkenhead. Sometimes his wife and children went to stay with him at Rainhill, and on other occasions Deeming visited his wife at Birkenhead. This is held to explain the circumstances connected with his conduct. His frequent absence from Rainhill, he explained, was occasioned by his visits to London, but were in reality occasioned by his visits to his wife at Birkenhead; and there is no doubt that the woman and the little ones – who visited him at Rainhill, and whose identity he was so anxious to conceal, and said were his sister and her family – were his own wife and children. Mrs Deeming was very much concerned by reason of what she described as the "carryings on" of her husband, and determined to bring matters to a crisis by taking her family with her to Rainhill and establishing herself at Dinham Villa. "DEEMING'S" VISIT TO MONTE VIDEO. HIS ARREST BY A HULL DETECTIVE. The Press Association Liverpool correspondent telegraphs with reference to the absconding of Deeming to South America and his arrest there, a gentleman who was on board the steamer Coleridge, in which he sailed from Southampton on March 16, 1890, says the saloon accommodation was fully engaged, but rather than miss his passage Deeming consented to occupy the ship's hospital, dining in the saloon. He soon became well known among the other passengers; he was placed at the head of the table, and was looked on as a person of some consequence, having in his possession cards bearing his name as managing director of the South African Gold Mining Company. On one occasion he told a gentleman that he knew a spot in South Africa where there were tons of gold. A couple of days before arriving at Monte Video, he presided at a concert on board, and headed the subscription list with a liberal donation. The subscription was in aid of the Seaman's Orphanage. Scarcely, however, had the vessel dropped anchor at Monte Video, on Easter Monday, when a steam launch came alongside, and a Hull officer stepped on board with a warrant for his arrest. The event caused a great sensation among the passengers, as no one suspected that a man of such courteous manner and apparent respectability could be wanted on so grave a charge.*

The Hull Daily Mail, March 21st 1892, P. 3,

> *MELBOURNE AND RAINHILL MURDERS. PRISONER BEFORE THE AUSTRALIAN MAGISTRATES. MORE REVELATIONS OF DEEMING'S CAREER. INTENSE EXCITEMENT AT RAINHILL. THE VILLAGE INVADED. PORTRAITS OF DEEMING'S VICTIMS. THE ACCUSED CHARGED. The greatest curiosity was exhibited by the public at Perth (western Australia) on Saturday as to "Swanston's" appearance in court, and, though the proceedings were purely formal, the court-room was packed to suffocation, and many who wished to gain admission were unable to do so. "Swanston" entered the dock with a jaunt, sir, and smiled from time to time with well affected indifference, but he*

nevertheless betrayed by his fidgety movements and restless glances a considerable amount of nervousness. The

Miss Emily Mather of Rainhill.

usual formal evidence having been given as to his arrest, and the nature of the charge preferred against him, he was remanded for a week, in order that the Court might be in possession of the result of the investigation which the police are *now actively prosecuting. EXAMINATION OF THE PRISONER'S LUGGAGE. The luggage which the prisoner had with him at the time of his arrest has been carefully examined. The result was the discovery of a considerable body of evidence bearing in a most pointed manner upon the identity of the accused. Among other important documents are a testimonial drawn up on parchment and signed "Benjamin Goodfellow, Hyde, Hampshire," a local time table of the trains from Rainhill to Liverpool and other centres, a Prayer-book, with the name "Emily" on the fly-leaf, a card of membership of the Rainhill Band of Hope bearing the name of Emily Mather, an autograph album which belonged to Emily Mather, and a book containing a number of addresses, mostly in England. There are also a pocket-flask bearing a monogram of the letters "B.F.D.," a Masonic apron inscribed with the same letters, a silver card case on which the name "Emily" is engraved, various photos, by Messrs Pettingall, Livrpool; Braybrook, West Hartlepool; and Clelland and Randugen, Rockhampton; and a Prayer Book marked "Sarah Oates." The name in the address book mentioned above included the following: - Mrs. Galtshell, Camebridge-road, Seaforth: Mrs. Canham, Camebridge: Jane McDonald, Birkenhead: Marshall, New York: and Mrs. Oshlon, Dronfield, Liverpool. WHOLESALE SWINDLING IN CANADA. The fact telegraphed to Cape Town on March 20th from London that Deeming, the supposed Rainhill murderer, visited the Cape a few years ago, has deepened the sensation caused by the crimes laid to his charge. Inquiries which have been instituted show that his name is well known at Johannesburg in con –*

Mike Covell

Mrs. Marie Deeming nee James

- nection with some extensive jewellery swindling in 1890, the specific charge against him being one brought by a Cape Town jeweler of having robbed him of £3,000 in the Transvaal. Additional interest attached to the crime from the fact that during Deeming's stay at Johannesburg, which lasted one month, two mysterious murders occurred there. EXCITEMENT AT RAINHILL. There is still no abatement in the public interest regarding what is now everywhere spoken of as the Rainhill tragedies. On Saturday the village was invaded from an early hour in the morning by men, woman and children from far and near, many travelling

long distances on foot, while others arrived by train and vehicles of various kinds. The day being fine, as the afternoon wore on some hundreds of bicyclists arrived at the village, and during the whole

Evening, and up to a late hour at night, the place presented the appearance of a popular fair. The chief interest of the crowd seemed to be centered on the graves of the victims and the villa where the tragedy was centered. It required a strong force of police to keep back the crowds at these places. DEEMING'S "PIETY." Some new incidents regarding Deeming, alias Williams, came to light on Saturday. There is now a prevalent opinion among those who knew Deeming at Rainhill, and it is also shared by the police, that he was a professional thief and burglar. Strange stories are afloat as to his having been soon with a large number of keys in his possession, and it is alleged that upon one occasion he obtained entrance into Rainhill Church by a key which he took out of his pocket. Deeming was well known in Prescot, and he was in the habit of attending mission services held at Holt, a short distance from the village. He is said to have at three times displayed a great deal of piety. DEEMING'S MARRIAGE TO MISS MATHER.

Mike Covell

Deeming's marriage to Miss Mather at Rainhill Parish Church appears to have been conducted in a somewhat clandestine way. The parties got into the church at any early hour by a private gate on the rectory grounds, and through the vestry. The main door was afterwards opened without being unlocked.

by pulling up the bolt at the bottom. Deeming and his bride then walked through the churchyard, and emerged by the west gate. No one who saw them come out could have suspected the peculiar secret arrangement by which they got into the sacred edifice. Deeming had arranged the matter beforehand with considerable straightness, and Mr. Johnson, the [illegible] costs, claimed in a very amiable way with murderer's plan, which to all appearances at the time had nothing [illegible passage] that the marriage might be conducted with as much secrecy as possible. When the fact that Miss Mather was being married leaked out a number of villagers went to the church, but found the whole thing over and the parties gone. When he gave the officiating clergyman and the sexton their foes, which were larger than usual, he

Mike Covell

SYDNEY FRANCIS.

Led them to understand that the excess was to be applied for the poor of Rainhill. Soon after the marriage an effort was made to sublet Dinham Villa on behalf of Deeming, and immediately prior to the terrible discovery negotiations were in progress with several persons for its [illegible] one of the parties being a Liverpool gentleman. Another gentleman had gone over the place, but found it too

small. A CHRONOLOGICAL TABLE. *The following table shows in chronological order some of the events in the career of the accused under his four aliases.*

DEEMING

Frederick Bailey Deeming marries Miss Mary James. Leaves England for Cape Town	1881
Joined by his wife (now identified as Mary James) in Sydney	1882
Receives six weeks' imprisonment for theft	1882
Absconds from Sydney on charge of fraudulent insolvency	1888
Swindles a jeweller at the Cape out of £2,921, and a bank at the Transvaal out of £4,000	1889–0
Returns to England (11th of August) and to Birkenhead, leaving that place and his wife about four months afterwards	1889

LAWSON

Arrives in Hull, and obtains jewellery on false pretences March 15th	1890
Marries Miss Matheson at Beverley, and deserts her a fortnight afterwards	1890
Arrested at Monte Video	1890
Tried at Hull Sessions on a prosecution of the jewellers, and sentenced to nine months' imprisonment ... October	1890

WILLIAMS

Arrives at Rainhill ... July	1891
Visits Birkenhead, taking Mrs Deeming and the children with him to Rainhill. Supposed murder ... August	1891
Marries Miss Mather at Rainhill ... September	1891
Arrives with his wife in Australia	1891
Murders Mrs Williams December 25th (supposed)	1891

SWANSTON

Arrested when on the eve of a fourth marriage ... March	1892

HOW DEEMING GOT HIS MONEY. *It appears that at the end of 1889 – just after Marie Deeming left him for Birkenhead – Deeming applied at a Transvaal bank for a sum of £1,000, giving as a security a number of deals – presumably forged – which identified him with the owner of a large amount of landed property in another part of South America. He gave also a further reference.*

Through a bank in Cape Town. In the course of a few days the money was paid over to him, and he disappeared. It was subsequently discovered that the whole transaction was a fraud, and the Government of the Transvaal put the matter into the hands of an English detective agency were making inquiries Deeming was in Birkenhead, and afterwards to Hull Gaol. In South Africa he gave his name as Fred Deeming, but when he went to Hull he was known as Harry Lawson, and therefore was not identified. DEEMING'S BANQUET AT RAINHILL. The

Newspapers from Hull Volume 2

following account of the banquet given at Rainhill by Deeming appeared in the Preston Recorder at the time the invitations for it were issued by the ill-fated Miss Mather – "On Wednesday evening Mr. Albert O. Williams, an inspector of the Indian Army Service, who is on a short visit to England, and who has taken up his residence in Rainhill while in the country, entertained at the Railway and Commercial Hotel, Rainhill, a number of the residents of the village whose friendship he has made during his sojourn among them. The menu was of an excellent character. After full justice had been done to the good things provided, Mr. Williams presided, and Mr. Short occupied the vice-chair. The usual loyal and patriotic toasts having been submitted and responded to, one of the guests, in a fallacious speech proposed "the health of their host, Mr. Williams." He said that whilst that gentleman had been with them at Rainhill he had made many friendships, which he sincerely hoped, now that he was going away again to foreign service, would tend for many hours when [illegible] set in to bring back to his mind the many pleasant and social evenings he had spent with them in Rainhill. – The toast was enthusiastically drunk with musical honours. – Mr. Williams, in reply, thanked his guests, for the hearty and kind way in which they had received his name. He had been in many climes and countries, and had mixed with many [illegible], but he must say he had never in his life met a more sociable number of friends than he had done at Rainhill. – During the evening musical selections were given by the host (Mr. Williams) and others. The party broke up at 11 o'clock, a happy evening having been spent.

The Hull Daily Mail, March 21st 1892, P. 4,

THE RAINHILL MURDER. FURTHER REVELATIONS. A VISIT OF WILLIAMS TO HASTINGS. A Hastings correspondent telegraphs: - In connection with the Rainhill tragedy it transpires that in October last Williams and his wife, Miss Mather, visited Hastings, where the latter had a distant relative, the couple spending five days at that watering place. During their stay it was noticed that Williams possessed a very handsome chronometer, the value of which was estimated at £100, besides other valuable articles. He stated that he was going to return to India for about two years in order that he might get his pension. During his day on the south coast those who had an opportunity of judging declare that he appeared to be a perfectly sane man. They returned to the hotel in Finsbury-square, London, on leaving Hastings. It is mentioned as a point not already stated that whilst at that hotel Mrs. Williams sent some blood stained linen to the laundry, and it is suggested that this linen belonged to the first wife. It is further suggested that Mr. Williams would account for the linen by saying that a man was occasionally called upon to act as a doctor in the parts he had visited. WILLIAMS UNDER THE NAME OF "WARD." A Reuter's telegram to-day from Adelaide

Mike Covell

says: - The man Deeming or Williams, suspected of murdering a woman at Windsor, near Melbourne, has been identified from a photograph as being the man who passed here as Ward in January, 1888, coming hither from Melbourne. He became very friendly with two brothers named Howe, and was suspected of robbing them. He eventually left for Cape Town, via St. Helens. HAD WILLIAMS A CONFEDERATE? In St. Helens the theory of Williams having a confederate or confederates is being accepted. The disappearance of the man who forged the cheque on Parr's Bank in the name of James Howarth and Co., who supplied the cement, and who gave tickets with their printed name on, lends colour to this view. The man had made inquiries at some stables as to the trade done by Mr. Berry, and when he walked into the shop in Tontine-street, and gave Mrs. Berry an order for £5 5s worth of provender, he said he knew they did a good business, and supplied both the St. Helens Corporation and Colonel R. Pilkington, of Rainford-hall, with provender Mrs. Berry, with characteristic business shrewdness, was not to be caught with the £17 cheque on Parr's Bank, and refused to hand £11 13s change. The same man called at the establishment of Alderman Wilcock, is Baldwin-street, on the same day, and inquired the price of provender, but he evidently felt it would be risky to offer the cheque to the manager, and left, saying he would send an order up. He told the manager he came from Rainhill, and to Mrs. Berry he said he lived opposite the Derby Arms, Rainhill, but there is no such house. SENSATIONAL STATEMENT BY A NATIVE OF RAINHILL. A representative of the Warrington Observer has interviewed Samuel Mercer, a native of Rainhill, who was well acquainted with Williams, the supposed murderer of five persons found in Dinham Villa, Rainhill. Mercer is employed by Councillor Plumpton, toolmaker, Warrington. In reply to questions, he said: "My name is Samuel Mercer, and I am a native of Rainhill, where I have lived practically all my life. About three weeks ago I left Rainhill and came to live at Warrington, and had been working as a toolmaker for Messrs Plumpton and Son. The first time I ever spoke to Williams was at the flower show, Rainhill, about the 25th July last year. I was in the Commercial Hotel with the landlord, Mr. Short. On another occasion – I believe it was on the first Sunday in August last – I was in the Commercial Hotel, and he asked me and another friend, and in the presence of two others, if I could get a man to cement a floor for him. I said I had a friend, a Mr. Davis, who lived next door to me, and who was a practical man, and could do it for him. He, however, could not do it for a week, as he was away. To that Williams said, "I can't wait so long," and I told him there was another practical man in the next street whom I knew, and I promised to bring the man with me. Being Bank Holiday I never thought more of the matter until Wednesday morning, when I went up to Williams's house, having promised to do some repairs for him in connection with looks, &c. He told me that I was too late, and that he had had the locks repaired. I went into the kitchen and stood on a board over the cement, *and Williams said to me, "Don't stand on the cement," to which I replied, "No; I am on the board." A man was cementing the floor, and was moving the board as he did the various parts. Williams had plenty of refreshments in the house, and I had some with him. He next showed me the various weapons, including swords, knives, spears, and an Arab [illegible] which he said he had got from Zululand. He next showed me a beautiful knife with a sheaf made of woven silver wire, and said that it had belonged to Cetewayo. He had given one similar to it to "the Museum," and he was also going to give that. Mercer went on to say that Williams said he was an Army inspector, and all Indian slaves went through his hands. He had held the position since he was 17 years old, his uncle, who had held the position before him, having got him the place. In 18 months' time he said he should be entitled to a pension. Williams once in company said that he was 35 years old, but he appeared to be about 45. "I little dreamt," concluded Mercer, who is a man of more than average intelligence, "as I stood on that plank over the cement that there were five dead bodies beneath my feet." WILLIAMS'S BOX. A Plymouth correspondent telegraphs that instructions have been received for the stationmaster at Friary Goods Station, Plymouth, of the London and South Western Railway, to forward the box sent by Deeming, addressed to Mrs. Holds, Goods Railway Station, and which contained wearing apparel of the murdered wife and children, to St. Helens Railway Station, Lancashire, whence it was despatched. The railway officials there will hand over the box and its contents to the Widnes police. DIGGING OPERATIONS TO BE RENEWED. A Liverpool correspondent says Rainhill is again crowded to-day with sightseers, Dinham Villa and the churchyard being the chief objects of attention. The police state that it has been decided to resume digging operations at the villa, and take up the remainder of the cement flooring in the kitchen and passage, with the view to setting at rest rumours which have got in circulation as to other disappearances.*

The Hull Daily Mail, March 22nd 1892, P. 4,

THE RAINHILL AND MELBOURNE MURDERS. INQUEST OF THE AUSTRALIAN VICTIM. Melbourne, Tuesday. – The inquest on the body of the woman known as Emily Williams, wife of Frederick Deeming, was resumed to-day, and after formal evidence was adjourned till April 5th, pending the arrival of Deeming from Perth. "DEEMING" MAKES AN ADMISSION. Reuter telegrams from Perth (Melbourne) as follows: - Deeming admits he is the same man who has been known as Williams, but attributes his wife's death to a man who, he said, was her lover. Among his luggage a pair of trousers, blood and cement stained, has been found. FINDING A SPADE. Our Liverpool correspondent telegraphs: - A portion of the furniture sold by Deeming when giving up Dinham Villa was purchased by Mr. Pickerting, Mrs. Mather's son in law. A result of the search

Mike Covell

> *amongst these article to-day was the discovery of a spade, which had been purchased at Mrs. Mather's shop. Cement was still adhering to it, and examination showed that upon the handle were spots evidently blood stains. The spade has been handed over to the police, and will be subjected to microscopical examination.*

The Hull Daily Mail, March 22nd 1892, P. 4,

> *THE RAINHILL AND MELBOURNE MURDERS. INQUEST ON THE AUSTRALIAN VICTIM. Melbourne, Tuesday. – The inquest on the body of the woman known as Emily Williams, wife of Frederick Deeming, was resumed to-day, and after formal evidence was adjourned till April 5th, pending the arrival of Deeming from Perth. FINDING A SPADE. Our Liverpool correspondent telegraphs: - A portion of the furniture sold by Deeming when giving up Dinham Villa was purchased by Mr. Pickerting, Mrs. Mather's son in law. A result of the search amongst these article to-day was the discovery of a spade, which had been purchased at Mrs. Mather's shop. Cement was still adhering to it, and examination showed that upon the handle were spots evidently blood stains. The spade has been handed over to the police, and will be subjected to microscopical examination.*

The Hull Daily Mail, March 23rd 1892, P. 4,

> *THE RAINHILL AND MELBOURNE MURDERS. INQUEST ON THE AUSTRALIAN VICTIM. MELBOURNE, TUESDAY. – The inquest on the body of the woman known as Emily Williams, wife of Frederick Deeming, was resumed to-day, and after formal evidence was adjourned till April 5th, pending the arrival of Deeming from Perth. "DEEMING" MAKES AN ADMISSION. Reuter telegraphs from Perth (Melbourne) as follows: - Deeming admits he is the same man who has been known as Williams, but attributes his wife's death to a man who, he said, was her lover. Among his luggage a pair of trousers, blood and cement stained, has been found. FINDING A SPADE. Our Liverpool correspondent telegraphs: - A portion of the furniture sold by Deeming when giving up Dinham Villa was purchased by Mr. Pickering, Mrs. Mather's son-in-law. A result of the search amongst these articles to-day was the discovery of a spade, which had been purchased at Mrs. Mather's shop. Cement was still adhering to it, and examination showed that upon the handle were spots, evidently blood stains. The spade has been handed over to the police, and will be subjected to microscopical examination.*

The Hull Daily Mail, March 24th 1892, P. 3,

> *MORE ABOUT DEEMING. LETTERS FROM AUSTRALIA. A letter has been received at the Commercial Hotel, Rainhill, bearing the Huddersfield postmark, and addressed to T. B. Deeming. Mr. Short, landlord, yesterday received three letters from Deeming, written before his arrest in Australia. Their contents will be made known at the inquest. Mr. Short also had yesterday a communication from Mr. J. H. Exley, of the firm of Messrs. Charles and Co., woollen merchants, Huddersfield, who have a branch at Johannesburg, South Africa, in which occurs the following: - "Will you oblige me by a few lines giving a description of Williams. My reason in writing is that I left Durban, Natal, last April by the Union steamship Moor, and a man named Williams was also a passenger by the same boat. This fact in itself is perhaps not of any moment, but the conduct of this man during the voyage leads me to think it is quite possible he may be the same. Most of our saloon passengers avoided him, and no one presumed to know anything about him except his statement that he had come down from Maitland, and his yarns, to put it mildly, were difficult to believe. He spoke of travels in other countries besides Africa, and there are other little matters which have come to memory that makes me think he is the same man." It is further stated that during the time Deeming lived in Birkenhead he was a regular customer at the shop of Mrs. F. A. Dobson, chemist, Bridge-street, to whom he represented that he was a doctor in practice at Manchester. He was in the shop one day, when a well-known Birkenhead doctor came in. Deeming accosted him familiarly, saying, "Good morning, doctor. Perhaps you do not know me. I am a fellow practitioner of yours." His greeting was not reciprocated by the doctor, who did not like the flashy appearance of the man.*

The Hull Daily Mail, March 24th 1892, P. 4,

> *THE MELBOURNE MURDER. DEEMING AGAIN BEFORE THE MAGISTRATES. Perth, Wednesday (Reuter's Telegram) – The hearing of the charge of murder against Frederick Bailey Deeming was resumed in the Police Court at Perth this morning. Mr. Haynes, who represents the prisoner, is striving to prevent Deeming's removal to Melbourne on Saturday. Should he succeed appeal will be made to a Supreme Court to delay the prisoner's extradition. NOTHING FURTHER TO BE FOUND AT RAINHILL. A Liverpool correspondent telegraphs: - The police concluded digging operations at Dinham Villa, Rainhill, having moved the whole of the cement in the kitchen and passage, and also the floor of the scullery, which, it will be remembered, had been filled with soil and boarded over by the instructions of Deeming, who thus got rid of the mould caused by his own excavations. No new discoveries have been made, and the police consider nothing further is to be found at Rainhill. THE MISSING BOX. The missing box alleged to have been sent to Plymouth by Deeming, and which*

Mike Covell

> was discovered at Friary Goods Station, Plymouth, was on Wednesday handed over to Superintendent Keighley at Widnes. No doubt remains that the box belonged to the murderer, it containing clothing worn by his unfortunate victims. Many of the articles are stained with what is believed to be blood. An immediate medical examination will be made, and the result made known at the adjourned inquest.

The Hull Daily Mail, March 25th 1892, P. 3,

> THE MELBOURNE AND RAINHILL MURDERS. DEEMING'S TECHNICAL DEFENCE. ANOTHER CEMENTED FLOOR DISCOVERED. A correspondent, telegraphing from Perth (Western Australia) under the date of March 24th, says: - Deeming's solicitor, Mr Haynes, is more confident than ever that he will succeed in upsetting the decision of the magistrate committing the prisoner for trial at Melbourne. He maintained that the unauthorised rectification of a clerical error in the original warrant by the alteration of a date, that of the murder at Windsor, from 1892 to 1891, is sufficient to invalidate the whole of the proceedings that have been taken upon it. The belief that this flaw is fatal to the legality of the remand receives pretty general support in legal circles here. The matter will be argued before the Supreme Court, when Mr Haynes, is accordance with the notice he gave yesterday, moves for a writ of habeas corpus. It has been discovered that the floor of the cottage which "Swanston" occupied at Southern Cross, where he was arrested, has been taken up and the excavations made underneath, filed up with cement in the same manner as in the case of the houses at Rainhill and Windsor. Digging operations will be begun at once, as it is though extremely probable that a considerable quantity of gold which the prisoner is suspected of having pilfered while employed as engineer at Fraser's Gold Mine will be found concealed there. The prospect of fresh revelations has still further stimulated the public interest in the case, and a very strong feeling is springing up against the prisoner. Meanwhile "Swanston" has to a great extent recovered his health and spirits, and maintains an appearance of the utmost concern, continuing to protest that he is perfectly innocent of the crimes laid to his charge. SCENE AT RAINHILL YESTERDAY. MORE REMINISCENCES OF DEEMING. A Liverpool correspondent telegraphs: - The Thursday half-holiday was the cause of a large influx of visitors to the scene of the Rainhill tragedy yesterday. The villa was stormed, and the solitary policeman in charge could not resist the crowd, bent on satisfying their morbid curiosity. They rushed pell-mell into the kitchen of Dinham Villa, there to satisfy their desire of seeing the open grave of Deeming's victims. The villa itself will be razed as soon as the police surrender charge of it, the owner, a lady of the neighbouring village of Huyton, feeling that there is no chance of re-letting it, having determined on its destruction. In view of the

> adjourned inquest next Monday, which is to be hoped may be concluded that day without further adjournment, the police are actively engaged in completing the chain of evidence against Deeming from his liberation from Hull gaol to the culmination of his career of crime in the Rainhill murders. Some 16 witnesses will, it is said, be called, and some startling evidence is anticipated. Reminiscences of the doing of Deeming locally continue to crop up. Mr W. Gastrell, formerly proprietor of the Falcon Restaurant at Liverpool, says he saw Deeming several times in the spring last year. He was a regular customer at the restaurant, spending money lavishly on all persons present. Just before taking Dinham Villa Deeming called at the Falcon and ordered luncheon for five persons, saying he had hired a Waggonette and was driving to Rainhill. He said he did not care what the luncheon cost so that the ladies were pleased. There were three ladies and two gentlemen in the party. They enjoyed the luncheon so much that Deeming insisted on seeing the chef and standing him a drink. On one occasion while conversing with Mr Gastrell, Deeming handed him a card bearing the name A. Williams, and commenced to relate his experiences in Johannesburg. Mr Gastrell desired to introduce him to a Liverpool silversmith and jeweller who had just returned from Johannesburg, and was at present in the restaurant. Deeming deprecated the notion, and seemed very much confused and disturbed. He left the restaurant, and was never seen again. Gastrell is certain A. Williams and Deeming are one and the same person. Yesterday two near relatives of Deeming visited Widnes and inspected the contents of the box that was received from Plymouth on Wednesday. They identified almost every article as having belonged to Deeming, and one of the relatives said he could tell the date upon which some of them were bought. The police have taken their statements down. The bassinetie, the child's chair, and rocking chair sent to Plymouth by Deeming arrived in Widnes yesterday morning, and have also been identified by the relatives of the prisoner.

The Hull Daily Mail, March 28th 1892, P. 2,

> MAIL MEMS: The London Daily News, commenting upon the charges against Deeming, said it would be a pity to lynch him, inasmuch as "he is a monster whose anatomisation in process of trial would yield valuable results."

The Hull Daily Mail, March 28th 1892, P. 2,

> MAIL MEMS: It is a singular coincidence that Deeming, on his removal from Perth (Australia) to Albany, passed through a railway station at Beverley.

The Hull Daily Mail, March 28th 1892, P. 3,

Mike Covell

> MELBOURNE AND RAINHILL TRAGEDIES. REMOVAL OF DEEMING. HOSTILE DEMONSTRATION OF WOMEN. VIOLENT CONDUCT OF THE PRISONER. DESPERATE STRUGGLE. On Saturday "Swanston" (Deeming) was removed from Perth (Western Australia) to Albany, and the journey was attended by scenes of great excitement. Large crowds awaited the arrival of the train at every station. At York a particularly hostile demonstration against the prisoner took place. A rush was made for the carriage in which he was travelling, and in the tumult the windows were broken. During the whole time the train was drawn up at the station the air was filled with hisses and groans, and loud cries of "LYNCH HIM" were here raised again and again. A large number of women were present in the crowd, and it was noted that they formed by far the most violent section of the mob. They made no attempt to restrain their feelings, and it was evident that if they could have got at the prisoner they would have torn him limb from limb. Deeming, who heard all this uproar, and was well aware that it was directed against himself, exhibited great alarm, and was intensely relieved when the train steamed out of the station. Similar demonstrations on a smaller scale occurred at other stations along the route. Shortly after leaving Beverley Deeming fainted. The train was stopped, and bucketfuls of water were thrown over him. When he recovered consciousness he KICKED AND WRITHED LIKE A MADMAN, and the detective in charge of him found it necessary to put on the handcuffs. At subsequent stages of the journey he was seized with fresh fits, during which four men were required to hold him down. So violent were his struggles that his wrists were terribly bruised by the handcuffs. They were covered with blood, and became greatly swollen. The detective Cawsey expresses belief that these fits were nothing more nor less than extremely clever pieces of acting. Towards the end of the journey Deeming became more composed. When the train arrived at Albany it was stopped at Parade-street, where there is a crossing, leading to the prison. A large crowd had collected, but there was no demonstration, and perfect order was maintained. The prisoner was taken into gaol, where he was searched. To this process he submitted quietly, remarking that he liked to give the authorities all the assistance in his power. "I thought," he added, "I WAS GOING TO PEG OUT LAST NIGHT." Subsequently in his cell, where two policemen had been told off to keep a constant watch upon him, the prisoner had another fit, and two doctors had to be called in to attend to him. He will be taken on board the Ballaratt with the least possible delay. Detective Cawsey will be accompanied on the voyage to Melbourne by Detective Smythe, of Perth. THE PRISONER'S CAREER. The following is a record drawn up from the newspaper reports of the prisoner's career under the various aliases he assumed and of events with some of which it is thought probable he was connected: -
>
> "FREDERICK BAYLEY DEEMING."

1881. – Feb. – Married Miss Marie James at St. Paul's Church, Higher Tranmere. Went alone to Australia.
1882. – Joined by his wife. Sent to gaol for six weeks for theft. He was at that time supposed to be working as a plumber.
1884. – Numerous bank robberies took place in Sydney, the perpetrators not being detected.
1885. – More robberies, burglaries, mysterious disappearances and tragedies.
1886. – Sets up shop in a large way, perpetrated a fraudulent bankruptcy, and absconds from Sydney.
1887. – Flies from Adelaide to Cape Town, after, it is stated, robbing two brothers whom he met, of £60.
1888. – Nothing known of him. During this year six of the Whitechapel murders were perpetrated.
1889. – Poses in Durban as a mining engineer going to Johannesburg, and succeeds in obtaining £600 by fraud.
June. – Has £3,500 advanced to him in Durban on bogus deeds, obtains £420 worth of jewellery and decamps. About the same time two murders were committed in the Transvaal, the murderer escaping.
July. 17. – The eight Whitechapel murder.
Sept. 10. – The ninth Whitechapel murder.
Oct. – Is tracked by a private detective, who wants him for the Transvaal robberies, to Camberwell, then to Stockton-on-Tees, and back again to London.
Nov. – Sails on the Jumna for Australia. Leaving the vessel at Port Said, he doubles on his pursuers and returns to Birkenhead.

"HARRY LAWSON."
1890, Jan. – Leaves Birkenhead.
Feb. 18. – Arrives at Beverley, and marries Miss Matheson a fortnight afterwards.
March. 16. – Obtains Jewellery by false pretences at Hull.
March 16. – Sails from Southampton for South America.
April 7. – Arrested at Monte Video.
Oct. 16. – Tried at Hull Assizes, and sentenced to nine months' imprisonment.
1891, July 16. – Liberated from Hull Gaol.
1891, July 19. – Miss Langley was murdered at Preston, near Hull, the murderer escaping.

"ALBERT OLIVER WILLIAMS."
July 21. – Makes his first appearance in Rainhill, to inquire about Dinham Villa, and takes up residence at the Commercial Hotel.

Mike Covell

> *July 22. – Has tea at the hotel with a dark lady, who turns out to be his wife, Mrs Deeming, of Birkenhead.*
> *July 23. – Lunches at the hotel with his wife. Is afterwards accompanied to Huyton by Miss Mather, and signs the agreement of tenancy.*
> *July 23. – The first barrel of cement supplied from St. Helens to Dinham Villa, to order of Miss Mather.*
> *July 25. – Mrs Deeming and four children arrive at Dinham Villa.*
> *July 20-7. – The fivefold murder is committed.*
> *July 27. – Returns to the hotel.*
> *July 30. – Obtains two more barrels of cement.*
> *Aug. 26. – "Williams" gives the Rainhill banquet.*
> *Sept. 27. – Leaves Rainhill.*
> *Sept. 22. – Marries Miss Emily Mather at Rainhill.*
> *Oct. 17. – Sails with his wife from London to Australia.*
> *Nov. 27. – Miss Mather's last letter posted on the way out, at Colombo.*
> *Dec. 15. – "Williams" and his wife arrive at Melbourne.*
> *Dec. 24. – Miss Mather murdered.*
>
> *"SWANSTON."*
> *1892. January. – Applied for another wife in a Melbourne matrimonial agency. Recognised in Sydney by a publican. Proposes to and is accepted by Miss Rounsevell, at Perth, Australia.*
> *February. – Wrote to Miss Matheson at Beverley, repeating a previously made request that she should rejoin him.*
> *March 8. – Arrested on the eve of his marriage to Miss Rounsevell.*

The Hull Daily Mail, March 28th 1892, P. 4,

> THE RAINHILL HORRORS. ADJOURNED INQUEST TO-DAY. A SISTER OF THE MURDERED WOMAN GIVES EVIDENCE. VERDICT OF THE JURY. Mr. S. Brighouse, the county coroner, commenced the adjourned inquest this morning at the Victoria Hotel, Rainhill, touching the death of Marie deeming (aged 38), and her four children, Bertha (aged 8), Marie (aged 6½), Sidney Francis (aged 4), and Martha (aged 2½ years). The former was the wife and the others the children of Frederick Bayley Deeming, alias Williams, Swanson, Levey, &c, who is now in the custody of the Australian police charged with the murder of his wife, Emily Mather, of Rainhill, whom he married on September 22nd, two months after his supposed murder of his wife and four children, whose bodies were found buried in the kitchen of Dinham Villa on the 16th inst. EVIDENCE OF BERTHA DEEMING. The jury were sworn at half past ten, and the inquiry at once proceeded. The first witness called was Bertha Deeming, sister of the deceased woman Marie

Deeming, who left her house at Birkenhead to go to Rainhill on Saturday, July 25th. Her sister's husband had come out of prison at Hull a week before, and on Saturday the 18th, Mrs Deeming went to Chester to meet her. On the 25th she said that she was going to Dinham Villa to stay until they went way. She saw her sister again on the Monday, and had been told by a Mrs McKenna, of Liverpool, that she had seen her on Tuesday, the 28th. She next saw her brother on August 23rd, when he told her they had gone to Brighton. He came three times afterwards, and told the same story, though once he suggested that they should come back. They heard of DEEMING'S MARRIAGE TO MISS MATHER subsequently, and she then heard that her sister and the children had gone to Calcutta. The witness stated that on July 24th Mrs Deeming's luggage went to Rainhill, and on Monday, the 27th her sister took back with her from Birkenhead a crate containing pictures. The witness also identified the contents of the box and the perambulator in the possession of the Widnes police. It was the same box which left Birkenhead on July 24th. DEEMING'S BOX: EVIDENCE OF A STATIONMASTER. The stationmaster at St. Helens Junction, James Lucas, was the next witness. He identified the photograph produced as that of Mrs Deeming, who, with her two children, arrived at the station sometime in July, and took a cab for Lawton-road, Rainhill. She had a cab with her. MRS. DEEMING'S DRIVE TO DINHAM VILLA. A cabman named Edward Rowlands deposed that he drove Mrs Deeming to Dinham Villa. She had no children with her, but she had a crate, which a man, whom he believed from the photograph to have been Deeming, assisted him to take it off the cab. She seemed to know the way to Dinham Villa, for she directed him. WHAT A CHARWOMAN SAW. Catherine Lally, a charwoman, next stated that on Wednesday, July 22nd, she was engaged by Miss Mather to clean Dinham Villa. On the Thursday and again on the Friday the man "Williams" came to see how she was getting on. On the Thursday she gave the key of the house to Williams, who then had a lady with him. That lady was Mrs Deeming, whom she now recognised by the photo. She gave the key to Miss Mather on Friday, and was paid by Miss Mather. When she remarked to Williams that there were marks on the flags he told her he was going to have it concreted. DEEMING'S VISIT TO THE HOTE: EVIDENCE OF THE LANDLORD. Edward Henry Short, landlord of the commercial Hotel, now came forward and detailed the circumstances connected with Deeming's stay at that house. He arrived on July 21st, and on the following Saturday, July 24th, he removed to Dinham Villa, which he said, he had taken for a Colonel Brookes, who had two fine daughters and would bring two Arabian horses with him. On Monday, the 27th, he returned unexpectedly, and had dinner at the hotel. There was nothing strange in his manner, either then or afterwards. The witness next spoke to finding a black serge jacket among Deeming's clothing, while he was tidying in his bedroom. There was blood upon both sleeves, but no more than he had often seen on a gentleman's shooting

Mike Covell

> *jacket. Witness cleaned this off, but did not tell deeming he had done so. He had only seen one lady at the hotel with Deeming, and he believed that was the lady now identified as Mrs Deeming. Witnesses went on the Thursday in that week to Dinham Villa with Deeming, where he saw the man Benson finishing the cementing. Deeming had been working at this also, for he told witness so, and showed him his sore hands. The witness next told the jury about the knives which Deeming possessed. One of them was Ceteway's knife, he said, while another was, according to Deeming, a poisoned dagger. THE HOUSEKEEPER'S EVIDENCE. The housekeeper at the hotel gave corroborative evidence as to Deeming's arrival and stay at the commercial Hotel. She stated that on the 27th he returned to the hotel, and told her that he was lonely at the house, but had left his sister there for the night. The Coroner interposed with the remark that this alone should have been sufficient enough to arouse suspicion. Deeming had always passed as an unmarried man. A BARMAID'S STATEMENT. Mary Jane Barry, barmaid at the hotel, also corroborated. She detailed the circumstances attending the two visits of a lady whom he described in her absence as his "sister." On the first occasion they had tea together, and on the next dinner. She identified the lady by hr photograph as Mrs Deeming. She never saw the lady again. HOW THE CEMENT BARRELS WERE CONVEYED TO DINHAM VILLA. A St. Helens carter, named Oliver Thomas Duxberry, next gave evidence as to bringing a number of barrels of cement to Dinham Villa on July 23rd, July 31st, August 1st, and August 4th. This, as well as some sand, was ordered and paid for my Miss Mather. "FINISHING" THE FLOORS. The two young men Young and Benson next gave evidence as to the helping Deeming to finish the cementing of the floors of Dinham Villa. BOARDING THE SCULLERY. Joseph Pickering, joiner, who married a sister of Miss Emily Mather, who was married to a Deeming on September 22nd, gave evidence as to being engaged by Deeming to board the scullery floor, and to shorten and rehang the doors, which Deeming himself had taken off. The witness told the jury what he had bought, and what he had given him by Deeming. Among the things given him, in addition to a number of Zulu spears, was a small clock, upon which was scratched the name "Deeming," some initials, and the date 1889. Witness thought nothing of this at the time. SPOTS ON DEEMING'S CLOTHES. A woman, named Jane Collins, next stated that she had cleaned some of Deeming's clothes, upon which she thought there had been some red paint spilled. She got most of it out, but not all. A few days after she was charring at the Commercial Hotel, when Deeming received a telegram, which he said had come from India, and had cost 10s a word. He read it aloud to her, and led her to believe that his master had changed his mind about taking Dinham Villa. MORE ABOUT THE BOX. Evidence was then given as to the removal from Dinham Villa to St. Helen's Goods station of a Box and other articles, on August 15th. The carrier stated that he remarked to Deeming that the box was heavy and that it*

might have contained bricks. MRS MATHER'S EVIDENCE. Mrs Mather, the mother of the ill-fated Emily Mather, was the next witness. She gave evidence as to "Williams" arrival at her house, on July 21st, to arrange for the tenancy of Dinham Villa, of which she was the agent. He said that he was taking the home for himself, but he afterwards spoke of a sister and her two children. He married the witness's daughter on September 22nd, and they sailed for Southampton on November 2nd. The last letter from her daughter was written on November 28th, and the last letter from Deeming was dated Melbourne, December 29th. Witness never heard her daughter speak of Williams's sister and her children. She heard some village gossip, but that was all. The Coroner here intimated that he only proposed to call Ann Morley, and Superintendent Keighley, and that would complete the inquiry. The other woman, whose name he had mentioned, was in an advanced state of consumption, and was quiet unable to attend. This was the woman who went to Chester with Mrs Deeming, and would also speak as to the time she saw the deceased woman last. Ann Morley was then called. She stated that she lived in Hall-lane, Liverpool. She had known Mrs. Deeming for 14 years. She knew her as Marie James when she was in service in Liverpool. She remembered her marriage and remembered Deeming, her husband, to whom she was introduced on July 25th last. Witness saw Mrs Deeming and her four children off from Lime-street Station. She did not know whether they were going to Rainhill or St Helens, but Mrs Deeming said that they were going there for a short time and were then going abroad. The previous Saturday witness's daughter went to Chester with Mrs Deeming to meet her husband, who was then coming out of prison. Witness was certain that she saw Mrs Deeming again on Tuesday, July 28th, when she came to Liverpool, bringing the baby with her, and saying that "Fred" was minding the other children. She then arranged to come the following Sunday – the day after the Bank Holiday, but witness never saw her alive again. She came to Rainhill sometime afterwards to see them, but found that they had left. She heard that a man named "Williams," whom they believed to be Deeming, had got worried again, but they only put it down to gossip at the time. His wife had known of his marriage in Beverley also, and knew that he had not only been in prison, but was also a bigamist. Witness did not know that she knew nothing else about him. She himself knew of his various aliases. In answer to the jury witness said that the family had often wondered where Deeming got his money. They put it down to his good luck. When he told them that they had sent his wife and family to Brighton, It did not occur to them to ask where he got his money, although he had only just come out of prison. POLICE EVIDENCE. The next and last witness, Supt. Keighley, who at the previous inquiry had explained how Dinham Villa came to be executed. He now described the contents of the box received by him from Plymouth, and the contents of which had been identified by Mrs Martha Deeming. The odd boot produced was taken out of the box. It was the

Mike Covell

> fellow boot to that taken from the floor of Dinham Villa. In reply to a Juryman, witness said that none of the local police had ever made reports to him with regard to "Williams" during his stay at Rainhill. If the residents had suspicions of the man they should have conveyed those suspicions to the police. CORONER'S SUMMING UP. At half past one the Coroner proceeded to sum up. He dealt with the evidence adduced, remarking that the jury would have little difficulty in deciding how the five persons came to their deaths. It would be for them so to decide, and to say who had caused their deaths. He said it certainly seemed to him that Mrs Deeming went to Dinham Villa by way of St. Helens Junction, in order that none of the Rainhill people should see her. The only discrepancy as to the dates occurred in the evidence of Mrs Morley, who, however, might have been mistaken. VERDICT OF THE JURY. After an absence of ten minutes, the jury returned a verdict of WILFUL MURDER against Frederick Bayley Deeming, alias Williams. DEEMING "ROMANCING." Reuter's agency, telegraphing from Melbourne this morning, says that the statement that Deeming had confessed to the murders at Rainhill and Whitechapel was based upon a communication made to Detective Cawsey. Regarding the Whitechapel crimes, the Argus says that an investigation on Deeming's movements shows that he has been romancing.

The Hull Daily Mail, March 29th 1892, P. 3

> THE WHITECHAPEL MURDERS. AN EXTRAORDINARY STORY FROM BELFAST. "THE RIPPER" SAID TO BE IN PRISON. A Belfast newspaper's London correspondent says: "The Scotland Yard authorities did not believe the alleged confession of the Whitechapel murders by Deeming. The fact is they consider, rightly or wrongly, that they have the author of the Whitechapel tragedies now under lock and key at Portland prison undergoing a sentence of 20 years penal servitude. He is a Belgian, and was tried and sentenced some six years ago for attempting to obtain money from ladies by threats of violence. There is just one link in the chain of evidence missing, and they expect, sooner or later, to be able to supply it. This information reached me yesterday, and a few hours later, strange to say, another letter from an alleged Jack the Ripper was received by Mr. Hopkins, stipendiary magistrate, at Lambeth Police Court. The police have in their possession the letters written on previous occasions by the mysterious personage, and they will be able to compare yesterday's communication with the hand writing of those epistles. The latest intimation is to the effect that "Jack the Ripper" means to commence his tricks about Cable and Flower and Dean-streets, and he asks the magistrates to see if the bluecoats have their eyes open.

Newspapers from Hull Volume 2

Charles Le Grand:

It is believed, by some, that the prisoner in Portland Prison, to which this article refers, was none other than Charles Le Grand. Le Grand, it is said, was Danish and had been in prison in 1877, and later in 1891. He was a member of the Whitechapel Vigilance Committee and was later involved in the Matthew Packer fiasco, where Packer claimed to have sold grapes to Elizabeth Stride.

The Hull Daily Mail, March 29th 1892,

THE RAINHILL FIEND. DEEMING'S INSURANCE POLICIES. The Mutual Provident Society of Sydney has reported to the authorities that a man named Frederick Bailey Deeming insured his life for £500 in the branch office of that society at Rockhampton in October, 1883, and in the course of the following month took out a second policy for a similar amount. The "proposal" which he filled up on each of these occasions contained some very interesting particulars as to his personality and antecedents. It states that he was born at Birkenhead on July 30th, 1854, that his occupation was that of an engineer and gas fitter, and that his address at the time of the proposal was East-street, Rockhampton. It further describes him as married, declares his father to be alive and his mother dead, and represents that at the date in question he had ten brothers and two sisters alive. As to his antecedent place of residence, the document asserts that Deeming had lived in England up to three years previously, and that since his arrival in Australia he had resided in Queensland. His height is set down at 5ft. 8in., and his weight at 11st 10lb. The medical certificate which accompanied the proposal reported him to be a "first class life," and states that he had not previously suffered any bodily injuries affecting his chances of life. Upon these insurances Deeming only paid two quarters' premiums, and both policies therefore lapsed in the summer of 1884. DEEMING AS "DICK TURPIN." Among the acquaintances of Deeming's younger days he was not a great favourite, his tastes not being such as to commend him to his associates. He earned the reputation of being very energetic in the pursuit of any object which he set before himself for attainment, and it was generally accepted that he would not stick at trifles to gain his end. The reading of sensational literature was a favourite amusement of young Deeming's, to whom the "penny dreadful" and the "threepenny thriller" offered irresistible attractions. His reading of this style of story together with his general dare-devil conduct, gained him the nick-name of "Dick Turpin," of which he was not at all ashamed but rather the reverse. He is said to have had a shifty look about the eyes, a failing which is usually looked upon with great distrust too well founded in this case. Although a somewhat regular frequenter of public houses, he was by no means what could be called a drinking man, and even at that time his stories of a

> small adventure were thought to be characterised more by brilliancy than veracity; indeed, some folk went so far as to endorse the well-known phrase applied by one to a famous writer, that he was "a most picturesque liar." In somewhat later life, when for some time he is said to have followed the sea, in one capacity or another, his tales assumed an even greater degree of pictoresquence; but there was not the same ground for doubt and denial since his auditors had not been where Deeming claimed to have visited. MISS ROUNSEVELL. A Teignmouth paper says that Miss Rounsevell's whom Deeming intended marrying in Australia, formerly residing in Teignmouth, Devon. Two of her brothers were nominated to serve with the Australian cricket team which last visited England, but through business were unable to accept the invitation. Miss Rounsevell is stated to be a beautiful and accomplished young lady, and now resides at Sydney. She is about 20 years of age.

The Hull Daily Mail, March 29th 1892, P. 4

> MORE ABOUT DEEMING. A Reuter's telegram from Melbourne to-day states that a plea of insanity will be put forward on Deeming's behalf. Detective Cawsay, who has charge of Deeming at Albany, expresses a conviction that the prisoner is "Jack the Ripper."

The Hull Daily Mail, March 30th 1892, P. 3,

> THE MELBOURNE AND RAINHILL MURDERS. THE IDENTIFICATION OF DEEMING. THE EX-GOVERNOR OF THE HULL GAOL A WITNESS. The Earl of Hopetown, Governor, has received a telegram from Lord Knutsford, pointing out that if Mr. Webster, the ex-Governor of Hull Gaol – who is now believed to be in or on the way to Australia – could identify Deeming with Lawson, his identity with the Rainhill murderer would be established. At Melbourne the expected arrival of the prisoner is looked forward to with the keenest curiosity. It is expected that he will be landed and conveyed to prison as secretly as possible, so as to avoid the hostile demonstration which would be certain to occur if the time and place of arrival were publicly announced. It is understood that he will be brought round all the way from Albany by sea.

The Hull Daily Mail, March 30th 1892, P. 4

> DEEMING AND HIS VICTIMS. ANOTHER SUPPOSED MURDER. A Melbourne telegram (Reuter's) this afternoon says that suspicions that Deeming is concerned in yet another murder have arisen. A man passing under the name of Lawson, one of Deeming's aliases, visited the Cape with a man named Keays in 1888, and

Newspapers from Hull Volume 2

> *subsequently wrote to Sydney announcing Keays death at the Transvaal gold fields. It is believed Keays was murdered.*

The Hull Daily Mail, March 31st 1892, P. 2,

> *A SHRINE OF CRIME. It was only to be expected that the famous firm of Tussauds should endeavour to bring their "collection" up to date by counterfeiting in wax, the notorious of Rainhill. Else, indeed, their thrilling chamber of horrors would have fallen in the rear of crime. But that they should have cast covetous eyes upon Dinham Villa itself comes as a decided surprise, and smacks somewhat of "Yankee" spirit. It is a case with them, evidently, of the man and his environment. Anyhow, Dinham Villa has been purchased by Tussauds, and very shortly it will be on its way to that London gallery, beloved of the "country cousin." The project of removal also savours of "The States." The roof will, practically, be removed intact, the walls will be sectionized and carefully put upon the railway; the floors, windows, even the exterior stucco will be conveyed to the Metropolis with tender care. The horrid floor of concrete with its ghastly hole will afford the coup de theatre, however. It will be laid down in its new home – that Shrine of Crime – with all watchfulness and solemnity. Photographs and plans will further aid the re-building of the villa, and we presume Deeming will be seen bending over his ghastly work. Tussauds are nothing if not realistic.*

The Hull Daily Mail, March 31st 1892, P. 3,

> *MELBOURNE AND RAINHILL MURDERS. ARRIVAL OF DEEMING AT ADELAIDE. THE ACCUSED INTERVIEWED. It was exactly a quarter to two o'clock yesterday whom the Ballarat cast anchor in Largs Bay, Adelaide. The weather was fine. Taking advantage of the fact that the Peninsular and Oriental steamer Valetts, homeward bound, was sailing yesterday with the English cricketers on board, I went (telegraphs a correspondent) out early with the Custom House launch, which took out to the vessel the revenue and health officers, and by this means I was enabled, together with these gentlemen, and a detective, to get on board the Ballarat before any of the officials and press representatives, who came out later in another launch. I found Deeming confined in a second class deck cabin facing the starboard bulwark. Detective Cawsey was standing at the door of the cabin, and allowed no one to enter. At the same time he was ready to answer the thousand and one questions with which he was assailed. Having obtained the necessary authority I was admitted to the cabin, where I found the prisoner sitting on a couch playing a game of draughts with Detective Williams, who arrested him at Southern Cross. The weather being rather sultry, Deeming had taken off his coat and rolled up his shirt sleeves, thereby displaying*

166

Mike Covell

a pair of brawny arms thickly covered with hair. His present appearance is quiet unlikely those of his photos which I have had an opportunity of inspecting. This is not wholly accounted for by the removal of his moustache. His eyes seem MORE FERRETY than those of the photos, and his mouth looks hard and cruel. His features generally appear to have grown sharper. The handcuffs had been removed from his wrists, and his eyes were bent upon the draught board, as if he were intent upon the game, but it was easy to see from an occasional twitching of the lips and from the beads of perspiration that stood upon his face that a terrible conflict of emotions was raging in his mind. In answer to the questions which I put to him Deeming stated that he felt very well and had no suffered from sea sickness. Most of his waking hours he told me, he spends in playing draughts. He is aware of the fact that the bodies of his wife and children have been discovered at Rainhill, and he complains bitterly that no written statement on the subject has been supplied to him. He also considers it a grievance that he has not been himself invited to make a formal declaration on the subject. As we conversed Deeming threw off altogether his air of assumed indifferences, and his face looked HAGGARD AND WORN. His eyes were restless, and his quick nervous movements betrayed to the most casual observer that he fully realises he is approaching the scene of his last fiendish work, where he will be confronted with overwhelming proof of his guilt. During the portion of the voyage which has been accomplished, the prisoner, after conversing for a while has usually lapsed into periods of profound silence and dozed fitfully. He does not sleep long, but wakes up at frequent intervals, and is altogether unable to conceal the wearing effect of the mental strain he is enduring. He is kept in irons all night, and there is always at least one watcher with him inside the cabin. The handcuffs are only removed at night while he is undressing, and then the door is locked on the outside, and GUARDED BY MARINES, who have been sworn is as special constables. Since leaving Albany the prisoner has never been allowed outside his cabin, except during short intervals when it is being ventilated, and then he is handcuffed to one of his guards. He has eaten fairly well, and it is expected that he will land in Melbourne in fairly good health. The police have in their possession the fragment of a broken bottle which Deeming used in getting rid of his moustache. With regard to the confession which Deeming is alleged to have made to the effect that he was the author of two of the Whitechapel murders, Detective Cawsey informed me that the report was freely circulated in Perth, but he had no personal knowledge of the matter, and could only suppose that if Deeming did confess he must have done so to his solicitor, Mr. Haynes. The bent of the prisoner's mind is well illustrated by a remark which Cawsey declares he made to him in reference to the Rainhill murder. "Well," he said, "if I have to swing I will swing like a man. I will be no coward. I do not wish to have a monument erected to my memory by the people of England." DINHAM VILLA TO BE BROUGHT TO LONDON.

Yesterday afternoon Mr Richardson, of Chelsea, arrived at Dinham Villa with a party of skilled workmen, and immediately proceeded to survey and take dimensions of the villa. There was at first some mystery about the operations, but it gradually leaked out that Mdme. Tussaud's has acquired the villa by purchase, and it is the intention of the famous exhibition proprietors to remove Dinham Villa from its present site and convey it to London. As much as can possibly be taken down without breakages will be carried off wholesale, and all the materials of the building will be preserved, so that it can be put together again exactly as it stands now. Most of the roofing will be easily enough removed intact. The only difficulty likely to arise will be the stucco wall. It is probable that in the near future a figure of Deeming may be seen at Tussaud's busy in his ghastly midnight operations, and the sight will be all the more impressive as the exact pit in which the bodies were concealed, in the kitchen range, and all appurtenances of the room will add reality to the act. The reconstruction will be done from plans and photographs. DEEMING'S LION CUB. The lion cub brought by Deeming from South Africa is at the present time in the possession of Messrs Wombwell and Bailey's travelling menagerie and circus. It now forms one of a group of performing animals, and it was trained to perform by the late lion-tamer, Delhi Montarua, who was killed only a week or two back. It has always evinced a very ferocious disposition, having attacked its trainer no fewer than on five or six different occasions. AN INTERESTING COINCIDENCE. The Central News Liverpool correspondent telegraphs: A singular coincidence that one of the blue jackets delegated to watch Deeming whilst on board the steamer Ballarat, en route to Melbourne, is named Layhe, his father being a gentleman's coachman at Rainhill, where Layhe spent three weeks of his furlong last August, when Deeming's doings were the theme of village gossip. At that time Layhe met Deeming at the flower shop and other places in the villages of Rainhill and Prescot, is well acquainted with him, and his evidence will, it is expected, conclusively establish the identity of Swanston, the Windsor murderer, with Williams, the Rainhill murderer. ALTERING HIS APPEARANCE. A Melbourne telegram says that Deeming continues to exhibit an extremely uncertain temper. He has succeeded in removing his moustache. However it was accomplished the operations must have been a painful one, since about 75 per cent. of the hair appears to have been plucked out by the roots. DEEMING'S ACCOUNT OF HIS FLIGHT FROM HULL. Deeming has given, it is reported, the following account of his departure from Hull: -- "On the 15th day of March, 1890, I was staying at the Station Hotel, Hull, with my wife. We had been married then only three weeks. I had promised my wife a present. I went to Reynoldson's, with whom I had done business in many instances before. I bought goods to the amount of £285. I then gave Reynoldson cheques in payment for the goods, as I had always paid him or by cheque before. I then wired to London to my agent to place money in the bank to meet those cheques, but received a wire

Mike Covell

back to say that Westheart had not been seen since the 12th. I took train to London at once. On arriving there I learned that he had gone to Monte Video. I then took train on Sunday morning for Southampton, thinking he would go by the Coleridge on Sunday, but I learned that he had gone by the boat on Thursday. I then wrote to my wife and asked her to be patient until my return, and sent her money to go on with, but I had not time to write to Reynoldson's. In fact, I thought they would wait until I returned, but on arriving at Monte Video I was arrested, for what I have never been told, but I can only think it is a debt, which I can, and which I am willing to pay. This statement I vouch to be true. "HARRY LAWSON." HIS GAOL TREATMENT AT MONTE VIDEO. During his detention in gaol at Monte Video he wrote to the British Consul complaining that the treatment he was experiencing was not fit for a dog, and that it was doing his health considerable injury. He threatened to take action against the Government, if it should cost him £4,000 to do it. He also reminded the Consul that he had taken no action against a man who had "eloped with £9,000 of his money." He appears to have been removed, and he thanked the Consul and asked him to help him to keep clean if he could not help him by any other means. He, therefore, requested that his luggage should be sent to him. On learning that he was to be transferred to England, he wrote asking that any letters that had arrived might be forwarded to him. He said he had suffered much, and "his poor dear wife must have suffered more." He asked to be allowed to go as privately as possible for the "sake of his family name." Three days afterwards he wrote complaining about being dirty and miserable, and asked for clean clothing and a few dollars. He moreover complained about the man with the £9,000 being still at liberty, whilst he (Deeming) was only owing 3285, which would be paid before he got to England. On the 28th April he wrote touching his solitary confinement and severe imprisonment. He said Mr. Westheart, who had his £9,000 was still at large, and he (Deeming) had received three letters from three gentlemen stating that a certain gentleman in Monte Video was acquainted with Westheart, "and was party man with him in his money." THREATENING THE BRITISH MINISTER. It is said that Mr. Chamberlain, the British Minister at Monte Video, received an anonymous letter whilst Lawson was in gaol. The handwriting was disguised, and the following is the text:

"Sir, - If my cousin Harry Lawson, now in the Central Police Station, is not released by the thirtieth day of May, as he is guilty of no charge and his debt is paid before now. As true as there is a God above, on or as soon after that date as possible you are a dead man. I have a Spaniard who will do the work for a few dollars, and my poor cousin has only been arrested for spite because he bought a piece of land in London that Reynoldson wanted. Be careful for your own sake and punish the innocent no longer. If you lot free him I will see that he goes home

at once. I have been to see him but have not been allowed to do so, and the poor boy does not even know I have arrived. – Yours, "CAUTIOUS."

Lawson, who had no relatives, it is said, in Monte Video at the time the letter was received, subsequently wrote, saying that he had been informed that Mr. Chamberlain had received threatening letters, which that gentleman seemed to think had been sent by him. He said he was aware that he had written many letters, but the only threat he had made was that he should lay the whole statement of his treatment before the British Government. He had not, however, intended to carry his threat into effect, for fear of doing him any harm.

The Hull Daily Mail, April 1st 1892, P. 3,

THE RAINHILL AND AUSTRALIAN MURDERS. THE SUSPECTED MURDER IN SOUTH AFRICA. Information has come to the knowledge of the police at Melbourne, which puts them, as they think, upon the track of an additional murder perpetrated by Deeming two or three years ago. The story is that in 1888 one Harry Lawson, who is believed to have been none other than Deeming, this being an alias which he adopted on other occasions, was engaged in mining operations at Charters Towers, Queensland, his "chum" being a man named James Keays. Lawson, who was of an extremely enterprising character, induced Keays and two other diggers to quit Charters Towers and start with him for South Africa. At the hotel where the party was put up in Sydney the two men, who had thrown in their lot with Lawson and Keays, were mysteriously robbed of all their earnings, which amounted to £170, and they were consequently unable to continue their journey. Lawson and his companion accordingly sailed for the Cape without the other two. Nothing was heard of them for some time, but at length a letter was received from South Africa in Lawson's handwriting, announcing that Keays had died in the goldfields there, and describing with great minuteness, his illness and last hours. The writer also gave an account of the funeral, at which, he said, he was the only person present. When Lawson left the South African goldfields he took with him a large sum of money, and the police strongly suspect that most of it belonged to the unfortunate Keays, and that his companion murdered him in order to obtained possession of it. DEEMING ALLEGES THAT HIS LODGINGS ARE HAUNTED. "A CORPULENT WOMAN." Further particulars have been obtained from the Sydney police as to Deeming's residence there. It appears that he arrived in July, 1881, by the Nerene, on which vessel he served as a steward. For a time he lodged in the house of a Mrs. Taft, but she gave him notice and got rid of him because he was continually complaining that the house was haunted by ghosts. He subsequently worked as a gasfitter in the employment of a Mr. Manley. In 1882 he asked for and obtained a holiday in order, as he said, to go upon a shooting

> *expedition, but Mr. Manley afterwards discovered that Deeming's real object in obtaining leave of absence was to appear at the police court in answer to a charge of stealing gasfittings. Of this charge he was convicted, and he was only discharged from prison on the morning that his first known wife – Marie James – the victim of the Rainhill murder – arrived at Sydney from England. Deeming, prior to his imprisonment for theft, lived with an extremely corpulent woman, whom he represented to be his wife. PRECAUTIONS AGAINST LYNCHING. Public excitement continues to grow in anticipation of the impending inquest and trial. The police authorities are anxious that the adjourned inquest on the body found at Windsor should be resumed, not at the morgue, where the inquiry was opened, but at the City Police Court, which is close to the gaol. The chief concern is to prevent a disorderly rush when the prisoner is conveyed to and from the inquiry. If the adjourned proceedings are held at the Morgue an escort of at least 100 mounted police will be necessary, besides a large force of unmounted constables. To provide such an escort detachments of police would have to be drafted in from other districts, which would thus be left for a time unprotected. In the event, however, of the sittings being transferred to the City Court an escort of some 25 constables would be amply sufficient, on accounts of the shorter distance to be traversed. The question is still undecided, but, whichever plan is adopted, no precautions will be neglected which can secure the safety of the prisoner.*

The Hull and North Lincolnshire Times, April 2nd 1892,

> *ANOTHER "RIPPER" STORY. A Belfast newspaper's London correspondent says: "The Scotland Yard authorities did not believe the alleged confession of the Whitechapel murders by Deeming. The fact is they consider, rightly or wrongly, that they have the author of the Whitechapel tragedies now under lock and key at Portland prison undergoing a sentence of 20 years penal servitude. He is a Belgian, and was tried and sentenced some six years ago for attempting to obtain money from ladies by threats of violence. There is just one link in the chain of evidence missing, and they expect, sooner or later, to be able to supply it. This information reached me yesterday, and a few hours later, strange to say, another letter from an alleged Jack the Ripper was received by Mr. Hopkins, stipendiary magistrate, at Lambeth Police Court. The police have in their possession the letters written on previous occasions by the mysterious personage, and they will be able to compare yesterday's communication with the hand writing of those epistles. The latest intimation is to the effect that "Jack the Ripper" means to commence his tricks about Cable and Flower and Dean-streets, and he asks the magistrates to see if the bluecoats have their eyes open.*

The Hull and East Yorkshire and Lincolnshire Times, April 2nd 1892, P. 5

FURTHER SENSATIONS ABOUT DEEMING. HE AND HIS WIFE RESIDE AT PORTSMOUTH. HE GOES TO LONDON: RESULT: A WHITECHAPEL MURDER. AN EARLIER VISIT TO BEVERLEY. Our Portsmouth correspondent says: - William Taylor, living at Chelsea-road, Southsea, and employed in the Gun Mounting Store in Portsmouth Dockyard yesterday, made a statement which it is believed, may throw some light upon the career of Deeming. Taylor says: - "In November, 1888, I was lodging at an eating house in William-street, Morice Town, Devonport, where Lawson and his wife took lodgings for a fortnight while on their honeymoon. Lawson appeared to be a gentleman, but was remarkably taciturn. It was generally believed that he only occupied such lodgings as he did out of consideration for his wife, who was a relation of the keepers of the house. Though Mrs Lawson had her meals with the other boarders, her husband took his in the bedroom. One evening Mrs Lawson returned to her lodgings alone, and announced that her husband had received a letter at Plymouth Post Office, calling him immediately to London, and that he left by train that night. Two days afterwards came a Whitechapel murder. He left no money with his wife, had not paid his bill, and had not given his address. His conduct generally was regarded as highly suspicious. The wife did not hear from Lawson until she received a telegram ordering her to Weymouth, and by that time she was much distressed, and had packed up intending to return to Jersey from whence she had come. The other lodgers thought Lawson was strange in his mind. Mrs Lawson did not say what her maiden name was, but she appeared tolerably well to do. Both she and the husband appeared of the same age, about 27. EARLIER VISIT TO BEVERLEY. LUCKY ESCAPE OF A LANDLADY. Information has just come to light that between four or five years ago, a stranger, giving the name of Williams, stayed at Forrester's Arms, Beverley, then kept by a widow, whose husband had recently died. He represented himself as a sheep farmer in Australia, owning three thousand acres, and said he had come to England to purchase sheep, and to sell some property at Nafferton, to which he was heir. He made the landlady an offer of marriage, promising to provide for her children, and laid on the table thirty £5 notes. She said she would talk to him in two years' time, and shortly afterwards he went away. Two years later he again appeared, the landlady having in the meantime removed from the Forrester's to the Sloop Inn. He renewed his offer of marriage, and she accepted him. All the arrangements were made, and the wedding dress provided, but she ascertained that one of the statements he made was untrue, and refused to have anything further to do with him, and he left shortly afterwards.

The Hull Daily Mail, April 4th 1892, P. 3,

Mike Covell

DEEMING AT MELBOURNE. MORE IMPORTANT DISCOVERIES. GRUESOME LOOKING WEAPONS FOUND. PRECAUTIONARY MEASURES: DEEMING IN A RAGE. After his incarceration at Melbourne Deeming was visited in his cell by numerous official personages, including the Hon. Allen M'Lean, Chief Secretary and Minister of Lands, and the Hon. T. H. Wilson, Under Secretary. The prisoner appeared greatly annoyed by these visits, which he resented as an intrusion. He flew into a violent passion and walked up and down his cell in a state of great excitement. The arrival of Mr. M. Marshall Lyle, his solicitor, is no way diminished his agitation. "What fresh intruder is this?" he demanded. In reply Mr. Lyle explained who he was, and produced a bundle of papers relating to the case. The prisoner, however, refused to look at the documents, and burst into a violent tirade against the authorities for having taken his spectacles from him and refusing to return them. He also roundly abused the prison officials for having stationed a warder in his cell, and declared he would not on any account touch the prison fare. An attempt was made to pacify him by suggesting that he might, if he desired, have his meals sent in from a neighbouring restaurant, but he absolutely declined to listen to reason and continued to behave in a highly excitable manner. Mr. Lyle endeavoured in vain to induce him to enter into conversation, though the warder retired into the further most corner of the cell. The solicitor was consequently obliged to postpone the discussion of the prisoner's affairs with him until he becomes more reasonable. With regard to the question of the spectacles, the police point out that nothing would be easier than for the accused to break and swallow the glass or use it to open an artery, and so defeat the ends of justice. OVERHAULING THE PRISONER'S LUGGAGE: A KNIFE AND AXE FOUND. Detectives have been overhauling the luggage of Williams, alias Deeming, alias Swanton, and have made some discoveries of great importance. The first of these is a marriage certificate, which is dated "Parish Church, Rainhill, September 22nd 1891." There is also a time table giving the arrivals and departures of the trains between Rainhill and Liverpool. There are also a lot of Christmas cards which had been sent to Emily Mather from friends at Rainhill and Liverpool, together with a number of Bibles, prayer books, and other devotional volumes bearing her name. A number of articles of dress belonging to the unfortunate woman have also been found, some of them being easily recognisable as her property in consequence of their familiar patterns. Among them some belts, a hat of unusual shape, and a gold ornament have already been identified as having been worn by her during the voyage out on the Kaiser. More gruesome in character are a knife and hammer headed axe, the possession of which will tell strongly against the prisoner. They are of a kind used only in medical examinations, the knife being a dissecting knife. Both bear evidence of usage, and as they are only employed in the post mortem work, they may lead to an explanation of William's morbid motive in his crimes, and his work on the *bodies of his victims.* **WHERE DEEMING MET MISS ROUNSEVELL.** *Callington, a small mining town on the borders of Devon and Cornwall, has for some few days discussing the probabilities of Deeming having at one period of his life paid it a visit. Anyway, about five years ago, a man who flashed plenty of money and jewellery put up at an hotel there, and, on one or two occasions, paid a band to play outside the house at which he was staying. In various other ways he acted in a manner similar to that which has since been proved to be characteristic of Deeming. When the man in question arrived at the little Cornish town he subscribed himself as Captain Tamblyn, and announced that his object was to look at the mines of the neighbourhood with a view to their purchase. During his visit he had opportunities of intercourse with two young woman, Elizabeth and Kate Rounsevell, who subsequently went to Australia. Their relatives still reside at Callington, and are now congratulating themselves on the fact that Kate escaped marriage with such a man. The advices from Australia all agree that Deeming was about to marry a Kate Rounsevell, and Callingtonisms have no doubt that it was the girl of that name who left them some time ago for Australia. Besides, Kate, not very long ago, wrote home to her friends that she had met a gentleman who had offered her marriage, and that he had made her presents of costly rings. Elizabeth sent a letter corroborating this, and stated that she had been invited to pay a visit to them after they were married, and that they intended settling down at Bathurst. One of the two brothers Rounsevell, who had also emigrated to Australia, has handed to the police a bundle of letters which Deeming had sent his sister. While at Callington Captain Tamblyn paid considerable attention to a married woman, whose husband, in consequence of their too frequent trips, left the country. Subsequently Tamblyn also went away, and soon after the married woman disappeared, and has not since been heard of.* **A CURIOUS LETTER.** *The fine weather yesterday attracted many thousands of visitors to Rainhill, the railway, bicycles, and vehicles of various kinds being used for their conveyance. The keenest interest was manifested in Dinham Villa, but the police kept the crowd from getting near it. The following letter, evidently written by a female, has been received by Mr. Short, landlord of the Commercial Hotel, Rainhill: - 89 Furnival-street, Holborn, E. C., Dear Sir. – Will you let me know if this man Deeming is in height 5 feet 6 inches, aged 39, stout, brown hair, sandy moustache, and something peculiar with one of his eyes. I have known this man from 1887 till February 1889, when he left London for Lancashire, and if he be the same man, I could give information that would greatly assist the police. – Trusting you will favour me with a reply, yours truly. Mr. A. Roberts.*

The letter bears no date. It has been handed to Superintendent Keighley, of Widnes, who has had charge of the Rainhill murders, and he will forward it to the London police.

Mike Covell

The letter from "A. Roberts was interesting and I searched the national newspapers for other references but found only one, in *The Glasgow Herald*, dated April 4th 1892, it stated,

> The Widnes police have received and sent to the London police a letter in female writing, signed A. Roberts, 89 Furnival Street, Holborn, E. C., describing a man whom the writer knew from 188 till February, 1890, when he left London for Lancashire, and stating, if Deeming, the writer can give information to useful to the police.

The Hull Daily Mail, April 7th 1892, P. 3

> DEEMING'S CRIME AT MELBOURNE. INQUEST ON MISS EMILY MATHER. YESTERDAY'S PROCEEDINGS. SENSATIONAL LETTER FROM THE PRISONER. MISS ROUNSEVELL GIVES EVIDENCE. THE PRISONER AS "BARON SWANSTON." An extraordinary letter which the prisoner Swanston wrote to Miss Rounsevell from Southern Cross on the Monday after his arrest was made public in Melbourne yesterday. After informing the young lady, who was on her way from Sydney to marry him, that he had been taken into custody and charged with a murder of which he was wholly ignorant, the writer assured her that he would have no trouble in clearing himself. Her love for him he knew was steadfast, and he asked her to give him some assurance that it was still unshaken. He knew that his position was a critical one, but many an innocent man had been hanged before now. If Miss Rounsevell were unable to marry him in consequence of his being charged with his crime, then death would be preferable to all else that could befall him. "But I have always," he added, "trusted in God, and He will not forsake me now." In conclusion, the prisoner asked "Katie" to remember him in her prayers. A postscript was added in which "Swanston" requested Miss Rounsevell to send money to his solicitors to pay for his defence, and suggested that if she were unable to do this she might sell a ring set with five stones which he had given her, and send whatever it would fetch. THE ADJOURNED INQUEST. The adjourned inquest upon the body of Mrs Williams (Emily Mather) was resumed in the City Court, Melbourne, at 10 o'clock yesterday morning. Deeming, who had eaten and slept well overnight, again attended in custody. He was brought from the gaol to the Watch house Yard half an hour before the time fixed for the resumption of the inquiry. Though closely guarded, he was not handcuffed. Both before and throughout the public proceedings he continued to manifest in utmost callousness as to his position. While waiting in the yard he attempted to be jocular, addressing to his jailors a variety of facetious observations as to the appearance and assertions of the witnesses examined yesterday. He asked whether the crowd outside was as large as ever, and, on being informed that it was nit, he

rejoined, "They are getting more sense." READING TUESDAY'S EVIDENCE. The evidence taken on Tuesday was then read over to the jury. Deeming meanwhile listened intently, and occasionally asked his solicitor a question in a low tone. The portion of the recital which seemed to irritate him most was the deposition of Mr Hirschfeldt, who was his fellow passenger on board the Kaiser Wilhelm. Interrupting the reading the accused exclaimed, "You ought to be ashamed at getting up and swearing such stuff." Each witness was put into the box whilst his disposition was being read. As Martha Buella, the laundry keeper, who spoke to calling at 57, Andrew-street, for washing, passed the prisoner on her way to the box, Deeming, who appeared to have forgotten the nature of her testimony, asked his solicitor what her connection with the case might be. Again, while another witness was identifying a number of photographs which were put in on Tuesday, Deeming showed that he had not understood their importance by asking what they were, and on being informed that they were pictures of the hearth and fireplace of the room where the remains were found, he expressed incredulity as to their authenticity. When Mr Woods, the ironmonger from whom the spade, trowel, and cement were purchased, reappeared, the accused lay back in his chair and GRINNED, but very soon afterwards his feature again assumed a position of doubt, and when the portion of the evidence relating to the cement was reached he put on a puzzled air as if asking himself the question, "what cement?" He then suddenly seemed to remember all about Mr Woods' deposition. At other stages of the reading he again affected apathy, but it was not the loss apparent that all the essential facts were carefully noted, especially Mr Spedding's evidence as to finding an invitation card for the banquet at the Commercial Hotel, Rainhill. While the remaining depositions are being read, the prisoner, having meanwhile conversed earnestly with his solicitor, signalled to Mr Hirschfeldt to come over from the other side of the court to where he was seated. Mr Hirschfeldt having compiled, Deeming said to him, "Why don't you send Miss Rounsevell to me?" He was evidently aware that his young lady had been residing with the Hirschfeldt family since her arrival in Melbourne. Mr Hirschfeldt replied that Miss Rounsevell must exercise her own discretion as to whether or not she should grant the accused an interview. Deeming then strongly upbraided Mr Hirschfeldt for the evidence he had given, asking that as if it was not true it would not suffice to hang him, "even if God did make little apples." This was in allusion to a remark which Mr Hirschfeldt had made to him on board the Ballarat between Albany and Melbourne to the effect that he would be hanged "as sure as God made little apples." YESTERDAY'S WITNESSES. Mrs Louisa Atkinson, a widow residing near Andrew-street, Windsor, deposed that one evening in December, about the 23rd or 24th, she heard the sound of two persons quarrelling at No. 57. The voices sounded like those of a man and woman, and she heard another noise like that of something heavy being thrown. Walking up to the side gate she saw a woman half way up the side walk coming towards the gate. The woman resembled the photograph of Mrs Williams produced. DAWSON'S TOOLS. Richard Leech, ironmonger's salesman, said he remembered a man who gave the name of Dawson calling at the shop where he was employed on December 23rd, and offering to sell him some tools, which included a turning lathe. The bargain was not concluded at that time, but Dawson called again in January, and said he must get rid of the things, even at a sacrifice. The witness went with him to a shop in Little Collins-street and saw the tools, which he finally purchased for £32. He observed also in the shop a number of pictures and books, a canary in a cage, and blankets. He identified the accused as the man Dawson in question. Mr Willmot, ironmonger, next deposed to buying at an auction held in a shop in Little Collins-street a zinc pan, a spade, a bucket, and some other articles. The pan had cement adhering to it, and the spade, which was slightly damaged, seemed to have been used as a lever to prise up a heavy weight. The bucket contained a small quantity of sand. Simeon Solomon, a general dealer, who also attended the sale, identified the prisoner as the owner of the goods disposed of. The canary and cage produced were knocked down to him for £3. When he paid in the money the prisoner gave him a receipt and asked him as a favour to take good care of the bird. LEVITY OF THE PRISONER. Here the prisoner burst out laughing and exclaimed, "As the witness how his eye is" (laughter). This it appeared, was the witness whom Deeming struck in the face yesterday while passing from his cell to the Court after the process of identification. "DAWSON'S JEWELLERY." Mr Vivian, salesman, in the employment of Messrs. Kilpatrick, jewellers and watchmakers, Collins-street, who was next examined, remembered the prisoner coming to the shop in December and buying a silver watch, the price of which was £7. He ordered it to be sent to Mr Dobbin, Criterion Hotel, Sale, Gippsland. As the watch was not paid for it was not sent, but the prisoner called again on January 4th and took it away with him. Three days later he returned and bought a field glass, paying the bill with a cheque signed "H. Dawson." Witness was perfectly certain that the prisoner was the customer in question. He afterwards bought another silver watch, on which he had his initials engraved, and paid for it with a cheque upon the Bank of Australasia. He also purchased a napkin ring, on which he had the initials "B. S." engraved, explaining that it was for a friend, and he also bought in January two rings, one at £30 and the other at £25. Mr Vivian further testified to having put a gold ring or the accused's walking stick, and to having seen a spirit flask bearing the initials "F.B.D." in his possession. Another article which he sold the prisoner was a match box, with the initials "B.S." About the time the prisoner was visiting the shop two rings which were now produced, and which the witness identified, were missed. DAWSON'S "DEAR LITTLE WOMAN." Mr Smith stated that he attended the sale of Deeming's effects on January 7. The goods realised £72. Prisoner said he had intended to furnish a house, but was leaving to join his wife. On the following day witness accompanied "Dawson" on board the Ophir, which was lying in harbour at Melbourne. Prisoner remarked, "I wish my dear little woman was here." A few days later he said he had received a letter from his wife, who was in Sydney, adding, "If anything happened to her I should have nothing left to live for." AN EFFECT EXAMINED. Mr Edward Shire, sub-manager of the Bank of Australia, was called and examined as an expert in handwriting. He stated that he believed letters address to Miss Rounsevell, dated Sydney the 18th and 21st of January, and signed "Your loving Baron," and another dated from Perth and signed "Your loving and affectionate Baron," as well as a letter signed "Duncan" and addressed to a matrimonial agency from the Cathedral Hotel, and another to Mr Vivian, signed "Dawson," in reference to a promised cheque, were all in the same handwriting. MISS ROUNSEVELL IN THE BOX: EXCITEMENT IN COURT. The next name called was that of Miss Kate Rounsevell. There was considerable excitement in court when she entered. She walked to the witness box unfalteringly, and having been sworn looked steadfastly at the prisoner, who returned her gaze. She stated, in reply to the questions addressed to her, that she was travelling from Adelaide, which called in at Melbourne on January 12th. After the vessel left Melbourne she was sitting in the saloon, when a gentleman who was passing stopped and asked her whether she felt sick. She replied in the negative. The same gentleman subsequently asked her to join a game of whist, introducing himself as BARON SWANSTON. On arrival at Sydney we went together to Coogee, a suburb of the city. In Sydney I stayed at the same hotel as Swanston – Wentworth House. The prisoner told me that he was very wealthy, and owned a property in Melbourne. On January 15 I travelled with Swanston to Bathurst. On the way I saw in a newspaper a list of passengers who had arrived in Adelaide, and observed that Swanston's name was not on there. In reply to a question on the subject, he told me that the omission was accounted for by the fact that he had booked after going on board. While we were in Sydney Swanston gave me the ring, produced. On the afternoon of the same day he asked me to marry him. I replied that I did not intend to marry, and Swanston then asked me to keep the ring as a memento of our acquaintance. He also gave me a small brooch. During the journey to Bathurst Swanston remarked that I looked fatigued, and produced a silver flask containing brandy, which he recommended me to sip, but I declined to taste it. When we arrived at Bathurst my sister met us at the station, and I introduced the prisoner. On January 16 he called upon us three times, and was admitted on the third occasion. He was staying at the Royal Hotel. On the following day he called again, and renewed his offer of marriage. I then expected him. He gave me the scent spray and the two diamond rings now produced. THE MURDERED WOMAN'S RING. Mr Walsh, Crown prosecutor, interposing, stated that one of the rings, which had a boat shaped setting, had been identified as having been worn by the murdered woman. Miss Rounsevell,

Mike Covell

further interrogated, said: Swanston left Bathurst on the evening of January 17. He said that if he had not met me he was going straight to America, and he asked me if I should like to go with him to England. I replied that I did not wish to go just then, but I added that I was willing to go to Western Australia. Swanston said that would be all right; he would go there. This he did shortly afterwards. The first letter I received from him after he left was dated Sydney, January 18th. On the two succeeding days I received letters from Sydney, dated respectively January 19th and January 20th. Then I had a letter from Melbourne, dated January 31st, and after that I did not hear from the prisoner till he reached Western Australia. The letter which then arrived was dated February 8th, and signed "Baron Swanston." February 15th was the date of the next letter, which bore the same signature. I also received from Swanston several telegrams, but I did not keep these. The correspondence was here put in and read by the Clerk of the Court. The letters were all couched in most affectionate terms, the writer professing unbounded devotion to Miss Rounsevell. In one of them Swanston said he was going to Perth, and their future home would soon be in readiness. He urged the witness to loose no time in joining him, and stated that he had obtained employment as engineer of Fraser's gold mine at Southern Cross, his salary being £6 a week. He added that she was to telegraph to him if she wanted money. While these letters were read Swanston sat stiffly on the edge of his chair, and never once removed his eyes from the witness. This concluded Miss Rounsevell's evidence. She was not cross examined either by Mr Lyle or any member of the jury. A RELIC OF RAINHILL. Mr Webster spoke to assisting at the exhumation of the body in the house at Andrew-street. He explained that the cement in which it was embedded was broken off as carefully as possible, and the body was then removed to the Morgue. During the removal the whole of the hair fell from the head of the deceased. Witness remembered Mr Spedding finding on March 18th the card of invitation to the dinner at Rainhill on August 8th. HOW DEEMING WAS ARRESTED. Evan Williams, a policeman from Western Australia, gave evidence as to "Swanston's" arrest at Southern Cross on the 11th of March. He stated that he placed his hand on the prisoner's shoulder and said to him, "I arrest you for the murder of Emily Williams at Windsor." Swanston replied, "I don't know anything about it. I never was at Windsor to my knowledge. I am innocent." He afterwards asked, "How did you come to pick on me, an innocent man?" Witness replied, "I don't know, innocent men are sometimes arrested." Swanston rejoined, "Yes, many an innocent man is hanged these days." At Albany, he stated, the prisoner was placed in the lock up in charge of two constables. During the night he contrived to remove his moustache; no one could explain how. Being asked whether he had omitted to repeat anything Swanston had said to him, witness recalled the remark that a man who had committed such a murder must have a terrible conscience, but if he had lived a good life up to the time of the murder he had nothing to fear, and *could only die once. A RAINHILL BAND OF HOPE CARD. Detective Cawsey spoke of finding the body. In other rooms of the house the remains of burnt papers and other debris were found, including a portion of a Liverpool newspaper and torn scraps of letters. Detective Cawsey described how dresses which were found among the prisoner's luggage had been ripped to pieces, and enumerated the other articles which his boxes contained. There was a card of membership of the Rainhill Band of Hope bearing Emily Mather's name, the certificate of her marriage with Williams, photographs of the deceased, and of a house, on the back of one being the name of "F. B. Deeming" in the prisoner's handwriting. There were other photographs of people taken in Liverpool, and a little book in which were written the words, "To dear Emily, with love," a spirit flask with the letters "F. B. D." engraved upon it, a Prayer Book, bearing the inscription "Emily from George, 1887," other articles bearing the initials of the deceased, and a sovereign case bearing Deeming's initials. There were also two gold brooches, and a silver one, a memoriam card of John Mather, two diamond rings, and one wedding ring. These articles were handed to witness by the Perth police. The inquest was adjourned. DRIVEN TO SUICIDE BY THE RAINHILL MURDERS. AN EXTRAORDINARY STORY. At the Aston (Birmingham) Police Court yesterday, before Messrs R. P. Yates, F. S. Bolton, R. Peyton, and Alderman Ash, a middle aged man named Matthew Lane, of 89, Wainwright-street, Aston, was charged with attempting to commit suicide by jumping into the canal at Witton on the 4th inst. – Mr W. Walker (the assistant magistrates clerk) asked the prisoner whether he was guilty or not. Prisoner replied in a low, deep voice, "As God is my witness, I am guilty." He went on to say that when he was in Africa some time ago he suffered from sunstroke, and was afterwards laid up in hospital with an abscess in the head. The latter illness had caused him some trouble ever since. He suffered from occasional aberration of the mind, and if he drank it made him much worse. He was a great reader, and had lately been carefully studying the Rainhill murders, the horrible details of which so moved upon his mind that he felt if he did not destroy himself he should surely murder his dear wife and children the same as Deeming had done. Prisoner (continuing in solemn tone): This made me mad, and it was either their life or mine. I could stand it no longer, so wrote a letter to my wife, saying I was about to visit some friends. I adopted this course, feeling that it would relieve my mind of the fearful hallucinations. I, however, drank, and the more I drank the worse I became. Devoid of money, I returned home and slept. When I awoke I saw before me a knife, which I took, intending to kill myself with it. I wrote to my wife to that effect; but I afterwards decided to drown myself, and accordingly went to the canal at Witton and jumped in. I sank twice, and on coming up for the third time I heard a voice bidding me to get out. I did so, and went to the police station and gave myself up, as stated by the constable. I hope the magistrates will punish me severely for what I have done, and not let me go*

Mike Covell

> home to my wife and children whom I dearly love, and whom I am afraid of injuring. – Prisoner's wife said he had always been a good husband and father: but a short time ago he lost his situation, and his mother died about the same time. These two events had caused great depression, and were responsible for his late conduct. – Prisoner was remanded in custody for a week, in order that he might be seen by a doctor in the meantime.

The Hull Daily Mail, April 8th 1892, P. 2,

> SHOULD DEEMING BE BROUGHT TO ENGLAND? No doubt many people would be glad if Deeming could be brought to England to take his trial. Apart from the love of sensation there is a feeling that the worst of the man's crimes was that at Rainhill – the one which, above all others, he should be made to expiate. The remoteness of the Australian case is calculated to try the patience of those morbid people who prefer to read of crime red hot in their own land. But there seems to be no real reason why the ordinary course should not be followed. Deeming was arrested on a definite charge. For this he must face Australian justice. Only in the event of his being acquitted by the Colonial Courts, will he be brought to England to answer what is no longer the Rainhill Mystery. The Attorney General made a statement to this effect in Parliament yesterday. But there is little likelihood of Deeming finding mercy in Australia. The probabilities are that he will be sent to his account with the Rainhill crime, unredeemed even by the forfeit of his life.

The Hull Daily Mail, April 13th 1892, P. 4,

> LATEST NEWS. DEEMING'S CRIMES AT RAINHILL. APPLICATION FOR A WARRANT AT WIDNES. A WITNESS SEVERELY CENSURED. The adjourned application for a warrant for the apprehension of Frederick Bayley Deeming for the murder of his wife and four children, at Rainhill, in July last, was heard at Widnes this morning. – The cart driver, Hackett, whose non-attendance on Monday caused the adjournment, said he did not come because his master told him it was not necessary. – The Magistrate severely censured Hackett, and, after hearing his evidence read over, granted the warrant asked for. He observed that the evidence before him certainly gave rise to a strong presumption that Deeming committed the offences alleged against him.

The Hull Daily Mail, April 19th 1892, P. 3,

> DEEMING AND THE MELBOURNE MURDER. MISS ROUNSEVELLE'S NARRATIVE. HOW SHE NARROWLY ESCAPED. The files of the Melbourne

Argus received by mail supply copious and interesting details respecting the tragedies at Windsor, and many romantic episodes connected with the crime. Deeming wrote to Mrs Mather, his wife's mother, at Rainhill, on December 29: - "We have spent a happy Christmas, and Emily is the happiest woman ever seen. She does enjoy herself." Emily is believed to have been murdered by him five days previously. On January 2, Williams, in the name of Duncan, sent the following extraordinary epistle to a matrimonial agent: - "Cathedral Hotel, Melbourne, January 2, 1892," "Matrimonial." "The undersigned, at the above address, wishes to meet with a young lady with the above intentions. She must be good looking, age 18 or 20, and know something of housekeeping. I myself am 32 years, engineer by trade. I have £360 in the bank, and am about to enter a good appointment. Am sober, steady man. Am just from England, and have 14 years' testimonials from one master. Please enclose photo of lady. – Yours &c., F. DUNCAN."

A letter acknowledging the receipt of this, and advising Mr "Duncan" that there were several "good looking ladies with the above intentions, age 18 to 20, who knew something of housekeeping" on the books of the office was sent to him, and to this he replied, promising to call on the following Saturday, but he failed to do so. The part played by Miss Kate Rounsevelle in the tragic story of the murder of Mrs Emily Williams and the pursuit of her murderer is a most romantic one. Miss Rounsevelle had been housekeeping for her brother, a storekeeper in Broken Hill, and in consequence of the unsuitability of the hot climate to her health she determined to go for a change to Bathurst, in New South Wales, where her sister resides. She left Adelaide by steamer, and arrived in Melbourne on the morning of January 12th, between one and two o'clock on that day the boat sailed for Sydney, and among her passengers in the first class was Williams. He persistently pressed her to marry him, and when she at length consented, he gave her a ring set with diamonds and sapphires, and two other rings, a large five-stoned diamond ring, and a boat shaped diamond ring, and also an opal broach set in gold. Miss Rounsevelle said: - "I remarked that it was curious that he should have the rings in his possession, and his answer was that he had courted a young lady in England and had bought the rings to present to her, when one night, as he was taking her into the box of one of the theatres, a gentleman tapped him on the shoulder, and said, "I trust you do not forget that is my wife you are escorting." He was astounded at the woman's duplicity that he left her standing at the entrance and walked away with the intention of renouncing her and the sex. After this little reminiscence he said that he had a lot of clothes which had belonged to his dead sister, and if I liked I might have them. I told him that I could not wear the clothes of a dead woman even if I could overcome my objection – which I did not think possible – to taking gifts of clothing from any man not my husband."

Mike Covell

> *Proceeding to a narrative of her journey to meet Deeming, Miss Rounsevelle says: - "When I arrived in Melbourne I was met by a friend who took me and my luggage to the Federal Coffee Palace. There I found awaiting me a telegram from my sister, "For God's sake go no further." I showed it to my friend, and he wired asking to know the reason. Naturally I was much distressed, and was unable to sit down or rest. I therefore asked my friend to walk with me down the crowded streets, that I might get some little distraction for my thoughts. Presently we noticed a crowd in front of a newspaper office, and inquiring the reason were informed that Williams, the murderer, had been arrested. I felt strangely moved, and I asked my companion to buy a paper. He did so, and read – "Williams, alias Swanson, arrested at Southern Cross." I knew then the meaning of the telegram from my sister, and, overcome with a nameless terror, I fainted. When I recovered I was at the Federal Coffee palace, and Detective Cawsey and Considine were there to question me. At first they seemed to believe that I was in some way connected with the crime, but I had little difficulty in satisfying them of my utter ignorance of it. The jewellery, which was, I am told, the jewellery of the poor dead woman, I handed over immediately, and it makes me shudder now to think I have worn it, and as a love gift too." THE STATEMENT BY A GRIMSBY MAN. SINGULAR THREATENING LETTER. The man Wilson, who made the statement concerning Deeming's conduct in Hull gaol, yesterday received the following letter, addressed, "Mr Fred Wilson, No. 4, Holne-street, Grimsby, near Hull," and bearing the Cardiff post mark: - "Frederick Wilson, you are a ____ ____. What do you want, rounding on poor old Deeming. How would you like anyone to round on you if you were arrested like him. I believe the statement you made is a false one; you want to get money from the Government, or you want a cheap trip over to Australia. You will get no luck all the days you live. Everybody calls you a dirty, sneaking cur. You will be in gaol again before you die. You are not an Englishman, or you would not have done the likes of that, you _____, and you had better leave Grimsby. What good will it do you? Everybody calls you an informer. You belong to the Carey family, and "Skin the goat" will be on your track." The letter further abounds in abuse of the lowest kind, and is signed, "Tom, the Fisherman." Wilson's comment upon the document is, "That's what you get for telling the truth." DEEMING PREPARING FOR HIS END. WRITING HIS AUTOBIOGRAPHY. It is understood that Mr Marshall Lyle, Deeming's solicitor, will instruct counsel to apply for a postponement of his trial. The grounds of the application are of a somewhat peculiar character, as they amount to a virtual admission on the prisoner's part of the hopelessness of attempting to invalidate the overwhelming weight of the evidence adduced against him. It is stated that Deeming has made revelations to his solicitor which will fully warrant the adjournment of the trial, not with the object of disputing the accused's guilt, but with the view of marking inquiries for the purpose of removing from innocent*

> *shoulders the suspicion of having committed crimes of which Deeming has confessed himself to have been perpetrator. An additional proof that Deeming has abandoned all hope of averting a capital sentence for the Windsor murder is afforded by the way in which is alludes, in conversation, to his impending fate. He now states his intention of bequeathing to Miss Rounsevelle the autobiography which for some days past he has been engaged in writing. The profits of which she may derive from its publication will, he expresses the hope, in some degree compensate her for the wrong and annoyance which, he has been the means of inflicting on her.*

The Hull Daily Mail, April 21st 1892, P. 4

> *DEEMING'S CRIMES. THE INHABITANTS OF RAINHILL AND DINHAM VILLA. At a public meeting in the parish of Rainhill, held after the vestry meeting on Tuesday, the Vicar occupying the chair, a reference was made to the recent tragedies at Dinham Villa, and a resolution was submitted thanking Mrs Hayes, of Huyton, who owns the property, for her thoughtfulness in not leaving a trace of the villa in which the murders were perpetrated. – Mr J. Johnson Owen introduced the subject. He said they were indebted to the chairman for giving them an early opportunity of discharging what many of the inhabitants regarded as a public duty- that was to tender to Mrs Hayes, the owner of Dinham Villa, a public expression of thanks for having demolished the house where the dreadful tragedy took place, which had caused so much painful excitement in the neighbourhood. With that object in view he submitted the following resolution: - "That this meeting of inhabitants of Rainhill desires to express its sincere thanks to Mrs Hayes for promptly demolishing Dinham Villa, the house where the Deeming murders were committed." Mrs Hayes had by this action conferred a benefit of residents, who might have been driven from the neighbourhood by the constant incursion of sightseers, and on landlords, whose property would have been consequently been depreciated. What was of more importance, she had rendered public service by removing what has undoubtedly proved a means of stimulating a morbid and degrading taste, and this she has generously done at her own cost, although she might have sold the house at a considerable price, or might reasonably have looked for compensation for its destruction (hear, hear). – The Vicar thought that the resolution should be in more genial terms, but it was ultimately adopted.*

The Hull Daily Mail, April 28th 1892, P. 3,

> *THE TRIAL OF DEEMING. ANOTHER APPLICATION FOR POSTPONEMENT. THE CASE TO PROCEED. At the Criminal Court, Melbourne, yesterday, before*

Mike Covell

> Mr Justice Hodges, Deeming's counsel, Messrs Deakin and Furlonge, made a fresh application to have the trial of the prisoner for the Rainhill murders postponed in order that further inquiry might be made as to his mental condition. There was not a large attendance of the public, the majority of those who sought admission being denied it. There was, however, a numerous attendance of barristers and solicitors, who are following with the keenest interest the various legal points which have been raised in connection with the case. The prisoner on this occasion was not brought into court. Mr Deakin asked that the case should be adjourned for one month. In support of the application he put in affidavits, signed by Drs Springthorpe and Fishbourne, and in which these gentlemen expressed their belief that the adjournment proposed was essential in the interests of justice. He also cited and enlarged upon a telegram which had been received from England by the newspapers to the effect that there was known to have been insanity in Deeming's family. The affidavits put me in, he submitted, contained new facts, of which the Court was entitled to take cognisance, and which fully justified the application. The Judge pointed out that the affidavits, which merely declared that a searching investigation ought to be made, were extremely vague. If the adjournment was asked for in order that such an examination might take place, that should have been done clearly and definitely stated in the affidavits. Mr Deakin replied that the medical examinations which had already been made had disclosed the fact the prisoner was suffering from tertiary symptoms of a contagious disease, epilepsy, and hereditary insanity, and in these circumstances he maintained it was essential that a reasonable opportunity should be afforded to procure further information as to Deeming's past history. The Judge said he did not know what the expression "further information" in the affidavits meant. This point seemed to have been studiously left vague. If the application were granted, similar demands might be put forward months after months, and six months hence they might be no nearer the trial of the accused. Mr Deakin observed that the Government medical officer acquiesced in the application. It was not proposed that there should be any unreasonable delay. The Judge: If I were to postpone the trial for a month without reasonable hope that during that interval further information essential to the case would be collected I should be merely hindering the progress of justice. Mr Deakin: But I hope to be able in a month to produce witnesses who will testify to the prisoner's mental condition. The Judge: Counsel for the defence must understand that cables received from Calcutta or other parts cannot be accepted as evidence. Mr Deakin remarked that apart from intelligence of that kind the prisoner's physical condition, especially the periodic epilepsy to which he was subject, suggested that he was not altogether responsible for his actions. In these circumstances he asked: Would it not be well to give the doctors time to thoroughly investigate the matter? The Judge: These attacks are not always periodic? Mr Deakin: No, Julius Cesar during one of the Gallic wars

recovered totally. The Judge: It is suggested that this disease leaves the prisoner permanently insane? Mr Deakin said he was unable to answer that question. The Judge: The question is not whether the accused is insane now, but whether he was insane when the murder was committed. Mr Deakin: This application is based on the physical symptoms present, and it is their probable connection with the mental condition of the accused which requires further investigation. Mr Walshe, Crown prosecutor, opposed the application that at some length. It was not even suggested, he said, that it could be proved the prisoner was insane at the date of the murder. He was sane now, and the question was whether he was insane when the murder was committed. The Judge acquiesced in this view, remarking that the prisoner had been sane enough to plead when last before the Court. Mr Deakin: It was not intended that he should be arraigned then. The Judge: The plea cannot be cancelled on the ground that it was taken by mistake. I am asked to give the doctors a further opportunity to test the prisoner's mental condition. That application I will not dispose of now, but tomorrow I will hear medical evidence on both sides. I feel that my position is one of great responsibility, but the interests of the community demand that a person accused of such a crime as this should be tried immediately, and if found guilty should suffer the extreme penalty of the law. If I am necessary I will grant it, but if the evidence on the point is not conclusive the trial must proceed. Deeming will accordingly be brought up for trial when the court resumes to-day. DEEMING'S HISTORY. The doctors who have examined Deeming state that they have elicited from him the following among other statements: - His name as a child was Frederick Deeming. He remembers nothing of his life before he reached the age of 12, except that he was sent by his father to an asylum near London. From that establishment he was taken away by his mother, and was under her care between the ages of 12 and 16. H was never in robust health, but was nevertheless always in mischief. His scrapes, however, never ended in his being sent to prison. He was generally called "Mad Fred" and on one occasion while still a boy he threw a girl into a canal for calling him that name. He afterwards changed his name to Harry, and when about 16 ran away to London, where he knocked about for some time, and having been reduced to a starving condition he was placed in an asylum as "Teddy Williams." He did not remain there long. He climbed over the wall and got away, but was subsequently arrested while tearing his clothing to pieces in the streets. He was sent to a house of correction, whither he was traced by the chaplain of the asylum where he had been confined. Instead of taking him back to the asylum, however, the chaplain got him sent to son. From early life he was in the habit of frequently changing his name and passing from one employment to another. He proved clever at almost everything he attempted. His object in changing his name was not to escape detection on account of any crimes he had committed, but to escape from himself by changing as much as possible his personality and mode of life. His desire for

Mike Covell

> *changes was habitual. His mother, he declares, still exercises a strange influence over him. His brother Albert, if asked, would be able to state what his ideas were respecting his mother's presence and influence, and could also explain why he had changed his name so frequently. His mother predicted that he would be hanged before he reached the age of 40. Ever since his boyhood he has been greatly addicted to the society of women. With regard to his family history he states that his father's mind was unhinged, that he was of a very violent temperament, and that he died in a lunatic asylum at Birkenhead. His mother he describes as good and kind, but she also was confined to a lunatic asylum until shortly before the prisoner's birth. His brother Sam, he asserts, has likewise been confined in a lunatic asylum, but this fact was only known to his other brother, Albert. When in England last year, the prisoner declares he vainly endeavoured to ascertain their whereabouts of his brother Sam. He has a sister who is employed as a housemaid at New Brighton, near Liverpool, and another who is "not right in her head." Deeming has also given as to some serious family trouble which he says occurred between 1880 and 1881.*

The Hull Daily Mail, May 3rd 1892, P. 3,

> *LATEST NEWS. DEEMING'S CONVICTION. SPEECH FROM THE DOCK. PERSONAL APPEAL TO THE JURY. HE PROTESTS HIS INNOCENCE. As stated in the special edition of the Mail last evening, Deeming was yesterday found guilty of murder and sentenced to death, the jury adding a [illegible] that the accused was not insane. Counsel for the prisoner, in concluding his address, which lasted over an hour, said: - "There is a possibility that what the prisoner has said is true. If you believe him to be sane and not guilty, then set him free; but if you say he has committed the crime, but is not responsible for his acts, then the doors of this court must only open to admit him into a lunatic asylum for life. Society is amply protected, and I implore you to weigh doubly, trebly, every circumstance surrounding this crime." Mr Walsh, Crown prosecutor, submitted that the crime had been brought home to the prisoner in the most satisfactory manner, and called upon the jury to dismiss this nonsense about insanity from their minds. The learned gentleman proceeded to review the circumstances adopted to conceal all traces of the crime. While Mr Walsh was addressing the Court Deeming sent a note to Mr Lyle, asking for a plan of the house at Windsor where the murder was committed. When it was supplied to him he studied it for some time and made a number of notes. He then stood up, and leaning over the front of the dock, exclaimed in a loud voice, "I wish to say a few words in my defence." The Judge: You can make any statement you choose. DEEMING ADDRESSES THE COURT. The Prisoner: I have not had a fair trial. It is not the law that is trying me, but the Press. The case was prejudiced even before my*

arrival by the exhibition of photographs in shop windows, and it was by means of these that I was identified. I leave it to the Jury to say if it did not the case that there are hundreds of people in Melbourne who would execute me without a trial. If I could believe that I committed the murder, I would plead guilty rather than SUBMIT TO THE GATE of the people in this court – the ugliest race of people I have ever seen. Woods swore he saw a copper standing in the yard, but he could not have done so. Is his evidence to have any weight? I leave it to the jury to judge of the value of his evidence, seeing he told a deliberate lie. I am told that whatever I say will not be believed, and even my own witnesses have been kept out of my way by counsel. It was the Press, not the public, that judged me. People have sworn to seeing me whom I have never seen in my life. Another objection I have to this trial is that no time has been allowed to communicate with witnesses in England and India. It is not a pleasant thing to confess to disease – mental or otherwise; but I am determined to do so, in justice to myself and the community. For weeks together I have suffered LAPSES OF MEMORY. In my own mind I know I am not guilty of this thing. So long as Emily Mather was my wife I dealt as gently and affectionately with her as it is possible for any man to deal with a woman. I cannot remember any incident which would have led to this awful crime: there was no reason for the murder. I know the people of Melbourne to-day have been so incited and infuriated by the Press that they would lynch me if they had the chance: but that would not settle the question of my guilt or innocence. Mr Hirscchfeldt swears that the body found at Windsor is that of Emily Mather; but it is a lie. My one comfort throughout this trouble is that EMILY MATHER IS ALIVE. If she were not I would tell you so. I think no more of my life than I do of this piece of paper. My life is ruined. If I were turned into the street to-night a free men, to-morrow would find me in the River Yarra Yarra – that is the best place for me now. I do not hesitate to give up my life; it would be a pleasure. I have fought the blacks on the Zambezi, and have fought with lions single handed. What is life to a man like me, whose prospects the newspapers and the public have blasted and ruined me for ever? I DON'T EXPECT JUSTICE; it is neither in the mind of the judges, nor of the jury, nor of the public to give me a fair trial. The case should have been postponed for two months, to enable evidence to be collected. Instead of that the trial was fixed, by premeditation, to take place at a time when the public is enraged against me. I have had great lapses of memory. I have made a voyage of six months' duration, and remembered nothing at the end of it. I cannot help these things, if God is pleased so to afflict me. What can I do here, without friends or relations? Still, the Crown throws every obstacle in the way of the doctors, of the lawyers, and of myself. Can you call this justice? LOOK AT THIS THING SQUARELY! One of the most unusual parts of these proceedings was the method of identification. I was placed among 19 other men, not one of whom was the least like myself. I was unfortunate in losing my moustache, which was removed by two

> *constables, but I won't give them away." The prisoner went on to comment upon the weakness of the identification of the body of the murdered woman. "A verdict of guilty," he continued, "would be the greatest relief to me. The doctor of Sydney Gaol should have been called to swear that I was treated for fits when confined there. There are also many people in England whose evidence should have been taken. My frequent change of name was AN HABITUAL FAD, and I must ask for an adjournment of the trial, if only to enable the evidence of Hirschfeldt to be more closely examined. I ask the jury to consider the evidence most carefully. A man swore he saw me in the verandah of the house in Andrew-street wearing a smoking cap – a thing I never wore in my life. I spent the whole of Christmas Day in the Exhibition Buildings. If I cannot tell the truth myself, I want the case put so that the jury may clearly understand it. In conclusion, he said: "I am as innocent as a man can be. That is my comfort." He spoke for nearly an hour, and betrayed no signs of hesitation or nervousness. The jury returned a verdict of guilty against Deeming, and added a rider that he was not insane. The Judge asked the prisoner whether he had anything to say. Deeming repeated that the trial throughout had been unfair, and requested the judge not to deliver any exhortation in passing sentence. The Judge accordingly passed sentence of death in the ordinary manner, without addressing the prisoner. Deeming listened to his condemnation with composure, and at its conclusion said "Thank you." His features then relaxed into a smile. DATE OF EXECUTION: DEEMING WRITING HIS BIOGRAPHY. A Reuter's telegram from Melbourne this morning states that it is expected Deeming's execution will be fixed for the 16th inst. On waking this morning in the condemned cell he resumed writing his biography. MRS MATHER INTERVIEWED. Mrs Mather was interviewed last evening at Rainhill. She stigmatised as atrocious the allegation of Deeming against her daughter Emily. Her daughter, he said, was never married before being united to Deeming, though she had been engaged to a Sheffield gentleman, which took place long before Deeming's coming to Rainhill. Mrs Mather also indignantly denied that her daughter sought marriage with Deeming, or was cognisant of the murder of Deeming's first wife. She never visited Dinham Villa except in the company of her youngest sister.*

The Hull Daily Mail, May 5th 1892,

> *IMITATING THE "WHITECHAPEL" MURDERER. The body of Elizabeth Walsh, a married woman, has been found at Chicago in a horribly mutilated condition, and bearing all the evidence of having been treated in the same fashion as that adopted by "Jack the Ripper" in Whitechapel. There is the greatest excitement in the city in consequence.*

The Hull Daily Mail, May 11th 1892, P. 3

DEEMING AS "LORD DUNN." HIS CAREER AT ANTWERP. FURTHER REVELATIONS OF HIS IMPUDENCE. *An Antwerp correspondent of the Belgian News writes an interesting account of Deeming's proceedings in November, 1889, when he passed himself as "Lord Dunn." He travelled to Antwerp from Hull on board the steamer Zebra. During the voyage, we are told, he made himself very agreeable to everybody on board; but excited a certain amount of distrust by an ostentatious display of money and jewellery. He took up his quarters at the Hotel de l'Europe, a house of the highest respectability, but as his conduct appeared to the management to be eccentric, if not suspicious, he was requested to leave, and went to another hotel. On the 17th of the month, he repaired to a photographer in the Place Meir, and there the man's [illegible] VANITY FOUND FULL PLAY in having his portrait taken in every conceivable attitude. He gave his name as "Lord Dunn," and the amount expanded for copies on this first visit was more than £6. He appears to have changed much of his gold for Belgian notes, for when requested to pay something in advance, he drew out a large bundle of notes, threw them on the table and exclaimed, "There, take it out of that." One of the poses chosen by himself was so arranged that the right hand, on the finger of which was a large diamond ring, should be prominent. He was also taken with a quantity of Masonic insignia, which the "initiated" at once perceived from his photograph (which is reproduced by the Belgian News,) that most of the "jewels" pinned to the coat have no meaning whatever, and the presumption is that Deeming was not a Freemason. A second visit was paid to the photographer's a day or two later, when further copies, to the value of £2 10s, were ordered. Those were duly supplied, but "Lord Dunn" appears to have forgotten the little account on this occasion, for the sum STILL STANDS TO HIS DEBT on the books of the establishment. That the man had some misgivings on the subject of police pursuit in suggested by the following fact. Deeming was asked to sign his name and address in the photographer's books. He was, however, unwilling to give a specimen of his handwriting, and though posing as a member of English aristocracy, and a millionaire, he refused to sign, actually alleging that he "did not know how to write!" When courteously reminded that this was impossible, he said "I mean I am too ill to write." And this let him to give the young lady in charge of the books, in explanation of his supposed inability to write, some few details of his personal history. He told her that he had come over "FOR A LARK" to Antwerp, but that he had been obliged to feign illness, in order to account for his absence from home and his duties in the House of Lords! He said he had been already caught by his wife and her mother, as in their solicitude for his health, they had followed him to the Continent; and, he added, "As they are coming here to-morrow I must keep up the trick, you know, and that is why I am ill." There is evidence to show that the wife, murdered at Rainhill, did come over with one of her children, a very fine little fellow of the Lord Fauntleroy type, and the party were then often seen in the café near the station, where by their "flashy" conduct they were put down as members of the English "music hall clan" who frequent the [illegible] in that quarter of the city. Deeming seems induced to have been HAUNTED BY THE FEAR OF ARREST when staying at Antwerp, for though he had his rooms at an hotel, he made one or two attempts to find shelter in private houses. One day, a family, having relatives at Liverpool, were at tea when a stranger called. He gave the name of the gentleman engaged to the lady's cousin; and seemed to be so well up on the family history, that his statement was credited, and he was invited to tea and to spend the night in the house. But the man was not long able to keep up the delusion, and before the evening was over he committed himself so much that the gentleman grew suspicion and politely REQUESTED HIM TO LEAVE. Nothing daunted, Deeming immediately went to a cousin of his entertainer, also resident there, and now furnished with additional facts gleaned from his recent interview, he proclaimed his "cousinship" and demanded hospitality. But the other cousin had reached the house first, and Deeming found that the only hospitality offered was a "cold shoulder." Deeming paid a visit to the house of another English resident, alleging that he wished to have some information in regard to the scheme for making a tunnel under Scheldt. He said that not being able to speak French he was forced to apply to a fellow countryman for assistance in carrying out some project, and said that the English chaplain had recommended him to apply to the gentleman in question. This latter promised to try and obtain the information required, and requested by Deeming to call on the morrow. He rose to leave, but, catching sight of a photograph of a daughter of the house, Deeming took it up in his hand and exclaimed "FINE GIRL THAT!" This remark, so utterly vulgar and out of place, adduced the gentleman to ask the chaplain who the man was. The Rev Gentleman refused all knowledge of him or his visit. Consequently on the morrow the gentleman refused to see Deeming when he called. "Like his impudence?" exclaimed he in English to the wondering servant. He appears very soon afterwards to have left the city and returned to Hull on board the steamer [illegible].*

The Hull Daily Mail, May 23rd 1892, P. 3,

DEEMING GONE. EXECUTED THIS MORNING. HOW HE SPENT SUNDAY. PROTESTATION OF INNOCENCE. THE SCENE AT THE GALLOWS. At three minutes past ten o'clock this morning Frederick Deeming, the Windsor murderer, expiated his crime on the scaffold within the precincts of the Melbourne prison. Long before the hour appointed for the execution an immense crowd of spectators assembled outside the gates of the gaol, but only about a hundred, who hold cards of admission signed by the Sheriff, were allowed to enter the corridor where the majesty of the law was vindicated. No case since the notorious Kelly gang paid the penalty for their many crimes has aroused in so pronounced a degree the curiosity and interest of the Australian public. It was not surprising under the circumstances that the LAST SCENE IN THE CONVICT'S EVENTFUL LIFE should have attracted many sightseers to the streets in the neighbourhood of the gaol. The feeling everywhere manifested was of intense but subdued excitement. The large assemblage was most orderly. It consisted of tradesmen, shop assistants, clerks, artisans and others, who had snatched a half hour from business to see they knew what, but to be near the place where the tragedy was being enacted. As soon as the announcement came that the sentence had been carried out, there was a heavy sigh of relief, and the gathering slowly dispersed. There had been numerous applications to the Sheriff for permission to witness the execution, but most of them were refused. Amongst those who were granted permits were several

Mike Covell

of the lawyers who had been engaged in the case, members of the medical profession, and about 40 representatives of the Press. The condemned cell where the convict spent his last night is in CLOSE PROXIMITY TO THE SCAFFOLD. There had been no previous execution in the gaol for 17 years, so the melancholy event was more elaborate than is usually necessary in the Colonial prisons. The work in connection with the erection of the scaffold was carried out in the hearing of the convict, who now and again would give an involuntary start as the pound of carpenters' tools would fall upon is ears. There had been during the past four days a marked change in the demeanour of the convict. He appeared to realise fully the gravity of his position, and although he professed indifference at his approaching end, he frequently gave vent to his feelings in a way that indicated that his thoughts were dismayed that his mind was haunted by visions of the dreadful fate awaiting him. He spent Sunday, on the whole, tranquilly. He read his Bible occasionally, and devoted the greater part of the day to alternately writing and SKETCHING GIBBETS AND COFFINS. His mind appeared to dwell morbidly upon the details of his execution, in regard to which he made frequent inquiries. To these he generally received evasive answers.

MRS MATHER.

He asked to be introduced to the executioner, but the request, it is almost needless to say, was refused. In the evening, before he lay down to rest, it was thought that the doomed man desired to relieve his mind by an avowal of his guilt. The Chaplain (the Rev Mr Scott) was sent for, but on the arrival of the rev gentleman Deeming not only made no confession, but he persisted in declaring himself innocent of the murders laid to his charge. He, however, hinted that he intended to hand a statement to the Governor of the Gaol at the last moment, which might be made public after his death. During the early part of the night Deeming was restless, constantly TOSSING ABOUT ON HIS BED. His mind was evidently uneasy, but about three o'clock he sank into a calm repose, and slept until six o'clock in a moderately peaceful way. At seven o'clock the executioner, Jones, and his assistant, entered the cell and removed the prisoner's irons. Breakfast was then served him. He took a moderate meal, such as he had been accustomed to receive since his sentence was pronounced. During the repost he was conversed cheerfully with the officials, and declared that he was perfectly resigned to his fate. The Rev Mr Scott (prison chaplain) and the Rev Mr Whitton arrived at eight o'clock, but the former left early, and was not present at the execution. It is impossible to ascertain what gave rise to the rumour which was circulated on Saturday that the convict would attempt to take his own life, and this escape the ignominy of the scaffold. There was apparently no foundation for it, though a vigilant watch was kept over his actions, but nothing was observed in any of his movements from which the inference that he contemplated suicide could be drawn, and at breakfast ridiculed the idea, and denied that the thought had ever entered his head. A little before ten o'clock the doors of the cell were opened, and Sheriff Anderson appeared to demand the body. The executioners, who had been in the gaol overnight, entered and pinpointed the prisoner's arms in the usual manner, Deeming submitting with quiet composure to the operation. A moment of BREATHLESS SUSPENSE, and then the spectators in the corridor beheld the condemned man walking between two clergymen – the Rev Mr Whitton and the Rev Mr Forbes. He was pale and somewhat haggard looking. He glanced quickly and eagerly at the crowd, but his eyes rested on no particular face. He walked with a firm, steady step to the gallows, the Rev Mr Whitton reading the Church of England Service for the Burial of the Dead until the fatal bolt was drawn. When the rope was adjusted round the prisoner's neck, he was asked the usual question by the Governor of the Gaol, "At this last moment have you anything to say?" Deeming murmured, in almost inaudible tones, "Lord, receive my spirit," or, according to the Governor, "Lord' have mercy on my soul." He had all the morning been in a penitent frame of mind, and was not averse to receiving the religious consolation which he had declined some days previously. Indeed, he added that he felt he knew where he was going, and was quiet resigned to his fate. The adjustment of the white cap over the eyes of the condemned man was the work of but a few seconds. Then the bolt was drawn, and the victim was LAUNCHED INTO ETERNITY. The body, which weighed 10st, was dropped 10ft 3in, and hung *motionless at the end of the rope. There was scarcely a quiver or motion of the limbs. The neck was evidently broken. Thirty seconds afterwards a curtain was lowered, and the body was screened from view. The spectators then left. There were still thousands of people outside the gates, and a portion of the crowd, which had thus far behaved in a most orderly manner, began HOOTING AND RUSHING TOWARDS THE GAOL GATES, which were guarded by a body of police, who had some difficulty in keeping the people back. As to the expected confession the evidence is contradictory. It is said that a paper which Deeming had been preparing for several days has been placed in the hands of the Sheriff. The Governor of the gaol, however, states that the convict left no statement of any kind behind him. This is a surprising fact, for it was well known that the man had been occupied several days writing what he himself more than once referred to as a confession, which he intended to appear in the Melbourne Press. After the post mortem examination, which will be held to-day, the body will be buried in prison grounds. There will be no examination of the brain, the final refusal of the Government to permit the removal of the cerebral organ from the rest of the body having been communicated to the prison authorities on Saturday. The reason alleged by the Government for refusing to comment to the examination of Deeming's brain after death is that they see nothing in the circumstances of the convict's case to justify an exceptional course being taken. [REUTERS TELEGRAM.] MELBOURNE, MONDAY. – Deeming was executed by hanging at one minute past ten this morning. The condemned man was quiet resigned, and said he had made his peace with God. He again denied committing the Rainhill murders. An immense crowd collected around the prison, but there was no demonstration. The hangman wore a false white beard and his assistant a false black one. Deeming walked firmly to the scaffold, but appeared to tremble slightly. On the Sheriff asking if he had anything to say he replied faintly, "May the Lord receive my spirit." After the chaplain read the Burial Service the bolt was drawn, and no movement of the body was observed. It was declared that death had been instantaneous. INQUEST ON THE BODY. (REUTER'S TELEGRAM.) MELBOURNE, MONDAY. – At the inquest on Deeming's body the jury found that deceased had been hanged in accordance with law. There is reason to believe that Deeming has not made any full confession.*

The *Hull Daily Mail*, May 24th 1892, P. 4,

DEEMING! CONFESSION OF THE RAINHILL MURDERS. Melbourne, May 24th. – Deeming wrote a letter on Saturday last to the Rev. Mr. Scott, in which he said he should die a penitent sinner and a Christian. He said, further, that he never had intended to murder his poor Emily. Yesterday he said that if they were to say that he murdered his wife and family at Rainhill they would be lying, but the

Mike Covell

> *Rev. Mr. Witton states that this morning he broke down completely before leaving the cell, fell on his knees, and implored forgiveness for sending his wife and family into eternity unprepared. This is his first and only confession of the Rainhill murders, and was due to the fear that overcame him at the last moment. He appears to have left a statement which is being held back by officials. Mr. Witton says further that when Deeming was being removed to the cell, near the gallows, he shuddered at the sight of the machine on which he was so soon to die, and clung tremblingly to the warder for support.*

The Hull Daily Mail, August 25th 1892,

> *DEEMING'S WILL. The relatives of Deeming, the perpetrator of the Rainhill and Sydney murders, have received an intimation that the authorities of Australia have decided to carry out the instructions contained in the will made by Deeming in gaol, in Sydney, as to the disposal of his property. He leaves a gold albert to one of his brothers, but the remainder of his effects, including some land in Australia, he leaves to Mr. Lyle (his solicitor), Miss Rounseville, some gaol officials, and others.*

1893 – More Ripper Scares

The Hull Daily Mail, March 3rd 1893,

> *LATEST NEWS. A "JACK THE RIPPER" IN KENT. DIABOLICAL OUTRAGE ON A CHILD. MUTILATED ON THE ROAD SIDE. A terrible outrage, accompanied by mutilation of a most atrocious kind, was committed last evening in Ladywell-lane, Brockley, Kent, upon Nelly Price, a little girl aged 10, who now lies in her aunt's home at Crofton Park, in a sadly injured condition. About half past six in the evening she was sent on an errand to a public house, about 200 yards from her home, and on her way there was ACCOSTED IN A LONELY PART of the road by a well-dressed young man, who said he had lost his purse and would give her two pence if she would help him find it. She agreeing to do so, he sent her to an oil shop a short distance away to buy a candle. When she returned he took her down Ladywell-lane, a little used thoroughfare branching off from the main road leading to Lewisham. Then, pretending to look for the purse, he seized and attempted to outrage the child, who, however, struggled and regained her feet. He knocked her down, partially stunned her, and then stuffed a handkerchief into her mouth. Failing still to accomplish his foul purpose, he took a knife and deliberately cut open the lower part of her abdomen, after which he ran down the road and disappeared. His victim CRYING AND BLEEDING, was found by two boys, who assisted her to her aunt's house. Dr. Boothroyd was called in, and then*

> *the terrible nature of the girl's injuries became manifest. She now lies in a sad, if not dangerous, condition. So far no arrest has been made. The only description which the girl can give of her assailant is that he seemed about 24 years of age, and was well dressed in dark coat and light trousers. It is alleged that several girls and young woman have been molested in the neighbourhood.*

The Hull Daily Mail, March 6th 1893,

> *SUICIDE OF JACK THE RIPPER. An extraordinary affair has occurred at Monmouth. A tramp entered the house of a florist named Woodhouse, from whose wife he demanded alms, saying he was "Jack the Ripper." The woman screamed, and a gentleman named Pryce, who happened to be passing, went to her assistance. The man thereupon made off, and, being pursued by Mr. Pryce, made for the river, into which he leaped and sank almost immediately.*

The Hull Daily Mail, May 3rd 1893,

> *JACK THE RIPPER LETTER. The detective department at New Scotland Yard are engaged in making inquiries as to the author of a letter received on Monday by Mr. Mead, the magistrate at the Thames Police Court, signed "Jack the Ripper." The letter stated that Jack the Ripper had again arrived in London, and would shortly resume operations. On the epistle was the outline of a coffin, drawn with blood or red ink, and in a piece of tissue paper was a portion of dried liver.*

The Hull Daily Mail, July 4th 1893,

> *THE RIPPER MURDERS. REVIVAL OF AN OLD THEORY. The recent murder of a woman at Rotherhithe and the circumstances attending it have revived in Lisbon the old report that the "Jack the Ripper" murders were committed by a Portuguese sailor. One of the Lisbon papers, discussing this matter, says that prior to the Whitechapel crimes several women were found murdered in Lisbon under circumstances similar to those attending the murders in London. The Portuguese police failed, it adds, to discover any clue to the assassin, though there was in each case evidence which pointed to the probability of the man being a sailor.*

The Hull Daily Mail, October 10th 1893,

> *JONG AND "JACK THE RIPPER." A STRANGE STORY. A strange story is, says a Dalziel telegram, going round the sailors' quarters at Gibraltar, emanating apparently from certain seamen formerly employed in the Dutch trade, to the*

Mike Covell

> *effect that some years ago it was a matter of common belief among the crews of vessels trading between London and Rotterdam that Jack the Ripper was identical with a Dutch ship's surgeon named Jungh or Jong.*

The Hull Daily Mail, October 12th 1893 featured a report on the German Jack the Ripper scare.

The Hull Daily Mail, October 16th 1893 features a report on a Jack the Ripper scare in Amsterdam.

The Hull Daily Mail, April 16th 1894,

> SAVAGE LIVERPOOL. ATTEMPTED "JACK THE RIPPER" OUTRAGE. WOMEN MURDEROUSLY ATTACKED. *A shocking case, illustrating the state of terrorism and insecurity which prevails in the lower parts of Liverpool, occurred about midnight last evening, when a woman giving the name of Margaret Ward, and the address 8, Cartright-place, off Byrom-street, crawled into the Detective Office, Dale-street, suffering from a severe wound in the abdomen, inflicted only a short while before in her own house. The wretched woman came in assisted by a neighbour, and immediately collapsed, falling upon the floor in the public office meaning that she was bleeding to death. Her features, as well as those of her companion, were disfigured by recent severe ill usage. Whilst the ambulance was coming round from the hospital, where a telephone message was immediately sent, the woman who had been assisted stated that not long before Ward's house was forcibly broken into by A GANG OF ROUGHS, whom they believed to be associated with a house of bad repute recently opened in the neighbourhood. The injured woman's husband was first brutally assaulted, and forced to fly for his life, whilst the wife was knocked down and beaten, and as she lay on the floor one of the gang attacked her with a knife inflicting a gaping wound on the abdomen. Then, whilst the woman weltered in blood, they proceeded to smash the windows and furniture, having done which they decamped, no one daring to molest them. The injured woman was then assisted into the detention room, where, after having been seen by the surgeon, she was taken on the police ambulance to the Workhouse Infirmary. Whilst the case was in progress another woman came in suffering from severe stabs in the arm, inflicted in the street shortly before. She was sent to the nearest public dispensary to be attended to.*

The Hull Daily Mail, June 6th 1894,

> THREATENING TO "PLAY JACK THE RIPPER." MAD FREAK IN HULL. DANGEROUS WOMAN ARMED WITH A KNIFE. *Last night Mary Mylett, a*

middle aged woman, was causing a crowd to assemble in a terrace in Tomlinson-street. On being told by P.C. Tavish (44) to go into her house she told him to mind his own business, and spat in his face. Tavish procured a handcart, and took her to the Gordon-street Police Station. This morning she had to face Mr. Twiss at the Police Court. – Defendant, when Tavish had given his evidence, called out, excitedly, "I have got a lump on my head that [illegible] (Tavish) made with his fist." – P. C. Hall, who took the charge at the Police station, said the defendant raved like a maniac for some hours after being put in a cell. She was made drunk. – Defendant (scornfully): Maniac! You can only give me two months, and it will do me good. You can give me six if you like. – Kate Anderson, a widow, and defendant's sister, said that last night defendant came to her house drunk. She had a large knife in her hand, and she said she would cut witness's throat and would play "Jack the Ripper." She broke nine squares of glass in witness's window, and broke the door, with the knife and her hand. The damage done was 6s 6d. – Defendant, with a laugh: You can let me off if you like, and I will go to work. – Mr. Twiss imposed a fine of 20s and costs on each charge, and ordered defendant to pay 6s 6d damage, or in default two month's imprisonment.

Mary Mylett:

It appears that Mary Mylett has a long colourful history in Hull with numerous offences and charges under her belt. The earliest can be found in the England and Wales Criminal Registers, 1791-1892 [HO27, Piece 175, Page 264] which states,

Name: Mary Mylett, Date of Trial: June 29 1876, Trial Year: 1876, Location of Trial: Yorkshire, East Riding, England, Sentence: 2 Months Imprisonment, Crime: Larceny

The charge made it into the local press, when *The Hull Packet and East Riding Times*, dated June 30th 1876, featured a report on the 18 year old who, had been caught shoplifting on May 24th 1876. The case also made it into *The York Herald*, dated July 1st 1876. On September 29th 1876, *The Hull Packet and East Riding Times,* featured a report on Mary Mylett stealing a watch, but with insufficient evidence the case was dropped.

England and Wales Criminal Registers, 1791-1892 [HO27, Piece 178, Page 231] Name: Mary Mylett, Date of Trial: Jan 4 1877, Trial Year: 1877, Location of Trial: Yorkshire, East Riding, England, Sentence: 8 Months Imprisonment, Crime: Larceny from the prison, one previous conviction

Mike Covell

The York Herald, dated July 30th 1878, reported that Mary Mylett had appeared at Hull charged with stealing a tobacco pouch from a man named James Murray, but once again there was insufficient evidence and the case was dropped.

England and Wales Criminal Registers, 1791-1892 [HO27, Piece 181, Page 301] Name: Mary Mylett, Date of Trial: Oct 17 1878, Trial Year: 1878, Location of Trial: Yorkshire, East Riding, England, Sentence: 8 Months Imprisonment, Crime: Larceny from the person, one previous conviction

England and Wales Criminal Registers, 1791-1892 [HO27, Piece 181, Page 301] Name: Mary Mylett, Date of Trial: Oct 17 1878, Trial Year: 1878, Location of Trial: Yorkshire, East Riding, England, Sentence: No Bill, Acquitted, Crime: Larceny from the person

The Hull Packet and East Riding Times, dated January 24th 1879, featured a report on Mary Mylett, which stated that she had assaulted a police officer named P.C. Smith (83) in Waterhouse-lane. It stated that Mylett was a known prostitute and had previously appeared before the court 15 times! She was sent to prison for three months.

The York Herald, dated July 22nd 1881, featured a report on Mary Mylett, claiming she had been drunk and disorderly with one other. It was stated that she had caused criminal damage and assaulted a police officer.

Tomlinson-street:

Tomlinson-street was situated in West Hull off Selby-street, which ran between Anlaby-road and St George's-road. Tomlinson-street has today been replaced by Doncaster-street. The original-street ran from Selby-street, which stood to the north, and Heron-street, which stood to the west. Several terraces came off the street including Emma's Terrace, on the western side, and St Andrew's and Lily's-terraces which stood on the eastern side. The entire street stood approximately 350 feet from one end to the other. Tomlinson-street stood approximately 0.5 miles from Gordon-street and walking the distance would have taken around 10 minutes.

P.C. Tavish (44):

Police Constable Willie McTavish was sworn in on March 7th 1894. He was awarded the badge number 44.

1901 Census, shows McTavish residing in Hull on Barnstable-street, Class RG13, P4506, F7, P6				
Willie McTavish	Head	34	Police Constable
Annie McTavish	Wife	35	
Florence McTavish	Dau	17	Scholar
James Rider	Boarder	36	Joiner

McTavish passed away in 1918, his death entry reads,
Name: Willie McTavish, Birth Date: abt 1868, Date of Registration: Oct- Nov- Dec 1918, Age at Death: 50, Registration District: Sculcoates, Inferred County: Yorkshire East Riding, Vol: 9d, Page: 456

Gordon-street Police Station:

Gordon-street Police Station is was built in 1885 at the corner of Redbourne-street and Gordon-street. In the 1930's some extension were made but these were destroyed in 2008. The building is mainly yellow bricks with red banding, with stone details, many of which still exist today. For some years it stood empty but in 2008 it was renovated using part of the old frontage and a more modern rear construction. *Bulmer's 1892 Trade Directory of Hull* lists John Nevile Drury as the resident sergeant at the station. For many historians the building has one claim to fame. When the popular British band, The Beatles, played in Hull at the ABC, they were escorted to the police station after the show to keep them safe!

P. C. Hall:

Given the time frame the only Police Constable with the surname Hall serving in the Hull Police at that time was William Ambrose Hall. He was sworn in on July 18th 1888 and was assigned badge number 73.

1891 Census, 42 Mayfield-street, Sculcoates, Hull, Class RG12, P3928, F34, P20, GSU6099038

Mike Covell

Francis Hall	*Head*	*31*	
Mary Jane Hall		28	
Francis Hall		2	
Charles Hall		1	
William Hall	Boarder	35	Policeman
Florence J. Foster		20	

Another version appeared in *The Yorkshire Herald, and The York Herald*, dated June 7th 1894,

A DANGEROUS WOMAN. – At the Hull Police court, yesterday, Mary Myllett was charged with being disorderly in Tomlinson-street. On being told by P.C. Tavish to go into her house, she told him to mind his own business and spat in his face. Tavish procured a handcart, and took her to the Gordon-street Police Station. – Kate Anderson, a widow and defendant's sister, said Mylett entered her house with a large knife and threatened to cut witness's throat. Instead, she broke nine squares of glass in the window. – A fine of 40s, and costs was imposed.

The Hull Daily Mail, September 25th 1894 features a report on Jack the Ripper in the Tyrol

The Hull Daily Mail, November 23rd 1894 features a report on Jack the Ripper in France.

The Hull Daily Mail, November 26th 1894,

ANOTHER LONDON MYSTERY. YOUNG WOMAN MURDERED AND MUTILATED. A young woman, apparently about 20 years of age, was found murdered early this morning in a quiet part of Holland Park-road, Kensington.

The deceased's throat had been cut almost from ear to ear, and the constable who made the discovery found near the body a walking stick which it is supposed the murderer left behind in his anxiety to escape. No cries were heard, and the crime is at present a complete mystery. Later inquiries tend to show that the deceased belonged to the unfortunate class, and it is now stated that the policeman who found the body previously heard a woman screaming, and that this was what attracted him to the spot. The police have no clue to the murderer beyond the walking stick, which is made of cherry wood. The deceased woman, who is of a dark complexion, was not well clad, and wore two common dress rings on the third finger of the left hand. – A woman residing near the scene of the murder states that she was roused from the bed shortly after midnight, and, on looking through the window, saw a dark bearded, tall elderly man leaning against the wall of the house opposite, with a woman on either side of him. They were all wrangling. The woman retired to bed again, and a quarter of an hour later was awoke by fearful screams and the tramp of horses hoofs, the murder having apparently been committed and discovered within a few minutes after she looked through the window. A later telegram states that the woman murdered at Kensington has been identified as Augusta Dudley, (30), of 36, St. Clement's-road, Notting-dale. She was a prostitute, and was identified by another woman living in the same house. No arrests have yet been made, nor has any further clue been obtained which would enable the police to track her murderer. Deceased's landlady says she last saw her alive at eight o'clock on Sunday night, when he went for a walk. Deceased, who was unmarried, leaves behind a three year old baby, which the landlady is in the habit of minding during the mother's absence. The landlady describes deceased as a needlewoman. IS IT "JACK THE RIPPER"? There appears to be no suggestion that the present murder is one of the "Ripper" crimes, but it is somewhat singular that, as in the "Ripper" murders, so in this instance, the knife was drawn across the woman's throat from left to right. The only difference in this case is that the knife has entered the throat a little more to the left, and has apparently been inserted with even more savagery.

Augusta Dawes, aka Agusta Dudley:

The Times, dated December 11th 1894 featured the following,

THE MURDERS IN THE WEST-END. THE HOLLAND-PARK-ROAD CRIME. *Colonel Saunderson, M.P., accompanied by Mr Llewellyn Saunderson, the father of the young man who is charged with the murder, was present during the enquiry.*

Mike Covell

[The report goes on to state] *Francis Rollison, one of the masters at Eastcote, Hampton Wick, said Reginald Saunderson was one of the pupils there, and he was well acquainted with his writing. He had no doubt that the letter and envelope produced, and dated November 27, 1894, had been written by Saunderson. Mr Avory - The letter is signed "Jack the Ripper," and is addressed to "The Police Station, Kensington, London, W., England." The witness went on to give details as to Saunderson's escape from Hampton Wick, and as to his possession of a knife similar to that found.*

Christening:
Name: Augusta Louisa Dawes, Gender: Female, Christening Date: December 9th 1866, Christening Place: Bristol, Gloustershire, England, Father's Name: Charles James Dawes, Mother's Name: Caroline.

1871 Census, Class RG10, P2557, F61, P10, GSU835265
5 Abbots home Place, Bristol, Gloucestershire, England

Charles J Dawes	Head	43	Wine Merchant Manager
Caroline Dawes	Wife	42	
Ada A Dawes	Dau	14	Scholar
Frank W Dawes	Son	8	Scholar
Florence E Dawes	Dau	6	Scholar
Agusta L Dawes	Dau	4	Scholar
Frederick Hiles	Lodger	21	Outfitters assistant

1881 Census, Class RG11, P2486, F122, P37, GSU1341598
13 Clarence House, Bristol, Gloucestershire, England

Charles James Dawes	Head	52	Commercial Traveller (Brewery)
Caroline Jane Dawes	Wife	49	
Charles Henry Dawes	Son	24	Clerk
Frank William Dawes	Son	18	Assistant to Wine Merchant
Augusta Louisa Dawes	Dau	14	Scholar B. Bristol
James Ernest Barter	Lodger	37	Lt Royal Navy
Ada Alice Barter	Lodger	24	James's Wife

Augusta Dawes death:
Name: Augusta Louise Dawes, Estimated Birth Year: abt 1865, Date of Registration: Oct- Nov- Dec- 1894, Age at Death: 29, Registration District: Kensington, Inferred County: London, Vol: 1a, Page: 92

The Hull Daily Mail, December 7th 1894,

THE WHITECHAPEL MURDER. THE ACCUSED INSANE. George Henry Matthews, the man charged with the murder of a woman in Whitechapel, was to have appeared before the magistrate in Worship-street to-day, but a further adjournment was asked for, it being stated that the prisoner had seriously assaulted several warders in Holloway Gaol. An opinion is expressed that the magisterial examination will not be concluded, but that Matthews will be removed to an asylum.

The Hull Daily Mail, February 12th 1895,

Mike Covell

> ANOTHER "JACK THE RIPPER" SENSATION. WOMAN SERIOUSLY STABBED. ARREST OF THE ASSAILANT. *At Worship-street Police Court, London, yesterday, a man named Grant was remanded on a charge of wounding in the abdomen Alice Graham, in Butter-street, Spitalfields, early on Sunday morning. A statement made in connection with the case gave a very serious aspect to the charge, and interest in the "Jack the Ripper" murders has been revived by facts alleged to have come into the possession of the police. A knife of a most peculiar pattern, marked with blood, was found 30 yards from the spot where the accused was found stooping over the woman, and there were clots of blood along the pavement between the injured woman and the place where the knife was found.*

The Hull Daily Mail, March 27th 1895,

> ONE OF "JACK THE RIPPER" SERIES. TEN YEARS FOR SEAMAN. *At the Central Criminal Court this afternoon, William Grant, seaman, was found guilty of feloniously wounding Alice Graham, whom he had accompanied to a house in Spitalfields, and then seriously stabbed her in the abdomen, the crime bearing a strange resemblance to the "Jack the Ripper series." Prisoner was sentenced to 10 years penal servitude.*

The Hull Daily Mail, April 10th 1895 features a Jack the Ripper scare in the Pola de Lena district of Austria. A woman by the name of Rosa Fernandez was found with her head severed and many dagger wounds in her chest, and her lower body mutilated. Another girl was also a attacked by a man described as a foreigner, with fair hair, and dressed as a miner.

The Hull Daily Mail, April 29th 1896,

> JACK THE RIPPER. HAS HE BEEN EXECUTED? *An impression, says a New York telegram, based on an eleventh hour confession and other evidence, prevails that Carl Feigenbaum, who was executed at Sing Sing yesterday, the real murderer of the New York outcast, nick-named Shakespeare, is possibly Jack the Ripper, of Whitechapel notoriety. The proofs, however, are far from positive.*

> *Carl Feigenbaum:*
>
> William Sanford Lawton, who was Feigenbaum's own solicitor, actually him forward as a viable suspect shortly after his execution on April 27th 1896. Whilst

the press had a field day with the claims, there was little evidence, and even Lawton's partner, and Feigenbaum's co-lawyer, Hugh Owen Pentecost, distanced himself from the claims. Lawton later shot himself on February 13th 1896. In more recent years he was proposed as a suspect in Trevor Marriott's Jack the Ripper: The 21st Century Investigation.

Further Reading
Jack the Ripper: The 21st Century Investigation, Trevor Marriott, Blake, 2005
Jack the Ripper: The 21st Century Investigation, Trevor Marriott, Blake, 2007
The Evil Within: The World's Worst Serial Killers, Trevor Marriott, 2008

The Hull Daily Mail, October 13th 1897 features an article on Vacher and his crimes, where he was named as "The Southern Jack the Ripper."

__Joseph Vacher:__

Joseph Vacher, who was born on November 16th 1869, was known in the press as "*The French Ripper*" or "*The South East Ripper.*" His crimes first appeared in the British press in 1897 when the press were reporting tales of "The French Ripper." *The Pall Mall Gazette*, dated October 18th 1897, gave an overview of Vacher's deeds, and stated that he had killed between 18 and 20, and had allegedly told *The Echo de Paris*, that he had more revelations to reveal! Vacher tried to plead insanity, but on October 28th 1898, he was sentenced to death and was executed by guillotine on December 31st 1898. According to the *Lloyd's Weekly Newspaper*, dated January 1st 1899, Vacher refused to listen to mass, claiming that "he would celebrate it with Jesus Christ himself!" The same newspaper also states that Vacher failed to move to the scaffold, and was subsequently dragged!

The Hull Daily Mail, February 25th 1898,

The statement that the Scotland Yard officials knew of the arrest and death of "Jack the Ripper" and of the whereabouts of the murderer of Miss Camp has received an emphatic denial from the police headquarters.

The Hull Daily Mail, March 8th 1898 states that the French Jack the Ripper, Vacher, is now writing his memoirs.

The Hull Daily Mail, October 12th 1898,

An experienced officer at Scotland Yard inclines to the opinion that Jack the Ripper was a Lascar sailor, who came to London at pretty frequent intervals.

Mike Covell

The Hull Daily Mail, November 28th 1898,

> TWO SISTERS. WOMAN'S INHUMANITY TO WOMAN. STABBED IN WHITECHAPEL. A shocking murder was committed shortly after midnight on Saturday in Dorset-street, Spitalfields. The house in which it was perpetrated is the one in which Mary Kelly was murdered and mutilated by the notorious "Jack the Ripper" ten years ago. Among the occupants were a man named David Roberts and his wife Elizabeth, aged 36, who occupied the back room on the first floor. For some time past Mrs. Roberts' sister, Kate Marshall – married, but separated from her husband – has also lived there. About half past twelve o'clock some of the other occupants of the house heard ominous sounds of a quarrel proceeding from Roberts' apartments. A little later a man named Amery, who lives on the main floor, heard a knock at his door, and opening it he discovered Roberts struggling on the landing with Marshall, a tall, powerful woman, who was brandishing a formidable looking knife, the blade and handle of which were covered with blood. Nearby Mrs. Roberts was leaning against the wall, her bodice torn open, and blood streaming from a fearful wound in her right breast. It seems that the two sisters had been in each other's company during the evening at a neighbouring public house, and returned home together, Kate Marshall going into the room of her sister, whose husband from all accounts had already retired to bed. This quarrel was occasioned, or aggravated, it is stated, by a taunting reference to the fact that one of the woman – Kate Marshall – had recently emerged from a term of imprisonment for using the knife upon her husband. Marshall, it would seem, in a fit of ungovernable rage, suddenly, knife in hand, made a savage attack on the other, and delivered one or more blows with such vigour upon her breasts that the poor woman almost instantly staggered a few yards out and fell dying on the landing. The murdered woman is spoken of in the neighbourhood in which she lived as hard working and industrious. Her sister on the contrary, bears a very indifferent character. It is stated that she has already undergone several terms of imprisonment for stabbing – viz, 18 months for wounding a blind man, another term for stabbing her father, and five years penal servitude for stabbing her husband.

The Hull Daily Mail, November 30th 1898 features a report on a Ripper scare in Amsterdam.

The Tamworth Herald, December 24th 1898,

> HULL "JACK THE RIPPER" RESPITED. The Governor of York Gaol has received a message from the Home Secretary respiting George Stoner, lying under sentence of death for the murder of Emily Hall, of Hull. The Governor at once

> *communicated the news to Stoner, who appeared greatly relieved. Stoner took the woman, an "unfortunate," to a house, and stabbed her repeatedly, Mr. Justice Darling saying in passing sentence, that the crime was too awful for words.*

George Stoner and Emily Hall:

A little after four o'clock on the afternoon of Friday July 22nd when George Stoner arrived at number 1 Princes-row, a small entry off Dock-street, in Hull City centre. The property was owned by a German lady named Mrs. Elizabeth Shikoffsky and as Stoner knocked on the door, with his companion, Mrs. Shikoffsky opened it and allowed them access to a room, which was paid for in advance. At about half past five the man came down from their room and informed Mrs. Shikoffsky that his partner needed to rest and that he would return, but never did. After approximately an hour Mrs. Shikoffsky went upstairs to find Emily Hall, who was apparently asleep on the bed fully clothed. Mrs. Shikoffsky left the room and went back downstairs, but a while later returned to check on Hall. Hall was awake and asked for help with her clothes, so Mrs. Shikoffsky helped undo her corset, but discovered that her skirt was covered in blood. Blood also covered the bed sheets and floor. A cab was called for and Emily Hall was removed to the Hull General Infirmary. Sadly, she passed away from her injuries at five minutes past midnight. It was subsequently discovered that a bar of soap had been pushed high up into Hall's vagina. George Stoner was well known in Hull and was subsequently caught and charged with the murder, before being removed to Parliament-street Police station. The City Analyst checked on the clothing work by Stoner and discovered blood in the right pocket and on the sleeve of the right arm of his shirt. Eventually the trial began at York Assizes and the Jury took only 30 minutes to find Stoner guilty of Hall's murder. The Judge sent them back to reconsider after the Jury stated that Stoner was guilty of committing grievous bodily harm, but without premeditation." The Jury returned again and after ten minutes found Stoner guilty of murder, but with a recommendation to mercy. The Judge passed the sentence of death, but the next day decided against this bearing in mind the Jury's inability to return a verdict, and on December 19th 1898 a reprieve was delivered and Stoner was sentenced to penal servitude for life!

Throughout the trial the British National press featured several stories regarding the case, nationally the *Lloyd's Weekly Newspaper*, dated July 31st 1898, was one of the earliest to publish details of the story, and especially the victim, Emily Hall, who it was stated was aged 37 years old.

The Aberdeen Weekly Journal, dated August 12th 1898, and *The Dundee Courier and Argus*, also dated August 12th 1898, stated that the George Stoner evidence was too revolting for publication. Bearing in mind that these newspapers had earlier covered the atrocities in Whitechapel! *The Lloyd's Weekly Newspaper*, dated August 14th 1898, *The Aberdeen Weekly Journal*, dated August 17th 1898, and *The North Eastern Daily Gazette*, dated November 30th 1898, featured several reports on the Grand Jury, at the York Assizes, and how they had eventually found a true bill against George Stoner, aged 35, who it was claimed was an engraver, and who is indicted for the wilful murder of Emily Hall at Hull on the 23rd July 1898. *The Reynolds's Newspaper*, dated December 11th 1898, stated that George Stoner's execution will take place on December 20th 1898, and the *Trewman's Exeter Flying Post or Plymouth and Cornish Advertiser*, dated December 17th 1898, George Stoner has been respited. *The North Eastern Daily Gazette*, dated December 19th 1898, featured a short statement that claimed George Stoner will be sentenced to life.

George Stoner's birth was registered thus:
Birth: Name George Stoner, Date of Registration: Jul- Aug- Sep- 1864, Registration District: Hull, Inferred County: Yorkshire, East Riding, Vol: 9d, Page: 189

George Stoner appears in the 1901 Census, at Portland Convict Establishment, Dorset, Weymouth. [1]

| George Stoner | 36 | Prisoner | Engraving Metal | B. abt 1865 Hull |

The 1911 Census, shows George Stoner at the H.M. Prison, County Gaol and Convict Prison, Maidstone, Kent thus: [2]

| George Stoner | 46 | Prisoner | Engineer Fitter | B. abt 1865 Hull |

Emily Hall's death is registered thus:
Name: Emily Hall, Estimated Birth Year: abt 1861, Year of Registration: 1898, Sub District: Humber, Region: Yorkshire, Ref: HUM/3A/22

Another version of her death is registered thus:

Name: Emily Hall, Estimated Birth Year: abt 1861, Date of Registration: Jul-Aug- Sep- 1898, Age at Death: 37, Registration District: Hull, Inferred County: Yorkshire, East Riding, Vol: 9d, Page: 175

It should be mentioned that no other newspaper report linked George Stoner with either Whitechapel or "Jack the Ripper."

References and Further Reading:
1. 1901 Census, Class RG13, P1997, F111, P27
2. 1911 Census, Class RG14, P4159
Murder and Crime – Kingston Upon Hull, Douglas Wynn, Tempus, 2008
The Wharncliffe A-Z of Yorkshire Murder, Stephen Wade, Wharncliffe Books, 2007
Yorkshire Murders and Misdemeanours, Stephen Wade, Amberley, 2009

1900's

The Hull Daily Mail, May 11th 1900 features a report on a Ripper scare in Paris.

The Hull Daily Mail, August 3rd 1900,

A correspondent records the interesting fact that the late King of Italy was fascinated by the horror of the series of murders committed years ago in Whitechapel, and ascribed to the legendary Jack the Ripper. So deeply was King Hubert impressed that when he came incognito to London in 1892, he made a point of visiting Buck's-row, Mitre-square, Dorset-street, and the other scenes of the crimes.

The Hull Daily Mail, May 28th 1901,

IN "JACK THE RIPPER'S" HAUNTS. ANOTHER WHITECHAPEL MURDER. WOMAN STABBED TO DEATH. Our London correspondent telegraphs this morning: - Within a stone's throw of the house in which Mary Kelly was murdered and mutilated in November, 1888 (when police and public alike were astounded by that extraordinary series of atrocities known as "The Ripper Murders"), a tragedy of somewhat similar character occurred in the early hours of Sunday morning. Dorset-street, Spitalfields, the scene of the murder, consists of dingy shops and common lodging houses, frequented by the poorest denizens of Whitechapel. At present the police are mystified by the peculiar circumstances surrounding the tragedy. The cosmopolitan character, too, of the population,

Mike Covell

> *makes the work of the investigation all the more trying. It is clear, however, that on Saturday night a woman, named Annie Austin (28), with a man not yet identified, occupied a cubicle at Dorset-street. On Sunday morning the woman was found alone, suffering from dreadful wounds, evidently inflicted by a sharp instrument. She was removed to the London Hospital, and died early yesterday morning. The police only became aware of the murder [illegible] hospital authorities, and the criminal thus obtained several hours start before the work of the investigation commenced. In conversation with a Press representative early this morning the manager of the lodging house referred to the above said he had 72 cubicles under his control. He was on duty all night. Nobody could leave till he opened the door at five in the morning. A regular female lodger first informed him she heard groans proceeding from a room on the second floor. He found a big, strapping woman in great pain, just able to say, "I am bad; what can I do? Help me." With the assistance of his wife he helped to dress her, but she was difficult to manage, owing to her sufferings. So far there have been no arrests.*

Mary Ann Austin:

It has been written that Mary Ann Austin was born in or around 1873.
Whilst no one was charged for the murder of Mary Ann Austin, there were suspects, the first of which was her estranged husband, William Austin, Daniel Sullivan, who was the brother in law of William Crossingham, who owned the lodging house, and later George Neating. No charges were brought against any of them.

Mary Ann Austin's death was registered thus:
Name: Mary Ann Austin, Estimated Birth Year: abt 1873, Date of Registration: Apr- May- Jun- 1901, Age at Death: 28, Registration District: Whitechapel, Inferred County: London, Vol: 1c, Page: 196

Further Reading:
Case File is held at the National Archives, Ref MEPO 3/162
The Complete Jack the Ripper A-Z, Paul Begg, Martin Fido, Keith Skinner, John Blake, 2010

The Hull Daily Mail, February 21st 1902 features a report that Jack the Ripper might be at work in San Francisco.

Newspapers from Hull Volume 2

1920's

The Hull Daily Mail, March 5th 1921,

> A HUNTER OF "JACK THE RIPPER." Lieut. – Colonel Sir Henry Smith, K.C.B., a former Commissioner of the City of London Police, who has died at Edinburgh, in his 86th year, rose from the rank of constable to that of commissioner. He was educated at Edinburgh Academy, and qualified as a chartered accountant. After serving in a Scottish county police as a constable, he went to London in 1879, and six years later became Chief Superintendent of the City of London Police, becoming Commissioner in 1890, and resigning that office in 1901. During his professional career Sir Henry Smith was associated with some outstanding historical cases, including the hunting of the famous "Jack the Ripper."

Henry Smith:

Henry Smith wrote in his memoirs, *From Constable to Commissioner: The Story of Sixty Years Most of them Misspent*, that Jack the Ripper "*...completely beat me and every Police officer in London.*" and that "*...I have no more idea now where he lived than I had twenty years ago.*" He also claimed that at one point "*....There is no man living who knows as much of those murders as I do....*" He also claimed that one evening he was "*....within five minutes of the perpetrator....*" His recollections came with some criticism though, and research shows that Smith was nowhere near the murders to be close enough to be five minutes away he also claims that the Mitre-square murder of Catherine Eddowes came after the Miller's-court murder of Mary Jane Kelly making his recollections less than reliable.

The Hull Daily Mail, July 27th 1922 features a report on a French Jack the Ripper scare.

The Hull Daily Mail, September 23rd 1922 features a report that the collection of Mr. George Sims is up for sale and includes "Jack the Ripper" photographs.

The Hull Daily Mail, October 26th 1923,

> THE WHITECHAPEL HORRORS. *Mr. William Le Quex has come forward with another theory about the infamous Whitechapel murders that filled England with sensation and horror in the later eighties of last century. The victims were all East*

Mike Covell

> End daughters of joy, whose bodies were fiendishly mutilated, but the author was never brought to justice. Many rumours have got around about these mysterious London crimes. It was said at one time that the murderer was a mad doctor, who has since died in an asylum. Again it was whispered that the murderer was a degenerate offspring of a great family, who came to a violent end in the toughest hinterland of the Empire. According to Mr. Le Quex he was a mad Russian doctor, formerly in a maternity hospital, who had his accomplices a Russian Secret Service agent, member of an East End anarchist club, and a disreputable of tailoress of Jewish descent. Mr. Le Quex claims to have seen official documents, written by the notorious Rasputin, the monk who ruined the Russian royal family and helped submerge Russia, giving intimate details of the Jack the Ripper crimes.

The Hull Daily Mail, December 5th 1924,

> In contrast with the new Chief of C.I.D., ex inspector Sagar, who has just died at Brighton, stepped straight from the hospital wards, where he was studying medicine, into a plain clothes detective's mufti. He was in charge of the Jack the Ripper case, and always held that the murderer, suspected by the police, died in an asylum.

The Hull Daily Mail, January 27th 1925,

> The Jack the Ripper terrorised the East End of London from Christmas 1887 until July 1889. Although a child was murdered in Hull in 1888, we do not know that Jack the Ripper ever terrorised Hull and district.

The Hull Daily Mail, November 15th 1929 German Jack the Ripper

The Hull Daily Mail, November 16th 1929 German Jack the Ripper

The Hull Daily Mail, November 20th 1929 German Jack the Ripper

The Hull Daily Mail, November 21st 1929 German Jack the Ripper

1930's

During the 1930's there was a popular greyhound that ran many of the Hull circuits named "*Jack the Ripper.*" As such a large number of articles were devoted to the animal which I have chosen not to include here.

The Hull Daily Mail, October 25th 1930,

> WHEN JACK THE RIPPER ROAMED. QUEEN VICTORIA'S ATTACK ON THE POLICE. Queen Victoria is revealed in the role of a sleuth, critical of the police and with her own ideas of the manner in which the hunt for Jack the Ripper should have been conducted, in the volume of her letters, edited by George Earle Buckle, published to-day by John Murray. The Queen was in residence at Balmoral Castle, where she was kept informed of the activities of the police, when another murder took place. "This new more ghastly murder," read like Marquis of Salisbury, "shows the absolute necessity for some very decided action. All of these courts must be lit, and our detectives improved. They are not what they should be." QUEEN'S SUGGESTIONS. "The Queen fears," she wrote a few days later, "that the detective department is not as efficient as it might be. No doubt the recent murders in Whitechapel were committed in circumstances which made detection very difficult and the Queen thinks that in the small area where these horrible crimes have been committed, a great number of detectives might be employed, and that every possible suggestion might be carefully examined and, if practical, followed. "Have the cattle boats and passenger boats been examined? Has any investigation been made as to the number of single men occupying rooms to themselves? The murderer's clothes must be saturated with blood and must be kept somewhere. Is there sufficient surveillance at night?" The effect of this caustic comment and advice is not revealed; we may be sure that Queen Victoria would ensure that it was not ignored.

The Hull Daily Mail, January 24th 1931 features a report on The Blackheath Ripper.

The Hull Daily Mail, April 11th 1931 German Jack the Ripper trial.

The Hull Daily Mail, April 13th 1931 German Jack the Ripper trial.

The Hull Daily Mail, May 7th 1932,

> SOME PEOPLE WILL BELIEVE ANYTHING. "Strong minded men, who would laugh if you accused them of superstition, lend a ready ear to the share pusher or believe that "perpetual motion" is a commercial position..." BY SIR MAX PEMBERTON. Many years ago, in the affrighting days of the Jack the Ripper crimes, the police made a close investigation into the cult of Black Magic in this country. The results were a poor tribute to the onward march of that incredulity which education should foster. One publisher, it appeared, made a handsome living by catering to the mad devotees of the blasphemous faith. To the same mind the fact would appear incredible, yet Scotland Yard, I imagine, could speak of the

Mike Covell

> *same "faith" to-day and its pursuit by the degenerates whom no country would willingly harbour.*

Sir Max Pemberton had previously written about Jack the Ripper and the Black Magic angle in a book about a true crime group that would meet in London and discuss cases with each other. The following snippet is taken from a lengthy article that appeared in *The Hull Daily Mail*, dated May 7th 1932, and once again touching on Jack the Ripper and Black Magic.

Stop the Press – Editors Comments

The creation of this book has been a long and often difficult road, but I hope you appreciate and enjoy the end result. Here, in one volume, is a collection of newspaper reports that you can read from start to finish, putting yourself into the terrible shoes of those in Hull, Whitechapel, and other locales during the "Autumn of Terror," or you can refer to over and over again as a point of reference for future research. Whilst researching and transcribing the articles I have learnt of many new letters to the police and the press, and names of witnesses and suspects that have often been overlooked, as well as crimes and criminals who have fell by the wayside in favour of what many refer to as "Celebrity Suspects," such as Lewis Carroll, Queen Victoria, and Walter Sickert. I have also seen and witnessed more scares and scandals associated with the case, and names that are rarely mentioned in connection with the case. I hope you, the reader, enjoy reading this volume as much as I have enjoyed researching and writing it, and hopefully, among the column inches, there is something of special interest that inspires you to read and research the case further.

Mike Covell

Appendix I - The 1900 Hull Ripper Scare

Researching the "Jack the Ripper" case in relation to Hull does often throw up a few surprises, but the biggest case to hit the headlines in conjunction with Hull was the 1900 Jack the Ripper scare. I was first made aware of the case just a few months prior to the 2010 Jack the Ripper Conference, held at the King's Stores in the East End of London, where I was due to lecture on Hull's connection to the case. I made several visits to the Hull History Centre and spent many hours going through newspaper reports on microfilm. Alongside this search was another search made on the 19th Century Newspaper's Online Archive, as well as several online newspaper resources both nationally and internationally. The case also gained my attention due to the locations mentioned, and the fact that the same police officer who brought Frederick Bailey Deeming to Hull was also involved in the case. One of the first stories I came across was featured in *The Dundee newspaper, Courier and Argus*. The report was published on Tuesday November 27th 1900, and stated,

> *"JACK THE RIPPER" SCARE AT HULL. The Hull police have received information to the effect that four women were stabbed on Saturday evening while walking along the road. One of them reports that she was stabbed by a man who came up behind her. She was taken to the infirmary, where within two hours three other cases were reported. In each case it was a woman who had been stabbed on the thigh. None of the woman can give a clear description of the assailant.*

> **"JACK THE RIPPER" SCARE AT HULL.**
>
> The Hull police have received information to the effect that four women were stabbed on Saturday evening while walking along the road. One of them reports that she was stabbed by a man who came up behind her. She was taken to the infirmary, where within two hours three other cases were reported. In each case it was a woman who had been stabbed on the thigh. None of the women can give a clear description of the assailant.

Typical announcement regarding a "Jack the Ripper" scare at Hull. Image Copyright Mike Covell.

With this new piece of information I decided to re-visit the Hull History Centre, which was closed and under construction when I uncovered the report, and found the following,

The Hull Daily Mail published the following, on Monday November 26th 1900,

> STABBING IN HULL STREETS. FIVE CASES: REMARKABLE OUTRAGES. No less than five cases of stabbing in the street were reported to the Hull police on Saturday night. In one case the wife of Thomas Broadwell, coal porter, residing in Fawcett-terrace, Derby-street, was walking along Beverley-road about 5.45 on Saturday afternoon, along with her friend, a young woman named Edith Hardy. When near Trafalgar-street a man walked by the left side of Miss Hardy and stabbed her in the thigh. He ran down Norfolk-street. Mrs. Broadwell took Miss Hardy to her house, but on realising the nature of the injury she was taken to the Infirmary, where Dr. Jackson found that she was also suffering from a stab

Mike Covell

> wound, but she was not detained. The man is described as of dark complexion, about 5ft, 3in, in height, and dressed in dirty black clothes. Further details appear in other pages of the Mail. The outrages are of an extraordinary character, and are giving the police great anxiety. Although it is stated that none of the cases are serious, it is too early to make any definite statement. It is believed that the assailant was the same man in each case, and it is, of course, assumed that he is insane.

The Hull Daily Mail published the following on Monday November 26th 1900,

> STABBING OUTRAGES IN HULL. FIVE WOMEN WOUNDED. On page 2 of the "Mail" to-day we report that five stabbing outrages upon women in Hull were made. The facts, gleaned in later enquiries to-day, appear to be that shortly before half past five o'clock on Saturday evening two women were walking past Adderbury-grove, Beverley-road, a locality which is sufficiently busy on Saturday evening to protect anybody from molestation, when a man of whom they can give only a vague description, sauntered quietly up and stabbed one of them in a dangerous part. The person attacked did not realise that she had been wounded – or even struck at – until the man had disappeared in the direction of the town, and of course she was unable to raise an alarm until he had made good his escape. From this point the man appears to have made his way rapidly into Prospect-street, and then to have doubled back as far as Gleadow's arcade, Beverley-road, for within the short space of 20 or 30 minutes he renewed his attacks on four other females. In each case he seems to have employed the same methods – walking unconcernedly up to his victim and delivering exactly the same blow, apparently with a sharp pen knife. In all the five cases the clothing was cut clean through and the flesh penetrated, but, fortunately the wounds, in no instance, was sufficient to justify the injured person being detained in the Infirmary. Only one case came under the notice of the authorities at this institution, but it was not serious. The name of the victim was Mrs. Broadwell, the wife of a coal porter, Fawcett-terrace, Derby-street. At first she was taken home by a friend named Mrs. Hardy, who was with her at the time of the attack, but later in the evening it was deemed advisable to remover her to the infirmary Dr. Jackson dressed a stab wound, and afterwards permitted Mrs. Broadwell to return home. Upon inquiry this morning we learn that none of the sufferers are in a serious condition, but that each might congratulate herself upon not having received a dangerous thrust. One of the victims, who lives in Harley-street, was fortunate, because had the knife point struck half an inch away from the place it entered, the result in all probability would have been fatal. It is needless to say that the greatest alarm has been created amongst the female residents, not only in the neighbourhood of Beverley-

road, but in others parts of Hull also. All the attacks were made at a time of the night when hundreds of persons were about, and in two of Hull's busiest thoroughfares. It is impossible to conceive the miscreant's motive, unless it be that the outrages are the work of a maniac suffering from a special form of malady – attacks with the knife upon woman. One is inclined to ask how I is that so many cases could occur without any of the victims being able to give an alarm, but, as it generally known, the effects of the stab are often not felt at the moment. So it was on Saturday night, and hence the ruffian got clear away. The Hull Police have little or no clue to guide them, but Detective Superintendent Chapman and Superintendent Grassby have been unceasing in their efforts to trace the criminal. It is satisfactory to notice that no other cases beyond the five are recorded have come to the knowledge of the Police, but unless the perpetrator is laid by the heels there is no knowing when he may break out again. Saturday night's incidents are similar to what occurred in Doncaster a year or two ago. There, we believe, seven woman were attacked in precisely the same manner as at Hull on Saturday night, the particulars corresponding strangely with each other. To make them more complete, the culprit has only to be captured, as was the case at Doncaster.

The Hull Daily News published the following on Monday November 26th 1900,

MYSTERIOUS OUTRAGES IN HULL. FIVE WOMEN STABBED. A "JACK THE STABBER" AT LARGE. SUPPOSED DANGEROUS LUNATIC. Considerable apprehension has been caused in Hull, especially among the weaker sex, in consequence of a number of remarkable and mysterious stabbing outrages. The feeling of alarm is intensified by the belief that they are the work of one individual of doubtful sanity, who has already been through the hands of the police. It will be remembered that some time ago there was a similar sensation at Doncaster, and the culprit on being caught got a term of nine months' imprisonment which has only just expired. The cases in Hull were reported on Saturday night as having occurred within a short interval of one another on the Beverley-road and in Prospect-street, and it is noted as a singular fact that those taking place later were nearer and nearer the town. The outrages number five, and though none appeared to have ended in very serious wounds, one victim at least had an exceedingly narrow escape. Had she been struck an inch away from where she was, one of the main arteries would have been severed. In one case, particulars of which have been recorded at Norfolk-street Police Station, the wife of Thomas Broadwell, a coal porter, residing in Fawcett-terrace, Derby-street, was walking along Beverley-road about 5.45 on Saturday afternoon, along with her friend, Edith Hardy, a young woman of 10. They were near the end of Trafalgar-street, when a strange man in an instantaneous manner walked by the end and stabbed

> *the latter with some sharp instrument at the thigh. Directly afterwards he made off down Norfolk-street, and was lost to view. The outrage had been committed so suddenly and quickly that the victim found it hard to realise how it had taken place. Mrs. Broadwell, however, at once came to her assistance, and helped her to her own house. There the nature of the injury was realised, and Miss Hardy was taken to the Royal Infirmary. Dr. Jackson found that she was suffering from a stab wound, and directly it had been attended to it was not considered necessary to detain her any longer. What became of the mysterious assailant is not known, but later in the evening a fifth outrage was committed in Prospect-street. To-day detectives are making a diligent search for the culprit, but they are finding themselves hampered to no small extent by the inability of the victims to give them anything like a definite description of him. The most that it seems possible to state is that he is of dark complexion, about 5ft 3in, in height, he was dressed in a [illegible] black suit. [illegible] nature of the attacks, the police have paced themselves in communication with the authorities in Doncaster, so as to ascertain whether the Hull assailant is identical with the individual who has just completed a term of imprisonment for a similar crime. Full description and particulars of the latter arrived in Hull this afternoon, and no pains will be spared to crown the inquiries with success. LATEST PARTICULARS. Further inquiries by a "News" representative this afternoon shows the victim having the narrowest escape was a Miss Beetham, residing in Ryde-street. It appears that she was returning home with her sister about half past five on Saturday evening when the assistant made his appearance. He seemed only to knock up against her, and the young lady was not aware of the injury until reaching her destination. Then she found she was bleeding. Dr. Martin dressed the wound, which was [illegible] an inch from the femoral artery. [The next paragraph, which is the last, is illegible due to the poor condition of the newspaper.]*

The Eastern Morning News published the following on Tuesday November 27th 1900,

> STABBING OUTRAGES IN HULL. MYSTERIOUS ATTACKS ON LADIES. ASSAILANT STILL AT LARGE. *Considerable apprehension has been caused in Hull, especially among the weaker sex, in consequence of a number of remarkable and mysterious stabbing outrages. The feeling of alarm is intensified by the belief that they are the work of one individual of doubtful sanity, who has already been through the hands of the police. It will be remembered that some time ago there was a similar sensation at Doncaster, and the culprit on being caught got a term of nine months' imprisonment which has only just expired. The cases in Hull were reported on Saturday night as having occurred within a short interval of one another on the Beverley-road and in Prospect-street, and it is noted as a singular*

fact that those taking place later were nearer and nearer the town. The outrages number five, and though none appeared to have ended in very serious wounds, one victim at least had an exceedingly narrow escape. Had she been struck an inch away from where she was, one of the main arteries would have been severed. In one case, particulars of which have been recorded at Norfolk-street Police Station, the wife of Thomas Broadwell, a coal porter, residing in Fawcett-terrace, Derby-street, was walking along Beverley-road about 5.45 on Saturday afternoon, along with her friend, Edith Hardy, a young woman of 10. They were near the end of Trafalgar-street, when a strange man in an instantaneous manner walked by the end and stabbed the latter with some sharp instrument at the thigh. Directly afterwards he made off down Norfolk-street, and was lost to view. The outrage had been committed so suddenly and quickly that the victim found it hard to realise how it had taken place. Mrs. Broadwell, however, at once came to her assistance, and helped her to her own house. There the nature of the injury was realised, and Miss Hardy was taken to the Royal Infirmary. Dr. Jackson found that she was suffering from a stab wound, and directly it had been attended to it was not considered necessary to detain her any longer. What became of the mysterious assailant is not known, but later in the evening a fifth outrage was committed in Prospect-street. To-day detectives are making a diligent search for the culprit, but they are finding themselves hampered to no small extent by the inability of the victims to give them anything like a definite description of him. The most that it seems possible to state is that he is of dark complexion, about 5ft 3in, in height, he was dressed in a [illegible] black suit. [illegible] nature of the attacks, the police have paced themselves in communication with the authorities in Doncaster, so as to ascertain whether the Hull assailant is identical with the individual who has just completed a term of imprisonment for a similar crime. Full description and particulars of the latter arrived in Hull yesterday afternoon. ARREST OF SUPPOSED ASSAILANT. The result of the efforts of the police was the arrest of a man whom they have reason to believe they will be able to identify as the person who assaulted one of the women. His name is James Gray (23), a hawker, of 3 Lawrence-square, Cuthbert-street, Hull, and he was arrested by Detective Baker last night. He was taken to the police station, and afterwards confronted by the woman, Edith Hardy, who picked him out of a group of other men as the man who stabbed her in the thigh when near Trafalgar-street on Saturday night. The man Gray was then locked up, and will be brought up at the City Police Court this morning. ANOTHER ALLEGED STABBING AFFRAY. COLOURED MAN ARRESTED. A coloured man, named James Smith, who has been residing at the Sailors Home lately, will be brought before the Hull Police Court this morning charged with unlawfully and maliciously wounding Valentine Strandlund, a Norwegian, residing in Paradise-place, by stabbing him with a knife. It is stated that Strandlund spent some time in the King William Inn in

Mike Covell

> Market-place last night with a few friends, and on coming out of the public house and walking down the Market-place, was followed by Smith, who, it is alleged, suddenly took hold of Strandlund by the shoulder and stabbed him in the right side of the head with a knife which he had in his other hand. Two police constables happened to be in the vicinity at the time, and promptly arrested Smith. Strandlund was bleeding profusely, and was conveyed at once to the Royal Infirmary, where it was found that his right ear was cut in two, the wound extending for several inches round the back of the head, necessitating the insertion of six stitches.

THE ACCUSED.

James Gray as he appeared in the contemporary Hull Press. Image Copyright Mike Covell

The Hull Daily News, published the following, on Tuesday November 27th 1900,

HULL'S REIGN OF TERROR. THREE MORE WOMEN STABBED. ARREST OF THE SUPPOSED ASSAILANT. TO-DAY'S POLICE COURT PROCEEDINGS. SENSATIONAL DEVELOPMENTS. The latest development in connection with the sensational crop of stabbing cases in the Beverley-road tend to increase rather than minimise the importance and serious nature of the whole affair. Reports of three more cases of young ladies have been wounded have reached the ears of the police, and a couple of detectives have succeeded in arresting the man whom they suppose to be the assailant. His name is James Gray, and he has been described as a hawker, only 23 years of age, residing No. 3, Lawrence-place, Cuthbert-street, Hull. It has transpired that the officers – Detectives Baker and Cherry – had been busily engaged in investigating the case [illegible] yesterday; and as the [illegible] came into their possession, they went in the evening to the house in Lawrence-square. There they found Gray, and to Barker fell the task of explaining the object of their visit. The detectives said that he was suspected of stabbing several women on the Beverley-road. "Not me," was the reply of the startled tenant; "I was never in Beverley-road." Then he asserted that he could call his mother to witness the statement. The detectives, however, quietly asked him to accompany them to the Central Police Station, Parliament-street. Upon arrival there he was placed with four men similarly attired, and picked out by the young woman, Edith Hardy, as her assailant. A charge of malicious and unlawful wounding was entered, and the prisoner was taken to the cells pending his appearance before the Stipendiary Magistrate (Mr. E. C. Twiss) this morning. The scene in the vicinity of the police court in the forenoon was one of subdued excitement. Few of the public gained admittance, but the attendance of the witness was enough to create bustle. It was shortly after eleven o'clock when, in response to the call of "James Gray," a rather young looking man of dark visage stumbled rather than walked through the spring doors at the rear of the dock. He [illegible] the court in a careful way, and directly the Deputy Chief Constable Mr. Jones, rose to open the case, fixed his gaze intently on him till the end of the proceedings. He wore an old black coat and a dirty green neckerchief. The charge against the accused was that he "did unlawfully and maliciously wound one Edith Hardy, with a certain weapon – a knife – on the 25th of Nov, 1900, with intent to do grievous bodily harm. Mr. Jones began by reciting the main circumstances of the case. He observed that the prosecutrix was a single woman, residing at 1, Fawcett-terrace, Darby-street. Around 8.45p.m. on Saturday the 28th of November, in company with her married sister, [illegible] Broadwell, who resides at the same address, she was walking along the Beverley-road in the direction of Wellington-lane. She was carrying her sister's child. When between Trafalgar-street and [illegible passage] the footpath, noticed a man approaching them. When within a few yards of them he stepped off on to the road, as if to cross to the other side, but when passing them he again stepped on to the footpath and struck the prosecutrix a violent blow

Mike Covell

on the left thigh. Then he ran away in the direction of Norfolk-street. On arriving home prosecutrix found that her dress and underclothing had been cut through, also she was bleeding from the wound in front of her thigh. She was taken by her sister to the infirmary, where she was examined by Dr. Jackson, who found it necessary to put four stitches in the wound. Information was given to the police, and about 6.45 p.m. yesterday Detectives Barker and Cherry saw prisoner at the house, 3, Lawrence-place, Cuthbert-street. When told by Barker that he was suspected of stabbing several women on the Beverley-road on Saturday night last he replied: "Not me! I was never on Beverley-road. My other can prove where I was." He was conveyed to the Parliament-street Police Station, placed with four others, and identified by the prosecutrix. He was then charged by Barker, and replied "I never did it." Mr Jones added that in one case the wound was half an inch in extent. Mr Twiss: Is this the case where there are several other charges? Mr Jones: Yes. Mr Twiss: The case I have seen noted in the papers. Does he belong to Hull? Mr Jones: No, sir; he has been in Hull a short time – a few weeks. Mr Twiss: Has he any occupation? Mr Jones: At present he is working on the docks. I believe he is a scissors-grinder or a hawker. Mr Twiss: Who do you call this morning? Mr Jones: I will call the prosecutrix. Mr Twiss: Yes, I think you must do so. Miss Edith Hardy, a respectable looking young woman residing in Fawcett-terrace, Derby-street, then entered the box and was sworn. Mr Jones (to witness): On Saturday night about a quarter to six, where you on Beverley-road with your sister? Witness: Yes, sir. Mr Jones: I think you were carrying a baby? Witness: Yes. Mr Jones: Did you see a man between Trafalgar-street and Leonard-street? Witness: Yes, sir. Mr Jones: Can you see him now? Miss Hardy answered in the affirmative and indicated the prisoner in the dock. Mr Jones: Are you sure that is the man? Witness: Yes. Mr Jones: When he was passing what did he do? Witness: He went as though he was going to cross to the other side of the road. Mr Jones: When he passed what did he do? Witness: He struck me with his doubled fist. The Stipendiary: Did it give you much pain? Witness: Yes. The Stipendiary: What part was it he hit you? Witness: On the backside. Mr Jones: I think you went home with your sister? Witness: Yes. Mr Jones: And when you got home did you know your dress was cut? Witness: Yes. Mr Jones: And up to examining your thigh did you find that also cut? Witness: Yes. Mr Jones: And did your sister take you to the infirmary? Witness: Yes. Mr Jones: And the doctor put in four stitches? Witness: Yes, sir. Mr Jones: And you have no doubt about the identity of this [illegible]? Witness: No. The Magistrates Clerk (to accused): Do you wish to ask any questions? Prisoner: Well, gentlemen, I never saw ------. The Stipendiary: That is not a question. The Stipendiary: How did the prosecutrix identify the prisoner? Mr Jones: He was placed with four more. The Stipendiary: Had she any difficulty in picking him out? Mr Jones answered in the negative, and said that all the men were dressed. He desired a [illegible] for eight days. In reply to the [illegible] question whether he had any cause to that was he should not be remanded, the prisoner replied: "Yes, I have, and proceeded to make a long rambling statement with [illegible line] that he was never on Beverley-road on Saturday night. After finishing work he said he went home and had something to eat. Then he left he left and spent a little time with his parents. On his return he had a drink with a neighbour, and then went on again with his mother. He stated until half past six when he came home again. Subsequently he went to a public house in Cuthbert-street, and [illegible line] with his neighbour. They had a glass of beer each round. Later he returned to his mother and found she was not very well. She was in a fainting condition and he stayed with her till 11 o'clock, when she bundled him off. He [illegible line] was not near the Beverley-road. The Stipendiary: You will have another opportunity of calling witnesses. Prisoner: I can prove it. The Stipendiary (to Mr Jones): Has he been identified by anyone else. Mr Jones: Not at present. But I should mentioned that from the same one in Prospect-street, another woman was stabbed, and I think he didn't understand the nature of the [illegible line] to run after the prisoner, or rather the [illegible] and she said "No., he needn't bother." This man, I believe, had the opportunity of seeing the man (the assailant) who stabbed her, but I don't know where he is. I thought perhaps if he saw the man he is the -------. The Stipendiary: Perhaps publicly will bring him to the authorities. Mr Jones: He might assist us. The Stipendiary (to the prisoner): I must order you to be remanded for eight days. Accused, with a [illegible] "thank you, sir," then [illegible] the dock. PRISONER'S ANTECEDENTS. THE TWO NEW VICTIMS. A SINGULAR AND STARTLING STORY. This afternoon a "News" representative provided further inquiries into the case, and learnt that the man Gray is indeed a man who was convicted at York some time ago for a similar offence at Doncaster. Consequently the task of the Hull detectives was greatly [illegible] by the full description which was sent on by train yesterday from the south Yorkshire racing town. The first think that struck the police was the [illegible line] and the vague account of the statement given by Mrs Henry and her fellow victims. Owing to the [illegible] of the [illegible paragraph]

Miss Bowers tells a similar story, and the most singular fact about it is that the attack upon her was made not more than five minutes later, and within a comparatively few yards of the spot where Miss Smith was struck. She was going along the road and was near Gleadows Arcade. Suddenly she realised that someone had struck her a sharp blow on the left thigh. She did not realise that anything serious had happened until she reached her home, then she found signs of bleeding and discovered a small flesh wound. Our representative obtained the names of the other five victims, which are – Miss Selina Officer, of Hardy-street, Miss Mary Beetham, of Earle-street, Mrs Whittaker, of Somerscales-street, Miss

> Edith Hardy, of Fawcett-terrace, and Miss Florence Amlas, of Hawthorne-avenue. It appears to have been the latter who was attacked in Prospect-street, and the fact that this occurred about ten minutes to six o'clock induces clearly that the assailant was coming in the direction of the City when he committed the disgraceful acts. What has puzzled the police so far as the nature of the instrument used to inflict the wound. None was found on the person of Gray at the time of his arrest, and the only conclusion that can be arrived at is that it was the small blade of a penknife.

ANOTHER HULL STABBING CASE. MAN'S EAR CUT IN TWO. SIX STITCHES PUT IN.

JAMES GRAY.
(Sketched in Court by one of our Special Artists.)

An illustration of James Gray as it appeared in the contemporary press. Image Copyright Mike Covell.

The Hull Times, published the following on December 1st 1900, it stated,

STABBING OUTRAGES. FIVE HULL WOMEN WOUNDED. No less than five cases of stabbing in the street were reported to the Hull police on Saturday. Shortly before half-past five o'clock in the evening two women were walking past Adderbury-grove, Beverley-road, a locality which is sufficiently busy on Saturday evening to protect anybody from molestation, when a man ran up and stabbed one of them in a dangerous part. The person attacked did not realise that she had been wounded – or even struck at – until the man had disappeared in the direction of the town, and of course she was unable to raise an alarm until he had made good his escape. From this point the man appears to have made his way rapidly into Prospect-street, and then to have doubled back as far as Gleadow's-arcade, Beverley-road, for within the short space of 20 or 30 minutes he renewed his attacks on four other females. In each case he seems to have employed the same methods – running quickly up to his victim and delivering exactly the same blow, apparently with a sharp pen knife. In all the five cases the clothing was cut clean through and the flesh penetrated, but, fortunately, the wounds, in no instance, were sufficient to justify the injured person being detained in the Infirmary. Only one case came under the notice of the authorities at this institution, but it was not serious. The name of the victim was Miss Hardy, sister of Mrs Broadwell, wife of a coal porter, Fawcett-terrace, Derby-street. At first she was taken home by Mrs Broadwell, who was with her at the time of the attack, but later in the evening it was deemed advisable to remove her to the infirmary. Dr Palmer dressed a stab wound, and afterwards permitted Miss Hardy to return home. It is needless to say that the greatest alarm was created among the female residents, not only in the neighbourhood of Beverley-road, but in other parts of Hull also. All the attacks were made at a time of the night when hundreds of persons were about, and in two of Hull's busiest thoroughfares. It is impossible to conceive the miscreant's motive, unless it be that the outrages were the work of a maniac suffering from a special form of malady – attacks with the knife upon women. One is inclined to ask how it is that so many cases could occur without any of the victims being able to give an alarm, but, as is generally known, the effects of a stab are often not felt at the moment. So it was on Saturday night, and hence the ruffian got clear away. The Hull Police have little or no clue to guide them, but Detective Superintendent Chapman and Superintendent Grassby have been unceasing in their efforts to trace the criminal. It is satisfactory to notice that no other cases beyond the five recorded have come to the knowledge of the police, but unless the perpetrator is laud by the heels there is no knowledge when he may break out again. Saturday night's incidents are similar to what occurred in Doncaster a year or two ago. There, we believe, seven women were attacked in precisely the same manner as at Hull on Saturday night, the particulars corresponding strangely with each other.

Mike Covell

> To make them more complete, the culprit has only to be captured, as was the case at Doncaster. MAN ARRESTED ON SUSPICION. On Monday Detectives Barker and Cherry saw prisoner at the house, 3, Lawrence-place, Cuthbert-street. When told by Barker that he was suspected of stabbing several women on the Beverley-road on Saturday night last he replied: "Not me! I was never on Beverley-road. My other can prove where I was." He was conveyed to the Parliament-street Police Station, placed with four others, and identified by the prosecutrix. He was then charged by Barker, and replied "I never did it." Mr Jones added that in one case the wound was half an inch in extent. Mr Twiss: Is this the case where there are several other charges? Mr Jones: Yes. Mr Twiss: The case I have seen noted in the papers. Does he belong to Hull? Mr Jones: No, sir; he has been in Hull a short time – a few weeks. Mr Twiss: Has he any occupation? Mr Jones: At present he is working on the docks. I believe he is a scissors-grinder or a hawker. Mr Twiss: Who do you call this morning? Mr Jones: I will call the prosecutrix. Mr Twiss: Yes, I think you must do so. Miss Edith Hardy, a respectable looking young woman residing in Fawcett-terrace, Derby-street, then entered the box and was sworn. Mr Jones (to witness): On Saturday night about a quarter to six, where you on Beverley-road with your sister? Witness: Yes, sir. Mr Jones: I think you were carrying a baby? Witness: Yes. Mr Jones: Did you see a man between Trafalgar-street and Leonard-street? Witness: Yes, sir. Mr Jones: Can you see him now? Miss Hardy answered in the affirmative and indicated the prisoner in the dock. Mr Jones: Are you sure that is the man? Witness: Yes. Mr Jones: When he was passing what did he do? Witness: He went as though he was going to cross to the other side of the road. Mr Jones: When he passed what did he do? Witness: He struck me with his doubled fist. The Stipendiary: Did it give you much pain? Witness: Yes. The Stipendiary: What part was it he hit you? Witness: On the backside. Mr Jones: I think you went home with your sister? Witness: Yes. Mr Jones: And when you got home did you know your dress was cut? Witness: Yes. Mr Jones: And up to examining your thigh did you find that also cut? Witness: Yes. Mr Jones: And did your sister take you to the infirmary? Witness: Yes. Mr Jones: And the doctor put in four stitches? Witness: Yes, sir. Mr Jones: And you have no doubt about the identity of this [illegible]? Witness: No. The Magistrates Clerk (to accused): Do you wish to ask any questions? Prisoner: Well, gentlemen, I never saw you. The Stipendiary: That is not a question. The Stipendiary: How did the prosecutrix identify the prisoner? Mr Jones: He was placed with four more. The Stipendiary: Had she any difficulty in picking him out? Mr Jones answered in the negative, and said that all the men were the same age and similar build. Mr Shackles (Magistrates Clerk): Have you anything to say why you should not be remanded for eight days? Gray thereupon made a long statement, which was somewhat disjointed and difficult to follow. He was understood to say that on Saturday evening, when he left work, he had a pint of ale with his "missus," and

he left her and went home. He then went and stayed a little time with his father and mother, and went home again. He and his neighbour had a little drink in the house. He stayed with his mother until half past six, and when he got home at half past seven, himself, his "missus," and the next door neighbour went inside the public house in Cuthbert-street. They had a glass of beer each round. They came out, and he went home to his mother. She had fainting fits, and he stayed with her until eleven o'clock. As to being on Beverley-road he would take his oath he was not. Mr Twiss: Has he been identified by anybody else in the neighbourhood? Mr Jones: Not at present. I should mention that another woman in Prospect-street was stabbed and a man offered to run after her assailant, but she said, "You need not bother." This man, I believe, had a good opportunity of seeing the man who committed the assault, but we do not know who he is, and I thought the Press might be of some assistance. Mr Twiss: Perhaps publicity will bring him to the authorities. (To prisoner) You must be remanded for eight days. PRISONER'S ANTECEDENTS. The prisoner has not been in Hull very long. He is said to be known at Doncaster. FRESH CASES. We understand that in addition to the five cases of stabbing on the Beverley-road and Prospect-street on Saturday night, three more have come under the notice of the police.

The Hull Daily Mail, December 5th 1900, P. 5,

FURTHER REMAND. ACCUSED OF BEVERLEY-ROAD STABBING CASE. The man, James Gray, who has been in custody upwards of a week, and who is suspected by the Hull police of being the author of the recent stabbing outrages in Beverley-road, Hull, was again brought up at the City Police Court this morning. The charge of maliciously wounding a young woman, Edith Hardy, on Beverley-road on the 24th November. D.C.C. Jones said he would require a further remand. Before a remand was granted Mr H. L, Redman, who appeared on the prisoner's behalf, said there was one question he had been instructed by the prisoner's friends to mention. It was with regard to the unfair comments which had appeared in the press. More particularly he was asked to mention the fact in open Court, that prisoner's photo had been freely exhibited in the local Press. When the prisoner was first accused of the crime he made an answer, in which he practically suggested an alibi. The question of identity, therefore, was a very important one. Prisoner had been confronted by a dozen or more people – some of them the unfortunate ones who had been stabbed – and although he had been identified by the prosecutrix, other men, he had been instructed to say, had been identified as the guilty persons by others who had been stabbed. He, therefore, thought it unfair that the prisoner's photo should have been so freely displayed. It was, in his opinion, unfair and unjust, and if the prisoner was committed for trial,

Mike Covell

> it might tend to prejudice him and defeat the ends of justice. He did not object to a further remand. Prisoner was accordingly remanded a further eight days.

The people involved in the case can be found in the 1901 census, thus,

1901 Census, Thomas Broadwell, 1 Fawcett-terrace, Hull [Class RG13, P4492, F10, P11]

Thomas Broadwell	Head	24	Coal Porter
Lily Broadwell	Wife	23	
Laura Broadwell	Dau	2	

1901 Census, Edith Hardy, 13 Ada's-terrace, St. Paul's-street, Hull, [Class RG13, P4495, F8, P7]

Samuel Hardy	Head	25	
H A Hardy	Wife	39	
Edith Hardy	Dau	11	

1901 Census, Miss Beetham, 85 Ryde-street [Class RG13, P4469, F18, P27]

Julia Beetham	Head	57	
Athel K Beetham	Dau	23	Board School
Adelina M Beetham	Dau	22	Short Hand Clerk

Edith E Beetham	Dau	21	Short Hand Clerk
Julia A Beetham	Dau	19	
William J Beetham	Son	17	Fitters Apprentice
John W Beetham	Son	17	Post Office Sorting Clerk
Erica Pearson	Servant	14	Domestic Servant

So who was James Gray, and what happened to him?

A quick search of the Michaelmas Quarter Sessions for the year 1900, held at the Hull History Centre, [1] failed to show any court case involving James Gray, so I made efforts to trace the Calendar of Prisoners, [2] which covers the years 1893 through to, and including, 1904. It was here that I discovered that the case of James Gray was recorded in the Epiphany Quarter Sessions of 1901. [3] The Calendar of Prisoners revealed that James Gray was sentenced to 9 calendar months hard labour on the 30th of December in the year 1898, at the Doncaster Quarter Sessions. On the 24th of November 1900, Gray had unlawfully and maliciously wounded Edith Hardy, it was this offence that Gray was charged with at the Hull Epiphany Quarter Sessions. The date that Gray entered into police custody was November 27th 1900, however; it wasn't until December 20th that a warrant was issued for his arrest. I find this odd, as Gray was in custody at this period. His age was listed as 23 years old, giving the birth date of 1877, and his occupation was listed as a Hawker. The magistrate for the case was E. C. Twiss, Esq., Stipendiary Magistrate, Hull. Twiss, or Edward Curtis Twiss M. A. was the Stipendiary for Hull, but lived out in Beverley, a small market town a few miles north of the city of Hull that also has some connections to the case, as we shall see. [4] Gray was charged on the 8th of January in the year 1901, before Twiss, and was sentenced to 12 Calendar months of hard

Mike Covell

labour. The prison at that time was the Hull Prison, a location that is still in use today to house young offenders.

The 1901 Census shows James Gray at Her Majesty's Prison, Sculcoates, St. Andrew, Hedon-road, Hull.

| James Gray | Prisoner | 22 | Hawker | b. abt 1879 Yorks, Hull. |

[Class RG13, P4487, F143, P3]

Hearing that James Gray had been involved in other similar attacks I searched for more newspaper articles and found the following case from 1898 and based in Doncaster.

The Isle of Man Times and General Advertiser, Friday December 1st 1898, featured the following,

> OUTRAGES BY A KNIFE GRINDER. By Telegraph, Doncaster, Friday. At Doncaster, top-day, James Gray, a knife grinder in Hull, was indicted for unlawfully wounding several young women, by stabbing them through the legs with a pocket knife in the public thoroughfare. The Recorder said the prisoner's conduct was outrageous and incomprehensible. He could only suppose that he was not in his right mind. Gray, who was sentenced to nine months with hard labour, admitted having been in Chesterfield and Worksop, where similar outrages had taken place.

The North Eastern Daily Gazette, Saturday December 24th 1898,

> EXTRAORDINARY STABBING. CASES AT DONCASTER. At Doncaster yesterday a grinder, belonging to Hull, named John James Gray, was remanded, charged with cutting and wounding a number of women on Wednesday night. The prisoner commenced his assaults near the racecourse. About eight o'clock Rose Smith and Mary Airton were near the Common Pond, when they met the prisoner coming towards Doncaster. He was swinging his right hand, and on passing Smith, hit her on the leg. On returning to town Smith and Airton heard of Rose Richmond being stabbed. It seems that Richmond, in company with Lily Wood, was near the White Bear, when the prisoner struck Richmond. She soon found herself soaked with blood. And, becoming faint, was taken into a house. Doctors were fetched, and she was removed to the Infirmary. Just after this smith and Airton again saw the prisoner in High-street, and prisoner struck Smith with

> *something in his right hand. She felt herself stabbed in the leg. A few yards farther on he met Florence Kenward, who, when passing him, felt herself hit on the leg. Still farther on he encountered Annie Nicholson coming from the Post-office. He ran "band against her," and she immediately felt something sharp strike her leg. In the meantime, Airton and Smith had met Inspector Cobb, and told him what had occurred. While speaking, prisoner came down High-street, and turned into Baxter-street. Cobb, who followed him, saw he had something bright in his right hand, with which he struck at the door jambs as he passed. Cobb went behind him, seized his hand, and in it found an open pocket knife. He brought prisoner to the Guildhall, and yesterday morning he was identified by five women, some of whom had been assaulted, others accompanying them at the time.*

Reynolds's Newspaper, Sunday, December 25th 1898,

> ALLEGED WHOLESALE STABBING OF WOMEN. At Doncaster on Friday John James Gray, of Hull, was remanded on a charge of cutting and wounding five women, where he met coming from a racecourse to Doncaster. According to the evidence the accused walked quickly along swinging his right hand, in which he held a pocket knife, and stabbed the women in the thigh as he passed. Another young women is in the infirmary and unable to give evidence. The prisoner, who was apprehended with the knife in his hand, was remanded until Tuesday.

The Royal Cornwall Gazette Falmouth Packet, Cornish Weekly News, & General Advertiser, Wednesday, December 29th 1898,

> WHOLESALE STABBING OF DONCASTER WOMEN. A series of mysterious stabbing outrages have been committed in Doncaster. A married woman named Kenward was the object of an attempt at stabbing. The next evening, while Mrs. Kenward was in High-street, another attempt to stab her was successful. About the same time, and in the same thoroughfare, two woman named Rose Richmond, of Catherine-street, and Olive Stacey, of St. Sepulchre's Gate, were also stabbed. All the women were injured about the legs and thighs. Just after the last occurrence the police effected the arrest of a man who is supposed to be the offender.

On Saturday December 31st 1898, *The Nottinghamshire Guardian* published the following,

> THE STABBING MANIA: A WORKSOP CASE:-On Wednesday a warrant was issued by Worksop magistrates against James Gray, the man who has been before the Doncaster Bench on a charge of unlawfully wounding a female, charging him

Mike Covell

> with a similar offence at Worksop on Dec 17*th*. The complainant, a young woman named Ada Alletson, living in Foley-place, Worksop, alleged on oath that between 9.30 and 10 o'clock on the night in question she was walking down Bridge-street when the defendant ran past her and stabbed her in her thigh. She did not realise the injury till a little time after, when she felt blood trickling down her leg. Execution of the warrant will be stayed till the conclusion of the trial pending at the next sessions.

The Nottinghamshire Guardian, Saturday December 31st 1898,

> THE DONCASTER OUTRAGES. PRISONER GIVES EVIDENCE. *There was an animated scene at the Doncaster Police-court on Tuesday when James Gray, the Hull grinder, who is charged with stabbing a number of females, was again before the magistrates. The court room was crowded by the number of ladies who occupied seats testifying to the sensation of the case has caused in the town. The appearance of Gray is dark and unkempt, and he has aquiline features. In the lobes of his ears are rings, and a dirty scarf, one gaudy of colour, covered his neck. The young lady who has been caused the greatest amount of suffering at the hands of the assailant is Ada Richmond, of 9, Catherine-street, Doncaster. She was conveyed from the Infirmary to the court house in a cab. Miss Richmond told the magistrates that she was in Aldgate with a friend named Lily Wood on December 22nd, They met prisoner, and has he was passing them she felt a "thump" on the thigh. She thought it was Gray, but he had a cap on at the time.*

The Isle of Man Times and General Advertiser, Friday December 31st 1898, featured the following,

> OUTRAGES BY A KNIFE GRINDER. *By Telegraph, Doncaster, Friday. At Doncaster, top-day, James Gray, a knife grinder in Hull, was indicted for unlawfully wounding several young women, by stabbing them through the legs with a pocket knife in the public thoroughfare. The Recorder said the prisoner's conduct was outrageous and incomprehensible. He could only suppose that he was not in his right mind. Gray, who was sentenced to nine months with hard labour, admitted having been in Chesterfield and Worksop, where similar outrages had taken place.*

The Nottinghamshire Guardian, Saturday December 31st 1898,

THE DONCASTER OUTRAGES. PRISONER GIVES EVIDENCE. There was an animated scene at the Doncaster Police-court on Tuesday when James Gray, the Hull grinder, who is charged with stabbing a number of females, was again before the magistrates. The court room was crowded, the number of ladies who occupied seats testifying to the sensation the case has caused in the town. The appearance of Gray is dark and unkempt, and he has aquiline features. In the lobes of his ears are rings, and a dirty scarf, once gaudy of colour, covered his neck. The young lady who has been caused the greatest amount of suffering at the hands of the assailant is Ada Richmond, of 9, Catherine-street, Doncaster. She was conveyed from the Infirmary to the court-house in a cab. Miss Richmond told the magistrates that she was in Aldgate with a friend named Lily Wood on December 22nd. They met prisoner, and as he was passing them she felt a "thump" on the thigh. She thought it was Gray, but he had a cap on at the time. Gray was accordingly asked to put his cap on. This he proceeded to do, in the calm and deliberate manner that characterised his behaviour all along, and Miss Richmond thereupon said she felt sure he was the man who assailed her. Witness, proceeding, said soon afterwards she found her clothing saturated with blood, and she and Miss Wood then followed prisoner down the street. She became faint, however, through loss of blood, and had to be taken to the Infirmary, where she was examined by Dr. Royle, the house surgeon. There was a wound in her thigh, and she had since been under treatment. The Magistrates' Clerk (to prisoner): Do you wish to ask the witness any question? Prisoner: No, sir: I never saw her before in my life, so I don't want to ask any questions. Lily Wood, who said she lived at St. James's-terrace, stated she was with the last witness on the night in question. It was about 8.30 when they were going up Aldgate, and prisoner came by swinging his right arm. She saw him hit her companion and they were following him when Miss Richmond turned faint and had to be taken to the infirmary. She did not see the man's face, but she saw his back as he was hurrying away, and she was certain Gray was the man. Dr. Royle, house surgeon at the Infirmary, said Miss Richmond was brought to the Infirmary about quarter to nine on Thursday night. On examining her he found a small punctured wound on the upper part of the left thigh, about a quarter of an inch long, and an inch deep. There had been a fair amount of haemorrhage, but the wound was now nearly healed up. The knife with which it is supposed the stabs were inflicted, was produced at this stage. It is a small clasp knife of ordinary pattern, with the blade considerably work owing to repeated sharpening. The blade, which was open, was capable, said the doctor, of inflicting such a wound as he had described. Mrs. Annie Mirfield, of Milner's-yard, Doncaster, at whose house prisoner had lodged from the 20th inst., was called next. Gray, she said, sharpened the clasp knife produced on Thursday afternoon last. He first rubbed it on the step and then on the stone, and it was while he was doing this that they talked of the Chesterfield case. Prisoner, she

Mike Covell

> added, went out between four and five o'clock. He sharpened his knife a second time, added the witness. Prisoner asked a few questions with a view to proving that the clasp knife he was carrying when arrested was not the same knife he was sharpening in the afternoon, but Mrs. Mirfield could not be shaken on the point. Another girl, whom prisoner is alleged to have stabbed, is Jane Elizabeth Howes, of 57, Irlam-road, Doncaster. This occurred about 8.20 the same night in Regent-square. "He came suddenly out of the darkness," Miss Howes said, "goodness only knows where from, and he struck me on the thigh with such force that I was nearly knocked over." Police-sergeant Cobb then deposed to arresting Gray on this same Thursday evening in Baxtergate. The man had the clasp knife in his right hand, and he was jabbing the blade at the doors of houses as he went along. Prisoner was then formally charged, and pleaded not guilty. He elected to give evidence on his own behalf. He said he had no regular place of abode. He was walking down High-street cleaning his finger nails when the officer saw him. He was closing the blade by pressing it against his trousers when he was first spoken to. This concluded the first case, and Mr. Hall, who prosecuted invited the Bench to decide there was a prima facie case which would justify them in committing Gray for trial to the Sessions.
>
> The Mayor (Councillor Birkenshaw), who was in the chair, accordingly committed prisoner for trial. The second charge against Gray was then proceeded with. Olive Stace, of 121, St. Sepulchre-gate, deposed to prisoner stabbing her in the thigh about 9.15 on Thursday night last, and similar evidence was given by Rose Smith, 19, Bentley-road; Mrs. Florence Kenward, 136, St. Mary's-road, Wheatley; and Annie Nicholson, of 38, Nether Hall-road. Evidence was also given by George Donald, a young man living at 25, Baker-street, Doncaster, who said he saw prisoner strike a young woman, and, following him, saw him strike two more. He told Police sergeant Cobb what he had seen. Mr. Hall briefly commended Police sergeant Cobb and Donald, and this concluded the case for prosecution. Prisoner said he did not desire to make another statement, and he was also committed for trial on this charge to the Borough Sessions.

A number of people involved in the case can be found in the 1901 census, thus,

Police Sergeant Cobb in the 1901 Census, 44 Bentinck-street, Doncaster [Class RG13, P4411, F123, P3]

| Reginald Belk Cobb | Head | 50 | Retired Police Sergeant |

| Lillie Cobb | | Wife | 44 | |

Dr. Royle in the 1901 Census, 67 Nether Hall-road [Class RG13, P4410, F114, P7]

| Thomas Clifford Royle | Head | 45 | Registrar Births and Deaths, Local |
| Mary E Royle | Wife | 35 | |

The Western Mail, Saturday, December 31, 1898,

DONCASTER OUTRAGE. *At Doncaster, on Friday, James Gray, a knife grinder in Hull, was indicted for unlawfully wounding several young women, by stabbing them through the legs with a pocket knife in the public thoroughfare. The Recorder said the prisoner's conduct was outrageous and incomprehensible. He could only suppose that he was not in his right mind. Gray, who was sentenced to nine months with hard labour, admitted having been in Chesterfield and Worksop, where similar outrages had taken place.*

The Dundee Courier and Argus, Saturday December 31st 1898,

The Stabbing of Young Women.- At Doncaster yesterday, James Gray was sentenced to nine months' hard labour for stabbing several young women in the legs in public thoroughfares. The Recorder thought he must be insane.

The Bristol Mercury and Daily Post, Saturday December 31st 1898,

DONCASTER OUTRAGES. LENIENT SENTENCE. *At Doncaster, on Friday, James Gray, a knife grinder in Hull, was indicted for unlawfully wounding several young women, by stabbing them through the legs with a pocket knife in the public thoroughfare. The Recorder said the prisoner's conduct was outrageous and incomprehensible. He could only suppose that he was not in his right mind. Gray, who was sentenced to nine months with hard labour, admitted having been in Chesterfield and Worksop, where similar outrages had taken place.*

The Western Mail, Saturday, December 31st 1898,

Mike Covell

> At Doncaster, on Friday, James Gray, a knife grinder in Hull, was indicted for unlawfully wounding several young women, by stabbing them through the legs with a pocket knife in the public thoroughfares. He was sentenced to nine months with hard labour.

The Belfast News-Letter, Saturday, December 31st 1898,

> At Doncaster yesterday James Gray was sentenced to nine months' imprisonment for stabbing several young women with a pocket knife.

The Lloyd's Weekly Newspaper, Sunday, January 1st 1899,

> James Gray, grinder, of Hull, was on Friday committed to prison for nine months by the Doncaster Recorder for stabbing young women in the streets with a knife.

The Derby Mercury, Wednesday, January 4th 1899,

> STABBING WOMEN AT DONCASTER. THE OUTRAGES AT CHESTERFIELD. At Doncaster, on Friday, James Gray, a knife grinder in Hull, was indicted for unlawfully wounding several young women, by stabbing them through the legs with a pocket knife in the public thoroughfare. The Recorder said the prisoner's conduct was outrageous and incomprehensible. He could only suppose that he was not in his right mind. Gray, who was sentenced to nine months with hard labour, admitted having been in Chesterfield and Worksop, where similar outrages had taken place.

Back to the Hull case I found more newspaper reports in the national press.

The Dundee Courier, November 27th 1900,

> "JACK THE RIPPER" SCARE AT HULL. The Hull police have received information to the effect that four women were stabbed on Saturday evening while walking along the road. One of them reports that she was stabbed by a man who came up behind her. She was taken to the infirmary, where within two hours three other cases were reported. In each case it was a woman who had been stabbed on the thigh. None of the women can give a clear description of the assailant.

The Evening Telegraph, November 27th 1900,

> CHARGED WITH STABBING FIVE WOMEN. James Gray, scissors grinder, was charged at Hull Police Court to-day with stabbing five women. Deputy Chief

Newspapers from Hull Volume 2

> *Constable Jones explained that the women were stabbed by a man identified as the prisoner by Edith Hardy. The man ran violently against the women and stabbed them in the lower parts of the body. Gray was remanded for eight days. About eleven months ago seven women were similarly stabbed at Doncaster.*

The Gloucester Citizen, November 27th 1900,

> *SCARE AT HULL. SIX CASES OF STABBING. At Hull to-day James Gray, a young man, now a dock labourer, and formerly a scissors grinder, was charged with unlawfully wounding Edith Harding on Saturday night. Prosecutrix was walking along the road on the night in question when it is alleged, prisoner stabbed her in the thigh with a knife, afterwards running away. Gray, who pleaded not guilty, was remanded. On the same day there were five other stabbing cases of a similar nature in Hull.*

The North-Eastern Daily Gazette, Tuesday, November 27th 1900, *The Daily Gazette for Middlesbrough*, November 27th 1900, *The Shields Daily Gazette*, November 27th 1900, and *The Derby Daily Telegraph*, November 27th 1900, all featured the following,

> *SENSATIONAL STABBING OF WOMEN AT HULL. At Hull to-day James Gray, a young man, now a dock labourer, and formerly a scissors grinder, was charged with unlawfully wounding Edith Harding on Saturday night. Prosecutrix was walking along the road on the night in question when it is alleged, prisoner stabbed her in the thigh with a knife, afterwards running away. Gray, who pleaded not guilty, was remanded. On the same day there were five other stabbing cases of a similar nature in Hull.*

The Morning Post, Wednesday, November 28, 1900, *The Sunderland Daily Echo and Shipping Gazette*, November 28th 1900, *The Morning Post*, November 28th 1900, and *The Western Daily Press*, November 28th 1900, all featured the following,

> *SERIOUS STABBING CHARGE.- James Gray, Scissors grinder, was charged at Hull Police Court yesterday with stabbing five women. Deputy Chief Constable Jones explained that the women were stabbed by a man, identified as Gray, who ran violently against the women and stabbed them in the lower part of the body. Gray was remanded for eight days. About eleven months since seven women were similarly stabbed at Doncaster.*

The *Glasgow Herald*, Wednesday November 28th 1900,

Mike Covell

> CHARGE OF STABBING AT HULL. At Hull to-day a man named Gray was charged with stabbing five women on Saturday night. A Miss Ward identified accused amongst four other men as the alleged assailant. In each case the women were stabbed on the inside of the thigh, and Miss Ward had four stitches put in at the infirmary. All five women were stabbed in one hour on Beverley-road, and within a mile from the first to the last woman. Other women could not identify Gray as the man. Some of the women stabbed were unable to appear in Court, being weak from loss of blood. The accused was remanded.

The *Huddersfield Daily Chronicle*, Wednesday November 28th 1900,

> At Hull on Tuesday a man named Gray was charged with stabbing five women on Saturday night. A Miss Ward identified accused amongst four other men as the alleged assailant. In each case the women were stabbed on the inside of the thigh, and Miss Ward had four stitches put in at the infirmary. All five women were stabbed in one hour on Beverley-road, and within a mile from the first to the last woman. Other women could not identify Gray as the man. Some of the women stabbed were unable to appear in Court, being weak from loss of blood. The prisoner was remanded.

The Leeds Mercury, Wednesday November 28th 1900,

> At Hull on Tuesday a man named Gray was charged with stabbing five women on Saturday night. In each case the women were stabbed on the inside of the thigh. Some of them were unable to appear in Court, being weak from loss of blood.

Northern Echo, Wednesday November 28th 1900,

> FIVE WOMEN STABBED. At Hull yesterday a man named Gray was charged with stabbing five women on Saturday night. A Miss Ward identified accused amongst four other men as the alleged assailant. In each case the women were stabbed on the inside of the thigh, and Miss Ward had four stitches put in at the infirmary. All five women were stabbed in one hour on Beverley-road, and within a mile from the first to the last woman. Other women could not identify Gray as the man. Some of the women stabbed were unable to appear in Court, being weak from loss of blood. The accused was remanded.

The Lichfield Mercury, November 30th 1900,

> At Hull, on Tuesday, James Gray, now a dock labourer, and formerly a scissor grinder, was charged with unlawful wounding of Edith Hardy on Saturday.

> *Prosecutrix was walking along the road when it is alleged prisoner stabbed her in the thigh with a knife, afterwards running away. Gray, who pleaded not guilty, was remanded. On the same day there were five other stabbing cases of a similar nature in Hull.*

Manchester Times, Friday November 30th 1900,

> STRANGE STABBING CASES AT HULL. *At Hull on Tuesday a man named Gray was charged with stabbing five women on Saturday night. A Miss Ward identified accused amongst four other men as the alleged assailant. In each case the women were stabbed on the inside of the thigh, and Miss Ward had four stitches put in at the infirmary. All five women were stabbed in one hour on Beverley-road, and within a mile from the first to the last woman. Other women could not identify Gray as the man. Some of the women stabbed were unable to appear in Court, being weak from loss of blood. The prisoner was remanded.*

The Weekly Standard and Express, Saturday, December 1st 1900, and *The Tamworth Herald*, December 1st 1900,

> *James Gray, a scissors-grinder, has been remanded at Hull, on a charge of stabbing five women. About eleven months since seven women were stabbed at Doncaster.*

The Nottinghamshire Guardian, Saturday December 1st 1900, *The Worcestershire Chronicle*, December 1st 1900, and *The Blackburn Standard*, December 1st 1900, all featured the following,

> HULL STREET OUTRAGES. *At Hull yesterday a man named Gray was charged with stabbing five women on Saturday night. A Miss Ward identified accused amongst four other men as the alleged assailant. In each case the women were stabbed on the inside of the thigh, and Miss Ward had four stitches put in at the infirmary. All five women were stabbed in one hour on Beverley-road, and within a mile from the first to the last woman. Other women could not identify Gray as the man. Some of the women stabbed were unable to appear in Court, being weak from loss of blood. The accused was remanded.*

The Leicester Chronicle and the Leicestershire Mercury, Saturday, December 1st 1900,

> FIVE WOMEN STABBED AT HULL. *James Gray was charged at Hull on Tuesday with stabbing five women in Beverley-road on Saturday night. One of the*

Mike Covell

> victims identified Gray as the assailant, though others of those assaulted were unable to do so. He was remanded.

Appendix I: - The 1900 Hull Ripper Scare References:

1. CQB436 Michaelmas Quarter Sessions 1900 C/O Hull History Centre

2. CQN/17 Calendar of prisoners 1893-1904 C/O Hull History Centre

3. CQB437 Epiphany Quarter Sessions 1901 C/O Hull History Centre

4. *Kelly's Trade Directory of Hull*, 1900

Appendix II - The 1988 – 1994 Hull Ripper Craze

The year of 1988 was the centenary of the five commonly accepted Jack the Ripper outrages in London and it saw a flurry of books, documentaries, television shows, radio shows, and magazines, with new theories and new suspects. It was an exciting time and more so because a suspect had been seriously posited by a Ripperologist, a suspect with links to Hull. The Ripperologist in question was the late Melvin Harris, who went on to write three Ripper books, released *Jack the Ripper – The Bloody Truth*, and the Hull press were keen to promote the book and look at the possible ramifications of the book on local tourism. Harris would follow this up with *The True Face of Jack the Ripper*, another book promoting Robert D'Onston Stephenson as Jack the Ripper in 1994, what followed between the two dates was a minor media frenzy in Hull, with Harris feeding the Hull press stories to both promote the book, and attract people to send information that might help crack the case. Here is a selection of articles from the period that I came across in my research into Robert D'Onston Stephenson;

The Hull Daily Mail, February 22nd 1988,

> *WAS RIPPER BORN IN HULL? Jack the Ripper, Britain's most chilling mass murderer, could have come from Hull. A Ripper expert believes a Hull doctor, the son of a wealthy local family, could have been the bloody murderer who slaughtered seven London prostitutes in an orgy of violence. But Scotland Yard police say that, although their century old file on the murders is still open, no fresh investigation will be launched. The finger of blame has been pointed at Dr. Roslyn D'Onston, a Hull born doctor living in Whitechapel, where the seven prostitutes were murdered and hideously mutilated 100 years ago. SOLDIER. Born Robert Donston Stephenson, in Hull, back in 1841, the bright doctor and journalist became the black sheep of his highly respected family when he turned into a drug addict and alcoholic, obsessed by black magic. Author and Ripper expert Melvin Harris claims D'Onston's time as a soldier helped him plan the murders with military like precision in the Whitechapel area he knew so well. His*

Mike Covell

> *medical knowledge would have enabled him to perform the almost ritualistic slaughters and removal organs in the dark alleyways where he attacked his victims. A black magician, Aleister Crowley, claimed to have a box of bloodstained ties, he said belonged to Jack the Ripper, but the box was originally owned by Dr. Roslyn D'Onston. TIME. But Scotland Yard police say the new evidence is too late for them to relaunch an investigation. "Although crimes are technically unsolved, everyone involved with the case is long since dead and it is too late for a police inquiry," said a spokesman.*

The Hull Daily Mail, February 24th 1988,

> *ON THE TRAIL OF THE RIPPER. The hideous Ripper murders that shook Victorian London and sent the police scurrying up endless blind alleys are a century old this year - still unsolved and still open on Scotland Yard's files. But only the fascinated few- authors and criminologists - still pursue the shadow of the murderer today. One such expert, who has painstakingly studied the seven slaughters of Whitechapel prostitutes claims the century's most infamous murderer was none other than a Hull doctor. JOURNALIST*
>
> *Born into a wealthy Hull family in 1840, Robert D'Onston Stephenson did not follow his father into the Dawber and Stephenson seed and bone mills in Church-street and Bankside, or his mother's relatives into the Dawber slating manufacturers. Educated in Munich, he became a doctor and a journalist. But, obsessed with Black Magic and fast becoming an alcoholic and drug addict, he left his family home in Charles-street, Hull, under a cloud of scandal, sill [illegible] today. Now, a council car park stands where his Victorian home would have been- hemmed in by shops and warehouses. Traders operate there today, unaware that the [illegible] of Whitechapel would once have walked that very street. It was an appropriate birthplace, however, if Stephenson WAS the Ripper, for Charles-street was known as "The Street pf the Butchers" with up to seven plying their trade there. But it seems no descendants of the man who could have been the ripper survive today. The Stephenson Mills are long gone and though his mother's maiden name lives on in one local building firm today, no direct Dawber descendant relatives can be traced. His chilling footsteps proved almost impossible to re-tread for Melvin Harris, Ripperologist, and author of the new book "Jack the Ripper- The Bloody Truth." When he arrived in Hull last year. "I had started my book as a means of exposing the false candidates who had emerged over the years." said, Mr. Harris, who lives in Essex. "But gradually, one man began to emerge from the shadows- Stephenson. "He was involved in the murders in more ways than any other person known." The authors pursuit of the man he calls the Magician from the Mist was complex. INVOLVEMENT*

> *Stephenson had moved from Hull and was living and practising in Whitechapel under the false name of Roslyn D'Onston ....a new identity taken on after his involvement in a crime or scandal in Hull? Also working on the Pall Mall Gazette, D'Onston wrote several articles on the murders and was even suspected of being the Ripper by his editor. Harris claims that the other facts that point the finger at D'Onston are, His 20-year study of Black Magic. The seven (a mystical number) of prostitutes could have been offered in human sacrifices in sites which form the shape of a cross on maps of Whitechapel. D'Onston became seriously ill at the time the murders ceased. And, after leaving hospital, he had a religious conversion, labouring for years over a detailed analysis of the gospel from the Greek and Hebrew texts, finally published in 1904. An act of atonement for his evil deeds, claims Harris. Another black magician claimed he owned a box of blood-stained ties once belonging to Jack the Ripper. And a woman friend of D'Onston's claimed she saw the ties in D'Onston's room- he later told her the Ripper cut out organs from the bodies and carried them off tucked inside his tie. Hull people can decide for themselves.*

The article was riddled with errors from assumptions on Robert D'Onston Stephenson's life, to the statement that there were no more members of the Dawber family residing in Hull. I was able to trace the family still residing in Hull and met them to donate some of my research to them to show them how their family lived in 19th Century Hull.

The Hull Daily Mail, March 2nd 1988,

> *HULL LINK WITH JACK THE RIPPER BUILDS UP. Hull's Jack the Ripper trail is hotting up. The man who slaughtered seven prostitutes in a series of gruesome murders of 100 years ago could have been Hull born doctor Robert Stephenson. Last week, the Mail reported that the grisly secret life of the mill owner's son was unveiled in a new book about the Ripper murders by Essex author Melvin Harris. And now the Ripperologist has uncovered more facts about the man who could be Hull's most infamous son of all. SMUGGLER. Stephenson – who changed his name to Roslyn D'Onson and moved to London – had studied toxicology, the subject of poisons. And this sudden move to London occurred after he became involved with a notorious Hull smuggler, Thomas Pile, in 1867 while working as a customs officer. "Stephenson became involved in some sort of smuggling racket and eventually was shot in the leg by Pile in 1868," said Mr. Harris, author of Jack the Ripper – The Bloody Truth. "Then he disappeared from his home in Norwood Terrace, Hull, around 1872," he added. Born in Charles Street in 1841, Stephenson had lived at 5 Regent Street around 1867 claims the author, and may have been the cousin of Hull solicitor Louis Stephenson. After arriving in London*

Mike Covell

> he started the Pompadour Cosmetics Company in Baker Street, manufacturing "the elixir of life" until the business suddenly folded in 1891: "I would like to hear any Hull residents who may have any recollections of the Stephenson family which would help in my research for a further book" Mr. Harris appealed.

The article is riddled with errors from start to finish making it difficult to ascertain where fact and fiction start and finish. Among the errors are:

Robert D'Onston Stephenson was never a doctor and never studied toxicology.

Robert D'Onston Stephenson never changed his name to Roslyn D'Onson.

Robert D'Onston Stephenson was a clerk for the Hull Customs, nothing more nothing less.

Robert D'Onston Stephenson's visit to Bridlington, where he was shot, was a family holiday his family appeared in the Bridlington press at the time of the shooting.

There is no evidence to support the claim that Thomas Pile was a smuggler, notorious or otherwise, and Pile never appears in the Hull or National press accused of such a crime.

Robert D'Onston Stephenson remained in Hull for another year after the shooting.

Robert D'Onston Stephenson never lived at 7 Norwood Terrace, this was another Robert Stephenson.

Robert D'Onston Stephenson never lived at 5 Regent Street.

Robert D'Onston Stephenson was never related to Hull Solicitor Louis Stephenson.

The Hull Daily Mail, July 1st 1988,

> TV SPECIAL ON "JACK" MAY SPARK BOOM. RIPPER TOURS SET FOR HULL. Hull is set for a macabre tourist boost....thanks to Jack the Ripper. By Jonathon Carr-Brown. For the centenary of London's Whitechapel murders this

August will be heralded by a prime time American TV show centering on new claims that the fiendish killer was the son of a Hull mill owner. An expert Melvyn Harris believes this will lead to hundreds of trans-Atlantic Ripper hunters swarming into the city. Hull City Council's tourism marketing officer, Val Woof says that, if necessary, she will put on coach tours for the enthusiasts seeking out the roots of prime suspect Robert Stephenson. CONCENTRATING. The major US TV network NBC plans to screen a two hour "special" on the murderer this October, concentrating on the theory that the Ripper came from Hull. The programme "The Secret Identity of Jack the Ripper" will be seen by millions across the United States and Canada. It will be in two parts and will feature lurid scenes of Hull born doctor Robert Stephenson practising black magic. FEATURES. Scenes from the lives of other suspects in the gruesome murders of seven prostitutes will also be featured. In the second part of the programme criminal specialists and computer experts will try to evaluate who the most likely culprit was.

But Melvyn Harris, has no doubts. He is now writing his second book which he believes will conclusively prove rich mill-owner's son Robert Stephenson was the slaughterer. He will be explaining his theory on the show, live via satellite from his home in Essex. There is some suggestion that some of the programme might be filmed in the back streets of Hull's Old Town. ADDICT. Born Robert Donston Stephenson, in Hull, in 1841, the bright doctor and journalist became the black sheep of his respectable family, when he became a drug addict and became obsessed with black magic, Mr Harris says. For some time he was a Customs officer, but after an argument with a smuggler in which he was shot in the thigh, he moved to London.

The Hull Daily Mail, August 18th 1988,

NEW RIPPER FILE TO SPARK TOURIST BOOM? By MATTHEW LIMB. NEW EVIDENCE from the Jack the Ripper case could shed light on speculation that Britain's most chilling mass murderer came from Hull. Original documents and photographs of the killers victims, which went missing from official records many years ago were put on show at Scotland Yard today. They could illuminate the mystery as to whether the murderer of prostitutes in Victorian London's East End was Hull born Dr Robert Donston Stephenson. And they are likely to fuel the City's predicted tourist boom for the centenary of the notorious crimes. The Ripper slaughtered seven women in Whitechapel between August and November 1888. It was first thought the complete file on the case was passed to the Public Records Office in 1951 and the public was given access in the early Seventies. DOCUMENTS. But last November a large brown envelope was sent anonymously

Mike Covell

> from the Croydon area to Scotland Yard. Its contents have been established as genuine Ripper documents which disappeared from Yard records many years ago. A Scotland Yard spokesman said "Within the last few months an album of photographs was found among the effects of a deceased senior officer." "His family forwarded them to the Yard, who discovered three photographs of Ripper victims which have never been published" A spokesman for the Metropolitan Police Museums Trusts aid "I am enormously pleased the documents and photographs have been restored to us, They are of great historical interest."
> BONANZA. Author and Ripper expert Melvin Harris wrote a book claiming the murderer was the son of a Hull mill owner. He believes a planned American TV series highlighting the Hull claims will spark a macabre tourist bonanza in the City. STOP THE PRESS: EDITORS FINAL THOUGHTS. So there we have it, a day by day, blow by blow account of what transpired in the Hull Press during the "Autumn of Terror". As seen through the eyes of the sensational pressmen, whose constant trawl for a good story, never got side tracked by the facts of the matter. From the "Torso Murders", to the "Whitechapel Murders", the victims, the suspects, theories, and those involved trying to apprehend the murder. It is interesting to see how the stories played out over the days and weeks, and how they became more and more sensational, with more and more details. Sadly, the more details that were covered, the greater the likelihood of mistakes, from simple spelling mistakes, to downright false statements and myths. What we have is an alternate history of events as they unfolded, which, at the time, where considered to be factual accounts of the events that unfolded, and without a doubt, adding to the terror that transpired.

The Hull Daily Mail, October 10th 1988,

> RIPPER NAME TO BE REVEALED. Recent research and alleged new evidence has tried to suggest that Jack the Ripper, Britain's most chilling mass murderer, came from Hull. The finger has been pointed at Hull born doctor Robert Stephenson. But tomorrow sees the start of a multimillion pound miniseries, n ITV also based on exhaustive research, that's almost certain to lay the blame in another direction. Michael Caine stars as Insp. Fred Abberline, who led the hunt for the man who brutally mutilated and murdered five prostitutes in the streets of Whitechapel in London's East End between August 31st and November 9th 1888.

On the morning of November 6th 1989, *The Hull Daily Mail* ran two front page news stories, one regarding teaching staff in Humberside, and the other about an explosion caused by lighter fuel. On the side bar was an interesting picture with the note, "Why is this former Hull doctor back in the news?"

Newspapers from Hull Volume 2

The side bar had a small image of Robert D'Onston Stephenson. On page 7 of that edition the following article, written by Simon Mander, was featured,

NEW EVIDENCE POINTS TO HULL MAN AS RIPPER. Ripperologist Melvin Harris has unveiled further evidence that the fiend of Whitechapel who slaughtered seven prostitutes in 1888 came from Hull. Using techniques pioneered by the FBI in America to track down modern sexual serial killers, the author claims to have discovered further proof that Hull-born Robert D'Onston Stephenson was guilty of the crimes that shook Victorian London. Mr. Harris told the Mail: "In my first book I name D'Onston Stephenson as the Ripper but my latest book examines information which has only become available in the meantime, which has filled in the missing links and confirmed my original suspicions. What I have done is compile a criminal profile of the Ripper by studying each murder and trying to build up a picture of the man who committed them, using techniques developed by the FBI's behavioral research unit. To the primitive way of thinking of the Victorian police the Ripper murders were the work of a madman – they were the first killings of their kind, and in fact the three suspects arrested at the time were all insane. But the FBI have found that a serial sexual murderer is more likely to be a quiet person, the nice guy next door, a bit of a loner, but someone who has a little difficulty mixing socially. Mr. Harris' latest book, The Ripper File, builds on his earlier suspicions about Stephenson, a former Hull Customs clerk, who lived under the false name of Roslyn D'Onston in Whitechapel during the Ripper's reign of terror. The case against Stephenson, whose family home was in Charles Street, Hull, is this: "The Ripper must have had an intimate knowledge of the East End in order to escape detection – Stephenson lived in Whitechapel. The Ripper must have had the physical prowess to carry out the gruesome attacks – Stephenson was described by contemporaries as an athletic, energetic person with nerves of steel and an iron will. The Ripper tore out organs from his victims' bodies with surgical precision – Stephenson trained as a doctor in Paris. Stephenson worked as a stringer for the Pall Mall Gazette – the perfect cover for the murderer who would not be a suspected by police at the scene of the crime. His articles also displayed more than was commonly known about the killings. Stephenson had already learnt how to kill – fighting as a lieutenant in Garibaldi's army during the Italian Civil Wars at the age of 18 he was used to the sight of blood and death. Stephenson, like some modern serial killers, was a drug addict, having become hooked on morphine after first taking it to ease the pain of a gunshot wound inflicted by a Hull smuggler in 1868. THREATS Harris adds that Stephenson was obsessed with black magic and hated prostitutes after his love affair with a Hull harlot was ended by his respectable parents using threats of refusing to pay for his gambling debts. Harris concluded by saying: "I once felt that we would never identify the

252

Mike Covell

> killer yet finally I came to name D'Onston Stephenson as the only man who can be taken seriously as the Ripper. He alone, of all the suspects, had the right profile, the opportunities, the motives and the ideal cover. His background, his personality, his skills, his frame of mind, all fitted him for the fateful role.

There are so many errors in this article, but here are just a few that are misleading and worthy of a closer look,

One of the first is the statement made by Harris that "*In my first book I name D'Onston Stephenson as the Ripper,*" but in two earlier books Harris looked at Stephenson and called him a fantasist. [1] Harris concludes this look at Stephenson with the statement, "*And as those imaginary heels click off into fairyland.*" [2]

Another claim made is that Robert D'Onston Stephenson "*lived under the false name of Roslyn D'Onston in Whitechapel during the Ripper's reign of terror.*" This is also false, Roslyn D'Onston was not a fake name, but a pen name, used from 1876 when Stephenson got married to his brother's servant girl in London, and later used for the writing of *The Patristic Gospels*.

Another false claim is that "*Stephenson lived in Whitechapel.*" At the time of the murders Robert D'Onston Stephenson was not living in Whitechapel but was an in-patient at the London Hospital, prior to this his only known addresses were in the Islington area of London, not Whitechapel. Another statement that is misleading is that "Stephenson was described by contemporaries as an athletic, energetic person with nerves of steel and an iron will," but George Marsh, who gave a statement that Stephenson was Jack the Ripper in 1888 stated, "*Age 48, height 5ft 10in, full face, sallow complexion, moustache is heavy- mouse coloured- waxed and turned up, hair brown going grey, and eyes are sunken. When looking at a stranger he generally has an eyeglass. Dress, grey suit and light brown felt hat all well-worn, military appearance and says he has been in 42 battles, well educated,*" whilst Inspector Thomas Roots gave no description on Stephenson's appearance at this moment in time. The claim that "Stephenson trained as a doctor in Paris," came from Inspector Thomas Roots, but it has never been proven with no records being found of Stephenson training in Paris, or gaining a diploma. Another claim that is false is that "*Stephenson worked as a stringer for the Pall Mall Gazette*" but during the murders no articles appeared in the press from Robert D'Onston

Stephenson, but he did write a letter to the newspaper on December 1st 1888. Another false claim is that "*Stephenson had already learnt how to kill – fighting as a lieutenant in Garibaldi's army during the Italian Civil Wars at the age of 18 he was used to the sight of blood and death.*" There is no evidence that Stephenson fought in the Italian campaigns, nor any evidence that he went to Italy. There is some evidence in the Muster Rolls, held at the Bishopsgate Institute that Stephenson applied to join, but no evidence that he left to fight. His timing certainly does not fit in with the known events of the English volunteers, or the 1861 census which shows him at home in Sculcoates on the night the census was taken.

Another false claim is that "*Stephenson, like some modern serial killers, was a drug addict, having become hooked on morphine after first taking it to ease the pain of a gunshot wound inflicted by a Hull smuggler in 1868.*" There is no evidence that Thomas Piles was a smuggler, his record is clean, and there are no articles or evidences of him being accused or charged with smuggling other than from Stephenson himself in a ghost story he wrote for William T. Stead. The final false claim is that "*Stephenson was obsessed with black magic and hated prostitutes after his love affair with a Hull harlot was ended by his respectable parents using threats of refusing to pay for his gambling debts.*" There is no evidence for this claim, other than a story that Stephenson told to a magazine. Stephenson eventually married his brother's servant. If his parents were so bothered why would they let him marry beneath him?

The Hull Daily Mail, May 30th 1994,

RIPPER MYSTERY WIDENS. *The spectre of Jack the Ripper has returned to haunt the city after a writer once again claims the murderer began life in Hull. More than a century after the killings, Melvin Harris claims to have proof that Jack was a member of a well-known Hull family. Six years after Harris first stated Dr Robert Stephenson of Charles Street, Hull, was the Ripper, he claims to have uncovered further evidence. In "The True Face of Jack the Ripper" (Michael O'Mara), Harris says he man addicted to drugs and obsessed with black magic. He was a doctor and a journalist, but sank into a world of depravity. Stephenson – who changed his name to Roslyn D'Onston – moved to London from his home in Norwood Terrace in 1872 after he became involved in smuggling. During the*

Mike Covell

> Ripper's reign, Stephenson was working on the Pall Mall Gazette and wrote several in depth articles on the murders, Harris claims.

The article is again riddled with errors, the main one being that Stephenson resided on Norwood-terrace. The Robert Stephenson who resided on Norwood-terrace was not the same Robert Stephenson who moved to London! The claim that Stephenson was involved in smuggling is also false, and there is no evidence to back up this statement, even the official Hull Customs Files show nothing of this alleged activity. It is also false that Stephenson worked on *The Pall Mall Gazette* at the time of the murders, it is now a proven fact that Stephenson was an in-patient in the London Hospital at the time of the murders, and only one article from Stephenson appeared in *The Pall Mall Gazette* on the murders, it being published on December 1st 1888, and weeks after the final murder in the murders commonly associated with "Jack the Ripper," which occurred on November 9th 1888.

References and further reading:

Appendix II - The 1988 – 1994 Hull Ripper Craze:

1. *Sorry You've Been Duped*, Melvin Harris, 1986, George Weidenfield & Nicholson Limited, P. VII
2. Ibid, P. 173

Newspapers from Hull Volume 2

Appendix III - Beverley Ripper Craze's

During my trawl of newspaper articles in the Hull press or relating to Hull, I came across a series of articles pertaining to Jack the Ripper in Beverley. Obviously having the market town on my doorstep I gained access to the articles and uncovered a treasure trove of articles pertaining to Jack the Ripper scares in Beverley to add to the material I already had on a number of suspects I had with links to the town.

Beverley is a small township on the outskirts of Kingston upon Hull, standing approximately 8 miles northwest of the city it is a popular market town with a long colourful history. The market town predates the Norman invasion and was, in the middle ages, one of the country's most prosperous townships. Walking around Beverley one certainly gets a feel for its rich history. The town is dominated by two key buildings, the medieval St Mary's Church, and the majestic Beverley Minster. Both churches are fascinating structural and architectural delights with numerous features that could fill guide book after guide book.

Connection to Ripper suspects:

For those theorists that posit Frederick Bailey Deeming as a suspect it should be mentioned that it was at St Mary's Church that Frederick Bailey Deeming was married, under the alias Harry Lawson, to Helen Matheson. Surprisingly the church has another link to the case, again depending upon who your suspect is, for the church has an unusual sculpture known as the Pilgrim Rabbit, which, it is said, was the inspiration for Lewis Carroll, who had friends in East Yorkshire and a maternal grandfather at Kingston upon Hull.

During the trial of Frederick Bailey Deeming in the first few months of 1892 a number of articles in both the Hull and Beverley press made statements about Deeming and his exploits in the area. As I have covered this ground previously I wish not to retread over old pastures, but to simply

Mike Covell

state that none of the Beverley or Hull articles stated that Deeming was Jack the Ripper or that Jack the Ripper had visited Beverley.

There are other links to the Yorkshire Region, for example anyone wishing to get to Bridlington, where Robert D'Onston Stephenson stayed at the Black Lion Hotel, they must pass via Beverley Railway Station, and further along the station line is Scarborough, where Scalby Mills is situated. It was here that the bloodhounds, belonging to Edwin Brough, Burgho and Barnaby resided, and their kennels are still present to day. I cover Frederick Bailey Deeming, Lewis Carroll, and Robert D'Onston Stephenson, in my *Jack the Ripper From Hell, From Hull* series.

But back to Beverley! This article is to concentrate on two key events in the history of Beverley in 1891 and 1894.

The 1891 Jack the Ripper Scare:

Despite the crime spree of "Jack the Ripper" ending on November 9th 1888 with the brutal murder of Mary Jane Kelly, the press were still eager to attach any and every criminal deed to "Jack the Ripper." As we have seen many of these cases featured the criminal claiming to be "Jack the Ripper," or claiming to "Jack the Ripper" the victims. In some cases we have seen threats made to "Rip" or "Whitechapel" the victims.

In Beverley in 1891 there was such a scare when a man by the name of William Jones, who it is stated came from Wrexham, made threats to a 14 year old Beverley girl. The first article appeared in the Yorkshire press when an article appeared that stated, [1]

> BEVERLEY. A "JACK THE RIPPER" SCARE AT BEVERLEY. – *A rough looking fellow, who gave the name of William Jones and stated he came from Wrexham, was charged at the Police court, yesterday, with stealing a bell, the property of Mr. George Bodger, of the Rose and Crown Inn. There was a further charge of being drunk and disorderly in the streets. The prisoner had gone to several shops on the previous afternoon where women and girls were and alarmed them very much. Annie Parks, aged 14, who kept for her father a fruit shop in Butcher-row, stated that the prisoner went into the shop and asked her if she would oblige "Jack the Ripper" by giving him a plum. She did so. He squeezed her hand and used bad language to her. He said he would go some time and rip her up. She was very much frightened and screamed out, when the neighbours went to her*

> *assistance. Superintendent Knight arrested the prisoner. He said there were several other cases of a similar character against the prisoner. The latter admitted being drunk, and said he did not insult any one. Evidence was given of the missing of the bell from the Rose and Crown, which was found in the prisoner's possession when taken into custody. He was remanded till Monday.*

Before investigating what the other reports were saying that were sat on my desk I wanted to gather more information about the people and places featured in the report. My first area of interest was The Rose and Crown Inn. The Rose and Crown is situated on North Bar Without, Beverley, and the current building dates from the early twentieth century. [2] Records dating from 1574 show that there was a public house here known as Bull with the property transferred from Robert Fayer to Stephen Smailes. As early as 1800 the public house was known as the Rose and Crown. In 1930 preparations were made to remodel the public house, and by June/July 1931 it was extensively remodelled and is now a Grade II listed building. George Bodger, who is listed in the newspaper report, is listed as the Victualler here from 1882 until 1892. [3] With the name of the Victualler named I decided to research George Bodger further and discovered him in the 1891 Census. The entry reads, [4]

Rose and Crown Inn, York-road, Beverley

George Bodger	42	Head	Innkeeper (Rose and Crown)
Rose Bodger	30	Wife	
Fred Bodger	17	Son	Cabinet Maker
Blanch Bodger	13	Dau	Scholar
Francis Bodger	1	Son	
Eria Bodger	1mo	Son	

Mike Covell

Fred Kelsey	24	Servant	
Ada Foster	18	Servant	
Agnes Birch	16	Servant	

The Rose and Crown Inn was originally listed as being on York-road before the 1930 renovations which made the public houses frontage closer to North Bar Without. [5] Other sources link George Bodger to the public house, with the following entry in a Beverley Trade Directory of the period, [6]
George Bodger, Vict, Rose and Crown, North Bar Without.
With details on the Rose and Crown Inn I searched for a 14 year old Beverley girl by the name of Annie Parks. Searches of the Census failed to find an Annie Parks, but they did throw up an Ann E Parks, with her family linked to a fruiterer. It was the only Parks listed in Beverley with links to a fruiterer, the age matched, but the father did not own the business as the articles stated. The 1891 Census for Ann E Parks reads, [7]

Wilbert-lane, Beverley

William Parks	50	Head	Basket Maker
Harriet Parks	48	Wife	
Rachel Cron	24	Dau	
Robert Cron	23	Son in Law	Labourer
Jane Parks	19	Dau General	Servant Domestic
Mary E Parks	16	Dau	Fruiterers Assistant

Ann E Parks	14	Dau	
Emily Crow	1	G. Dau	
Emily Crow	1mo	G. Dau	

> Wilbert-lane is a long lane that stretches from Mill-lane in the north, passing the William Crosskill Iron Works down to Butcher Row, approximately 1750 feet, to the south. Searching a trade directory of Beverley during this period I found two fruiterers on Butcher-row, these are F. Jameson, and W. Wilson. Again, neither of these are the father of Ann E. Parks.
>
> Searches for William Jones residing in Beverley in 1891 failed to reveal a suitable match and none that resided at the town. It is quite possible, as it was known to happen, that Jones was passing through. Many people would travel from town to town, village to village seeking work. A search of the East Riding Archives also failed to turn up a William Jones in the town during this period. Searches are ongoing.
>
> Searches for Superintendent Knight were, however, more successful, with two possible police officers discovered that was in active service in the East Riding Police during the period. These are, George Henry Knight, who joined the police force November 16th 1872, and Henry Knight, who joined the police force October 25th 1870. [9] A trade directory of the period also revealed a tantalising clue, with a listing for George Henry Knight, Head Constable, Borough Police Station, Guildhall. [10]

The Beverley Guardian, October 3rd 1891,

> *A "JACK THE RIPPER"SCARE. William Jones, a rough looking man, who said he came from Wrexham, was placed in the dock to answer to three charges, viz., stealing a table bell, the property of Mr. George Bodger, Rose and crown Inn; drunk and disorderly in Butcher Row and other parts of the town; and assaulting Annie Parks; all of which offences were committed on the previous day. – Supt. Knight said prisoner had gone into several shops where females were, and alarmed them very much. – Prisoner pleaded guilty to being drunk, but denied the other charges. – Annie Parks, aged 14, stated that she kept her father's shop in Butcher Row. About four o'clock on the previous afternoon, the prisoner, who was*

Mike Covell

> *very drunk, went in and asked her if she would oblige "Jack the Ripper" with a plum. She gave him one, and he took hold of her hand and used some very bad language to her. She said he would go in the night time and zip her up. She was very frightened and screamed out, when some neighbours came to her assistance. – Supt. Knight stated that in consequence of a number of complaints he arrested the prisoner, who was very drunk, about four o'clock. He (Mr. Knight) saw the girl shortly after and found her in a terrible condition owing to fear and excitement. With regard to Bell, prisoner had it in his possession when arrested, and it was ascertained that he had been trying to sell it at several places in the town. – Ada Foster, maid at the Rose and Crown Inn was called, and gave evidence as to the two bells being on the table in the first class bar, at 9-30 the previous day, and missing one of them about five o'clock. She identified the one produced as one of her master's bells. – Supt. Knight asked for a remand until Monday morning, and this the Bench granted.*

The Yorkshire Gazette, October 3rd 1891,

> *A "JACK THE RIPPER" SCARE. – A rough looking fellow, "William Jones, from Wrexham," was charged on Tuesday with stealing a bell, the property of Mr. George Bodger, of the Rose and Crown Inn, and with being drunk and disorderly. Annie Parks (14), who kept for her father a fruit shop in Butcher-row, stated that the prisoner went into the shop and asked her if she would oblige "Jack the Ripper," by giving him a plum. She did so. He squeezed her hand and frightened her. He was remanded till Monday.*

The Yorkshire Herald, October 3rd 1891,

> *BEVERLEY. A "JACK THE RIPPER" SCARE AT BEVERLEY. – A rough looking fellow, who gave the name of William Jones and stated he came from Wrexham, was charged at the Police court, yesterday, with stealing a bell, the property of Mr. George Bodger, of the Rose and Crown Inn. There was a further charge of being drunk and disorderly in the streets. The prisoner had gone to several shops on the previous afternoon where women and girls were and alarmed them very much. Annie Parks, aged 14, who kept for her father a fruit shop in Butcher-row, stated that the prisoner went into the shop and asked her if she would oblige "Jack the Ripper" by giving him a plum. She did so. He squeezed her hand and used bad language to her. He said he would go some time and rip her up. She was very much frightened and screamed out, when the neighbours went to her assistance. Superintendent Knight arrested the prisoner. He said there were several other cases of a similar character against the prisoner. The latter admitted being drunk, and said he did not insult any one. Evidence was given of the missing*

> *of the bell from the Rose and Crown, which was found in the prisoner's possession when taken into custody. He was remanded till Monday.*

The York Herald, October 6th 1891,

> BEVERLEY. A "JACK THE RIPPER" FRIGHTENER AT BEVERLEY. – At the Guildhall, yesterday, before the Mayor and Mr. R. Hill, William Jones, a repulsive looking man, who stated he came from Wrexham, was charged with being drunk and disorderly and assaulting a girl named Annie Park. There was a further charge of stealing a brass table bell from the Rose and Crown Inn. Evidence was given to show that the prisoner had gone to a shop in Butcher-row, which was kept by the girl's father. He asked for a plum for "Jack the Ripper." She gave him one, and he made use of bad language, said he was "Jack the Ripper," and that he would go at night and rip her up. She was very much terrified. Superintendent Knight said several young persons had been alarmed by the prisoner in a similar manner. He apprehended him after hearing the complaints, and found in his pocket a bell which it was ascertained had been stolen from the Rose and Crown Inn. Prisoner, who denied the charges, was sent to prison for six weeks.

The Yorkshire Gazette, October 10th 1891,

> BEVERLEY. A "JACK THE RIPPER" SCARE. – At the Guildhall, yesterday, before the Mayor and Mr. R. Hill, William Jones, a repulsive looking man, who stated he came from Wrexham, was charged with being drunk and disorderly and assaulting a girl named Annie Park. There was a further charge of stealing a brass table bell from the Rose and Crown Inn. Evidence was given to show that the prisoner had gone to a shop in Butcher-row, which was kept by the girl's father. He asked for a plum for "Jack the Ripper." She gave him one, and he made use of bad language, said he was "Jack the Ripper," and that he would go at night and rip her up. She was very much terrified. Superintendent Knight said several young persons had been alarmed by the prisoner in a similar manner. He apprehended him after hearing the complaints, and found in his pocket a bell which it was ascertained had been stolen from the Rose and Crown Inn. Prisoner, who denied the charges, was sent to prison for six weeks.

The Beverley Guardian, October 10th 1891,

> ALLEGED "JACK THE RIPPER" SAFELY BOXED UP. – William Jones, a stranger, was charged on remand with being drunk and disorderly, and with stealing a bell from the Rose and Crown, and also with assaulting Annie Parks. The evidence previously given was read, after which Annie Oxley, wife of Richard

Mike Covell

> Oxley, butcher, North Bar-street, was called, and stated that the prisoner came to their shop about half past 11 in the morning to beg. He came from the direction of York-road and the Rose and Crown smoke-room. He frightened witness by his strange conduct, and refused to go away unless they gave him something. – Supt. Knight said prisoner did not appear to know what he was doing at the time of his arrest. – Defendant said he had not styled himself on "Jack the Ripper," and it was very wrong of the last witness to say so. He did not steal the bell, but bought it of a man for 6d. – The Mayor said he would have to go to prison for 21 days with hard labour for being drunk and disorderly, and for stealing the bell he would be imprisoned for a similar period.

The York Herald, October 10th 1891,

> BEVERLEY. A "JACK THE RIPPER" FRIGHTENER AT BEVERLEY. – At the Guildhall, yesterday, before the Mayor and Mr. R. Hill, William Jones, a repulsive looking man, who stated he came from Wrexham, was charged with being drunk and disorderly and assaulting a girl named Annie Park. There was a further charge of stealing a brass table bell from the Rose and Crown Inn. Evidence was given to show that the prisoner had gone to a shop in Butcher-row, which was kept by the girl's father. He asked for a plum for "Jack the Ripper." She gave him one, and he made use of bad language, said he was "Jack the Ripper," and that he would go at night and rip her up. She was very much terrified. Superintendent Knight said several young persons had been alarmed by the prisoner in a similar manner. He apprehended him after hearing the complaints, and found in his pocket a bell which it was ascertained had been stolen from the Rose and Crown Inn. Prisoner, who denied the charges, was sent to prison for six weeks.

References:

Beverley Ripper Craze's:

The 1891 Jack the Ripper Scare:

1. *The York Herald*, September 30th 1891

2. *The Inn Places of Beverley*, Frank Pinfold and George Higginson, Hutton Press Ltd, 1988, P. 33

3. A Toast to the Town – A History of Beverley's Public Houses, Paul Gibson, Kingston Press, 2001, PP. 84 – 87

4. 1891 Census George Bodger Class RG12, P3907, F12, P15, GSU6099017

5. A Toast to the Town – A History of Beverley's Public Houses, Paul Gibson, Kingston Press, 2001, PP. 84 – 87

6. *Bulmer's Trade Directory of Beverley*, 1892

7. 1891 Census Ann E Parks Class RG12, P3908, F49, P10, GSU6099018

8. *Bulmer's Trade Directory of Beverley*, 1892

9. *Country Coppers – The Story of the East Riding Police*, A. A. Clarke, Arton Books, 1993, P. 138

10. *Bulmer's Trade Directory of Beverley*, 1892

The 1894 Beverley Jack the Ripper Scare:

The next "Jack the Ripper" scare occurred in 1894, just three years after the 1891 scare and a full 6 years after the 1888 "Jack the Ripper" murders in Whitechapel. One of the earliest articles that covered the case was published in *The Northern Echo*, dated August 8th 1894,

> THE NEWCASTLE MURDERS. CAPTURE OF THE SUPPOSED CULPRIT. A LOCAL "JACK THE RIPPER." The Beverley Police have made what is believed to be a most important capture in connection with the series of mysterious murders of women at Gosforth and on the Newcastle Town Moor. They have taken into custody a man named Henry Dale (23), said to hail from Thornley, alleged to be a dangerous lunatic, who has been lately seen hanging about in that neighbourhood. The prisoner is believed to be a maniac type of the author of the terrible series of "Jack the Ripper" murders and mutilations in London, and the alleged similarity in the character of the murders appears to give point to the theory. The prisoner was brought before the Beverley magistrates yesterday morning, and was by them remanded to Newcastle for trial, and handed over to the Newcastle police, who were in attendance. Superintendent Spencer, with the man in his company, arrived at the Central Station, Newcastle, by the South Express shortly before four o'clock in the afternoon. He was met by Inspector Taylor, and the man was marched to the portico, where a cab was in readiness to convey him to the police station. The passage of the man through the station attracted little attention, whilst the man himself appeared so indifferent to his position that he walked along unconcernedly smoking a dirty broken clay pipe

Mike Covell

> locally known as a "cutty." He appeared to be a man of some 35 years of age, of dark hair and complexion, and he was poorly dressed.

Sunderland Echo and Shipping Gazette, August 7th 1894, and the *Evening Telegraph*, August 7th 1894,

> THE NEWCASTLE MURDERS. AN ARREST AT BEVERLEY. The police at Beverley have apprehended a man named Dales, with several aliases, on suspicion of being concerned in the recent "Jack the Ripper" murders at Newcastle. When arrested he was armed with a knife. He was handed over this morning to a detective superintendent from Newcastle, who has the case in hand. The prisoner is believed to be a dangerous lunatic.

The same report was also featured in the *Manchester Evening News*, August 7th 1894, the *Coventry Evening Telegraph*, August 7th 1894, the *Manchester Courier and Lancashire General Advertiser*, August 8th 1894, the *Western Times*, August 8th 1894, and the *Dundee Courier*, August 8th 1894, it stated,

> THE NEWCASTLE MURDERS. AN ARREST AT BEVERLEY. The police at Beverley have apprehended a man named Dales, with several aliases, on suspicion of being concerned in the recent "Jack the Ripper" murders at Newcastle. When arrested he was armed with a knife. He was handed over this morning to a detective superintendent from Newcastle, who has the case in hand. The prisoner is believed to be a dangerous lunatic.

The Star, August 7th 1894,

> ARREST OF A SUPPOSED "JACK THE RIPPER." BEVERLEY. August 7. a man named Dales has been arrested at Beverley, suspected of participation in the Jack the Ripper murders at Newcastle. He is believed to be a dangerous lunatic.

The Hull Daily Mail, August 6th 1894,

> THE LOW MOOR MURDER, AN ARREST AT BEVERLEY. (From our Beverley correspondent.) The Beverley Police have in custody a man who is suspected of having committed the atrocious murders which caused such consternation in Newcastle at the end of last June. He gives the name of Henry Dale, alias Johnson, and his age as 23, but he looks a little older than this. He has been staying in a common lodging house in Beverley a little over a fortnight, and the police authorities in Newcastle, having heard of his whereabouts, Superintendent Spencer, of the Newcastle force, was sent down to make enquiries. As a result

> Dale was arrested on Sunday night at the lodging house by Sergeant Haldenby, accompanied by Superintendent Spencer. The murders of which he is suspected as being the perpetrator were both committed at Newcastle in June. Both victims were women of the unfortunate class, and were done to death with a knife in a most brutal manner, one of them having no less than eleven gashes in the neck and face. The murders took place on the Town Moor, and about a month intervened between each. The assassin has since been at large, and the only clue which the police had was the description of a man who had been in the company of one the victims shortly before the crime. The man which the Beverley police have in custody is supposed to be this individual. There is additional evidence against Dale in the fact that when he returned to his lodgings in Newcastle on the morning after the latter murder his clothes were, as the police have since ascertained, STAINED WITH BLOOD. Dale has been an inmate of the Durham County Asylum on four occasions, and is evidently a most dangerous character. He has been very violent at his lodgings in Beverley, and it was noticed by his fellow lodgers that he had a knife secreted in his coat sleeve. It was this fact which, being reported to the police, first brought him under observation. He was brought before the Beverley Justices at the Borough Police Court this morning, charged with being A WANDERING LUNATIC. No reference was made to the graver offence, as the inquiries are not yet completed. – Superintendent Knight mentioned that Dale had been in the town about a fortnight, and his conduct had given rise to suspicions as to his state of mind. – Prisoner (excitedly): "My mind is all right; don't you tell any damnable falsehoods." – Superintendent Knight: - "I should like a remand for 24 hours," – The Mayor: "You stand remanded until to-morrow morning." – Prisoner: "What am I remanded for. You have a right to tell me what charge there is against me." – Superintendent Knight: "He is undoubtedly not fit to be at large." – Dr. Appleton (one of the Justices on the Bench) "He has not only a dangerous mind, but is also a man who is dangerous to society." – Prisoner was then removed to the cells, the while using violent language. – Superintendent Spencer, who watched the proceedings, remains in Beverley awaiting instructions from Newcastle.

The York Herald, August 7th 1894,

> BEVERLEY. – Henry dale, 23, labourer, of no fixed residence, was charged with being a suspected person. Superintendent Knight asked that a remand be granted for inquiries to be made. The remand was granted.

The Hull Daily Mail, August 7th 1894,

Mike Covell

> LOW MOOR "RIPPER" MURDERS. THE ARREST AT BEVERLEY. HANDED OVER TO THE NEWCASTLE POLICE. Considerable excitement was caused in Hull and the district yesterday. This was occasioned through currency given to a report (which appeared in the Daily Mail) that the Beverley police had in custody a man who, there was reason to believe, would be charged on suspicion with having been concerned in one at least of the Low Moor murders. These deeds were committed at Newcastle during June, and were of an atrocious nature. For about a fortnight or three weeks a man had been known to be residing in Beverley at a lodging house. His behaviour gave rise to suspicion. From circumstances that afterwards transpired he was arrested on Sunday. Then he gave the name of Henry Dale, and described himself as a labourer, 23 years of age. It was afterwards ascertained that he had several aliases, among them being Solomon Francis, Arthur Fallas, Wreham Bainbridge, and William Johnson. He is a man of slight build, with black hair, and a dark moustache. He was shabbily dressed. Yesterday morning he was placed in the dock at the Borough Police Court. Superintendent Knight informed the Bench that the man's conduct had given rise to suspicion as to the state of his mind. The prisoner then behaved in A VERY EXCITED MANNER. When the Superintendent alluded to his state of mind he exclaimed "My mind is all right; don't you tell any damnable falsehoods." He demanded to know what the charge against him was. During the time he was taken into custody and his appearance at the Court, very little opportunity had been afforded for making complete inquiries. Therefore he was remanded for 24 hours. When the case came on for hearing this morning there were many persons in Court. The Justices upon the Bench were the Mayor (Mr. T. Turner), Dr. Appleton, and Mr. A. Crosskill. The demeanour of the prisoner had undergone a complete change, and he conducted himself quietly as compared with the attitude he assumed on the previous day. He listened to all remarks with the closest attention. Superintendent Knight repeated what he stated on Monday. He added that the prisoner had admitted that he had been on four occasions in the Durham County Asylum. He was at times subject to fits of violence, and was then not fit to be at large. His recovery might only be temporary. The Superintendent from that district was in court, and was WILLING TO TAKE THE PRISONER BACK in order that he might be dealt with in the form thought most desirable. Prisoner protested against this course being pursued. He was in regular work at Beverley, he said. If there was any charge against him he would prove his whereabouts since the 30th June. – Superintendent Knight said the attention of the police was drawn to the man through a disturbance in a lodging house, and, as it was alleged, the prisoner behaving in a suspicious manner with regard to a woman. He had a KNIFE UP HIS SLEEVE. The man was arrested in consequence of a complaint made to the police as to the apparently dangerous state of his mind. – The Bench agreed to hand the man over to Superintendent Spencer, of the Newcastle Constabulary.

> Dale was subsequently removed from Beverley. He was taken by two officers to the Railway Station to await the arrival of the 12.36 train from Hull. Very few persons were aware of the departure. During the period he was waiting at the station one of the private rooms of the company's servants was requisitioned to hide him from the gaze of the curious. There is considerable doubt as to the prisoner's mental condition. We are informed that he was discharged from the 10th Hussars owing to his mind being unhinged. It was understood that he would be charged, on suspicion, with having murdered a woman named Harland, at Low Moor, on the 30th June. We cannot give an official verification of this statement, as the police are very reticent about giving information to anyone.

The Beverley Guardian, August 11th 1894,

> THE TYNESIDE MURDERS. The man Dale, who was arrested in Beverley last Sunday and handed over to the Newcastle police on suspicion of having some connection with the murder of two women on the Town Moor at Newcastle, has been liberated, and is now in Beverley again, having returned on Thursday evening accompanied by a detective.

The Beverley Guardian, August 11th 1894,

> THE TYNESIDE MURDERS. A MAN ARRESTED IN BEVERLEY. A man who is supposed to have some connection with the murders committed in Newcastle some weeks ago, was arrested in Beverley on Sunday morning last, by the Beverley police, on a charge of being a wandering lunatic. He gave the name of Henry Dale, but has a number of aliases, and his age as 23, but looks a little older. He had been in Beverley a fortnight or three weeks, and the Newcastle police hearing of his whereabouts, Supt. Spencer, of the detective department, came down last Saturday and requested that Dale might be arrested. This was accomplished on Sunday morning by Sergeant Haldenby who found Dale in a common lodging house in Keld Gate. His conduct while there had been of a most violent nature, and on one occasion it was noticed that he had a knife secreted in his coat sleeve. Had he not been wanted by the Newcastle authorities, the police here would have been obliged to take charge of him, as he is undoubtedly a man whose temperament is such that he is not fit to be at large. It has been ascertained that he was formerly in the 10th Hussars, and was discharged from that regiment as a dangerous lunatic, and also that he has been four times in the Durham County Asylum. The murders of which he is suspected as being the perpetrator, were both committed on the Town Moor, at Newcastle, an extensive area of grass land at the north end of the city. Both victims were women of the unfortunate class, to which Dale is known to have a great aversion, and both were murdered with a knife. The

Mike Covell

latter crime took place on the 30th June last, the name of the victim being Harland, and her age 32. The other murder was committed about five weeks previously in the same locality. In both instances desperate struggles had taken place, the woman being almost cut to pieces. No clue was obtained of the assassin at the time, but the police were furnished with a description of a man who had been seen in the company of each woman shortly before each of the crimes, and who it was also noted had returned to his lodging with blood stained clothes, after the last murder. He disappeared, however, before the police could lay hands upon him, and it supposed from the description given that Dale is the man. He has not, up to the present been able to give a satisfactory account of his whereabouts at the time of the murders. Dale, whose aliases are Solomon Francis, Arthur Fallas, William Baimbridge, and William Johnson, and against whom there are numerous convictions, including horse stealing, was brought up on Monday before the Mayor (Mr. Tom Turner) Mr. B. Hodgson, Junior, and Dr. Appleton, on a charge of being a wandering lunatic. – Supt. Knight mentioned that Dale had been in the town about a fortnight, and his conduct had given rise to suspicions as to his state of mind. – Prisoner (excitedly): "My mind is all right; don't you tell any damned falsehoods." Supt. Knight: "I should like a remand for 24 hours." – The Mayor: "You stand remanded until tomorrow morning." – Prisoner: "What am I remanded for? You have a right to tell me what charge there is against me." – Supt. Knight: "He is undoubtedly not fit to be at large." – Dr. Appleton (who had seen Dale in his cell): "He has not only a dangerous mind, but is also a man who is dangerous to society." Prisoner was then removed to the cells, the while using violent language. – Supt. Spencer, who was in court, remained in Beverley, awaiting instructions from Newcastle. Dale was again placed in the dock on Tuesday morning, the magistrates on the bench being the Mayor (Mr. Tom Turner), Dr. Appleton, and Mr. Alfred Crosskill. – Supt. Knight informed the justices that Supt. Spencer was prepared to take the prisoner to Newcastle to be dealt with there as the authorities might deem best, and he suggested therefore that Dale be handed over to him. – The Bench acceded to this course. – Supt. Spencer and his prisoner left Beverley for Newcastle at midday. ARRIVAL OF THE PRISONER AT NEWCASTLE. Superintendent Spencer, arrived with his prisoner at the Central Station by the south express shortly before four o'clock. He was met by Inspector Taylor, and the man was marched to the portion where a cab was in readiness to convey him to the police station. The passage pf the man through the station attracted little attention, whilst the man himself appeared so indifferent to his position that he walked along unconcernedly smoking a dirty broken clay pipe locally known as a "cutty." He appeared to be a man of some 35 years of age, of dark hair and complexion, and was poorly clad. NOT THE MAN WANTED. The man who was arrested at Beverley on Sunday and conveyed to Newcastle by the police on suspicion of being the man wanted in conjunction with

Newspapers from Hull Volume 2

> *the murder of two woman near Newcastle, turned out not be the man the police are in search of. After being brought to Newcastle, he was seen by a man who had given some information on the subject of the murder. This person, it appears on the morning immediately after the Town Moor tragedy, had been in Jesmond-road, when he was accosted by a man wearing a peaked cap, who asked him the way to Chester-le-street. He directed him the way, at the same time taking a good look at the questioner. Afterwards he gave information to the police, and as the description tallied with that of a man who had been missing from his home once or twice in the County of Durham, the suspicion of the authorities was aroused. A description of the man was issued to the various police authorities. The person apprehended at Beverley and brought to Newcastle by Detective Spencer on Tuesday seemed to answer the description; but when he was brought before the man who gave the information respecting the Jesmond-road incident, that person failed entirely to identify him. He stated that it was not the man he had seen.*

The North Eastern Daily Gazette, July 2nd 1894,

> IS "JACK THE RIPPER" IN NEWCASTLE? TWO MYSTERIOUS MURDERS ON THE TOWN MOOR. NO CLUE TO THE CRIMES. *A shocking tragedy was discovered yesterday morning at Newcastle on Tyne. On the Town Moor, an extensive area of grass land at the north end of the city, a little after four o'clock, the body of Annie Harland, a married woman, but an unfortunate, aged 32, was found by a man who was taking his cows to pasture. The throat was cut in such a way that death must have been almost instantaneous. The police surgeon states that the woman must have been dead four hours or more. At ten o'clock on Saturday night she was seen going in the direction of the Town Moor with a stout man dressed in dark clothing. This is the latest that is known of her. The head and neck were cut and disfigured in a shocking manner. The body was removed on a stretcher to the mortuary, and the police immediately commenced to institute a search for the perpetrator of the murder. Within a short space of time Superintendent Spencer, of the Detective Department, together with several smart members of this staff, were on the scene, and a careful examination was made of the ground, with a view of finding footprints, or some other evidence that would lead to the capture of the murderer. Their efforts to detect footprints were in vain, as the ground was hard, owing to the recent fine weather. They also failed to discover any weapon, or to glean anything that would be serviceable to them in their investigations. A description of the murderer bears a striking resemblance to that of the supposed Gosforth murderer, and the opinion is strongly entertained by several members of the detective department that the Newcastle murderer is the same person. This opinion is further strengthened by the fact that the police are in possession of information regarding the recent extraordinary train of incidents*

> that took place at Gosforth, but they do not consider it wise to disclose these facts at present. The husband of the victim, John Harland, is in custody, but though he has been known to thrash his wife and threaten her life, the police do not think he has been involved in the tragedy. During the afternoon a boy found a knife with blood upon the handle, which was taken from him by an elderly man, who assured the boy that he would forward it to the police. The weapon, however, has not been yet handed to the police, and a search is now being made for the man who obtained it. If this be the instrument which killed the deceased the line of route indicates that the murderer made his escape in the direction of Spital Tongue. Hundreds of people visited the scene of the tragedy yesterday, where the blood stains are plainly visible. The murdered woman comes of a respectable family in Newcastle. Her father, who is still living, and who, along with his wife, will no doubt be deeply distressed at his daughter's sad end, is a minor official at a local colliery, and is well respected by his fellow workmen. The poor woman had been of a wayward disposition, and on the course of her career has come under the notice of the police for some ten or twelve years past. The Gosforth murder took place only a month ago not far from the same spot, the victim in that case also being an unfortunate. The opinion of the chiefs of police is that the murder is the work of the same hand. UNDETECTED MURDERS IN NEW CASTLE AND GATESHEAD. The murder of Annie Harland makes the fifth capital crime that has taken place during the last few years without any conviction having taken place. There was the first murder of Lizzie Tait in the Low Bridge, Newcastle, and though in this case the police succeeded in arresting a man he was acquitted at the assizes. Then there came the murder of a young man in Pipewellgate, Gateshead, followed by the still more mysterious shooting of Robert Turbot, in Scotswood, a little over twelve months ago, and not even a clue to the perpetrators of either of these crimes was ever discovered. Five weeks ago the woman Bucham was found dead at Gosforth, and now there is the latest crime in the murder of Annie Harland.

The *Bristol Mercury*, July 3rd 1894 and the *Liverpool Mercury*, July 3rd 1894, both published the following,

> THE NEWCASTLE MURDER. An inquest was held at Newcastle, last night, on the body of Jane Harland, 32, whose body was found on the Town Moor on Sunday with the throat cut. The evidence showed that a desperate struggle must have occurred, as indicated by the cuts and bruises on the hands. There were 11 gashes in the neck and face. A verdict of wilful murder against some person unknown was returned. A man, whose clothing is said to have been blood-stained, was arrested by the Durham constabulary yesterday, and detained on suspicion.

The Sunderland Daily Echo and Shipping Gazette, July 5th 1894,

THE NEWCASTLE MURDER. – Yesterday the police made no further progress towards elucidating the mysterious murder of Annie Harland on the Town Moor at a late hour last Saturday. To-day the deceased woman will be buried at St. Andrew's Cemetery, North-road.

Mike Covell

Appendix IV - Frederick Bailey Deeming in the Hull press 1890

In 1890 a gentleman arrived at Hull and began making transactions with a local jewellery story. He carried out, what today would be considered a long fraud, where he gradually bought larger and larger items for more and more cash, gaining the confidence of the team at Messrs Reynoldson and Son, who were situated on Whitefriargate, Hull. He eventually bought a number of items and tendered several cheques for the items, but all was not as it seems, and when the cheques bounced, an international manhunt was on the cards for the Hull police.

The Hull press began to follow the case on April 10th 1890 when the following article appeared in both *The Hull Daily Mail*, dated April 10th 1890, and *The Hull and East Yorkshire and Lincolnshire Times*, dated April 12th 1890,

> ALLEGED GREAT FRAUD ON HULL JEWELLERS. ARREST AT MONTE VIDEO. Particulars have just come to hand of the arrest of a person named Harry Lawson, at Monte Video, on a charge of having obtained a large amount of jewellery from Messrs. T. Reynoldson and Son, Jewellers, Whitefriargate. It appears that this interesting gentleman entered into the bonds of holy matrimony during February last, and the following month he obtained £286 worth of jewellery, for which he tendered what proved to be fictitious cheques. Shortly after he left the shores of dear old England, and the matter was placed in the hands of the police, with the result that a telegram was received in Hull on Wednesday intimating that the gentleman had been arrested at Monte Video. These are somewhat meager facts but no doubt more will be heard of this interesting matter within the next few days.

The Hull Daily News, April 10th 1890, and *The Hull News*, April 12th 1890, featured the following,

> ARREST OF AN ALLEGED HULL SWINDLER AT MONTE VIDEO. On Wednesday, the Hull Police received a telegram from Scotland Yard that a man

Newspapers from Hull Volume 2

> *named Harry Lawson, who is wanted in Hull for obtaining £285 worth of jewellery by fraud from Messrs. Reynoldson of Whitefriargate, had been arrested at Monte Video. It appears that early this year Lawson, who stated that he was a wool merchant from Australia, married a young lady at Beverley, and in March obtained jewellery to the amount named, of Messrs. Reynoldson. He tendered cheques in payment for the same, but these on being represented where, it is said, dishonoured. It was then found that Lawson had absconded, leaving his newly married bride. He was traced to Southampton, but he had sailed to Monte Video. Application was made to the Foreign Office, by whose instrumentality the arrest has been elicited.*

The Hull Daily Mail, dated July 11th 1890, and *The Hull and East Yorkshire and Lincolnshire Times*, dated July 12th 1890,

> THE ALLEGED FRAUDS ON HULL JEWELLERS. TO MONTE VIDEO AND BACK BY A HULL DETECTIVE. *Detective Sergeant Grasby, of the Hull Police Force, sailed from Liverpool on Thursday by the steamer Dom, for Monte Video, with a warrant from the Foreign Office, signed by the Marquis of Salisbury, to bring back to Hull Harry Lawson, who was arrested in Monte Video in April last and charged with fraudulently obtaining of Messrs Thomas Reynoldson and Son, Jewellers, Whitefriargate, some very valuable diamond jewellery, and absconding with the same. This is the first case of extradition granted under the new treaty between Great Britain and the Argentine Republic, which only came into operation on the 1st of January 1890. Owing to the great distance between the two countries, unavoidable delays, caused by the arranging of preliminaries for his extradition, have arisen, so that the prisoner could not be brought back before. He may now be expected to arrive, under charge of Sergeant Grasby, in about two months' time.*

The Hull Daily News, 1st September 1890 featured the following lengthy report on the Deeming case,

> THE ALLEGED JEWEL FRAUDS IN HULL, ARRIVAL OF THE ACCUSED *Detective Grasby of the Hull police force, arrived in Hull on Saturday night from Monte Video, having in custody Harry Lawson, alias Deeming, who is accused of obtaining £235 worth of jewellery from Messrs. Thomas Reynoldson and Son, jewellers, Whitefriargate, Hull, by means of fictitious cheques in March last. The detective and his charge, on whom nearly all the property was found, were landed at Southampton by the Royal Mail steamer Thames, and immediately proceeded by Hull, at 8-25 p.m. Some account of Lawson's alleged frauds has already been given in these columns, but the story of his career, as far as it is connected with*

Mike Covell

Hull, will doubtless be heard again with interest. The public is probably destined to hear a good deal about him and it shortly [illegible] took apartments at Beverley in October last, and he stated he came from Queensland, and he was connected with the Australian wool trade. He lived and behaved in a manner that suggested the substantial man. He bought expensive things, and paid for them- "The best recommendation I can give you," he said to the salesman, "is cash." He seemed to be a young man- aged about thirty- of good education, and his manners were pleasant. By and bye, it became known that he was engaged to a young lady of good social connections, and in February last (we believe) the wedding took place. It was about that time that he commenced to have dealings with several jewellers in Hull- amongst them Messrs. Reynoldson. He purchased articles of jewellery, and paid promptly for them, sometimes by cash and sometimes by means of cheques, which were duly honoured at the bank. Up to the early part of March he had business with the firm to the extent of about £100. On the afternoon of the 15th of the month, a Saturday, Lawson- who had just returned from his honeymoon- stopped at Messrs. Reynoldson's, and, after inspecting some articles, bought a diamond bracelet and a couple of diamond rings, worth £285. He gave a payment of two cheques, one for £120 and the other for £165, and took the jewellery away with him, it being after banking hours, the jewellers had no opportunity of cashing the cheques that day. On Monday they were presented in the ordinary course, when the banker informed the payees that Lawson's account had then closed some days previously. We believe that at some other tradesmen had already been the receivers of similar unpleasant information. The police were at once communicated with, and a warrant was [illegible] with all possible speed. It was soon found that the bird had flown, though he had left with his wife behind in Beverley. The Hull detective staff made energetic efforts to trace him, and the promptitude and thoroughness of their action resulted in the discovery that Lawson had shipped on board the Coleridge, bound for Monte Video. Mr. Thomas Reynoldson, the head of the firm of jewellers, was at the office in London, and upon receipt of this intelligence, then took immediate steps to procure Lawson's extradition. He went to the Foreign Office, and had an interview with Lord Salisbury, offering to pay all the expenses, as [illegible] indemnity. Thereupon, negotiations are opened up, and, after some delay, the necessary extradition papers were signed, it being, we believe, the first transaction of the kind between our Government and Uruguay, the treaty having only recently been concluded. Detective Grasby was entrusted with the impossible duty of proceeding to Monte Video to bring back the prisoner, and this duty he was successfully turned out, being able to put his hand on the man's shoulder upon the latter's arrival. H was found in possession of two diamond rings, 63 loose diamonds and three valuable Masonic emblems- one set with diamonds the others being from Messrs. Reynoldson have identical to the two diamond rings as their property, and they

> *believe that the loose stones were those belonging to the bracelet and Lawson obtained from them, the supposition being that the setting has been destroyed. It is thought that the he had obtained the other jewellery in Berlin and Antwerp.*

The Hull Daily Mail, 1st September 1890, also featured their take on the Deeming case.

> THE ALLEGED JEWELLERY FRAUD IN HULL, THE ACCUSED AT THE POLICE COURT
>
> *At the Hull Police Court this day, before Mr. EC. Twiss (stipendiary magistrate) Henry Lawson, alias Deeing, was charged for obtaining two diamond rings and a diamond bracelet from Messrs T. Reynoldson and Son, Whitefriargate, Hull, by means of certain false pretenses on the 15th March last.- Mr. Laverack appeared for the prosecution, and the accused was represented by Mr. Holdich. Mr. Laverack in his opening statement to the Court, said that the prisoner was charged with obtaining two diamond rings, and a diamond bracelet, by means of certain false pretenses. This was a case in which the prisoner had been brought a very considerable distance- from Monte Video upon that charge.*
>
> *Without making any lengthy statement it was sufficient to say that on the 15th March last, the prisoner went into Messrs Reynoldson and Sons establishment, and purchased, or agreed to purchase two rings for £120, and a diamond bracelet for £165. This was on a Saturday afternoon after banking hours, and he (Mr. Laverack), should say that the defendant had previously had transactions with the prosecutors, in some cases paying by cash, and in others by cheque upon the Yorkshire Banking Company, which had been duly met. On this occasion he purchased the rings first and gave a cheque for the amount of £126. This cheque was dated March 15th and was drawn upon the Yorkshire Banking Company. When he purchased the bracelet he gave another cheque for £165, and dated it March 18th and asked Mr. Reynoldson to agree to this, as he should have further remittance by that date, which he should pay into the bank, intimating that his banking account would not be sufficient to meet the two cheques at the same time. Under these circumstances he took the rings and bracelet away. He also promised to return on the following Monday morning with his wife to see certain silver plate which he had mentioned. It appeared from inquiries which subsequently were made that the prisoner left Hull that same afternoon, and never returned until he came with a policeman on Saturday afternoon last. That this was a deliberately planned fraud there could not be the slightest doubt, because not only did the prisoner leave for London that night, but it appeared he was staying with his wife- a lady with whom he went through the ceremony of marriage at any rate, whether*

> she was his wife or not is open to question. He was staying with the lady who it was expected is his wife at the Station Hotel, Hull, and he had told her, that he should not return until Monday morning. Mr. Twiss: Of course this you cannot prove. Mr. Laverack: Well, if she is his wife. Mr. Twiss: You are opening it on the supposition that she is not his wife? Mr. Laverack: Yes. He left for Hull and went to London, and then on the Sunday morning he left London by train which would enable him to catch the mail boat leaving Southampton for Monte Video. So that the whole of this was planned before he went to Messrs Reynoldson's shop and purchased the articles for which he had tendered these cheques. Well, on Monday morning the next cheque was presented at the bank, and it was found that the prisoner closed his account on the 12th March. It seemed that he opened an account at the bank on the 20th January, when he deposited the sum of £310. At the time he described himself as a wool broker and large sheep farmer, and that he wanted to open an account as he had large dealings in wool. He never deposited any further sums, but continued to draw on the sum first deposited until his funds were exhausted and his account finally closed on the 12th March. He knew, therefore, that the cheque he was giving for £120, and another that he gave for £163, could not be honoured; and, beyond that, he also knew that he had arranged to leave England the next day for Monte Video, and that this was for the purpose of using these valuable items in order that he might raise money upon them. Mr. Reynoldson took steps for having the defendant arrested immediately after his arrival at Monte Video. An officer was sent on and had brought him back here. Mr. Laverack, concluding his statement applied for remand in order that proper evidence might be furnished to the court. Detective Grassby said that he arrested the defendant at Monte Video on the 8th August. He had with him a warrant which he read over, and the defendant made no reply. He brought him to this country, and arrived in Hull on Saturday afternoon. Mr. Laverack then asked for a remand, and his Worship granted one until Saturday next, it being understood that the case will be completed on that day if possible, so his Worship will be absent from Hull sometime after that, which would consequently necessitate a series of remands. Mr. Holdich offered no objection to the remand granted.

The Hull Daily Mail, 2nd September 1890, featured a follow up report, note the misspelling of the first name, Henry, not Harry, and the surname, Deeing, not Deeming.

> THE ALLEGED JEWELLERY FRAUD IN HULL, THE ACCUSED AT THE POLICE COURT. At the Hull Police Court on Monday, before Mr. EC. Twiss (stipendiary magistrate) Henry Lawson, alias Deeing, was charged for obtaining two diamond rings and a diamond bracelet from Messrs T. Reynoldson and Son, Whitefriargate, Hull, by means of certain false pretenses on the 15th March last.-

Mr. Laverack appeared for the prosecution, and the accused was represented by Mr. Holdich. Mr Laverack in his opening statement to the Court, said that the prisoner was charged with obtaining two diamond rings, and a diamond bracelet, by means of certain false pretenses. This was a case in which the prisoner had been brought a very considerable distance- from Monte Video upon that charge.

Without making any lengthy statement it was sufficient to say that on the 15th March last, the prisoner went into Messrs Reynoldson and Sons establishment, and purchased, or agreed to purchase two rings for £120, and a diamond bracelet for £165. This was on a Saturday afternoon after banking hours, and he (Mr. Laverack), should say that the defendant had previously had transactions with the prosecutors, in some cases paying by cash, and in others by cheque upon the Yorkshire Banking Company, which had been duly met. On this occasion he purchased the rings first and gave a cheque for the amount of £126. This cheque was dated March 15th and was drawn upon the Yorkshire Banking Company. When he purchased the bracelet he gave another cheque for £165, and dated it March 18th and asked Mr. Reynoldson to agree to this, as he should have further remittance by that date, which he should pay into the bank, intimating that his banking account would not be sufficient to meet the two cheques at the same time. Under these circumstances he took the rings and bracelet away. He also promised to return on the following Monday morning with his wife to see certain silver plate which he had mentioned. It appeared from inquiries which subsequently were made that the prisoner left Hull that same afternoon, and never returned until he came with a policeman on Saturday afternoon last. That this was a deliberately planned fraud there could not be the slightest doubt, because not only did the prisoner leave for London that night, but it appeared he was staying with his wife- a lady with whom he went through the ceremony of marriage at any rate, whether she was his wife or not is open to question. He was staying with the lady who it was expected is his wife at the Station Hotel, Hull, and he had told her, that he should not return until Monday morning. Mr. Twiss: Of course this you cannot prove. Mr. Laverack: Well, if she is his wife. Mr. Twiss: You are opening it on the supposition that she is not his wife? Mr. Laverack: Yes. He left for Hull and went to London, and then on the Sunday morning he left London by train which would enable him to catch the mail boat leaving Southampton for Monte Video. So that the whole of this was planned before he went to Messrs Reynoldson's shop and purchased the articles for which he had tendered these cheques. Well, on Monday morning the next cheque was presented at the bank, and it was found that the prisoner closed his account on the 12th March. It seemed that he opened an account at the bank on the 20th January, when he deposited the sum of £310. At the time he described himself as a wool broker and large sheep farmer, and that he wanted to open an account as he had large dealings in wool. He never deposited

Mike Covell

> any further sums, but continued to draw on the sum first deposited until his funds were exhausted and his account finally closed on the 12th March. He knew, therefore, that the cheque he was giving for £120, and another that he gave for £163, could not be honoured; and, beyond that, he also knew that he had arranged to leave England the next day for Monte Video, and that this was for the purpose of using these valuable items in order that he might raise money upon them. Mr. Reynoldson took steps for having the defendant arrested immediately after his arrival at Monte Video. An officer was sent on and had brought him back here. Mr. Laverack, concluding his statement applied for remand in order that proper evidence might be furnished to the court. Detective Grassby said that he arrested the defendant at Monte Video on the 8th August. He had with him a warrant which he read over, and the defendant made no reply. He brought him to this country, and arrived in Hull on Saturday afternoon. Mr. Laverack then asked for a remand, and his Worship granted one until Saturday next, it being understood that the case will be completed on that day if possible, so his Worship will be absent from Hull sometime after that, which would consequently necessitate a series of remands. Mr. Holdich offered no objection to the remand granted.

The Hull Daily News, September 2nd 1890 featured the following report, this time getting the first name correct, but again calling Deeming Deeing.

> THE FRAUD ON HULL JEWELLERS, PRISONER BEFORE THE STIPENDIARY MAGISTRATE. On Monday, at the Hull Police court, Harry Lawson, alias Deeming, was brought in custody on a warrant, which charged him with obtaining £285 worth of jewellery from Messrs. T Reynoldson and Son, jewellers, Whitefriargate, by means of false pretenses in March last. Mr. Laverack was instructed to prosecute; the accused was represented by Mr. Holdich. Mr. Laverack, in his opening statement to the Court said the prisoner was charged with obtaining two diamond rings and a diamond bracelet by means of certain false pretenses. This was a case in which the prisoner had been brought a very considerable distance- from Monte Video- upon that charge. Without making any lengthy statement it was sufficient to say that on the 15th March last, the defendant went into Messrs. Reynoldson and Son's establishment and purchased, or agreed to purchase, two rings for £120 and a diamond bracelet for £165. This was on a Saturday afternoon after banking hours, and he (Mr. Laverack) should say that the defendant had previously had transactions with the prosecutors, in some cases paying by cash, and in others by cheque on the Yorkshire Banking Company, which had been duly met. On this occasion he purchased the rings first and gave a cheque for the amount of £120. This cheque was dated March 15th, and was drawn upon the Yorkshire Banking Company. When he purchased the bracelet he gave another cheque for £185, and dated it March 18th, and asked Mr. Reynoldson to

agree this, as he should have a further remittance by that date, which he should pay into the bank, intimating his bank account would not be sufficient to meet the two cheques at the same time. Under these circumstances he took the rings and bracelet away. He also promised to return on the following Monday morning with his wife to see a certain silver plate which he had mentioned. It appeared from inquiries which subsequently were made, that the prisoner left Hull that same afternoon, and never returned until he came with a policeman on Saturday afternoon last. That this was a deliberately planned fraud there could not be the slightest doubt, because not only did the prisoner leave for London that night, but it appeared he was staying with his wife- a lady with whom he went through the ceremony of marriage, at any rate, whether she was his wife or not was open to question. He was staying with this lady who it was expected was his wife at the Station Hotel, Hull, and he had told her he was about to purchase some presents for her, and that he should not return until Monday morning.- Mr. Twiss: Of course, this you cannot prove?- Mr. Laverack: Well, if she is his wife.- Mr. Twiss: You are opening it on the supposition that she is not his wife?- Mr. Laverack: Yes. He left Hull and went to London, and then on Sunday morning he left London by the train which would enable him to catch the mail boat leaving Southampton for Monte Video. So that the whole of this was planned before he went to Messrs. Reynoldson's shop and he purchased the articles, for which he tendered these cheques. Well, on the Monday morning the first cheque was presented at the bank, and it was found that the prisoner closed his account on the 12th March. It seemed he opened an account at the bank on the 20th January, when he deposited a sum of £310. At the time he described himself as a wool broker and large sheep farmer and that he wanted to open an account, as he had large dealings in wool. He never deposited any further sums, but continued to draw on the first sum deposited until his funds were exhausted, and his account was finally closed on the 12th March. He knew, therefore that the cheque he was giving for £120, and another he gave for £165 could not be honoured, and beyond that he also knew he had arranged to leave England the very next day for Monte Video, and that this was for the purpose of using those valuable articles in order that he might raise money upon them. Mr. Reynoldson took steps for having the defendant arrested immediately after his arrival at Monte Video. An officer was sent out, and brought him back here. Mr. Laverack, concluding his statement, applied for a remand in order that proper evidence might be furnished to the Court. Detective Grasby said that he arrested the defendant at Monte Video on the 8th August. He had with him a warrant which he read over, and the defendant made no reply. He brought him to this country, and arrived in Hull on Saturday afternoon.

Mr. Laverack then asked for a remand, and his Worship granted one until Saturday next, it being understood that the case will be completed on that day if

Mike Covell

> possible, as his Worship was will be absent from Hull sometime after that, and would consequently necessitate a series of remands. Mr. Holdich had no objection to the offer of remand, but asked, if he was not prepared to go on in the interest of his client, a further adjournment should be taken.

The Hull Daily Mail, September 3rd 1890 featured the following account by Detective Grasby,

> A HULL DETECTIVE'S VOYAGE TO MONTE VIDEO, AMUSING INCIDENTS AND EXPERIENCES, "It's an ill wind that blows nobody good," and the issue of a warrant for the extradition of a prisoner at Monte Video afforded me the opportunity of enjoying a trip which terminated last Saturday by my return to Hull. It was on the 8th of July that I was armed with the warrant, and having made all preparations for my voyage over the equator, I took train at Paragon Station and started across country for Liverpool, where I selected a berth in the steamer Sorrato, which sailed FOR THE RIVER PLATE The next day with a general cargo and about 200 passengers. It was a pleasant company, but the great majority were very susceptible to the feeling engendered by the tumbling and jostling of the sea. We had scarcely got into St George's Channel before all around me were in the throes of sea sickness. Several ladies bravely tried to become better sailors, while big burly fellows, bound for South of America to rough life and make a fortune, struggled to their feet, duly, however to sink once more under the excessive painfulness of their condition, which was at the same time highly disagreeable to myself and two others in the second class saloon. I myself proved to be AN EXCELLENT SAILOR On deck I roamed with a pipe in my mouth and scanned the ocean, at one time buffeting a stiffish breeze and again lounging leisurely on the lee side of the Sorrato. The voyage through the Bay of Biscay was on the whole a pleasant one. Very few of the passengers, however, were able to be up and about, so that there was only a select number to catch the first glimpse of the home of the gay Frenchman. The port to which we wave at the outset bound was, I learned, in the neighbourhood of Bordeaux. The name conjured up in my mind ideas as I pensively gazed over the bulwarks. As I stood there I dreamed, as it were, of a ball lighted by a thousand jets of gas, all [illegible] a radiant glare upon a happy hilarious throng, whose merry laugh and shouts of hurrah (as in Bosso's Empire) parched their throats, which they moistened with good old Bordeaux port or some other palatable wines from the same rich country. I am not, though, given to musings of this description, and soon my whole attention was riveted on the landscape on the other side of the river Gironde, up which we were travelling to Peuilliac, a place only a few miles from Bordeaux. It was on the 12th of the same month when we again sailed, this time to for Lisbon, where we would witness a sight that would surely TICKLE THE FANCY Of our leaders in Hull. The place

looked very well and the weather was fine, so we landed and made a tour of inspection. The spectacle that most tickled my fancy, and to which I have referred, was the number of women who were [illegible] vessels. The members of the female sex displayed fine muscular prowess as they carried large baskets of coal on their heads, while the men lazily sauntered in the neighbourhood performing the excessive labour attaching to the duties of tallymen. A captain named Osiris, from Caledonia, stern and wild, had an uncomfortable experience a few days afterwards whistling loudly, and the sea rose to an angry surge which swept part of the deck, a wave dashing through porthole and sweeping the captain's clothes about the cabin, at the same time leaving this "old salt" up to the knees in water. The storm did not last more than a day, and next morning we started to play at quoits, bragger &c.. The sport was witnessed by the passengers, the ladies taking shelter under parasols, and the gentlemen making things as comfortable as possible in caps and seasonable garments. St Vincent was not reached until the 21st of July, and as soon as we anchored BLACK DIVERS Came around in boats. They set up a babble which was almost deafening, and when any passenger through a silver coin into the sea, away went a swarm of these yelling amphibi, who, quickly diving to the bottom scrambled for the coin, the victorious diver rising to the surface with a shout of excitement. We left there at one o'clock in the afternoon, crossed "the line" on the 25th and on the same day we commenced ATHLETIC SPORTS Arrangements had been made for an obstacle race, a pick-a-back race, a 50 yards handicap, throwing the heavy weight and tilting the bucket. About 21 Englishmen and 16 Frenchmen entered the obstacle race, and great amusement it created. The track was round the ship, up a ladder, along a pole, which was about 10 feet above the deck, and through the wind sheet, which was partially filled with flour. A light young fellow named Clark, a native of Truro in Cornwall, carried off the premier award; and I got the principle prize 2s 6d for throwing the heavy weight. The sports did not conclude on that day, and were resumed on Saturday. I was the referee in the competition as to who was the best at tilting the bucket, and before this contest was over the whole of those who entered were wet to the skin. The Sorrato called at Pernambuco and Pabia, and arrived in Monte Video on the morning of Wednesday 6th August. The weather being rough we were unable to land until the next day, when I proceeded IN SEARCH OF THE PRISONER For whom I had been sent. I first called on the Consul, next arranged for two second class berths in the S.S. Thames, and on the 8th of August the military conducted the prisoner and myself to the vessel. There was a large number of passengers on board, but I was now on duty night and day, and stood sentry over the accused man who had been passed in my custody. Occasionally I heard reports of concerts on board; every day I gave the prisoner some exercise, and on the morning of the 30th August was delighted to set foot

Mike Covell

> once more on English soil at Southampton, from whence we at once departed, reaching Hull in the evening.

The Hull and East Yorkshire and Lincolnshire Times, September 6th 1890, and *The Hull Daily Mail*, September 8th 1890,

> THE ALLEGED FRAUDS ON JEWELLERS IN HULL. A PROBABLE CHARGE OF BIGAMY. At the Hull Police Court on Saturday, before Mr. E. C. Twiss, stipendiary magistrate, Henry Lawson appeared on remand charged with having obtained two diamond rings and a diamond bracelet from Messrs T. Reynoldson and Son, Jewellers, Whitefriargate, by means of false pretenses. – Mr. Laverack appeared for the prosecution, and Mr. Holdich defended. – Mr. Laverack, in asking for a further remand, stated that the inquiries instituted during the interval had resulted that it would be almost conclusively proved that the defendant was a married man at the time he went through the form of marriage with a young lady at Beverley. Under these circumstances he did not think it would be advisable to proceed with the case – Mr. Twiss: Do I understand that there will be a charge of bigamy in all probability entered. – Mr. Laverack replied that that was so. – Mr. Holdich offered no objection to the remand, but hinted that as further adjournments were necessary he should apply for bail. – Remanded for seven days.

The Hull Daily Mail, September 8th 1890,

> THE HEAVY FRAUD ON HULL JEWELLERS. ALLEGED BIGAMY BY THE PRISONER. At the Hull Police court, on Saturday, Henry Lawson, wool merchant, was engaged before the Stipendiary Magistrate, on remand, with obtaining a large quantity of jewellery from Messrs. Reynoldson and Son, jewellers, Whitefriargate, by means of fraud. – Mr. Laverack, who appeared for the prosecution, said he had to apply for a further remand in this case. His Worship would remember that it would, he thought, show that the accused that came before him whether they would be able to proceed with the evidence to-day. He had since found that the evidence of some witnesses living at a distance would be [illegible]. It would, he thought, show that the accused was a married man at the time he went through the ceremony of marriage with a young lady at Beverley. Under these circumstances he was sorry he could not go on with the case that day, and he therefore had to ask for a further remand. – Mr. Twiss: Do I understand there will be a charge of bigamy entered against him. – Mr. Laverack: Yes, your Worship. – Mr. Holdich, who represented prisoner, had no objection to other to a remand, and the prisoner was further remanded for seven days.

The Hull Daily News, September 15th 1890,

> THE ROBBERY OF JEWELLERY IN HULL. *Before Mr. J. Fisher and Mr. W. Bailey, at the Hull Police-court, on Saturday,* Henry Lawson *appeared on remand charged with obtaining two diamond rings and a diamond bracelet from Messrs. T. Reynoldson and Son, jewellers, Whitefriargate, Hull, by means of false pretenses. – Mr. E. A. Laverack appeared for the prosecution and Mr. T. W. Holdich defended. – Mr. Laverack asked for a further remand until Thursday next, when he said the case would be proceeded with. – Mr. Holdich offered no objection to the remand, but at the same time he thought that the case should now be proceeded with, as there had already been two remands. – Mr. Laverack replied that the reason for the adjournment was that there were other charges against the prisoner which were being investigated. – Mr. Holdich: And which we have not heard of yet. I think if there are any other charges, the defendant should be charged with them, and have an opportunity of meeting them. We have heard vague statements, but if there are any further charges they should be put in order, so that we might deal with them. – The remand was then granted until Thursday, the 18th inst.*

The Hull Daily News, September 18th 1890,

> THE ALLEGED FRAUDS ON A HULL JEWELLER. *Before Messrs. Robert Jameson and R. M. Craven, at the Hull Police court this morning,* Harry Lawson, *appeared on remand charged with obtaining two diamond rings and a diamond bracelet from Messrs. T. Reynoldson and Son, jewellers, Whitefriargate. – Mr. E. A. Laverack appeared for the prosecution and Mr. T. W. Holdich represented the defendant. – Mr. Laverack asked for a further remand in consequence of his inability to obtain witnesses from Southampton. He should not be able to complete the case in one day, and the Magistrates Clerk preferred that the case should be completed in one day. – Mr. Holdich asked that a day should be fixed for the case to be completed and a remand was granted for eight days.*

The Hull Daily News, September 26th 1890,

> THE ALLEGED EXTENSIVE JEWELLERY FRAUDS IN HULL. POLICE COURT PROCEEDINGS TO-DAY. *At the Hull Police court, this morning before Mr. T. W. Palmer and Ald Toozes,* Harry Lawson alias Deening, *stated that he was a native of Birkenhead, was charged on remand with obtaining two diamond rings and a diamond bracelet by means of fictitious cheques on the 15th March last, from Messrs. Reynoldson and Son. – Considerable interest was manifested on the case, which was conducted by Mr. E. A. Laverack, the prisoner being represented by*

Mike Covell

> Mr. Holdich (Messrs. Locking and Holdich). Mr. Laverack having recapitulated the facts at some length said that considerable credit was due to the police for the tact and skill they had displayed in tracing the whereabouts of the prisoner. When he left home the matter was placed in the hands of Detective Superintendent Clapham and Detective Grasby, and it was entirely due to their prompt and energetic action that the prisoner now stood before the Court. – Evidence was then called. Mr. Thos. Chas. Reynoldson, a member of the prosecuting firm, said that on the 17th March last he received a cheque for £120, which he endorsed, and presented to the Yorkshire Banking Company, which was dishonoured. The following morning he presented a cheque for £165 at the same bank, and this was also dishonoured. He had seen the diamonds found on the prisoner at the time of his arrest, and they were 73 in number, and similar to those supplied to the defendant.

The Hull Daily News, September 27th 1890,

> THE ALLEGED EXTENSIVE JEWELLERY FRAUDS IN HULL. At the Hull Police Court, yesterday, before Mr. T. W. Palmer and Ald. Toozes, Harry Lawson, alias Deening, who said he was a native of Birkenhead, was charged on remand with obtaining two diamond rings and one diamond bracelet by means of fictitious cheques on the 15th of March last, from Messrs. Reynoldson and son. – Considerable interest was manifested in the case, which was conducted by Mr. E. A. Laverack, the prisoner being represented by Mr. Holdich (Messrs. Locking and Holdich). Mr. Laverack having recapitulated the facts at some length, said that considerable credit was due to the police for the tact and skill they had displayed in tracing the whereabouts of the prisoner. When he left home the matter was placed in the hands of Detective Superintendent Clapham and Detective Grasby, and it was entirely due to their prompt and energetic action that the prisoner now stood before the Court. – Evidence was then called. Mr. Thomas Charles Reynoldson, a member of the prosecuting firm, said that on the 17th of March last he received a cheque for £122, which he endorsed and presented to the Yorkshire Banking Company, which was dishonoured. The following morning he presented a cheque for £165 at the same bank, and this was also dishonoured. He had seen the diamonds found on the prisoner at the time of his arrest, and they were 73 in number, and similar to those supplied by the defendant. By Mr. Holdich – They had other transactions with the defendant, who had paid them by cash and by cheque. They had entries in their books of an account with the defendant during January and February last, to the amount of £39. 17s. 6d. About five weeks previous to the purchase of the rings in question, they had negotiations with the defendant, respecting them, and he had the rings in his possession before the 15th March. Both rings were sent to the defendant at Beverley on the 17th February,

and on the same afternoon witness, who had been over to Beverley to see him, but had failed to do so, saw him at the Paragon Station, Hull, and he asked him why he had not complied to their rules. Defendant said he had not intended to pay them until the 15th March. Witness did not ask for a cheque for the payment of half, and never said they were not in a hurry for the balance. Defendant on leaving him said he would call at their shop that day. He did call eventually, and objected to witness having gone over to Beverley to see him. Defendant then had a conversation with witness's father. On the following day witness saw the defendant at the Station Hotel, Hull, and said that if he gave them payment for half they would give him a bill for the reminder. The rings were then in witness's possession, he having received them that morning. Witness said he would let the matter rest as he was going away, and would be back again in a month. Mr. Charles Wm. Moxon, manager of the Yorkshire Bank, Hull, said that on the 20th January last the defendant opened an account, which he closed on 12th March. By Mr. Holdich- He opened an account with a deposit of £310, and he drew against it as required. On the 12th March he sent a cheque which exhausted the balance. Mr. George Waterman, chief clerk at the parcels office of the London and South Western Railway at Southampton, said that on the 17th February last he received a letter from the defendant, who signed himself F. Deening, saying that he was sending some luggage by train, and asked that they might be kept until he arrived on the 14th March. On the following day nine articles came by passenger train. Alfred Jefferies, clerk in the employ of the last witness, said the defendant came to Southampton on the 8th March, and paid for his luggage. On the 16th witness again saw the defendant, who came for his luggage, which he took away in a cab. Witness asked if he should direct the cabman where to drive to, defendant declined. Albert Windsor, booking clerk in the employ of the owners of the steamer Coleridge, Liverpool, said that on the 16th March the defendant applied at Liverpool for a first class passage on the steamer Coleridge, bound for Buenos Ayres. Witness informed him that all the berths were taken up, and defendant said that it was of the greatest importance that he went in the steamer, and he really must go. Eventually it was arranged to make up a temporary berth, for which he paid £30. He booked in the name of "Mr. Deening." After the adjournment Mr. T. Reynoldson went into the box. The statement made by him to the court was to the effect that the accused went to his firm's premises on the afternoon of the 15th March, and purchased two rings for £120. He wrote out a cheque for this amount on the Yorkshire Banking Company. He then purchased a diamond bracelet for £165, giving a cheque for the same dated the 18th, explaining that his account in the bank would not be sufficient to meet the two cheques, but he should have money in the bank in a day or two, and the cheque would be met on the 18th. Believing this statement to be true the goods were supplied to the prisoner. – Detective Grasby deposed to apprehending the defendant at Monte Video, and

Mike Covell

> charging him with the offence, when he made no reply. Witness produced two diamond rings and 73 loose diamonds, which he received from the authorities at Monte Video. – This concluded the case for the prosecution, and the defendant, who reserved his defense, was committed for trial at the next borough sessions. – An application for bail made by Mr. Holdich, on behalf of his client, was refused, the prosecution objecting strongly to the application.

Appendix V - Newspapers Featured

Post – 1888

The Hull Daily Mail, January 1st 1889 Transcribed
The Hull Daily Mail, January 1st 1889 Transcribed
The Eastern Morning News, January 2nd 1889 Transcribed
The Eastern Morning News, January 3rd 1889
The Hull Daily Mail, January 3rd 1889 Transcribed
The Hull Daily Mail, January 10th 1889 Transcribed
The Hull Daily Mail, January 11th 1889 Transcribed
The Hull Times, January 12th 1889 Transcribed
The Hull Times, January 12th 1889 Transcribed
The Hull and East Yorkshire and Lincolnshire Times, January 12th 1889
The Hull Daily Mail, January 15th 1889 Discussed
The Hull Daily Mail, January 17th 1889 Transcribed
The Hull Daily Mail, January 19th 1889 Transcribed
The Hull Daily Mail, January 22nd 1889 Discussed
The Hull Daily Mail, February 6th 1889 Transcribed
The York Herald, February 7th 1889 Transcribed
The Hull News, February 1889
The York Herald, March 5th 1889 Transcribed
The Yorkshire Gazette, March 9th 1889 Transcribed
The York Herald, March 9th 1889 Transcribed
The Daily News, March 15th 1889
The Huddersfield Daily Chronicle, March 15th 1889
The Leeds Mercury, March 15th 1889
The Sheffield and Rotherham Independent, March 15th 1889 "Jack the Ripper" on a Grimsby Smack.
The Sheffield and Rotherham Independent, March 15th 1889
The Morning Post, March 15th 1889
The Standard, March 15th 1889
The York Herald, March 15th 1889
The Belfast News Letter, March 16th 1889
Birmingham Daily Post, March 16th 1889
The Huddersfield Daily Chronicle, March 16th 1889
The Leeds Mercury, March 16th 1889

Mike Covell

Manchester Times, March 16th 1889
The Nottinghamshire Guardian, March 16th 1889
The Standard, March 16th 1889
The York Herald, March 16th 1889
The Leeds Mercury, March 19th 1889
The Lancaster Gazette and General Advertiser for Lancashire, Westmorland, and Yorkshire, March 20th 1889
Berrow's Worcester Journal, March 23rd 1889
The Newcastle Weekly Courant, March 23rd 1889
The Sheffield and Rotherham Independent, July 15th 1889
The Hull Daily Mail, February 18th 1889 Discussed
The Hull Daily Mail, February 19th 1889 Discussed
The Hull Daily Mail, March 14th 1889 Transcribed
The Hull Daily Mail, March 18th 1889
The Hull Daily Mail, March 20th 1889 Transcribed
The Hull Daily Mail, April 8th 1889 Transcribed
The Hull Daily Mail, April 30th 1889 Transcribed
The Hull Daily Mail, June 4th 1889 Transcribed
The Hull Daily Mail, June 7th 1889 Transcribed
The Hull Daily Mail, June 11th 1889 Transcribed
The Hull Daily Mail, June 17th 1889 Transcribed
The Hull Daily Mail, June 26th 1889 Transcribed
The Hull Daily Mail, July 17th 1889
The Hull Daily Mail, July 18th 1889 Transcribed
The Hull Daily Mail, July 22nd 1889 Transcribed
The Hull Daily Mail, July 29th 1889 Transcribed
The Hull Daily Mail, August 27th 1889 Transcribed
The Hull Daily Mail, September 10th 1889 Transcribed
The Hull Daily Mail, September 11th 1889 Transcribed
The Hull Daily Mail, September 30th 1889 Transcribed
The Hull Daily Mail, October 14th 1889 Transcribed
The Hull Daily Mail, October 14th 1889 Transcribed
The Hull Daily Mail, October 18th 1889 Transcribed
The Hull Daily Mail, October 28th 1889 Transcribed
The Hull Daily Mail, January 8th 1890 Transcribed
The Hull Daily Mail, January 13th 1890 Discussed
The Hull Daily Mail, January 13th 1890 Transcribed
The Hull Daily Mail, March 19th 1890 Transcribed
The Hull Daily Mail, April 8th 1890 Transcribed
The Hull Daily Mail, April 9th 1890 Transcribed
The Hull Daily Mail, July 11th 1890 Transcribed

The Daily Gazette for Midlesborough, July 19th 1890
The Leeds Mercury, July 19th 1890
The Hull Daily Mail, July 25th 1890 Transcribed
The Hull Daily Mail, September 17th 1890 Transcribed
The Hull Daily Mail, October 2nd 1890 Transcribed
The Hull Daily Mail, October 3rd 1890 Discussed
The Hull Daily Mail, October 14th 1890 Transcribed
The Hull Daily Mail, February 7th 1891 Transcribed
The Hull and East Yorkshire and Lincolnshire Times, February 14th 1891 Transcribed
The Hull Times, February 21st 1891 Transcribed
The Hull and East Yorkshire and Lincolnshire Times, February 21st 1891 Transcribed
The Hull Times, February 28th 1891 Transcribed
The Hull Times, March 7th 1891 Transcribed
The Hull Times, March 7th 1891 Transcribed
The Hull and East Yorkshire and Lincolnshire Times, March 17th 1891
The Hull Daily Mail, May 1891 Transcribed *
The Hull Daily Mail, May 1891 Transcribed *
The Hull Daily Mail, May 20th 1891 Transcribed
The Hull Daily Mail, May 21st 1891 Transcribed
The Hull Daily Mail, May 22nd 1891 Transcribed
The Hull and North Lincolnshire Times, April 2nd 1892 Transcribed
The Hull and North Lincolnshire Times, April 2nd 1892 Transcribed
The Hull Daily Mail, March 3rd 1893 Transcribed
The Hull Daily Mail, March 6th 1893 Transcribed
The Hull Daily Mail, May 3rd 1893 Transcribed
The Hull Daily Mail, July 4th 1893 Transcribed
The Hull Daily Mail, October 10th 1893 Transcribed
The Hull Daily Mail, October 12th 1893 Discussed
The Hull Daily Mail, October 16th 1893 Discussed
The Hull Daily Mail, April 16th 1894 Transcribed
The Hull Daily Mail, June 6th 1894 Transcribed
The Hull Daily Mail, September 25th 1894 Discussed
The Hull Daily Mail, November 23rd 1894 Discussed
The Hull Daily Mail, November 26th 1894 Transcribed
The Hull Daily Mail, February 12th 1895 Transcribed
The Hull Daily Mail, March 27th 1895 Transcribed
The Hull Daily Mail, April 10th 1895 Discussed
The Hull Daily Mail, April 29th 1896 Transcribed
The Hull Daily Mail, October 13th 1897 Discussed

Mike Covell

The Hull Daily Mail, October 14th 1897 Discussed
The Hull Daily Mail, February 25th 1898 Transcribed
The Hull Daily Mail, March 8th 1898 Discussed
The Hull Daily Mail, October 12th 1898 Transcribed
The Hull Daily Mail, November 28th 1898 Transcribed
The Hull Daily Mail, November 30th 1898 Discussed
The Hull Daily Mail, May 11th 1900 Discussed
The Hull Daily Mail, August 3rd 1900 Transcribed
The Hull Daily Mail, February 21st 1902 Discussed
The Hull Daily Mail, March 5th 1921 Transcribed
The Hull Daily Mail, July 27th 1922 Discussed
The Hull Daily Mail, September 23rd 1922 Discussed
The Hull Daily Mail, October 26th 1923 Transcribed
The Hull Daily Mail, December 5th 1924 Transcribed
The Hull Daily Mail, January 27th 1925 Transcribed
The Hull Daily Mail, November 15th 1929 Discussed
The Hull Daily Mail, November 16th 1929 Discussed
The Hull Daily Mail, November 20th 1929 Discussed
The Hull Daily Mail, November 21st 1929 Discussed
The Hull Daily Mail, October 25th 1930 Transcribed
The Hull Daily Mail, January 24th 1931 Discussed
The Hull Daily Mail, April 11th 1931 Discussed
The Hull Daily Mail, April 13th 1931 Discussed
The Hull Daily Mail, May 7th 1932 Transcribed

1900 Hull Ripper Scare

The Dundee newspaper, Courier and Argus, November 27th 1900
The Hull Daily News published the following, on Monday November 26th 1900
The Hull Daily Mail published the following on Monday November 26th 1900
The Hull Daily Mail published the following on Monday November 26th 1900
The Eastern Morning News published the following on Tuesday November 27th 1900
The Hull Daily News published the following, on Tuesday November 27th 1900
The Hull Daily Mail, November 5th 1900 p. 4
The Hull Times published the following on December 1st 1900
The Hull Daily Mail, December 5th 1900 p.4 on British Newspapers
The Isle of Man Times and General Advertiser, Friday December 1st 1898,
The North Eastern Daily Gazette, Saturday 24th 1898
Reynolds's Newspaper, Sunday, December 25th 1898
The Royal Cornwall Gazette Falmouth Packet, Cornish Weekly News, & General Advertiser, Wednesday, December 29th 1898

The Nottinghamshire Guardian, Saturday December 31st 1898,
The Isle of Man Times and General Advertiser, Friday December 31st 1898
Nottinghamshire Guardian, Saturday December 31st 1898
Western Mail, Saturday, December 31, 1898
The Dundee Courier and Argus, Saturday December 31st 1898
The Bristol Mercury and Daily Post, Saturday December 31st 1898
Western Mail, Saturday, December 31st 1898
The Belfast News-Letter, Saturday, December 31st 1898
Lloyd's Weekly Newspaper, Sunday, January 1st 1899
The Derby Mercury, Wednesday, January 4th 1899
Dundee Courier, November 27th 1900
The Evening Telegraph, November 27th 1900
The Gloucester Citizen, November 27th 1900
The North-Eastern Daily Gazette, Tuesday, November 27th 1900
The Daily Gazette for Middlesbrough, November 27th 1900
The Shields Daily Gazette, November 27th 1900
The Derby Daily Telegraph, November 27th 1900
The Morning Post, Wednesday, November 28, 1900
The Sunderland Daily Echo and Shipping Gazette, November 28th 1900
The Morning Post, November 28th 1900
The Western Daily Press, November 28th 1900
The Glasgow Herald, Wednesday November 28th 1900,
The Huddersfield Daily Chronicle, Wednesday November 28th 1900
The Leeds Mercury, Wednesday November 28th 1900
Northern Echo, Wednesday November 28th 1900
The Lichfield Mercury, November 30th 1900
Manchester Times, Friday November 30th 1900
The Weekly Standard and Express, Saturday, December 1st 1900;
The Tamworth Herald, December 1st 1900
Nottinghamshire Guardian, Saturday December 1st 1900;
Worcestershire Chronicle, December 1st 1900
Blackburn Standard, December 1st 1900
Leicester Chronicle and the Leicestershire Mercury, Saturday, December 1st 1900

The 1988 Hull Ripper Craze

The Hull Daily Mail, February 22nd 1988 Transcribed
The Hull Daily Mail, February 24th 1988 Transcribed
The Hull Daily Mail, March 2nd 1988
The Hull Daily Mail, July 1st 1988 Transcribed
The Hull Daily Mail, August 18th 1988 Transcribed
The Hull Daily Mail, November 6th 1989

Mike Covell

The Hull Daily Mail, May 30th 1994

Jack the Ripper Scare in Beverley – The 1891 Scare
The York Herald, September 30th 1891 Transcribed
The Yorkshire Gazette, October 3rd 1891 Transcribed
The Yorkshire Herald, October 3rd 1891 Transcribed
The York Herald, October 6th 1891 Transcribed
The Yorkshire Gazette, October 10th 1891 Transcribed
The York Herald, October 10th 1891 Transcribed

Jack the Ripper Scare in Beverley – The 1894 Scare
Northern Echo, August 8th 1894
Evening Telegraph, August 7th 1894
Sunderland Echo and Shipping Gazette, August 7th 1894
Manchester Evening News, August 7th 1894
Coventry Evening Telegraph, August 7th 1894
Manchester Courier and Lancashire General Advertiser, August 8th 1894
Western Times, August 8th 1894
Dundee Courier, August 8th 1894
The Star, August 7th 1894
The Hull Daily Mail, August 6th 1894
The York Herald, August 7th 1894
The Hull Daily Mail, August 7th 1894

Jack the Ripper - General Reference
American Murders of Jack the Ripper, R. Michael Gordon, Lyons Press, 2005
Autobiography of Jack the Ripper, The, James Carnac, Bantam Press, 2012
Beaver Book of Horror, The, Daniel Farson, Beaver Books, 2007
Bell Tower, The, Robert Graysmith, Regnery, 1999
By Ear and Eyes, Karyo Magellan, Longshot Publishing, 2005
Carroty Nell – The Last Victim of Jack the Ripper, John E. Keefe, Menotomy Publishing, 2010
Carroty Nell – The Last Victim of Jack the Ripper, John E. Keefe, Menotomy Publishing, 2012
Complete History of Jack the Ripper, The, Philip Sugden, Robinson Publishing, 2002
Complete Jack the Ripper, The, Donald Rumbelow, W. H. Allen, 1976
Complete Jack the Ripper, The, Donald Rumbelow, Penguin Books, 1988
Complete Jack the Ripper, The, Donald Rumbelow, Penguin Books, 2004
Crimes and Times of Jack the Ripper, The, Tom Cullen, Fontana, 1973

Crimes, Detection and Death of Jack the Ripper, Martin Fido, George Weidenfield and Nicholson Ltd,

1987

Crimes, Detection and Death of Jack the Ripper, Martin Fido, Orion Books, 1993
Crimes of Jack the Ripper, The, Paul Roland, Arcturus Publishing, 2006
Diary of Jack the Ripper, The, Shirley Harrison, Hyperion Publishing, 1993
Diary of Jack the Ripper, The, Shirley Harrison, Blake Publishing, 1998
Diary of Jack the Ripper, The, - Another Chapter, James Stettler, Area Nine Publishing, 2009
Dracula Secrets, The, Jack the Ripper and the Darkest Sources of Bram Stoker, Neil R. Storey, History

Press, 2012

E1- A Journey Through Whitechapel and Spitalfields, John G. Bennett, Five Leaves Publishing, 2009
Enigma of Jack the Ripper, The, John de Locksley, 1994
Epiphany of the Whitechapel Murders, Karen Trenouth, Author House, 2006
First Jack the Ripper Victim Photographs, The, Robert J. McLaughlin, Zwerghaus Books, 2005
Fox and the Flies, The, Charles Van Onselen, Vintage, 2008
From Hell- The Jack the Ripper Mystery, Bob Hinton, Old Bakehouse Publications, 1998
Identity of Jack the Ripper, The, Donald McCormick, Arrow Books, 1970
Illustrated Guide to Jack the Ripper, An, Peter Fisher, P. and D. Riley, 1996
In the Footsteps of the Whitechapel Murders, John F. Plimmer, The Book Guild, 1998
Jack the Ripper, Andrew Cook, Amberley, 2009
Jack the Ripper, Daniel Farson, Sphere, 1973
Jack the Ripper, John McIlwain, Pitkin Guides, Jarrold Publishing
Jack the Ripper, Mark Whitehead and Miriam Rivett, Pocket Essentials, 2001
Jack the Ripper, Mark Whitehead and Miriam Rivett, Pocket Essentials, 2006
Jack the Ripper, Susan McNicoll, Altitude Publishing, 2005
Jack the Ripper- A Bibliography and Review of the Literature, Andrew Kelly, Association of Assistant

Librarians, 1973

Jack the Ripper- A Bibliography and Review of the Literature, Andrew Kelly, Association of Assistant

Mike Covell

Librarians, 1984

Jack the Ripper- A Bibliography and Review of the Literature, Andrew Kelly, Association of Assistant

Librarians, 1994

Jack the Ripper- A Bibliography and Review of the Literature, Andrew Kelly, Association of Assistant

Librarians, 1995

Jack the Ripper- A to Z, Paul Begg, Martin Fido, and Keith Skinner, Headline Book Publishing, 1991
Jack the Ripper- A to Z, Paul Begg, Martin Fido, and Keith Skinner, Headline Book Publishing, 1992
Jack the Ripper- A to Z, Paul Begg, Martin Fido, and Keith Skinner, Headline Book Publishing, 1994
Jack the Ripper- A to Z, Paul Begg, Martin Fido, and Keith Skinner, Headline Book Publishing, 1996
Jack the Ripper- A to Z, Paul Begg, Martin Fido, and Keith Skinner, John Blake, 2010
Jack the Ripper- American Hero, Jacob Corbett, Amazon, 2012
Jack the Ripper- An Encyclopaedia, John J. Eddleston, Metro Publishing, 2002
Jack the Ripper- An Encyclopaedia, John J. Eddleston, Metro Publishing, 2010
Jack the Ripper- Anatomy of a Myth, William Beadle, Wat Tyler Books, 1995
Jack the Ripper- And Black Magic, Spiro Dimolianis, McFarland, 2011
Jack the Ripper- And the East End, Alex Werner, Chatto and Windus, 2008
Jack the Ripper- And the Irish Press, Alan Sharp, Ashfield Press, 2005
Jack the Ripper- And the London Press, Lewis Perry Curtis, Yale University, 2001
Jack the Ripper- Black Magic Rituals, Ivor Edwards, John Blake Publishing, 2003
Jack the Ripper- Casebook, Richard Jones, Andre Deutsch, 2008
Jack the Ripper- Crime Archive, Val Horsler, National Archives, 2007
Jack the Ripper- End of a Legend, Calum Reuben Knight, Athena Press, 2005
Jack the Ripper- His Life and Crimes in Popular Entertainment, Gary Colville and Patrick Lucanio,

McFarland, 2009

Jack the Ripper- Infamous Serial Killer, Filiquarian Publications, 2008
Jack the Ripper- In Fact and Fiction, Robin Odell, Mandrake Publishing, 2009
Jack the Ripper- Letters from Hell, Stewart P. Evans and Keith Skinner, Sutton Publishing, 2004

Jack the Ripper- Light Hearted Friend, Richard Wallace, Gemini Press, 1997
Jack the Ripper- Location Photographs, The, Philip Hutchinson, Amberley Publishing, 2009
Jack the Ripper- Media, Culture, History, Alexandra Warwick and Martin Willis, Manchester University

Press, 2007

Jack the Ripper- One Hundred Years of Mystery, Peter Underwood, Blandford Press, 1987
Jack the Ripper- Opposing Viewpoints, Katie Colby-Newton, Greenhaven, 1990
Jack the Ripper- Quest for a Killer, M. J. Trow, Wharncliffe True Crime, 2009
Jack the Ripper- Revealed and Revisited, John Wilding, Express Newspapers, 2006
Jack the Ripper- Scotland Yard Investigates, Stewart P. Evans and Donald Rumbelow, Sutton Publishing,

2006

Jack the Ripper- Summing up and Verdict, Colin Wilson and Robin Odell, Corgi Books, 1992
Jack the Ripper- The 21st Century Investigation, Trevor Marriott, John Blake Publishing, 2005
Jack the Ripper- The 21st Century Investigation, Trevor Marriott, John Blake Publishing, 2007
Jack the Ripper- The American Connection, Shirley Harrison, Blake Publishing, 2003
Jack the Ripper- The Bloody Truth, Melvin Harris, Columbus Books, 1987
Jack the Ripper- The Celebrity Suspects, Mike Holgate, History Press, 2008
Jack the Ripper- The Definitive History, Paul Begg, Pearson Education Limited, 2004
Jack the Ripper- The Facts, Paul Begg, Robson Books, 2006
Jack the Ripper- The Final Chapter, Paul H. Feldman, Virgin Books, 2002
Jack the Ripper- The Final Chapter, Paul H. Feldman, Virgin Books, 2007
Jack the Ripper- The Final Solution, Stephen Knight, Harrap, 1976
Jack the Ripper- The Final Solution, Stephen Knight, Panther, 1981
Jack the Ripper- The Final Solution, Stephen Knight, Harper Collins, 1994
Jack the Ripper- The Hand of a Woman, John Morris, Seren Books, 2012
Jack the Ripper- The Murders and the Movies, Denis Meikle, Reynolds and Hearn Ltd, 2002
Jack the Ripper- The Mystery Solved, Paul Harrison, Robert Hale, 1993
Jack the Ripper- The Satanic Team, Karen Trenouth, Author House, 2007
Jack the Ripper- The Simple Truth, Bruce Paley, Headline Publishing, 1996

Mike Covell

Jack the Ripper- The Uncensored Facts, Paul Begg, Robson Books, 1989
Jack the Ripper, The Whitechapel Murderer, Terry Lynch, Wordsworth Editions, 2008
Jack the Ripper- Unmasked, William Beadle, John Blake Publishing, 2009
Jack the Ripper- Unveiled, John de Locksley, 1994
Jack the Ripper- Walk, The, Paul Garner, Louis London Walks, 2002
Jack the Ripper- Whitechapel Murders, The, Kevin O'Donnell, Andy and Sue Parlour, Ten Bells

Publishing, 1997

Jimmy Kelly's Year of the Ripper Murders, 1888, John Morrison, 1983
Last Victim, The, Anne E. Graham and Carol Emmas, Headline Publishing, 1998
Lodger- Arrest and Escape of Jack the Ripper, The, Stewart P. Evans and Paul Gainey, Century Publishing,

1995

London of Jack the Ripper Then and Now, The, Robert Clack and Philip Hutchinson, Breedon Books, 2007
London of Jack the Ripper Then and Now, The, 2nd Edition, Robert Clack and Philip Hutchinson, Breedon

Books, 2009

Mammoth Book of Jack the Ripper, The, Maxim Jakubowski and Nathan Braund, Constable and Robinson,

1999

Mammoth Book of Jack the Ripper, The, Maxim Jakubowski and Nathan Braund, Castle Books, 2005
Mammoth Book of Jack the Ripper, The, Maxim Jakubowski and Nathan Braund, Constable and Robinson,

2008

Man that Hunted Jack the Ripper, The, Nicholas Connell and Stewart P. Evans, Amberley, 2009
Many Faces of Jack the Ripper, The, M. J. Trow, Summersdale Publishing, 1997
Murder and Madness- The Secret Life of Jack the Ripper, David Abrahamsen M.D., F.A.C.Pn., Avon

Books, 1993

Mystery of Jack the Ripper, The, Leonard Matters, Arrow Books, 1964
News from Whitechapel, The, Alexander Chisholm, Christopher Michael DiGrazia, Dave Yost, McFarland

And Co, 2002

Portrait of a Serial Killer-Jack the Ripper-Case Closed, Patricia Cornwell, Little Brown, 2002
Portrait of a Serial Killer-Jack the Ripper-Case Closed, Patricia Cornwell, Time Warner, 2003
Prince Jack- The True Story of Jack the Ripper, Frank Spiering, Jove Books, 1980
Public Reactions to Jack the Ripper, Stephen P. Ryder (Ed) Inklings Press, 2006
Ramble with Jack the Ripper, A, John de Locksley, 1996
Ripper and the Royals, The, Melvyn Fairclough, Duckbacks, 2002
Ripper Code, The, Thomas Toughill, Sutton Publishing, 2008
Ripper File, The, Elwyn Jones and John Lloyd, Futura Publications, 1975
Ripper File, The, Melvin Harris, W. H. Allen and Co., 1989
Ripper in Ramsgate, The, Christopher Scott, Michaels Bookshop, 2008
Ripper Legacy, The, Martin Howells and Keith Skinner, Sphere Books Ltd, 1988
Ripper Suspect, D. J. Leighton, Sutton Publishing, 2006
Ripperology, Paul Begg (Ed) Barnes and Noble, 2007
Ripperology, Robin Odell, Kent State University Press, 2006
Saucy Jack- The Elusive Ripper, Paul Woods and Gavin Baddeley, Ian Allan Publishing, 2009
Sickert and the Ripper Crimes, Jean Overton Fuller, Mandrake Publishing, 2003
Search For Jack the Ripper- A Psychic Investigation, Pamela Ball, Midpoint Press, 2006
Secret of Prisoner 1167- Was this man Jack the Ripper?, James Tully, Robinson Publishing, 1998
The Harlot Killer- The story of Jack the Ripper in Fact and Fiction, Alan Barnard, Dodd Mead, 1953
The Man who would be Jack – The Hunt for the real Ripper, David Bullock, Robson Press, 2012
The Prince, His Tutor, and the Ripper, Deborah McDonald, McFarland and Company Inc. 2007
The Trial of Jack the Ripper, Euan Macpherson, Mainstream Publishing, 2005
Thames Torso Murders, The, M. J. Trow, Wharncliffe Books, 2011
Ultimate Jack the Ripper Sourcebook, The, Stewart P. Evans and Keith Skinner, Robinson Publishing, 2001
Uncle Jack, Tony Williams and Humphrey Price, Orion Books, 2006
Uncovering Jack the Ripper's London, Richard Jones, New Holland, 2007
Victims of Jack the Ripper, The, Neal Stubbings Sheldon, Inklings Press, 2007

Mike Covell

Whitechapel Murders Solved, The, John Plimmer, House of Stratus, 2003
Who was Jack the Ripper? Winston Forbes-Jones, Pipeline Promotions, 1988
Will the Real jack the Ripper, Arthur Douglas, Countryside Publications, 1979

Jack the Ripper – Press Associated

Illustrated Police News, Steve Jones, Wicked Publications, 2002
Jack the Ripper, Andrew Cook
Jack the Ripper and the London Press, L. Perry Curtis, Jnr, Yale University, 2001
London Correspondence: Jack the Ripper and the Irish Press, Alan Sharp, Ashfield Press, 2005
News From Whitechapel-Jack the Ripper in the Daily Telegraph, Alexander Chisholm, Christopher Michael DiGrazia, and Dave Yost, McFarland and Company Inc, Publishers, 2002
Public Reactions to Jack the Ripper, Stephen P. Ryder, Inklings Press, 2006
Ripper Notes-How the Newspapers Covered the Jack the Ripper Murders, Issue 21, Edited by Dan Norder, Inklings Press, January 2005

Hull History

Architecture of the Victorian era of Kingston upon Hull 1830-1914, Highgate Press, Ian N Goldthorpe, 2005.
Aspects of Hull, David Goodman, (Ed,) Wharncliffe Books,
Aspects of the Yorkshire Coast, Alan Whitworth, (Ed,) Wharncliffe Books,
Aspects of the Yorkshire Coast 2, Alan Whitworth, (Ed,) Wharncliffe Books, 2000
Atkinson's Trade Directory of Hull 1888
The Book of Hull, John Markham, Barracuda Books Limited, 1989
Breath of Sculcoates, A, Hull and District Local History Research Group, Heitage Lottery Fund, Developing our Communities, 2007
East Riding Chapels and Meeting Houses, East Yorkshire Local History Society, David Neave and Susan Neave, 1990
Forgotten Hull Kingston Press, Graham Wilkinson
Forgotten Hull 2, Kingston Press, Graham Wilkinson, 2000
Fourth Estate in Hull - The Life and Times of the Daily Press, The, Geoffrey Boland, Hull Local Studies, 2005
Georgian Hull, Ivan and Elisabeth Hall, William Sessions Ltd, 1978
Historical Atlas of East Yorkshire, An, Susan Neave and Stephen Ellis, (Ed,) University of Hull Press, 1996
History of the Yorkshire Coast Fishing Industry 1780-1914, Roy Robinson, Hull University Press, 1987
History of Seed Crushing in Great Britain, Harold W. Brace, Land Books, 1960
Hull and Scarborough Railway, C. T. Goode, Burstwick Publicity Services, 2000

Hull Schools in Victorian Times, Pete Railton, 1995
Illustrated History of Hull's Railways, Irwell Press, M Nicholson and W.B.Yeadon, 1993
Images of Victorian Hull - F.S. Smith's drawings of the Old Town, Text by Caroline Aldridge, Hutton Press, 1989
Innes Heritage Collection of Hull, The, Michael Thompson, Hutton Press, 1994
Kelly's Trade Directory of Hull 1889
Lost Churches and Chapels of Hull, Hutton Press, David Neave, 1991
Lost Pubs of Hull, Kingston Press, Paul Gibson and Graham Wilkinson, 1999
Lost Railways of Holderness, the Hull-Hornsea lines, the Hull-Withernsea lines, Hutton Press, Peter Price, 1989
More Illustrated History of Hull's Railways, Challenger Publications, W.B.Yeadon, 1995
Old and New Hull, T. Tindall Willdridge, M. C. Peck and Son, 1884
Railways of Hull, C. T. Goode, Burstwick Publicity Services, 1992
Sculcoates- Ancient and Modern, Christine Gould and David Knappett, Oriel Printing Company, 1991

Maps

Jack the Ripper, Whitechapel Map 1888, Geoff Cooper and Gordon Punter, 2003
Whitechapel, Spitalfields and the Bank 1873, Alan Godfrey Maps, 2006
Whitechapel, Spitalfields and the Bank 1894, Alan Godfrey Maps, 2006
Highbury and Islington 1871, Alan Godfrey Maps, 2006
Highbury and Islington 1894, Alan Godfrey Maps, 2006
Highbury and Islington 1914, Alan Godfrey Maps, 2006
Upper Holloway 1869, Alan Godfrey Maps, 1999
Upper Holloway 1894, Alan Godfrey Maps, 2005
Upper Holloway 1914, Alan Godfrey Maps, 1997
Hull Old Town 1853, Alan Godfrey Maps, 1988
Hull Railway Dock and Paragon Stn 1853, Alan Godfrey Maps, 2008
Hull Alexandra Dock 1908, Alan Godfrey Maps, 2007
Hull Hessle Road 1928, Alan Godfrey Maps, 1987
Hull East 1908, Alan Godfrey Maps, 2007
Hull East 1928, Alan Godfrey Maps, 1987
Hull North East 1980, Alan Godfrey Maps, 2007
Hull West 1908, Alan Godfrey Maps, 2006
Hull West 1928, Alan Godfrey Maps, 1987
I also consulted numerous maps held on file at Hull Local Studies Library.

Mike Covell

Miscellaneous Files

CQB436 Michaelmas Quarter Sessions 1900
CQB437 Epiphany Quarter Sessions 1901
CQN/1 Calendar of Prisoners 1893-1904
CDPM/2/6 Minute Book January – April 1891

Acknowledgments

First and foremost I would like to acknowledge the support of my family, who have stood by my crazy ideas and decisions and sat quietly whilst I tried to type this up! My wife Susan has been a rock and I wish to take this opportunity to thank her for her love and support, my children Bradley, Alyssa, and William, for their cuddles and smiles. My Mother and Father, for their constant support, inspiration and technical help. During the time of writing my Father passed away but his ongoing support and encouragement helped me along this path. We have seen some dark times, and hopefully this is the start of something positive. No book on Hull Newspapers would be complete without the invaluable help of all the staff at Hull Local Studies Library. Each and every question was asked and each and every need catered for. Every time the staff went above and beyond the call of duty, and for that I truly thank them. I also offer my deepest thanks to Hull City Council's Archives Department, who again helped me in every step I took. Their hard work and dedication did not go unnoticed. At the time of writing the Hull Local History unit and the Hull City Council's Archives have amalgamated with the Hull University Archives to form the Hull History Centre. I have had the pleasure of lecturing at the Hull History Centre on several occasions and they building, staff and crowd are always fantastic. My thanks also go to the hardworking staff at The Carnegie Heritage Centre, whose warm and knowledgeable staff make every visit one to remember. Special thanks must go to Liz Shepard and Paul Gibson of the Carnegie Heritage Action Group for their help and advice. I have had the pleasure of lecturing on the Ripper and my research at Carnegie and it is always a warm welcome and great atmosphere with a cracking cuppa! Special thanks and acknowledgements to Howard and Nina Brown of the JTR Forums, http://www.jtrforums.com/ Howard and Nina have helped shape and mould my many theories and helped provide a sound stage for my research. Not only that, but they have become close friends, and for that alone I thank them. Thank you to Stephen P Ryder of the Ripper Casebook http://www.casebook.org/intro.html, who provided me with a stage for my research and a casebook blog for my work to be presented. Stephen is a major force in the community and an inspiration to all Ripperologists. Thank you to all of the *Hull Daily Mail "Yourmail"* team who provided me with an excellent site to write about my passions! Whilst the site has since gone, the feedback that my work received inspired me to work on projects such as this. It also opened up several doors and avenues of research for me, and made me many friends and contacts for life. To Alan Brigham, Michael Lake, and Nicholas Evans, all have helped shape and inspire me to continue in this work. A special thank you must go to Richard Sutherland who was working at Waterstones in Hull when I began this book. Richard helped in the early stages, and is a very knowledgeable, friendly young man. To all the Ripperologists, whom I am lucky enough to call friends, who have helped along the way, I have put you all in alphabetical order to avoid you all arguing in the forums over who I mentioned first! Alan Sharp, Ali and Lee Bevan, Brian L. Porter, Bob Hinton, Chris George, Chris Scott, Chris Jones, Colin Cobb, Dave and Sandra Yost, Debra Arif, Gareth Williams, Jon Rees, John Savage, Martin Fido, Paul Begg, Philip Hutchinson, Ricky Cobb, Robert Clark, Robert J. McLaughlin, Richard Jones, Suzi Haney, and everyone else who has taken time out to discuss my research. To all the team at *Ripperologist Magazine*, including Adam Wood, Chris George, Chris Scott, and Paul Begg, who have helped me with my research, offered me a platform to talk about Ripper related blogs and all things connected to Hull. Thank you!! I would also like to thank everyone at the *Rippercast Podcast*, especially the main man Jonathan Menges for his help and support. I would also like to take this opportunity to thank the listeners who have contacted me from across the globe as far away as Australia, New Zealand, Japan, China, Canada, America and of course Kingston upon Hull. I would like to take this opportunity to thank everyone on the social media circuit that has supported my work, with fantastic help and advice from the gang on Facebook and Twitter, and of course all those who have visited my Jack the Ripper blog.

Mike Covell

Other works by Mike Covell

Jack the Ripper related:
Jack the Ripper, From Hell, From Hull? Volume I
Jack the Ripper, From Hell, From Hull? Volume II
Jack the Ripper, From Hell, From Hull? Volume III
Jack the Ripper Newspaper From Hull Volume I
Researching Jack the Ripper
Walking Jack the Ripper's Hull

True Crime:
Mike Covell presents The Marfleet Mystery
Mike Covell presents The Caughey Street Murder
Mike Covell presents Ethel Major – The Last Woman Hanged at Hull

Paranormal related:
Mike Covell's Paranormal Hull – The Paranormal Files
Mike Covell's Paranormal Hull – The Ghost Files
Mike Covell's Paranormal Hull – The UFO Files
Mike Covell's Paranormal Hull – The Cryptozoology Files
Mike Covell's Paranormal Hull – The Paranormal Press Perspective
Mike Covell's Paranormal Hull – Researching the Paranormal
Walking Mike Covell's Paranormal Hull

Printed in Great Britain
by Amazon